CW01262062

Planning to Fail

BRIDGING THE GAP

Series Editors
James Goldgeier
Bruce Jentleson
Steven Weber

*The Logic of American Nuclear Strategy:
Why Strategic Superiority Matters*
Matthew Kroenig

*Planning to Fail:
The US Wars in Vietnam, Iraq, and Afghanistan*
James H. Lebovic

Planning to Fail

The US Wars in Vietnam, Iraq, and Afghanistan

JAMES H. LEBOVIC

OXFORD
UNIVERSITY PRESS

OXFORD
UNIVERSITY PRESS

Oxford University Press is a department of the University of Oxford. It furthers the University's objective of excellence in research, scholarship, and education by publishing worldwide. Oxford is a registered trade mark of Oxford University Press in the UK and certain other countries.

Published in the United States of America by Oxford University Press
198 Madison Avenue, New York, NY 10016, United States of America.

© Oxford University Press 2019

All rights reserved. No part of this publication may be reproduced, stored in a retrieval system, or transmitted, in any form or by any means, without the prior permission in writing of Oxford University Press, or as expressly permitted by law, by license, or under terms agreed with the appropriate reproduction rights organization. Inquiries concerning reproduction outside the scope of the above should be sent to the Rights Department, Oxford University Press, at the address above.

You must not circulate this work in any other form
and you must impose this same condition on any acquirer.

Library of Congress Cataloging-in-Publication Data
Names: Lebovic, James H., author.
Title: Planning to fail : the US wars in Vietnam, Iraq, and Afghanistan / James H. Lebovic.
Other titles: US wars in Vietnam, Iraq, and Afghanistan
Description: New York, NY : Oxford University Press, [2019] | Includes bibliographical references.
Identifiers: LCCN 2018032423 | ISBN 9780190935320 (hc : alk. paper)
Subjects: LCSH: United States—Military policy—Decision making—Case studies. | National security—United States—Decision making—Case studies. | Vietnam War, 1961–1975. | Iraq War, 2003-2011. | Afghan War, 2001– | United States—History, Military—Case studies.
Classification: LCC UA23 .L4477 2019 | DDC 355.020973—dc23
LC record available at https://lccn.loc.gov/2018032423

1 3 5 7 9 8 6 4 2

Printed by Sheridan Books, Inc., United States of America

CONTENTS

Preface vii
Acknowledgments ix

1. The US Wars in Vietnam, Iraq, and Afghanistan   1

2. The Vietnam War, 1965–1973   17

3. The Iraq War, 2003–2011   64

4. The Afghanistan War, 2001–?   119

5. Three Long and Costly Wars: What Can We Learn?   181

Notes   193
References   221
Index   233

PREFACE

This book, fifty years in the making, assesses US decision-making in the Vietnam, Iraq, and Afghanistan conflicts, the three longest US wars of the post–World War II period. Those who speak of the Iraq and Afghanistan Wars often dismiss Vietnam as the exception or an aberration. But the Vietnam War serves as an essential introduction to the deficiencies of US wartime decision-making. In the Vietnam War, like its successors, US decision makers struggled less than they should have when conditions permitted good choices, and then struggled more than could matter when conditions left them with only bad choices.

History, finally, is what we make of it. To repurpose William Faulkner, "The past is never dead. It's not even past."

ACKNOWLEDGMENTS

I started this book early in the second term of the Obama administration. A book on the challenges of US decision-making in the Vietnam, Iraq, and Afghanistan Wars seemed a fitting companion to the book on the limits of US military capability in the Vietnam and Iraq Wars that I had completed in Barack Obama's first year in office.

As I wrote, I profited enormously from conversations with my department colleagues, often in discussions on seemingly unrelated subjects. I owe special thanks to Elizabeth Saunders for her willingness to talk about all things Vietnam—and Iraq, and occasionally even Afghanistan. Steve Biddle also deserves mention in that regard. He contributed to this book in ways he does not appreciate. Steve lectured on the Iraq surge to my undergraduate seminar, The United States at War, eight semesters in a row, providing me each time with new insights on decision-making in that crucial period. Perhaps his biggest contribution to this book came, however, at a public session, when he warned against the temptation to make low cost the overriding consideration in deciding among wartime options. I hope he does not mind that I enshrined his cautionary advice here in a "stage of conflict."

Outside of George Washington University, I gained useful perspective and information from a lengthy discussion (via email) about the Iraq surge with Peter Feaver. I appreciate the time he took answering my questions and providing answers when I did not realize I should have had questions. Also deserving thanks for helpful feedback are James Morris for his comments on a manuscript draft (and suggestions for a book cover) and the participants on my panel at the 2016 conference of the International Security Studies Section and International Security and Arms Control Section (of the International Studies Association and American Political Science Association, respectively), where I presented the theory from this book. I owe a special debt to the academic editors of the new Bridging the Gap series—Jim Goldgeier, Bruce Jentleson, and Steve Weber—and two anonymous reviewers for their extremely useful comments on early drafts of this manuscript. I also express my appreciation to Dave McBride, my editor at Oxford University Press, for seeing value in this manuscript and, along with Holly Mitchell, helping to shepherd it through the publication process.

Finally, I wish to acknowledge my wife Holly for the opportunity and support she gave me to complete this project. We never actually discussed the book. But some things in life are more important than in-house, manuscript feedback. If the truth be told, I live quite comfortably without it.

1

The US Wars in Vietnam, Iraq, and Afghanistan

Despite its planning, the United States has failed to meet its early objectives in almost every one of its major post–World War II conflicts. Of these troubled efforts, the US wars in Vietnam (1965–1973), Iraq (2003–2011), and Afghanistan (2001–present) stand out for their endurance, resource investment, human cost, and common decisional failings. US policy makers allowed these wars to sap available capabilities, push US forces to the breaking point, and exhaust public support.[1] They finally accepted terms for a US departure that they, or their predecessors, would have rejected earlier in these conflicts. I argue that the reason is found in asking *how* the United States fights—not just *why* it fights—and in seeking answers in the confluence of conceptual, organizational, and political forces that lead to goal displacement and replacement.

Most criticism of US war policy, however, centers on the question *why*. Why did the George W. Bush administration go to war in 2003 against Iraq? Why, after seizing Baghdad, did the administration choose to expand its objectives to remake Iraq as a democracy? Analysts are correct to focus a critical lens on key decisions that initiate the potential stages of war. US leaders, after all, do make decisions—to intervene militarily, escalate or de-escalate, or withdraw from combat—that determine the severity, length, and outcome of a war effort. Yet analysts can gain much from exploring how policy makers engage in war. How do US policy makers define war purposes? How do they prioritize their options? How do they redefine missions? How do they finally leave a conflict? I show that answers, at four stages of intervention, help explain why the United States fought; chose to increase, decrease, or end its involvement in a conflict; encountered a progressively reduced set of options; and ultimately settled for suboptimal results. In short, I establish that US leaders were effectively *planning to fail*, whatever their hopes and thoughts at the time.

Wartime Decisional Bias: The Primacy of Means

My basic argument is simple: policy makers are myopic. They craft polices around visible elements *as if they were the whole picture*. Because overarching policy goals are distant and open to interpretation, policy makers ground their decisions in the immediate world of short-term objectives, salient tasks and tactics, policy constraints, and fixed time schedules. In consequence, they exaggerate the benefits of preferred policies, neglect their accompanying costs and requirements, and ignore beneficial alternatives. These tendencies, though pervasive in decision-making, become disabling problems in the complex environment of asymmetric conflicts. With their many interdependent parts, these demanding environments confound planning and tax resources. The result—in Vietnam, Iraq, and Afghanistan—was shortsighted, suboptimal policies that failed to live up to ever-diminishing expectations.

Drawing from studies of psychological and organizational behavior, I assume individuals employ indicators to gauge the effects of proximate goals that serve, in turn, as surrogates for more abstract goals (March and Simon 1993; Steinbruner 1974). I draw also from cognitive research (Jervis 1976; Kahneman and Tversky 1979; Levy 1997; McDermott 2001) that highlights the stability of beliefs and explores heuristics by which individuals make decisions "quickly and frugally" (Gigerenzer and Gaissmaier 2011: 455). These studies establish that individuals, in opting for salient (or "available") referents to understand complex policy problems, defy the principle of rational value maximization. They do not consider their goals, much less evaluate their importance, compatibility, or feasibility. Nor do they search dutifully for policy alternatives, seek information necessary to assess those options, or choose logically and systematically from among them to maximize gains, reduce risks, or minimize costs. They anchor their decisions instead in referents that define the decisional problem.[2]

To be sure, any number of heuristics might account for the decisional failings of a policy maker or group at a given stage in a conflict. The suspect heuristics include the framing of decisions, the structure and particulars of competing options, how and when information becomes available (i.e., the manner and order of its presentation), the fact of prior losses or gains, and the illogical processing of probabilistic information. For instance, an option's deficiency on but one dimension can bias decisions toward an alternative that, by contrast, performs well on that dimension, or a middle option can appear more viable when juxtaposed with extreme alternatives (McDermott 2001: 24–25).[3]

A rich variety of heuristics can account for the thinking of particular decision makers at critical junctures in the Vietnam, Iraq, and Afghanistan Wars. I seek the explanatory and predictive benefits, however, of a macro approach that focuses analysis on persistent or recurrent cognitive influences on governmental behavior.[4] I argue that—across decisional bodies and throughout these wars—immediate goals, critical tasks, mission costs, and time schedules (as salient referents) supplanted broad-based goals.[5] Biased decisions (and non-decisions) helped create the strategic and political conditions (with accompanying referents) that influenced decisions in the next stage of these conflicts.

I accept that a number of factors could mitigate or exacerbate such decisional bias. These factors, long touted by international politics theorists, include a country's level of power, democratic governance, bureaucratic politics and competition, and organizational traditions and practices. Because these factors might promote *or* reduce bias, depending on the circumstances, their explanatory impact nonetheless remains unclear.

Enormous power arguably positioned the United States to pursue global interests and accept global responsibilities and to act with necessary deliberation and restraint. Big decisions provoke painful questioning and introspection (as time permits); reversible or low-stake decisions come more easily, with little thought for the consequences of failure. The process by which people decide whether to undergo a surgical procedure differs substantially from the process by which *most* people decide where to go for lunch. Yet such power also gave US leaders a cushion, safety net, or margin of error to survive mistakes, which permitted US leaders to act (in Vietnam, Iraq, and Afghanistan) without duly considering the pros and cons.

Likewise, the democratic character of a government might ameliorate wartime decisional bias or make it worse.[6] Bias might decline if open and accountable governance exposes decision makers to divergent points of view. Diverse opinions are introduced, for instance, when US presidents create a "coalition of rivals" by bringing political opponents into government; when they construct a broad tent in pursuit of bipartisan policies; or when they weigh options carefully (with input from policy and intelligence professionals), out of fear that the public will punish policy failure at the ballot box. Yet an open government, with widespread participation in policy, can have the opposite effect. It can lead instead to policy stalemate; a diffusion of authority that leaves no one in charge; or lowest-common-denominator policies meant to appeal to various constituencies, not serve policy goals.

Bureaucratic politics and organizational dynamics within government can similarly yield conflicting effects. Bias lessens when bureaucratic competition provokes constructive debate and a free flow of information or when organizational cultures, traditions, and practices—honed through professional experience and expertise—influence policy. Bias ensues, however, when the relative capability of the contenders, not the quality of ideas, determines who wins and who loses the argument.[7] Bias afflicts policymaking too when maintaining organizational traditions and observing past practices quash innovation and useful dissent.

Stronger evidence suggests that, apart from these other influences, a myopic bias blinds policy makers to the (bad) consequences of their choices. Indeed, such bias helps account for the decisional impact of factors such as national power. For example, it tells us why US policy makers exaggerated US power in the "bipolar" and "unipolar" systems of the postwar period.[8] An illusion of US power thus led US decision makers into conflicts that presented unexpected challenges. Only with time would US policy makers recognize that even vast US assets could not procure wins against ostensibly weak opponents.[9] The power asymmetry favoring the United States in Vietnam, Iraq, and Afghanistan proved elusive against local adversaries capable of using unconventional tactics to their advantage. The US failure to achieve a satisfactory outcome under these circumstances prolonged the conflict, deepened the country's involvement, and absorbed available resources, even as it created conditions that permitted bias to thrive.

A myopic bias can work in tandem with other forms of psychological bias. Take, for example, the "chasing of sunk costs" that has policy makers yielding to the non-rational logic that "we've sacrificed too much to quit." By this logic, they seek to recover losses, not weigh the marginal return on the additional units invested. They might even exaggerate the value of units lost relative to the potential benefits of some alternative course of action (Kahneman and Tversky 1979; Levy 1997; McDermott 2001). Yet a misplaced focus can bolster these tendencies. Chasing sunk costs seems a viable approach to policy makers because they focus excessively on immediate problems, solutions, and constraints, neglecting long-term goals.

The Stages of Wartime Decision-Making

Critiques of wartime decision-making center on the decision to go to war. Lost in these analyses, however, is the fact that how combatants choose to fight—whether and how they understand their initial goals and adapt later to adversary tactics and the wartime environment—critically affect military outcomes. A war is not necessarily "lost" when states choose war, ill advisedly, over potential alternatives, nor is it "won" when propitious conditions at the onset of battle promise a favorable result.

The prelude to war is undoubtedly a major part of any path-dependent explanation of wartime outcomes. Because the decision to go to war sets the basic parameters (the "where, why, and how") of the mission, the decision to fight is more consequential, in almost all respects, than decisions to change strategy, reallocate resources, or escalate or de-escalate a conflict. Moreover, policy makers invest politically and psychologically in initial decisions and resist changes in course that they believe, or their opponents will think, amount to conceding failure. Still, policy makers make consequential decisions (and non-decisions) at each of four stages of a conflict. For reasons of bias, policy makers might extend or expand the mission in its early stages; pursue the mission in some abbreviated, suboptimal form in a later stage; or finally, interpret the mission to serve an exit from the conflict. These decisions exacerbate performance challenges, waste and divert available resources, limit future choices, prolong the conflict, and lead eventually to exhaustion.

Stage I

Policy Choice: Engagement of Military Forces
Decision Dynamic: Fixation (Focus on Immediate Mission Goals)

Stage I, the engagement phase, commences when immediate mission goals come together in a war plan. The unmet challenge in policymaking, however, is aligning war plans with broad policy goals. In Vietnam, near-term goals were imprecise, nonconsensual, and eternally malleable. Still, these goals, which centered on efforts to punish the enemy and prevent it from making any gains, loomed larger than fundamental purposes of the US mission. In planning for the US operations in Iraq and Afghanistan, US policy makers were far more attentive to the proximate goal of regime change than to how it might serve (or undermine) US regional and global objectives. That would prove a critical deficiency as ensuing challenges tested US forces, and confounded US officials, when the governments in both countries fell.[10]

The unanswered question in all three conflicts, however, was, "How exactly would immediate goals serve broader national purposes?" Policy makers saw little reason to explore policy alternatives or to probe the potential negative consequences of their own preferred options.

Stage II

Policy Choice: Extension of Military Operations
Decision Dynamic: Disjunction (Focus on Separate Tasks, Apart from Implementation)

Stage II commences when government leaders extend or expand the mission, having accomplished, or failed to accomplish, their immediate goals. At this point, civilian leaders are twice encumbered. First, in conducting some core set of tasks—aerial bombing, remaking a host country's institutions, attacking insurgents, and the like—they inadequately attend to broad mission goals. In effect, they allow these tasks to replace these goals. Second, they stand distant from the battlefield, *detached* from wartime operations and realities and *deferent* to government officials and organizations charged with implementing policy. Thinking about policy remains undeveloped and fails to cohere (vertically or horizontally) within government. Thus, what passes for strategy amounts to less than the sum of its parts.

Stage II does not follow inevitably from stage I. With or without initial success, policy makers can exercise options. They might choose, for instance, to exit the conflict. The George H. W. Bush administration did just that in the 1991 Desert Storm Operation when it decided not to pursue Iraqi troops fleeing Kuwait. Conversely, policy makers might try to build on prior "success" by expanding the mission. In 1950 the Harry S. Truman administration took that path in Korea: once the US-led

United Nations force sent North Korean troops into retreat, Truman chose to resolve the dispute forcefully—and permanently—by unifying Korea, throwing the war into an eventual stalemate.[11] In 2003 the George W. Bush administration chose similarly to build on its success in overthrowing the Iraqi regime by attempting to remake Iraqi governing institutions in the Western image. Spurning both alternatives, policy makers might opt for a middle path. They might persevere, doing more of the same, to avoid the costs and risks of escalation or departure. The Lyndon B. Johnson administration chose that course in Vietnam when a limited bombing campaign and the introduction of ground troops failed to produce concessions from the adversary.

Whatever the course, the decisions can have a rational basis. Leaders might expand their immediate goals, for example, after determining (quite rationally) that meeting them requires accomplishing additional goals or will create opportunities to serve still others. For that matter, they might recognize, correctly, that expanding or extending the war is the cost-effective strategy. All things being equal, building on prior action is often cost effective, by merit of the prior investment.

Yet enlarging the mission can also stem from non-rational influences. Social scientists recount a litany of non-rational factors that can induce undue boldness (risk acceptance) or extreme caution (risk averseness) in decision-making and can blind participants entirely to the requirements of success, available options, their consequences, or the actual costs and risks of defeat. These influences include the perversities of group decision-making, known as "groupthink" (Janis 1982); wishful thinking and tunnel vision; the misapplication of historical analogies; anchored thinking; the inappropriate reading of probabilistic information; and the numerous psychological maladies that stem from motivated and unmotivated bias (Yetiv 2013). Non-rational influences also include the chasing of sunk costs and risk-taking when experiencing losses. These pervasive influences are behind the familiar refrain that missions tend to expand beyond sustainable levels, a phenomenon known widely as *mission creep* (Adams and Shoon 2014). The belated US shift in policy toward nation-building in Iraq stands as the virtual "poster child" for the argument that missions tend to grow beyond the will and capability to support them.[12]

At this stage in a conflict, civilian leaders are unlikely to have a well-developed plan should they decide to extend or expand the mission. Having fixated on immediate goals in the prewar period, they will not have fully considered the implications of failure, the opportunities and challenges of expanding or extending mission purposes, the links and trade-offs among these purposes, or the practical requisites of preferred policies. Adding to these failings, structural conditions distance leaders from both wartime realities and government organizations charged with policy implementation.[13] Leaders might not know that implementing organizations have sidelined some mission elements, pursued them only as preexisting procedures or country conditions allowed, or effectively redefined the mission by establishing guidelines (making "small" executive decisions) or relying on long-standing organizational practices. Indeed, leaders might not know that these organizations are struggling to achieve progress despite their resources, training, experience, personnel, and tactical know-how. The struggles might stem from a lack of preparedness, complications on the ground, or from poor coordination among organizations that diverge in their understandings of a mission and approaches to it. One organization might duplicate or contravene the actions of another or allow vital tasks to languish, having mistakenly assumed that some other organization would pick up the slack.

Leaders can certainly try to overcome the gap between declared policy and practice, yet they operate from a fundamental disadvantage. They must evaluate policy from a distance using *supplied* information, *standard* indicators, *anecdotal* evidence, or *mixed* news that ambiguously signals net gains and losses. They lack the access and specialized knowledge to grasp the intricacies of military planning, strategy, tactics, and performance; to recognize the full resource demands of an operation and the limited supply of capability; or to appreciate when and how US responses to war zone challenges might compromise policy goals. Through ignorance and indifference, they empower subordinates by default.

Stage III

Policy Choice: Limitation in Resources Committed
Decision Dynamic: Constriction (Recognize Limits, Focus on Cost Constraints)

Compounding challenges threaten to undermine all a president has sought to accomplish at home and abroad. Problems on the war front, tight resources, competing priorities, and declining public support now press visibly and immediately. Stage III commences when government leaders reach their limit. They recognize impediments to wartime success and restrict the resources available to the mission.

These constraints were apparent in 1967, when President Johnson (and Secretary of Defense Robert McNamara) set a ceiling of (roughly) half a million US troops in Vietnam. Indeed, these constraints were apparent in early 2007, when President Bush announced a US troop *increase* (the "surge")—a desperate effort to suppress the violence in Iraq—knowing that the US military could not long sustain those force levels. They were apparent as well in 2009, when President Barack Obama ordered a US troop *surge* in Afghanistan with a dictate that US forces commence a withdrawal eighteen months later.

US leaders took these actions, perhaps feeling hopeful, but never sanguine, about the likely outcome. President Johnson imposed his limit recognizing that at current strength US forces could not win in Vietnam in the foreseeable future. President Bush knew the surge was but a short-term fix—a Hail Mary pass of sorts—that if successful would still leave Iraq on the precipice of failure. President Obama set his force and time limits without a clear sense of what would constitute military success or failure a year and a half later. Indeed, these leaders accepted a cap on resources that could well impose additional costs by constraining future choices.

To be sure, a president can *rationally* cap an investment when resources become scarce, other priorities beckon, or the investment offers limited marginal returns. But rationality is impugned when cost curtailment—that is, getting the price down—becomes a driving and decisive factor in decision-making. At this point in the conflict, escalating involvement or exiting entirely might constitute better options.

Stage IV

Policy Choice: Disengagement of Military Forces
Decision Dynamic: Extrication (Prioritize Exit, Focus on Time Constraints)

Stage IV commences when rising costs and dwindling war support push policy makers to exit the conflict. Although they might strive for a graceful departure or reengage (even escalate the conflict) for abbreviated periods, "leaving on schedule" is now an overriding objective.

The war, around which much of the public rallied with the initial intervention, has now lost substantial support. Indeed, declining public support could produce an electoral mandate for change. Both President Richard M. Nixon and President Obama entered office unshackled; that they did not "own" their predecessor's policies eased the steps toward the door. Whether the impetus for change comes from the public or passes from elites to the public, the policy focus shifts to evacuation.

Consequently, policy makers turn their attention to establishing exit timelines, sticking to them, and coining justifications to cover the exit. Departure milestones are set without regard for the state of the conflict, efficient resource use, or the capability of allied forces to take charge. Policy makers might speak of a mission accomplished, the transferring of responsibility to local forces, or constraints that limit US options. Or they might try somehow to obscure the fact of retreat by blaming allies or local forces, handing over responsibilities to an international organization, escalating militarily for short-term gains, highlighting the achievement of some finite set of goals, or redefining the security problem to allow for an exit (on these strategies, see Tierney 2015: 224–228). Yet any such device thinly masks a palpable reality: withdrawing from the conflict has become *the* objective.

Leaving is plausibly the rational course here, at the point of exhaustion. Yet rational explanations for the pace and timing of departure fall short. Why did policy makers invest so heavily in a losing venture rather than hedge their bets, change strategies, or seek an earlier exit from the conflict? No less significantly, why would policy makers abandon their effort rather than plan to make efficient use of available resources in the time that remains or even extend the operation—somehow, in some way—to accomplish key objectives?

Contributory but Incomplete Explanations

To recognize that policymaking conforms to a means-driven process is not to deny the direct explanatory contribution of the psychological, organizational/bureaucratic, and political factors that foreign policy analysts have long credited with influencing the behavior of government leaders and officials. These factors nonetheless remain deficient explanations for lapses in national security decision-making.

Psychological Influences

That the beliefs of government leaders and officials bias their judgments, surviving logical and evidentiary challenges, amounts to a truism in the psychologically oriented foreign policy literature. The underlying principle is simple: "Beliefs are quick to form and then resist change." The resiliency of beliefs is attributable in part to cognitive bias, in which individuals unconsciously filter evidence and mold it to serve their preexisting beliefs. The accompanying cure is shock treatment: a surprising development or barrage of evidence that challenges the beliefs. By contrast, motivated bias—active resistance to arguments and facts that challenge coveted beliefs—acquires strength through confrontation. Individuals rationalize, discount the source of the information, look actively for confirmatory evidence, and interpret facts to support their own prior thinking—anything to salvage those beliefs.

Yet attributing the failings of policymaking to psychological bias invites a host of criticism, for good reason.[14] First, studying the beliefs of individual decision makers typically shifts the explanatory focus to idiosyncratic influences in policymaking. The danger for researchers is that having committed to a psychological explanation, they can always find a belief (maybe particular to a situation) that *can* explain behavior. Second, beliefs vary in importance with the decisional role of the individuals who hold them. "Who did what?" is often difficult to determine and a matter of continuing controversy. Third, beliefs *can* change with time. The problem for researchers, then, is distinguishing evidence of belief change from evidence that offers a fuller articulation of a long-standing belief. Fourth, attributing behavior to beliefs typically leaves multiple suspects. Analysts are left to ask whether an action reflects some general belief or one that applies only to a given situation. Finally, beliefs are elusive. They are often difficult to gauge from the public record, in no small part because it is the "public" record.

Together, these challenges best position individual-centered, cognitive-oriented foreign policy research to explain events rather than to predict them. A focus on the impact of influential and pervasive decisional referents in decision-making directly addresses that deficiency.

Organizational/Bureaucratic Influences

Writings on organizational and bureaucratic influences in wartime decision-making go a long way toward explaining the failings of wartime policies. Academic researchers and policy makers usefully attribute policy deficiencies to the short-sighted, narrow-minded practices of governmental organizations or the self-interested behavior of the governmental bureaucracy.

With either focus, the point is that governments act as they are structured. Whether and how policy translates into action reflects redundancies, relationships, missions, and interests across the governmental bureaucracy. Yet the literature is not without its weaknesses and limitations.

First, writers frequently conflate organizational processes and bureaucratic politics. They therefore leave unanswered whether, or when, bureaucratic politics and organizational processes amount to competitive, complementary, or interchangeable explanations.

As outlined in Allison's (1971) classic study of the Cuban Missile Crisis, organizations are "means-driven," whereas bureaucracies are "goal-driven."[15] Indeed, Allison sees self-interested bureaucracies acting much like rational states in realist theory: they employ available resources—here, horizontally and vertically within government—to serve their own interests at the expense of collective purposes. By contrast, organizations "offer solutions in search of a problem." They perform in set ways regardless of the situation. Even military organizations, in wartime, act as they were designed to act (Rosen 1991), whether or not that is necessary or appropriate. Whereas high stakes might weed out outmoded, ineffective, or counterproductive practices, organizations cannot easily recognize lapses in performance *as deficiencies*. Ambiguous information (e.g., in the fog of war) leaves them open to more favorable interpretations of evidence, playing to existing practice. Organizations can always dismiss failure as an exception or an insignificant setback, that is, the result of mistakes, inadequate resources or engagement, measurement flaws, or an inappropriate use or reading of the evidence. When acknowledging failure, organizations will try to rescue missions by doing more of the same—doubling down, for example, on established methods—and relying on standard performance indicators.[16] They have little incentive to change; adaptation takes time and absorbs resources—including those for training and equipment—when the demands of the moment (battlefield) press with urgency. Organizations answer novel challenges then with at most incremental changes in practice, not a comprehensive rethinking of the problem or its solution.[17]

Second, bureaucratic "interests" are subject to dispute. The literature is unclear, for example, on whether they lead organizations to protect some core mission or extend bureaucratic turf, and perhaps to pursue larger budgets (see Lebovic 1994). Bureaucracies cannot pursue all of these interests simultaneously without accepting trade-offs. What happens, for instance, if the desire to protect a core mission compromises the organization's long-term budgetary health?[18] The literature cannot tell us how a bureau (or bureaucrat) will respond in general to any given threat or opportunity.

Third, the behavior of a bureaucracy or organization is not always wrongheaded. Bureaucracies are not necessarily beholden to parochial interests and practices. The principal-agent literature, for one, assumes that decision makers can engineer decisions and invoke mechanisms to counter and deflect bureaucratic tendencies (Moe 1984). Moreover, government organizations might do the "right thing" without prodding. Organizations—including military organizations—can innovate to solve problems, even adapt to overcome the lapses and shortsightedness of government leaders. Scholars have increasingly recognized "horizontal and bottom-up innovation, in which actors across the military organization adapt to battlefield lessons and experiments to develop new ways of approaching operational problems" (Jensen 2016: 8). James Russell (2011) depicts military innovation in Iraq, for example, as largely a bottom-up and somewhat spontaneous process. Whereas observers frequently credit General David Petraeus with turning the tide in the Iraq War (by introducing counterinsurgency principles with the 2007 US troop surge), US troops innovated much earlier to address wartime challenges (absent concrete directives or enthusiasm from top military officials). These results were not limited to Iraq. In the first years after dethroning the Taliban, the US military command in Afghanistan adopted a counterinsurgency strategy, despite Secretary of Defense Donald Rumsfeld's disdain for the nation-building enterprise.

Fourth, and most relevant to the decisional focus of this study, maladies arise from above, not just from below. The literature on bureaucratic politics and organizational processes tends to offer a one-sided look at a two-sided problem. It depicts a rational decision maker who confronts or overcomes self-interested bureaucratic or non-rational organizational behavior,[19] when bureaucracies and organizations can act as directed and resourced.[20] Policy incoherence might stem then from *detachment* when leaders and organizations, rational or not, lack the mutual awareness to work from the same script, or from *deference* when leaders choose to delegate responsibilities to these organizations.

Domestic Political Influences

Domestic political explanations for the failings of wartime policies draw from compelling evidence, including public opinion polls that show the public rallying behind a presidential decision to take the country to war (Baker and Oneal 2001; Lian and Oneal 1993). Evidence suggests a president can realize political benefits through forceful action abroad. Researchers provoke greater controversy, however, when asking why war approval declines over time and whether declining approval constrains presidential options.

In 1971 John Mueller sparked considerable debate when he argued that US public support for war efforts falls with mounting US troop casualties. Researchers subsequently asked whether dwindling public support owes to rival elites who challenged war policy (Berinsky 2007);[21] insufficient leadership cues that a war is succeeding (Gelpi, Feaver, and Reifler 2005: 8); and the accumulation of bad news, as visible losses trump ambiguous gains in asymmetric conflicts (Lebovic 2010). They also asked, given a perceived relationship between military casualties and public support, whether governments avoid casualties by selecting to enter wars that they know they can win (Reiter and Stam 2002), inflict high civilian casualties to protect their own troops by using force indiscriminately (Downes 2009; Valentino, Huth, and Balch-Lindsay 2004), or limit their troop investments from the start. In this regard, John Caverley (2014) argues that US civilian leaders pursued a strategy in Vietnam that substituted capital for manpower to avoid politically injurious costs to the US mission. Although the fundamental issues remain unsettled, four points from the intellectual give and take deserve mention.

First, the public's support for any given war declines sharply over time.[22] Indeed, it has declined more quickly in recent years and dramatically once a war became a partisan issue. Just as the Vietnam War became "Nixon's war" and a subject of public division, the domestic Iraq War coalition splintered eventually along party and ideological lines. Wars that had not been major election issues in 1968 and 2004 became highly charged issues in 1972 and 2008, ironically as US intervention in Vietnam and Iraq, respectively, was ending.

Second, a change in administration can bring change to a US military mission. A new administration might enjoy a mandate to end an unpopular war or to at least alter the operative strategy. The US approach to the Vietnam, Iraq, and Afghanistan Wars did change markedly under new leaders, becoming less invested (politically and psychologically) in prior policies. The new leadership preferred not to hitch its own governing agenda to the failing priorities of the past.[23]

Third, public support is connected, but loosely, to the actions of US leaders. True, President Nixon reduced US reliance on the draft to quell public outrage against US involvement in the Vietnam War, just as President Obama realized opportunity in reducing the US troop presence in Afghanistan, absent public support for the Afghan mission. Yet presidential action (and inaction) during the Iraq and Vietnam Wars suggests that political leaders can act with little regard for current public support. Indeed, the long war in Afghanistan shows that a war can drag on long after the public has left it. Despite the polarization of American politics, neither Republicans nor Democrats saw potential gains in making the Afghanistan War an issue in the 2012 and 2016 presidential elections.

Fourth, public opinion is arguably less important to leaders than what they believe the public thinks about some present or likely administration action. On that score, Leslie Gelb and Richard Betts (1979) offer a compelling explanation of why, with US forces bogged down in Vietnam, President Johnson chose to stay the course. In their view, Johnson took the path of least (public) resistance; by enforcing a troop ceiling, he avoided the potential fallout and high political risks of an outright retreat or dangerous escalation. Although no one can say with certainty how the public would have responded to either escalation or withdrawal, Johnson had his fears and acted accordingly.

Johnson's choice of the middle course serves here as a building block for a more general explanation of leadership behavior. It is useful because Gelb and Betts establish that leaders do not necessarily change their policies to conform with existing public opinion and because they suggest further that some key referent—in Johnson's case, a US troop ceiling in Vietnam—can constrain decisions. No doubt Johnson's choice had the rational basis that Gelb and Betts suppose; rising public discontent and the untoward consequences of losing in Vietnam certainly influenced Johnson's thinking.[24] Yet the question remains whether Johnson locked into the war freeze option in no small part because it left him short of a critical domestic threshold *and* came without the glaring costs of escalation or withdrawal. Questions like this one, acknowledging the non-rational influence of salient decisional referents, fuel the analysis to follow.

A Less Useful Explanation: The Rational Theory of War

I offer this book, then, as a critique of the much-heralded rational theory of war, which attributes failings in military conflict to uncertainty over an opponent's capabilities and intentions. The theory poses a simple question, "Why does war occur if it is a losing proposition for at least one of the participants?" Put differently, if realists are correct that states are rational and that wars are costly (especially for the losing side), why do states fight rather than compromise? In the end, both parties would have been better off had they chosen to avoid war. James Fearon (1995) popularized the question and provided an answer: short of battle, states lack sufficient information to judge their adversary's capabilities and intentions.[25] Having reduced uncertainty through war, states can adjust their strategies, tactics, and level of commitment.

The rational theory holds advantages over its theoretical rivals in various respects, including parsimony, modest testing requirements, and apparent fit with available evidence. After all, the United States *has*, much like other major powers, gone to war expecting favorable outcomes, only to concede ground conspicuously when recognizing that its "capability advantages" were not all they seemed. The rational theory nonetheless suffers as an explanation in attributing non-rational decisional shortfalls to informational deficiencies. Whereas the rational theory of war supposes that policy makers adapt efficiently to an unfolding reality—that is, they choose war when it *is* the best option and depart a conflict when leaving offers the best return—I argue that the bigger challenge to viable war policy is not uncertainty but rather bias that overrides policy goals. In other words, sound policy suffers considerably not from uncertainty but rather from a "misplaced certainty" (Mitzen and Schweller 2011: 3).[26]

A rational policy maker will assess the likely payoff from pursuing one goal over another, husband resources to achieve critical objectives, and abandon policies that prove ineffective or promise disappointment. Yet US decision makers (in peacetime and wartime) fall well short of the ideal. They defer to immediate objectives and policy constraints with little thought to broader purposes. For a number of reasons, then, overarching objectives deficiently guide policy.

First, overarching goals are remote from "view." Policy makers therefore confuse what they can "see" for what remains out of sight. The contours and demands of a concept like "US security requirements in the Middle East" are sufficiently ambiguous that they play little active role in guiding policy deliberations. Policy makers are more likely to think about US security in light of a regional military balance, conceived in terms of force levels and weapons quality, and to see "imbalances" in departures from that configuration. Thus, policy makers are inclined to think and act as if these overarching goals reduced to such referents.

Second, overarching goals mean different things to different people. The Bush administration saw the fight against the Afghan Taliban and Iraqi insurgency as critical components in the war against "global terrorism." Policy experts certainly agreed that terrorism was a scourge, regardless of its location; they disagreed fundamentally over what combating terrorism meant in practice. Whereas some advocates pressed for forceful offensive military action, others hoped to address the root causes of terrorism by eradicating poverty, supporting democratic change, engaging in political outreach, and reducing the US profile in conflicts that make the United States an inviting target for attack. Likewise, US policy makers of the Vietnam era agreed on the need to preserve the "credibility" of US threats and promises in the world. Policy experts disagreed, however, on whether credibility stemmed from absorbing pain in Vietnam to show that the United States would stick to its guns or from acting rationally by leaving Vietnam to avoid the likely costs of the conflict. Decades later, US policy makers disagreed over the requisites of "stability" in Iraq and Afghanistan—the level of violence, institutional shortfalls, and political feuding—that would permit a US exit from these conflicts.

Third, the link between ends and means provokes tough questions, asked all too infrequently. Will the means produce desired ends, and if so, under what conditions, with what probability, and with a greater payoff than other options? Missing from internal debates over Vietnam, Iraq, and Afghanistan war strategy is evidence, for example, that US leaders asked whether they could best serve US security interests by withdrawing US forces—saving them for some more important fight—rather than by continuing to invest heavily in these war efforts.[27] The lapse is understandable. All assessments of fundamental goals and their relationship to policy instruments invite controversy and defy consensus. Reconciling the differences in policy perspectives was perhaps impossible, and certainly dangerous politically, should airing views derail a consensus or give ammunition to political rivals and policy critics.

Fourth, US goals depend on adversaries' intentions and capabilities. What *we* should do depends inevitably on what we think *they* want to do and what they can do. A challenge, as realists acknowledge, is judging intentions that are variable, opaque, and knowable only through inference from an adversary's behavior and capabilities. Yet assessing capabilities is more challenging than realists acknowledge. It requires an answer to the difficult question (Baldwin 1979), "power to do what?" Conclusions concerning these capabilities are actually quite sensitive to assumptions about the adversary's intentions (priorities and strategies). Whether the adversary is strong or weak depends on whether (and when) it seeks to maintain the status quo, perform within its comfort zone, rely on allies for support, or pursue small or big gains. Answering the key question becomes more difficult still when the adversary actively manipulates the information flow, perhaps spinning, managing, and staging events to exaggerate its will and capability to fight (Johnson and Tierney 2006). Hanoi certainly followed this script. In the 1968 Tet Offensive, it sought to create an aura of success by directing the Vietcong to seize cities throughout South Vietnam.[28]

Inasmuch as overarching goals remain elusive and remote, policy makers focus on tangible referents. They defer rhetorically to broad, ambitious goals. They claim they seek to preserve the peace in some part of the world, maintain US credibility abroad, spread democracy, defeat terrorism, or combat the spread of weapons of mass destruction. But merely stating broad goals is not enough to inject rationality into policy. Policies inevitably fall short when those who devise them fail to ask, "What precisely do we want to achieve, and how do we plan to achieve it?"

Thus, the rational take on war serves effectively as the "counterfactual" outcome in this study of wartime decisional outcomes. Goal-directed policy makers select from among feasible options when considering their relative costs and benefits with available information. Misdirected policies prove correctable, then, with the resolution of uncertainty. The indicators of rational assessment contrast sharply with the symptoms of decisional bias. Biased policy makers opt for war with little sense of whether and how it might serve their overarching purposes, they direct their efforts toward some immediate goal without fully comprehending the consequences of success or failure, and they do little to prepare for contingencies should unforeseen problems arise. Existing practices and priorities drive policy positions.

US decision-making in Vietnam, Iraq, and Afghanistan certainly approximated rationality in various respects. Decision makers exercised judgment, acquired information, planned the future, and adjusted policy when its costs became apparent. Yet as will become increasingly clear, appearances are deceiving.

The Argument in Brief

In focusing on the "how" of US policymaking, I highlight the sources and impact of a means-driven process that had policy makers gravitating toward limited solutions to complex and demanding policy problems. Eschewing rationality, policy makers defined US goals first to serve *proximate* goals; then to serve *disjoined* tasks; eventually to serve *available* US (political, economic, and military) resources; and finally to serve a *fixed-exit* schedule, at which point leaving became the primary objective. In other words, US leaders went to war to serve a narrowly conceived purpose; they pursued, and even expanded, the mission without fully appreciating the relationship among its parts or their practical requisites and potential consequences; they later defined their mission goals mainly to serve diminished US resources; and finally, they subordinated these modest goals to an exit strategy.

Organizational and bureaucratic influences helped distance US leaders from mission challenges and specifics from the air and on the ground, and domestic politics helped finally to define limits to the human and material resources that US leaders would invest in the conflict. Yet policy makers did not deal rationally with these constraints. They failed to reconcile goals with capabilities to make necessary trade-off decisions; to scrutinize the costs, benefits, and consequences of policy alternatives; or to adjust their policies assiduously when acquiring information about adversary capabilities and intentions. In consequence, they had to cope with an ever-smaller range of choice.

2

The Vietnam War, 1965–1973

In many respects the Vietnam War stands alone. As the bloodiest US war of the post–World War II period, it cost the lives of over fifty thousand Americans and a million Vietnamese. It also created unparalleled divisions at home. It provoked massive domestic protests, drove a wedge between the US citizenry and government, and survived thereafter as a cautionary tale and powerful analogy for disparaging foreign intervention. Warnings that the United States is involved in "another Vietnam" serve to strengthen accusations that US policy makers have taken the country blindly into battle, with a false sense of optimism or no sense of the likely costs and gains.

Despite its exceptional features, the Vietnam War—much like its successors in Iraq and Afghanistan—followed a familiar decisional pattern. The Johnson administration committed early to a US military solution without fully appreciating the "problem" or considering how available solutions might solve it (*fixation*). Once engaged in Vietnam, the administration extended the US mission to include a full-blown air war that was true to neither a political nor a military strategy, and it fought a ground war, at the military's direction, without concern for the war's critical political dimension (*disjunction*). Then, when reaching its limit, the government sought mainly to manage the US mission's costs (*constriction*). Finally, when victory proved elusive, the Nixon administration prioritized an exit from the conflict (*extrication*).

Backdrop to the War

In the aftermath of World War II, the United States sought, with mixed success, to prevent Communist gains in Southeast Asia. The Dwight D. Eisenhower administration backed French efforts to re-establish a hold in the region. It kept some distance from the French operation, however, preferring not to identify the United States with a colonial cause or join France in battle—in a losing effort, no less, that might leave US forces fighting the Vietminh alone (Gelb and Betts 1979: 58). When the French evacuated, the administration was unwilling to surrender the country to a Communist government. Although the 1954 Geneva Accords mandated an election to determine the fate of a unified Vietnam, provisionally divided between a Communist north and a non-Communist south, the administration recognized South Vietnam (the Republic of Vietnam) as an independent country. It stood by the southern government's refusal to hold the election, believing (correctly) that an election would favor Ho Chi Minh, the Vietminh leader and legendary independence hero. It also sent the country massive amounts of economic aid and hundreds of US military advisers. The Eisenhower administration thus laid the foundation for a growing US commitment to South Vietnamese sovereignty.

President John F. Kennedy built on his predecessor's policies by helping the Republic of Vietnam grapple with a growing Communist insurgency. He weighed recommendations for sending US combat troops to the country in a limited role and number. Although some of his advisers wanted to put the military option on hold and others chafed at a *limited* troop commitment, they generally agreed that a strong and overt US military commitment to the struggle was necessary, absent future military progress (Gelb and Betts 1979: 75–77). Over the course of his administration, Kennedy committed over ten thousand military personnel to Vietnam and created "a command structure that could encompass combat troops in addition to advisers and support personnel" (Talmadge 2015: 47).[1] He also increased the US role in South Vietnamese governance. He directed administration officials to press the corrupt and increasingly abusive leadership in Saigon to adopt political and economic reforms. When pressure alone proved insufficient, he backed a military coup d'état against South Vietnam's president, Ngo Dinh Diem, hoping that a new Saigon government would draw public support away from the Hanoi-backed National Liberation Front (or NLF, of which the Vietcong, the indigenous Communist movement in South Vietnam, was a part). But the coup left the United States trading one set of "problems" for another. The country's new regime took a more conciliatory stance toward the NLF and North Vietnam, and like the regimes that would rapidly succeed it, was too weak to secure a national power base, let alone engage in meaningful reforms.

Kennedy did not long endure this situation. Bullets took his life a few weeks after Diem's murder in the 1963 coup. Had Kennedy survived, he might have stepped back from the abyss. Some of his advisers have said as much; they cite Kennedy's acumen (McNamara 1995: 96), or confidences, to show that he would have extricated the United States from the conflict. Indeed, Gordon Goldstein (2008: 229–248), in his much-heralded book, recounts the suggestive conversations that allude to an early Kennedy exit from Vietnam. Goldstein also reveals a consistency in Kennedy's foreign policy record that by implication holds Johnson responsible for the misbegotten decision to opt for war. Kennedy supposedly revealed his conciliatory impulses in Laos and in *higher* stakes battles in Cuba, where he accepted defeat in the Bay of Pigs fiasco and a compromise to end the Cuban Missile Crisis by agreeing to remove US missiles from Turkey. The evidence here is more than circumstantial. Kennedy repeatedly thwarted recommendations from his top advisers to introduce combat troops directly into the Vietnam fighting (Goldstein 2008: 57, 63).[2]

Yet Kennedy's actions, purported instincts, and private comments to tangential participants hardly convey the full range and equivocation of his thinking, much less his likely course of action as conflict conditions evolved. At most, his cryptic verbal asides establish that Kennedy struggled over how best to handle the deteriorating situation in Vietnam. If Kennedy had truly committed to an early exit, why did he keep his actual plans for an exit from his inner circle of policy advisers? Their counsel was required to ease the transition to a new policy and sell a reversal more broadly. Why, also, did his policies and public rhetoric not reflect the "new reality?" After all, staying the current course—investing US resources and credibility in the war effort—only made an imminent US departure more difficult to achieve (Cuddy 2003: 360). If anything, Kennedy's actions had the United States moving in the opposite direction. By backing the coup against Diem, Kennedy had at once signaled his commitment to, and increased the US investment in, South Vietnam's future (Trachtenberg 2014: 23).

Shortly before his death, Kennedy had indeed backed plans to remove a thousand US troops from Vietnam as a step toward withdrawing all US troops from Vietnam by the end of 1965. His private conversations with Secretary of Defense Robert McNamara reveal, however, that these plans assumed that South Vietnamese security conditions would improve (Logevall 1999: 70; Selverstone 2010: 493). As one prominent historian, Marc Trachtenberg (2014: 21), concluded upon reviewing the historical documentation, "one comes away from that material with the distinct impression that the withdrawal plan was predicated on the assumption that the South Vietnamese army would eventually be able essentially to stand on its own."

Like his predecessor and his successor, Kennedy found himself caught in the middle. Had he lived, he might have succumbed to the decisional forces that engulfed the Johnson administration. Although Kennedy's commitment to South Vietnam had potential limits—"the President seemed to draw the line at the introduction of combat troops" (Trachtenberg 2014: 17)—those constraints would most certainly have changed with circumstances and increasing US involvement in the conflict. Thus, hunches about Kennedy's instincts—even his aversion to substituting US troops for South Vietnamese manpower and economic and political reforms—do not account for future conditions, at home and abroad, that might have pushed him toward war. Even Eisenhower emerged, in the Johnson administration, as an ardent, behind-the-scenes advocate for a decisive US response to Communist transgressions in Vietnam (Brands 1985). All of Johnson's top advisers—holdovers from the Kennedy administration—believed that the United States had to employ military force in Vietnam. They disagreed over the quantity and nature of the forces that the United States should deploy and the chances for meaningful negotiations with Hanoi; they largely shared the view, however, that the US stakes and the intensifying conflict proscribed a lesser response. For that matter, McNamara, who had pressed for the thousand-troop withdrawal and devised an exit schedule in the Kennedy administration (Selverstone 2010: 495), quickly became a strong proponent of escalating US involvement as secretary of defense under Johnson.

Stage I, Engagement: Fixation

Whereas his predecessors had sought to address the Communist challenge in Southeast Asia with supplies, subversion, and subterfuge, in 1965 Lyndon Johnson took US involvement to the next level by sending US combat troops to Vietnam. His was not clearly a "big" decision, if understood as an explicit choice at some key moment among well-specified options. Nor was it an "incremental" decision, that is, a series of small, successive decisions that finally took the United States to war. No wonder some critics chastised the administration for having no real plan and stumbling and bumbling its way into the conflict, while others assailed the administration for contriving a case for a war that it had secretly planned.

The decision most definitely had small, but also large, elements. Johnson acted with caution, even painful deliberation. His decisions to employ, and then increase, US forces in Vietnam were made slowly, in response to adversary provocations, and were built on his past decisions. His tepid, conditional, and selective responses brought the United States successively into, never out of, the conflict. Yet a critical, early decision to use US conventional forces as necessary to preserve the territorial integrity of South Vietnam drove the eventual outcome. Johnson decided at that point to act with sufficient force in Vietnam to win.[3] He shed his reserve and qualified thinking when, in the ensuing months, military conditions in South Vietnam continued to deteriorate. What he did not do was reconcile the views of his policy advisers on whether or how US military action, of any nature or scale, would produce a favorable outcome.

The Road to War

Early on, President Johnson received proposals for a strong US response to deteriorating conditions in the South Vietnamese countryside. South Vietnamese forces proved unable to hold territory throughout much of the country, and the peasantry had little reason to support the Saigon government. In January 1964 the Joint Chiefs of Staff (JCS) proposed bombing North Vietnamese targets and the "commitment of US forces as necessary," presuming that the administration would eventually move into the conflict (Warner 2003: 831). Although Johnson vetoed proposals that would place the United States squarely in the conflict, he nonetheless sought military options to press Hanoi to stop aiding the insurgency in the south, and continued to build up US advisory support to the South Vietnamese military.[4]

McNamara, who had visited South Vietnam the prior December, returned in March 1964.[5] In his subsequent report to the president,[6] he laid out the case for an "independent non-Communist South Vietnam." The stakes were high: "Unless we can achieve this objective in South Vietnam, almost all of Southeast Asia will probably fall under Communist dominance (all of Vietnam, Laos, and Cambodia), accommodate to Communism so as to remove effective U.S. and anti-Communist influence (Burma), or fall under the domination of forces not now explicitly Communist but likely then to become so (Indonesia taking over Malaysia)." The effects would reverberate more widely, reaching India—and even New Zealand and Australia. Despite his sense that the "South Vietnamese must win their own fight," McNamara called for US military assistance and recognized that "it may be necessary at some time in the future to put demonstrable retaliatory pressure on the North."

The stark choice might have sparked significant pushback under different conditions. In the current context, it did not. Indeed, the report initiated an onslaught of official reports recommending a deepening US military commitment or preparation for one, outlining military-option packages and sequences. In May 1964 Johnson asked McNamara (on his return from a third trip to Vietnam) for two plans: the first, a three- to six-month plan for a "major stiffening" of the US effort, and the second, for "an integrated political-military plan for graduated action against North Vietnam." When delivered, the second of these plans presented a scenario "culminating in air strikes of gradually increasing scope and intensity against North Vietnamese targets" (Warner 2003: 831–832). The same month, the president's national security adviser, McGeorge Bundy, sent the president a draft memo distilling, it said, the thoughts of Secretary of State Dean Rusk and Secretary of Defense McNamara. Barring improved conditions in South Vietnam and Laos,[7] and assuming that the diplomacy and politics were right, it recommended that Johnson "make a Presidential decision that the U.S. will use selected and carefully graduated military force against North Vietnam."[8] In its readiness to use military force, the recommendation was unequivocal: "It is our recommendation that these deployments be on a very large scale, from the beginning, so as to maximize their deterrent impact and their menace. We repeat our view that a pound of threat is worth an ounce of action—*as long as we are not bluffing* [emphasis added]."

While the planning continued, US forces saw limited military action. In August 1964 the administration retaliated forcefully for the Gulf of Tonkin "attacks" (discussed later in the chapter), hitting a number of naval bases and oil storage facilities. Then the administration backed off. It still lacked a strategy to address the growing threat. With the presidential election looming in November 1964, Johnson was risk averse and wanted to avoid the appearance that he had committed to a Southeast Asian war or that the JCS was pressing him toward combat (McMaster 1997: 70–71). Despite military and political pressure to respond forcefully, Johnson thus acted with some restraint to the deadly Vietcong attack in October on the Bien

Hoa airbase just north of Saigon. Yet that attack, like the subsequent (December 24) attack on the Brink Hotel officers' quarters in Saigon, hardened Johnson's resolve.

In November 1964 the president met with his national security team—McNamara, Rusk, and Bundy—for a discussion that centered on the ongoing progress of a working group assigned to consider US alternatives in Vietnam.[9] The alternatives all involved some degree of military force, with option A being to continue the current course with reprisal attacks as necessary; option B being a "'hard/fast squeeze'" of "attacks of increasing intensity against North Vietnam," and option C being a "slow, controlled squeeze" against the North. McNamara informed the president that thus far option C was preferred, though "work was also well advanced on Option B." Military options, and their preparation, dominated the discussion. Nonmilitary options were almost an afterthought. In Bundy's words, the "devil's advocate" exercise, entrusted to Undersecretary of State George Ball, "had not advanced." Ball was apparently "preoccupied with other assignments." Left unsaid was that in early October Ball *had* completed an exhaustive analysis—sixty-seven pages of single-spaced text—opposing a war that was "getting out of hand." Bundy, Rusk, and (a "horrified") McNamara had convinced Ball to bury it (Preston 2006: 158).[10]

In December 1964 the president approved a two-phase program that echoed the directive to McNamara earlier the same year. For the first month, the United States would seek to improve the South Vietnamese government's effectiveness, possibly bomb North Vietnam's infiltration routes, and strike North Vietnamese targets, if it were deemed necessary to avenge additional deadly attacks on US personnel in the south. The follow-on phase, predicated on improved South Vietnamese government effectiveness, called for air strikes of increasing intensity against North Vietnam. The military would first target infiltration routes south of the 19th parallel and then move, if required, to attack all major North Vietnamese military targets, mine North Vietnamese ports, and enforce a naval blockade of North Vietnam (Warner 2003: 841). In the revealing—indeed, prophetic—words of the National Security Council (NSC) principals, "Such a program would consist principally of progressively more serious air strikes, of a weight and tempo adjusted to the situation as it develops (possibly running from two to six months) and of appropriate US deployments to handle any contingency."[11]

In January 1965 the march toward war received further impetus with Bundy's (infamous) "fork-in the road" memo. Expressing the beliefs of both Bundy and McNamara in advance of a meeting with Johnson, it stated that the two advisers were "now pretty well convinced that our current policy can lead only to disastrous defeat." The preferred course was "to use our military power in the Far East and force a change of Communist policy." Taking explicit exception to Rusk's appeal for caution, it argued that "the time has come for harder choices."[12] Bundy would later claim that the intent was "to push President Johnson out of the zone of indecision that had characterized the 1964 campaign year" (Goldstein 2008: 153).

The stage was set. Phase 2 commenced with the Rolling Thunder bombing campaign in March 1965, ostensibly in retaliation for another deadly Vietcong attack, the prior month, on the US airbase at Pleiku. Johnson linked US retaliation to his prior decision to scale the combat effort as necessary (Warner 2003: 843). With the administration now seeking more "expansive proposals," the military responded favorably; "by the end of March, [General William Westmoreland, the US commander in South Vietnam], the chief of staff of the Army, and the Joint Chiefs of Staff all had recommended commitment of large numbers of U.S. troops to ground combat" (Cosmas 2006: 206).

In March 1965 Johnson responded to a request from Westmoreland by sending 3,500 Marines to guard the Da Nang airbase. The contingent was small, in relative terms, with 23,700 US military personnel already in South Vietnam. Yet their presence as a repellent force signaled a momentous shift toward active US combat (Warner 2003: 844). Preparations were under way for a still larger US combat presence. The following month Johnson approved the deployment of two additional Marine battalions, a Marine aircraft squadron, and 18,000–20,000 support troops, with the understanding that they would establish coastal bases sufficient to support the multiple army divisions that the JCS had recommended for deployment (Cosmas 2006: 208). Just as ominously, the force increase came with implicit presidential support for a US land-combat role in the form of an unspecified "'change of mission'" for the Marine battalions in Vietnam (Warner 2003: 845). Johnson "altered the mission of all Marine battalions in Vietnam 'to permit their more active use under conditions to be established and approved by the Secretary of Defense in consultation with the Secretary of State'" (Cosmas 2006: 208). The Marines deployed in defense of a larger perimeter, with "defense" now understood to include offensive action.[13]

The focus now, at all levels of government, was on establishing a meaningful ground combat presence. The internal debate centered on how and when—not whether—to introduce additional US troops. In July Johnson ordered US troop levels increased from 75,000 to 125,000 troops, with the promise of additional forces as requested (Gelb and Betts 1979: 129). The floodgates had opened.

Rational Explanations for US Intervention

Scholars offer two prominent rational explanations for the Johnson administration's decision to intervene in Vietnam with full force. The second of these is more persuasive than the first.

First, Johnson supposedly acted in Vietnam in paradoxical pursuit of his *domestic* agenda (see Bator 2008). His thinking was supposedly that, by not confronting "Communist aggression" in Vietnam, he would place the administration on the defensive at home, losing leverage for pursuing his cherished civil rights, educational, and antipoverty legislation (or "Great Society" programs). Claims that Johnson acted rationally, to serve domestic political purposes, acquire credibility from his preoccupation with challenges from the Right (Gelb and Betts 1979: 158; Logevall 1999: 76), which could accuse him of "losing Vietnam," much as Harry S. Truman had supposedly "lost China" (Herring 1991: 109).

Second, Johnson supposedly thought that by not responding to the Communist threat in Vietnam, he would unsettle US allies and embolden US adversaries, mortally damaging US credibility internationally. Johnson did not slavishly accept the so-called domino theory (as articulated by Eisenhower in the preceding decade); he did not believe that the loss to Communism of any one country would necessarily endanger surrounding countries. He focused instead on the effects of a US loss in Vietnam on the overall integrity of US commitments (Cuddy 2003: 361–362; Gelb and Betts 1979: 189).[14] He was backed in his thinking by McNamara, who argued that the loss of Vietnam would reverberate widely as a (failed) test of US will and capabilities (Warner 2003: 830–831)—a position that echoed also in Secretary of State Rusk's warnings that in Vietnam the very "integrity of the US commitment" was at risk (Warner 2003: 848). Johnson therefore resolved to hold the line. Whereas some of his advisers sought to limit US involvement in Vietnam to "symbolic action"—"doing just enough to say we tried" (McMaster 1997: 184)—Johnson took a strong stance in warning of the consequences of a US defeat.

Contrary to the somewhat cynical, domestic-political thesis, Johnson clearly cared about the outcome of the Vietnam conflict. It is difficult to imagine that he would otherwise have incurred the risks and costs of US military intervention.[15] Indeed, he believed that by engaging the United States more fully in Vietnam with limited success, he might actually *sacrifice* his domestic agenda. Few quotations express this sentiment more clearly than his later reflection to a biographer: "I knew from the start that if I left the woman I love—the Great Society—in order to fight that bitch of a war, then I would lose everything. All my programs. All my hopes. All my dreams" (Goodwin 1991: 233).

From a domestic-political standpoint, the odds actually seemed stacked in favor of Johnson extricating the United States from a potential war in Asia. No strong domestic contingent was pressing hard to take the country to war (Logevall 2004). On the contrary, Johnson won a landslide victory in the 1964 election by positioning himself as the peace candidate (Logevall 1999: 254). He also maintained strong personal ties to both dovish and hawkish Democratic leaders in Congress, who were sympathetic to the president's decisional plight. Indeed, he benefited from a prevailing bipartisan ethic and deference to the executive on matters of national security. The public would probably support a Vietnam engagement, but most Americans initially backed a negotiated solution to the conflict. Johnson could actually have made a strong public case against US military action. He might have argued that Hanoi's peace feelers could lead to a united but neutral Vietnam (following the precedent set in Laos in the Kennedy administration) or that the inept and venal Saigon government deserved blame for its own sorry plight. He could even have highlighted the confounding dimensions of the conflict: Hanoi's nationalist ambitions and appeal would challenge any *US-led* war effort yet create political space between Hanoi and its allies in Russia and China. In its earlier years, the Vietnamese revolution under Ho Chi Minh had grown without external support, and in later years, "the support provided by the Soviet Union and China was neither unlimited, unconditional nor unequivocal" (Herring 1991: 106).

That Johnson acted with great secretiveness, alone, impugns the argument that he would have benefited politically from going to war. Before the 1964 election Johnson withheld US war preparations from the US public; after his decisive win, he still preferred low-profile escalation—such as through interdiction strikes in Laos on North Vietnamese infiltration routes (Greenstein and Burke 1989/ 1990: 116)—and did little to prepare the public for the long road ahead. Indeed, the Johnson administration felt it necessary to hide *and manufacture* facts to support its push toward war in Vietnam.[16]

No set of disputable facts was more important in that regard than the collection of "events" that provoked Congress, in August 1964, to pass the Gulf of Tonkin Resolution. In the official version, North Vietnamese gunboats attacked the destroyer USS *Maddox* in international waters on August 2 and again—along with the destroyer USS *Turner Joy*—two days later. The US Senate passed the infamous Tonkin resolution authorizing the president to take "all necessary measures to repel any armed attack against the forces of the United States and to prevent further aggression"—indeed, to do what was necessary to promote peace and security in Southeast Asia. The strength of the resolution, with almost universal backing (it passed with a 466–0 vote in the House and 88–2 vote in the Senate), goes a long way toward explaining the feelings of betrayal that Johnson's former Senate colleagues felt toward the administration once the precipitating events came into question.[17]

The resolution gave Johnson a virtual blank check for prosecuting the war. The legislative outcome might have differed, however, had the Senate known about some combination of the following.[18] Specifically, (a) the *Maddox* was engaged in intelligence gathering off the North Vietnamese coast, where the United States was backing South Vietnamese sabotage operations; (b) South Vietnamese commandos had attacked North Vietnamese targets in the vicinity just a couple of days earlier; (c) the US military knew that North Vietnam was responding with increasing aggression to the South Vietnamese raids; (d) the US (Pacific and Vietnam) commands had acknowledged beforehand that the two operations might somehow conflict, but simply assumed that North Vietnam would know the operations were unrelated; (e) the *Maddox* actually fired first in the initial (and only) encounter (damaging two North Vietnamese vessels and disabling a third); (f) Johnson and McNamara suspected at the time that the North Vietnamese attack was a response to the South Vietnamese attack (Central Intelligence Agency [CIA] director John McCone told Johnson, in an NSC meeting, that the North Vietnamese attacked the *Maddox* for that reason);[19] (g) the administration was looking for a pretext to justify US military action and had crafted a supportive Senate resolution *before* the Tonkin encounter;[20] (h) after the *Maddox* attack, Johnson and McNamara discussed responses to a possible second attack and thus presumably could have avoided one; (i) North Vietnam sought to avoid, not initiate, another naval confrontation after the *Maddox* incident; and (j) McNamara had received word that the second "attack" might not have occurred—evidence suggesting a "second attack" was far more ambiguous and contradictory than the administration indicated at the time. Indeed, the subsequent "attack" amounted to little more than a misreading of radar signals.[21]

As the Senate would not rescind the resolution for another six years, it served as a touchstone for growing public skepticism of presidential claims and promises. In evaluating Johnson's war decision-making, it serves another critical function. It begs the question, "Why the deceit if the public was clamoring for war or Johnson knew that everything would work out politically for him in the end?"

Standard Non-Rational Explanations for US Intervention

These rational explanations have considerable explanatory merit, but so do alternative non-rational explanations of the progression toward war. Scholars disagree about which non-rational influences best explain failings and lapses in the Johnson administration's decision-making.

First, some scholars assert that a false promise of victory lured Johnson into war. Accordingly, they highlight evidence of wishful thinking—beliefs (or hopes) that active US military involvement in the conflict might compel Hanoi to back down—but also various decisional breakdowns and dysfunctional group dynamics within the administration. For instance, Johnson ignored policy specifics that cautioned against precipitous action; his focus, instead, was on the politics of making policy, not its particulars or intellectual underpinnings (Greenstein and Burke 1989/1990: 560). Put differently, "he had no interest in, or patience with, intellectual give and take" (Logevall 1999: 78).[22] He was predisposed, moreover, toward closeted decision-making: "He disliked large meetings or widely circulated written documents, which could lead to leaks showing dissent or disloyalty" (Kaiser 2000: 287). Indeed, he was prone to shut out advisers who voiced dissent, except privately, or who chose to look backward, not move forward, once a decision had been made. Hubert Humphrey became persona non grata in Vietnam-related discussions (Barrett 1988/1989: 642–648) after sharing his dovish views in an early, small-group advisory session with Johnson, just as McNamara would "lose his effectiveness" as a policy adviser years later when he expressed doubts about likely US military success. Further inhibiting rational action, Johnson's hawkish advisers purportedly controlled the information and limited the perspectives introduced in decisions. Johnson greatly respected and repeatedly consulted his team of national security advisers (Barrett 1988/1989: 660; Best 1988: 539). He held McNamara in particular in high regard: "He was the ablest man that Lyndon Johnson had ever dealt with, the President told people; there was no one like him for service to his country" (Halberstam 1969: 405). Johnson's inexperience, deference in matters of foreign policy, and dependence on his advisers supposedly left him unprepared to resist.

Yet overoptimism, underthinking, and excessive deference only take us so far as explanations. Despite assertions that Johnson, like Kennedy before him, led the United States blindly into a quagmire—"not really understanding the depth of the problems in Vietnam and convinced that it could win"—neither Kennedy, Johnson, nor their advisers were optimistic that intervention would soon bring a positive outcome: "Vietnam was indeed a quagmire, but most American leaders knew it." "At best, they *hoped* they might be lucky, but they did not *expect* to be" (Gelb and Betts 1979: 3, 19, 24). Johnson pushed repeatedly for more information and options to support his decisions, requested and received formal intelligence and policy assessments, agonized under the weight of these decisions in the presence of confidants, and sought the counsel of a broad circle of knowledgeable advisers from within and outside the government. Thus, he was reasonably well informed and clearly burdened by his belief that a US victory in Vietnam would not come easily. He understood, too, that sending US troops to Vietnam was a slippery slope: withdrawing them short of success would invite prohibitive domestic political costs. Getting into war, he knew, was far easier than getting out (Cuddy 2003: 363).

Second, other scholars look more to anonymous forces in arguing that a slow cascade of events drew the administration progressively, and somewhat unwarily, into the conflict. To make that case, scholars view the events of the period in sequence to show that tit-for-tat retribution for adversary acts pulled the United States incrementally into the conflict. After all, "the commitment of US combat troops, as opposed to advisors, had barely been mentioned during the many discussions on Vietnam during 1964," and "escalation had almost invariably been discussed in the form of air action against the DRV" (Warner 2003: 842). Indeed, Maxwell Taylor reflected with displeasure on the relative ease with which the administration introduced ground troops into the conflict: "It was curious how hard it had been to get authority for the initiation of the air campaign against the North and how relatively easy to get the marines ashore" (Taylor 1972: 338). Taylor—as JCS chair—had pressed hard against the seemingly sudden, growing sentiment in Washington for an increased US ground presence in the conflict. He had been wary of introducing the Marines into the conflict (Goldstein 2008: 163), and he now believed that the introduction of army troops, however the military sold it, would lead to an ever-larger US combat presence in Vietnam.[23]

Whether Taylor was right or wrong about the rashness of the deployment decision depends on the time horizon: whether the decision in mid-1965 came "out of nowhere" or followed, instead, from the prevailing understanding, as articulated in the two-phase program from December of the prior year, that the United States would move as necessary into the conflict. Even that decision followed from McNamara's report, which was approved by Taylor (Logevall 1999: 128), presented by the defense secretary in March 1964 upon his return from Vietnam. Formally sanctioned, as National Security Action Memorandum 288, it committed the United States to defend and preserve a non-Communist South Vietnam and "remained the bedrock upon which all proposals were to be built" (Logevall 1999: 256).

Of course incremental decision-making could account for the growing US force commitment in the months (and years) that followed. It is possible, for instance, that Johnson was progressively convinced—by events and by his advisers—to up the ante in the conflict after his initial commitment of ground forces. From March through July 1964, Johnson consulted inordinately with his small inner circle of advisers (Best 1988: 542), in particular, Robert McNamara, who was pushing for aggressive military action.[24] Had he convened regular meetings of his NSC, its diverse membership (including both Vice President Humphrey and the JCS chair) would have exposed him to a wider range of views (Burke and Greenstein 1989: 85; McMaster 1997: 89). But the company that Johnson kept also *reflected* his prior decision to pursue a military course in Vietnam. His advisory circle tightened because Johnson knew where he was heading. Thus, "Johnson did not want a debating forum in which such diverse views would be regularly and systematically argued" (Burke and Greenstein 1989: 86).[25]

That Johnson's eventual decision was made with relative ease despite the debates and deliberative struggles of the prior year is itself evidence that the introduction of US ground troops was not an afterthought or follow-on to the air war, much less that the call for additional forces emerged as an extension of the expanding base-perimeter mission. As David Kaiser (2000) succinctly put it, "Johnson clearly did not eagerly seek war in Southeast Asia, but he never questioned the need for the United States to resist the Communist threat to South Vietnam by any necessary means. He certainly wanted to avoid war before the November elections, but he always seems to have been ready to undertake it should the situation become critical enough, and he never seriously considered the alternatives of neutralization and withdrawal." The Johnson administration had cautiously committed to a course in late 1964; by the spring of 1965 it had accepted the seemingly inevitable and moved into the conflict to win (Gelb and Betts 1979: 278; Kaiser 2000: 409).[26]

Each of the administration's military steps facilitated the next, but each also stemmed from a recognition that the United States might eventually have to commit to a full-blown war in Asia. The issue for the administration had quickly become not *whether* the United States would act but *when* it should act and with *what* and *how many* forces. Whether the participants had illusions of victory or lacked a sense of the dangers ahead is somewhat beside the point. The key question is how they arrived at their conclusions. The answer directly impugns the rational basis of the Johnson administration's decision-making.

An Alternative Non-Rational Explanation: Mission Fixation

The case for the primacy of non-rational influences in decision-making is most strongly backed by evidence that the US decision to intervene with all necessary force in Vietnam came relatively early in the Johnson administration but at the price of hard thinking about US goals, including the immediate rationale behind preferred military options. The president and his advisers moved tentatively—but still too quickly—over the first intellectual (and emotional) hurdle in deciding to involve US forces directly in the fighting. Whereas Johnson's advisers disagreed over the appropriate steps, including the relative utility of air strikes and the rationale for military action, they chose not to engage their differences. Instead, they settled for agreement that military action, if done right, *might* work and that effective options were otherwise limited. Once Johnson concluded that forestalling impending losses in South Vietnam required US military intervention and that US forces in country were not up to the task, he too easily resolved that full US involvement in Vietnam, including ground forces, was the only viable alternative.

Notwithstanding his small inner circle, Johnson received a range of opinions; they came, however, with diverging assumptions about the war. Johnson guaranteed an unsatisfactory outcome when he chose to split the difference in opinion with a *solution* that followed from competing *diagnostics*. Even Bundy, the president's national security adviser, lamented "the discrepancy between the magnitude of the decisions the administration had taken over a short period and the limited extent to which it had assessed the premises of action" (Greenstein and Burke 1989/1990: 569). Simply put, the president received an abundance of views from a variety of participants; *exposure* was not the main problem. The problem was that these perspectives were inadequately reconciled: "The Johnson advisory process was so disorderly that they floated around the president in a giant swirl and never were channeled into focused debate" (Greenstein and Burke 1989/1990: 569). The resulting policy was bound to be ineffective, even self-defeating. It was intended to serve a military solution; it was not true to a well-defined strategy or to a consistent set of assumptions. The policy failings were apparent in multiple respects.

First, the administration extended its short-term policies apart from assessing their long-term viability. Throughout 1964 Johnson's advisers had recognized that a successful US bombing campaign required an effective and stable partner in Saigon. General Paul Harkins, commander of the Military Assistance Command in Vietnam, and his deputy (and later replacement), General Westmoreland, had actually cautioned against aggressive US bombing of North Vietnam before the Saigon government could capably combat the Vietcong in the South (Cosmas 2006: 158).[27] Otherwise, the bombing might provoke the Vietcong to intensify a fight that Saigon was unprepared to win or induce Saigon to shirk by passing the full burden of fighting the war to the United States. South Vietnamese leaders did not take the military and political action required to compete successfully with the Vietcong among the peasantry. Instead, they chose the path of personal empowerment and enrichment, condoning corruption; rewarding loyalty over competence in recruitment, promotions, and the distributing of resources; and structuring military forces to prevent coups from within, not to fight the adversary (on these liabilities, see Talmadge 2015). By early 1965, however, thinking had changed as the Vietcong grew stronger and more active. Westmoreland argued that intensive US bombing was needed, for instance, to buy time to allow the South Vietnamese military to expand (Cosmas 2006: 203).

The South Vietnamese government did not mend its ways; instead, it took backward steps when General Khang moved to strengthen his internal grip, in part by stripping civilians of oversight powers (Warner 2003: 841–842). When the bombing failed to reduce enemy activities, the Johnson administration intensified the bombing campaign without re-evaluating its essential purposes—indeed, by contravening its initial purposes. Administration officials now thought bombing would facilitate effective and stable South Vietnamese governance; it would presumably weaken internal opposition and strengthen government resolve by establishing that military progress was forthcoming and that the Saigon government had US support (Gelb and Betts 1979: 253; Kaiser 2000: 303; Logevall 1999: 123; McMaster 1997: 145, 150).

Second, the administration placed tactics ahead of strategy. The December 1964 plan was designed for options (Warner 2003: 841), like much of the administration's temporizing to follow. Johnson preferred to focus on short-term steps—grabbing the "middle option" in the policy debate—to maintain control of the war, limit its political costs, and avoid a decisive commitment that would invite discord within his inner circle (Cosmas 2006: 206). In Bundy's thinking, "Johnson wanted a bureaucratic consensus on combat troops relating to a number, not a strategy or use" (Goldstein 2008: 221). In place of strategy, the participants united only in crude consensus: "They found the prospects of defeat through withdrawal too costly to accept" (Garofano 2002: 164).

Yet options are only as good as underlying strategic principles, which in the critical early months of the war were poorly developed, insufficiently communicated, and applied too flexibly. Thus, administration officials made a case for sending ground troops to Vietnam without resolving key strategic issues: where and how to deploy these forces; when and how they would fight; and why, how, and when they might leave. The frail underpinnings of policy were on display, for instance, when various officials (including the president, Bundy, and Rusk) asserted that US ground troop deployments in Vietnam, much like bombing, could signal US resolve.[28] They failed to ask whether an appearance of resolve might depend on a combat commitment *and* its eventual result.

Similarly, the administration insufficiently weighed the conditions under which a bombing strategy could succeed. It intended the Rolling Thunder bombing campaign to signal Hanoi that its costs would increase with its intransigence. The plan was to squeeze the adversary through increasing pressure—upping the intensity, value, or geographical sensitivity of targets—to leave the enemy always with something more to lose (Pape 1996: 179). With McNamara taking the lead, the administration had embraced "graduated pressure" for its coercive and political benefits; it "could be calculated carefully to minimize the risk of escalation and avoid domestic and international opposition to widening the war" (McMaster 1997: 75).[29] Presumably the administration could communicate its desire to stand by a sovereign South Vietnam and its desire to settle the conflict, and do so at the lowest possible military and political cost.

Despite near-unanimous backing for the initial bombing campaign, administration officials differed substantially in their justifications, which should have provoked a critical interrogation of policy assumptions. All-important questions were asked too infrequently, and they were never answered definitively (McMaster 1997: 235–236). Should the United States design its bombing campaign to bring Hanoi to the negotiating table or to inflict hurt to get Hanoi to accept an agreement? Was bombing a substitute for ground troops—militarily or politically (McMaster 1997: 202, 230)—or an anticipated first step toward an eventual US ground war? Was selective bombing more a "reprisal" for specific enemy actions or a foot in the door for a full-blown air war intended to bring Hanoi to its knees? That was certainly the hope when the JCS tepidly, and often derisively, backed Johnson's "minimalist" strategy and even adopted "the language of graduated pressure to strengthen their argument that restrictions on military actions should be relaxed" (McMaster 1997: 189). For that matter, was bombing at all effective? Bombing might actually signal the limits, not the depth, of US resoluteness, by betraying the US preference to avoid the potentially prohibitive costs of full engagement. As one analyst observes, "gradual escalation of military action on the part of the strong tends to confirm the weaker party's optimism that domestic or international constraints will in the end prevent the strong from bringing the full weight of their military capability to bear" (Wirtz 2012: 24). What else could the adversary reasonably conclude? After all, the administration relied initially on aerial bombing, hoping to press Hanoi to concede, while nevertheless knowing that the targets were too few, scattered, and indirect to inflict significant damage on the war-fighting capabilities of either North Vietnam or the Vietcong. If bombing imposed insufficient costs, McNamara was arguably wrong to judge air strikes as at least a partial success—signaling that the United States would impose costs—when US bombers were inflicting relatively light damage for the number of sorties flown (McMaster 1997: 222).

To the extent that Johnson and his advisers asked these questions, the answers varied. But that did not seem to matter. Perversely, that the bombing required no fixed purpose and preserved US flexibility was for Bundy a big plus (McMaster 1997: 236).

Third, administration officials failed to recognize that preferred options have unanticipated consequences that pave the way for competing policies. While forestalling the introduction of ground forces, McNamara, by his own admission, ignored the possibility that US bomber bases in South Vietnam would create inviting targets for the Vietcong, necessitating a protective ground troop presence (McMaster 1997: 226–227). Likewise, backers of a graduated-pressure strategy should have recognized that the failure of the bombing campaign would position the military to argue convincingly that the United States must now invest fully in the war effort. The JCS had actually accepted the administration's limits on bombing, predicting that they would eventually erode (McMaster 1997: 328). Indeed, with the introduction of ground troops, the US mission in Vietnam shifted, by April 1965, from coercing Hanoi to fighting the war in the South. The United States now sought, through available means (including air power), to deny the Communists a victory in the South (McMaster 1997: 279–280, 289). By mid-1965, though McNamara continued to believe in the coercive virtues of air power, the administration had changed the US goal to taking the lead in defeating the insurgency (Cosmas 2006: 227, 241).

Fourth, the administration adopted policies without fully committing in theory or practice to a single view of the conflict: Was it a civil war (in the South), international war (between North and South), or some combination of the two? The administration escalated the air war and introduced US ground forces to the conflict in response to Vietcong attacks in the South and agonized early on about the dysfunctional nature of the Saigon regime, which kept the regime from extending its base and engaging effectively in the war effort (Saunders 2009: 150–151). Yet the administration's focus was clearly on North Vietnam and its direct and indirect roles in the fighting in South Vietnam. Johnson and his advisers assumed that Hanoi, through its command structure and supply lines, controlled the pace and nature of combat in South Vietnam; that US forces must target North Vietnamese (and Vietcong) main units; and that absent a strong US defensive position, Hanoi might seize ground by sending large numbers of regular troops into the South. For that reason, the administration coveted stability above all else in the Saigon government, so that it might aid—but certainly not contravene—the war effort. Johnson actually had serious misgivings about the 1963 coup that had deposed Diem, and he generally placed the requisites of war fighting in South Vietnam over its government's political reform: "Johnson diagnosed the source of South Vietnam's vulnerability to a communist takeover in terms of external aggression from the North" (Saunders 2009: 151).

Fifth, the administration pursued its policies without considering the limits of "half measures" and thus the potential requisites of fighting the war to a successful conclusion. Pressed to increase forces, Johnson was slow—indeed, hesitant—to rise to the challenge (Burke and Greenstein 1989: 83). He was hypersensitive to the public appearance of a growing military commitment to South Vietnam's security. He thereby avoided public disclosures of US military action or framed them to minimize their significance (Burke and Greenstein 1989: 82). What Johnson did not do was explore the military and political implications of holding back. He failed to ask whether a tepid or reluctant response might actually pass the initiative to the adversary and only delay the inevitable introduction of US forces. More important, he failed to recognize that his own reluctance to introduce US troops was an occasion to weigh the stakes of the conflict against the potential costs of a US commitment. Thus, he failed to acknowledge what it might take to "win" in Vietnam and whether he—and the country—would willingly accept the price in political, material, and human resources.

In sum, the Johnson administration decided relatively early to employ US conventional military capabilities, if necessary, in Vietnam. In this it arguably responded rationally to a perceived threat to US interests, should the administration fail to rise to the challenge. A bombing campaign, which played to US comparative military advantage, offered the administration a powerful and efficient tool to address the Communist threat, and the gradual introduction of combat troops created opportunities to gauge military and political effects before the administration committed to a full troop engagement. Still, we could argue that the administration acted rationally if it had taken the opposite course—that is, had it chosen to exit the conflict once it recognized the potential costs of the war, the continuing instability of the Saigon government, and the limited effects of an early departure on US credibility.

What makes rationality suspect here is not what option the administration selected but how it selected it. The administration failed to examine means-ends relationships to determine "how American troops would contribute to the achievement of the overall U.S. military and political objectives in South Vietnam" (Cosmas 2006: 219). Administration officials failed to reassess their courses of action when the underlying justifications changed; they converged on options without reconciling underlying assumptions; and they failed to appreciate that options, once selected, might come to serve very different policies. No less important, they never sought answers to critical questions that would undoubtedly have provoked contentious disputes. How committed was Hanoi to victory in the South? How dependent was the Vietcong insurgency on northern supplies and labor? Could the United States succeed over the long term, absent a competent and reliable partner in Saigon? If victory was not likely in the short term, might US intervention amount to an open commitment that might drain US resources and sap the US commitment to address more vital challenges elsewhere in the world at some point in the future? Absent hard questioning, the president and his secretary of defense sent US forces to Vietnam without a clear sense of what they would do or why they were needed. That left the military command to devise a workable plan (Cosmas 2006: 397).

Stage II, Extension: Disjunction

The administration prosecuted its war, being true to the requirements of neither a political nor a military strategy. From the air, the administration sought to use bombing to political effect yet subordinated political to military considerations. Indeed, it never duly considered what a political strategy required or how the war's conduct might compromise that strategy in practice. On the ground, it deferred to the army's military strategy yet assumed that it would somehow produce political dividends in the form of a stable South and compliant North. To its misfortune, the administration played to the adversary's political strategy.

The War from the Air

The conduct of the US air war, unlike the ground war, was a source of contention between US civilian and military leaders. The US military had emerged from World War II, a war without limits, convinced of the value and necessity of strategic bombing, and it blamed civilian-imposed constraints for the stalemate that the Korean War became.[30] American military leaders insisted that the United States, not the enemy, should determine the conditions of fighting, and they argued for hitting North Vietnam hard to destroy its industrial base (Pape 1996: 180; Spector 1993: 13). US civilian leaders, by contrast, sought to use bombing for coercive effect while avoiding an expanding war; they remembered that Chinese intervention had turned the tide against US forces in Korea. Due partly to this disconnect—though more to the aversions and intellectual lapses of US civilian leaders—the bombing campaign was never true to a viable, coherent, and consistent set of principles. As a political tool, the bombing revealed its inherent weaknesses in multiple respects.

First, the aerial strategy was pursued within ad hoc limits. The administration enforced restrictions on when and where US forces could act—keen on keeping Russia and China, in particular, out of the fighting. The Johnson administration prohibited (immensely lethal) B-52 bombers from operating over much of North Vietnam, restricted US targeting in and around Hanoi and along the Chinese border, forbade the targeting of surface-to-air-missile sites except in self-defense, and ruled out the mining of Haiphong Harbor to stem the flow of Soviet war supplies. Indeed, the administration prohibited US aircraft (initially) from bombing North Vietnamese airbases (to destroy enemy aircraft and prevent their launching) even when North Vietnamese MiG fighters were exacting a toll on US aircraft (Van Staaveren 1977: 83). Johnson personally had to approve targets—selected in weekly packages[31]—for the US strike list.

Johnson's fears had some basis in reality. By 1967 over a thousand Soviet military specialists were engaged in military tasks in North Vietnam, including piloting military aircraft and manning surface-to-air missile sites. Hundreds of thousands of

Chinese troops were in the country, engaged in reconstruction and military support such as operating antiaircraft guns (Warner 2005: 198-199; Zhai 2000: 135-137). Yet the administration's targeting limits largely reflected its *own* sensitivities; US intelligence analyses actually minimized the chances of direct Russian or Chinese intervention (Gelb and Betts 1979: 269). For example, in May 1964 a Special National Intelligence Estimate concluded, "Communist China almost certainly would not wish to become involved in hostilities with US forces."[32] The Nixon administration would eventually breach these very limits—with massive force—without provoking big-power intervention.[33]

In fearing a repeat of the Korean War, which had provoked Chinese intervention, the administration missed key distinctions between the Korean and Vietnamese conflicts. In Korea, the United States was seeking to seize control of a Communist country ruled by a Soviet-imposed government that was backed by a relatively strong Sino-Soviet alliance. In Vietnam, by contrast, the United States was seeking to maintain the sovereignty of a non-Communist government, opposed by a nationalist government with support from a fractured Sino-Soviet alliance. The Soviet and Chinese stakes were thus lower in Vietnam than they had been in Korea: North Vietnamese sovereignty was not at issue, the Vietnamese Communists had the political base to continue to fight, and neither power felt bound by ideological solidarity to invest fully in the conflict. Under these conditions, why would the administration assume that either power would intervene—massively, no less—to avenge the loss of property and personnel, which it had intentionally delivered to the war effort? Likewise, why would the administration assume that China would intervene to avenge attacks along the *North Vietnamese* side of the Chinese border? The administration posed no immediate threat to North Vietnamese, let alone Chinese, territory; it had established, through word and deed, that it had no intent of reversing the status quo in the North. For that matter, given its thinking, why would the administration *not worry* that Russia or China would intervene if the United States forced Hanoi to capitulate by abandoning its goals in the South? Would that not place Russia and China in the equally difficult political position of failing to assist an ally in distress as it sought to further Communist gains?

The point is not that the administration erred in assuming that extending the bombing would provoke big-power intervention or that bombing less discriminately would have produced a more favorable outcome. Instead, the point is that the administration never fully explored the underpinnings of its thinking. Its justification for the war effort lay in the ideological solidarity or affinity among Communist states, which minimally required the United States to stand up to Communist encroachments and challenges. Yet its prohibitions on bombing were set around concerns that Russia and China were "normal" states, motivated by traditional concerns like the integrity of their own borders and losses in national material and personnel. If ideology was a motivating factor, the proximity and intensity of the US bombing was not really the issue. The issue was how the US campaign would affect shared Communist goals. Worth remembering (albeit unappreciated in Johnson's time) in this regard is that the US threat to North Korea (in crossing the 38th parallel), not the direct threat to the Chinese border presented by advancing United Nations (UN) troops, had triggered Chinese intervention.

Second, the aerial strategy ignored the limits of bombing as a messaging device. The strategy assumed incorrectly that bombing could send unambiguous messages, that the target was receptive and could read messages for their intent, and that these messages stood out above the noise in a very noisy environment.

The administration's strategy of graduated pressure assumed, at its core, that Hanoi could read messages for their resolve and restraint, when Hanoi could easily read them for one or the other, but not both. The United States initially limited its attacks to radar and bridges below the 19th parallel, but by mid-1965 it was hitting targets above the 20th parallel, including bridges and rail lines linking Hanoi to China (Van Staaveren 1977: 70). The number of strikes rose accordingly. "From the first handful of strikes over the North in early 1965, Air Force and Navy attack sorties rose from 1,500 in April to a peak of about 4,000 in September" (Van Staaveren 1977: 74). By the time Rolling Thunder ended, "the Air Force and the other services had flown approximately 304,000 tactical and 2,380 B-52 sorties and dropped 643,000 tons of bombs on North Vietnam's war-making industry, transportation net, and air defense complex" (Van Staaveren 1977: 89). Although the United States left potential targets standing, why should Hanoi see that as restraint against the backdrop of bombs dropped and damage inflicted?[34]

Yet even "strong" signals had to overcome target resistance; the aerial strategy could only send "messages" that Hanoi was ready to receive. Hanoi's leaders, now decades into the struggle, had prepared for a long fight that would eventually bring victory. That lens was the one through which Hanoi viewed US actions. From Hanoi's perspective, US promises to stop the bombing for appropriate concessions could actually signal weakening US resolve. Indeed, US threats of more forceful action had to reinforce Hanoi's expectations that the United States believed its wartime costs were unsustainable and now was seeking ways to end the war sooner rather than later.

Even this assumes that the US messages were not weak, distorted, or lost to unintended messages in the clamorous war environment. The bombing was hardly optimized for sending clear signals; Westmoreland lacked full control of aircraft. In consequence, he had to contend with air force efforts to maintain operational independence, and secure a larger role in MACV headquarters, and the outright refusal of the Marines to place their aerial assets under his command (Cosmas 2006: 321–327, 333, 483). The assortment of participants in the bombing campaign—along with the practicalities of conducting such a campaign—inevitably yielded a cacophony of signals.

The US military consistently focused its bombing on interdicting manpower and supplies bound for the war in the South; it bombed targets both near and distant from Hanoi with regularity and on schedule; it bombed targets as they were identified not for their relative value; it adopted tactics meant specifically to maximize bombing sorties, to increase the efficiency of US aircraft, to avoid bad weather, and to minimize the danger to US aircraft without intending to send any particular message; it anticipated bans on certain targets by accelerating attacks on them; and it conducted its bombing campaign without considering effects on the negotiating environment (Lebovic 2010: 133).[35]

Noise often emerged from the signal itself. Johnson's 1968 bombing halt over North Vietnam—ostensibly a peace gesture—had to seem more like a "redirection" of effort to Hanoi, even a ruse, when US bombers intensified their attacks on targets in the Plain of Jars and along the Ho Chi Minh trail in Laos. The fact is that US aircraft did not hold a monopoly on signaling. What was Hanoi to make of continuing US losses in the land war, the changing pace of the US buildup, contradictory statements and false claims by US public officials, and the rising tide of dissatisfaction within the US public? Did they not provide a deafening chorus of signals that Hanoi had to hear?

Third, the aerial strategy ignored the limits of bombing as an instrument of coercion. North Vietnam was hardly the ideal target of a strategic bombing campaign, with its undeveloped infrastructure, lack of critical production bottlenecks, decentralized economy, low resource dependence, and ability to improvise and adapt to safeguard resources and limit their usage. Thus, the bombing yielded no political return in 1966, when the administration first hit petroleum and lubricant facilities and, later in the year, various industrial and electric-power-generating targets. Nor did the US prospects improve in 1967, when the Johnson administration finally decided to hit industrial and transportation targets that were previously off limits, including targets in and around Hanoi and near the Chinese border (Pape 1996: 184). North Vietnam could compensate: its populace turned to portable generators and dispersed fuel in small containers, deployed ferries to replace destroyed bridges, and easily repaired roads (Griffith 1995: 40; Herring 1986: 147–148).

Fourth, the aerial strategy suffered as both a political and a military instrument because it focused on abetting the ground war by interdicting resources heading to the South. The adversary could tolerate these attacks, even profit from them, for a host of reasons. Bombing proved deficient because (a) the Vietcong acquired resources locally and could control their usage by avoiding confrontations (Pape 1996: 192; Record 2007: 48); (b) US bombers dropped enormous tonnages on primitive, isolated, and evasive targets, inflicting impermanent, limited, and cost-ineffective damage; (c) the Vietcong harvested dud bombs for explosive materials for use in killing and maiming US and South Vietnamese troops (Schelling 1981: 14; Krepinevich 1986: 201); and (d) US attacks, focusing on supply lines (and elusive enemy main units) elsewhere in South Vietnam and along its borders, enabled the Vietcong to operate unhindered in hamlets and villages throughout much of the country.

To be sure, evidence, through 1967, challenges the common characterization of a self-contained Southern insurgency.[36] It points to growing North Vietnamese infiltration rates,[37] difficulties in insurgent recruitment,[38] and Vietcong reliance on supplies and weapons transited through, and from, Cambodia.[39] Still, these revelations do little to vindicate US aerial strategy. The strategy implicitly understated the indigenous (human and material) resources—and overstated the capability of bombing to stem the flow of resources—available to the insurgency. Thus, signals that the United States intended to send through the air would have to contend with a parallel message of misdirected, ineffective, and wasted US effort, from the air and on the ground.

The administration eventually discovered that even a ramped-up bombing campaign against North Vietnamese strategic targets would not bring Hanoi closer to accepting US terms for a settlement. "Civilian officials from the State Department and CIA, and increasingly from the Department of Defense [including the secretary of defense], challenged the political wisdom and military value of Rolling Thunder and urged that Johnson reduce the program or even halt it entirely" (Cosmas 2006: 383). Johnson's response, as always, was to split the difference in opinion. He opted for expanding the air campaign, as the military recommended, but short of the levels that the military preferred (Cosmas 2006: 383).

What the administration did not do was assess the requisites for success of a political or a military strategy. It might not have succeeded with either. Caught between the two, however, it floundered.

The War on the Ground

Johnson ruled out the invasion of North Vietnam and neighboring Laos and Cambodia, which served as supply routes and bases for action in South Vietnam, to prevent the war from spreading (and Russia and China from intervening). Beyond that, he left the ground war largely to his military commanders. For all his hopes that *communicating* the "right signals" could convince the adversary to back down, he shared the main aspirations of his commanders: he wanted to leave Vietnam with a win. This point of agreement brought tension to his strategy. He tried to raise the costs to Hanoi of prosecuting its war, hoping that it would sue for peace. He was thus competing against Hanoi in a contest that favored the party with greater commitment and staying power. At the same time, he sought to defeat adversary forces in the South, apart from the political payoff of the military effort. That was a critical lapse, insofar as "winning" militarily in the South might have little effect on the final outcome of the war. A US victory in the South might actually come too late, at too great a cost, to matter, given depleted US resolve. With little in reserve to claim the ultimate prize, the United States would lose the war in Vietnam precisely *because* it had won the battle in the South.

The military command, with Johnson's blessing, nonetheless went about fighting its war with an "attrition strategy" that played to US military advantages in mobility and sheer firepower.[40] The idea was to locate and then pound the enemy with all available force (Nagl 2005: 154–155). Westmoreland presumed that the US military, with its superior assets, would eventually reach the threshold—or crossover point—where it would kill enemy troops faster than they could be replaced (Lewy 1978: 83–84).

Westmoreland's strategy suffered from a reliance on the adversary "body count" to measure wartime success. Lacking a traditional battlefield, on which net progress was measurable through territorial gains and losses, the US command settled for an approximation in numbers of battle deaths and related measures that gave tacit support to the attrition campaign (Long 2016: 117). While these numbers served the attrition strategy—the count rose in lethal combat—they also increased, nefariously, when competing services each took credit for a kill and units fudged on the high side to get credit for good work or hide the fact of high civilian casualties. The problems with the body count ran deeper than its reliability as a measure. It was an invalid indicator. It played to existing US military strategy while neglecting the adversary's offsetting *political* strategy.

Reliance on the body count was not the cause but rather a reflection of a fundamental strategic problem. As a flawed performance indicator, it reinforced a ground strategy that suffered in multiple respects.

First, the US ground strategy ignored the enemy's willingness to accept heavy losses because it was playing for time. Rather than counting deaths, Hanoi watched the clock, knowing that the United States, like France before it, would eventually tire and seek a way out of the conflict. As Henry Kissinger (1969: 214) famously put it, "The guerrilla wins if he does not lose." Even that characterization understates the guerrilla's advantage, for "insurgents may gain political victory from a situation of military stalemate or *even defeat*" (Mack 1975: 177). The United States might depart the conflict with some semblance of victory, but what would remain behind when it did? Popular grievances? An inept and corrupt host government? A shadow insurgent infrastructure? An adversary across the border, positioned by virtue of proximity, ethnicity, and heritage to resume the fight, at an advantage? Should the adversary decide to reignite the conflict, would the United States resume a fight that it had, at great cost, finally "won?"

Second, the US ground strategy allowed the enemy to dictate when, where, and how fighting occurred to cut its losses. Battles occurred in places and on terms that the enemy dictated, far more often than the reverse (Thayer 1985: 46, 92–93). Small US operations tended not to make contact with the enemy, and increases in US military action did not yield higher enemy casualties (Lewy 1978: 83). When seizing the initiative, the adversary adopted tactics that negated US military advantages. It fought at close quarters, disappeared rather than fight, set booby traps and conducted ambushes, and kept US forces tied down and spread thin through hit-and-run tactics (Arreguín-Toft 2005: 154–155; Thayer 1985: 95). All the while, the adversary played to false US beliefs about where and how it would strike. Westmoreland, believing the Communists were losing the war in the South, prioritized securing the border regions to stop North Vietnamese infiltration and maximize the enemy body count (Wirtz 1991: 112–113, 168). Thus, when Westmoreland got the big fight that he had wanted, in late 1967—as North Vietnamese regulars encircled the Marine base at Khe Sanh, near the Laotian border—Hanoi had staged the battle as a ruse. Playing to US military tendencies, Hanoi meant the battle to draw US forces away from the cities to open them to a Vietcong assault early the following year. Westmoreland sought to hold the line in the far north of the country, dismissing warnings (even from JCS chair Earle Wheeler) that the attack on Khe Sanh was possibly a feint. In Westmoreland's words, the enemy had "put too much effort into this buildup to support the diversion theory."[41] However, the diversion theory was validated—convincingly—when the enemy attacked in force from the west (the border regions with Cambodia) across the north-south range of the country in the 1968 Tet Offensive.

Third, the US ground strategy failed to reconcile the demands, or recognize the full implications, of fighting two wars in Vietnam, one against North Vietnamese troops and supplies and another against an indigenous Communist adversary. Success against either adversary required success against the other. Indeed, the two US adversaries could work in tandem to outwit and outmaneuver the US military; North Vietnamese troops repeatedly lured US forces into the Central Highlands, away from the populated coastal regions where the Vietcong lived, recruited, operated, and thrived. Because its limited resources required the US military to focus on one of the two adversaries at a time, victory against either—if possible—might occur only after the point of US exhaustion.

In selecting which of the two enemies to fight, Westmoreland was admittedly "damned if he did and damned if he didn't." Alternatively, he could have adopted a counterinsurgency approach. Whereas traditional military operations are intended to fight the enemy, counterinsurgency is intended to deprive it of sustenance by securing the confidence and support of villagers (who supply and staff the insurgency) and eventually winning support for (by partnering with) the central government (Biddle 2008; Krepinevich 1986; Nagl 2005). Yet emphasis on either war freed the enemy to prosecute the other. Westmoreland maintained that the US military could not simultaneously fight enemy main units, provide security at the village level, and oversee programs and engage in outreach to build popular support for the Saigon government and deprive the Vietcong of a popular base.[42] He thus made his choice, quite reasonably, to focus on Vietcong and North

Vietnamese main units and, more generally, the enemy from the North. After all, North Vietnamese forces could strike quickly and seize ground, and the United States was advantaged in mobility and sheer manpower to combat such a threat. Thus the prevailing US Army–led mission absorbed US special forces and Marine personnel and their once distinctive counterinsurgency missions with the intensification in the ground war, integration of units into the military's Vietnam command structure, and growing army and Marine combat presence (Long 2016: 105–138). Special operations forces engaged in reconnaissance and sabotage in support of conventional operations (Avant 1993), and Marine units paralleled the efforts of army units. In practice counterinsurgency operations often reduced to "counter-guerrilla" operations, focused on hitting the enemy, not depriving it of its support base (Hamilton 1998: 6–7, 109).

To Westmoreland the issue was not whether pacification was important—he believed it was—but whether it could succeed in a hostile environment, given available US resources.[43] Indeed, the opposite choice, a dedicated counterinsurgency effort, would have required the recalcitrant government in Saigon to commit to the fight. The US military could not go it alone; it lacked the trained personnel, organizational preparedness, cultural sensitivities, and linguistic capabilities to establish an effective security presence in villages and hamlets throughout South Vietnam, much less build public allegiance or support for the central government. The US government tried to push the Saigon government to join the fight, but it pushed back or simply ignored US entreaties when recommended reforms threatened the leadership's political interests. In Westmoreland's thinking, going after the enemy still offered long-term payoffs in counterinsurgency. "Once the situation had stabilized and sufficient reinforcements had arrived, he planned to take the offensive in 1966 with the purpose of destroying the Communists' main forces, driving them away from populated areas, and pacifying high-priority areas as a prelude to the progressive pacification of all of South Vietnam over the ensuing years" (Birtle 2008: 1222).[44]

One frequently offered criticism is not entirely fair to General Westmoreland; he valued pacification more than critics typically acknowledge. "Westmoreland's strategy was not a matter of choosing search-and-destroy operations over counterinsurgency, but rather of emphasizing the use of Americans for one element of a complex and diverse mission" (Daddis 2011: 72). Indeed, the idea of counterinsurgency was not foreign to the US military. General Harold K. Johnson, US Army chief of staff, actively favored pacification; "A Program for the Pacification and Long-Term Development of Vietnam" (PROVN), which Johnson had commissioned, was briefed in 1966 to top US civilian and military war leaders. The voluminous study recommended a fundamental restructuring of the US approach around counterinsurgency principles.[45] In addition, the concept was already enshrined in recent field manuals of both the army and Marines. Thus, in the early years of US involvement in Vietnam, US Army special force units and the Marines, most notably through combined action platoons, invested heavily in pacification through small unit operations working in tandem with indigenous units.[46]

Westmoreland's approach nevertheless exaggerated the compatibility between an attrition strategy and a counterinsurgency strategy. Even if Westmoreland could defeat enemy main units—and Hanoi did not reconstitute these units—pacification would hardly be automatic. American military and civilian officials had thus far failed to embrace the effort. Indeed, US forces had contravened counterinsurgency principles in adhering to an attrition strategy and its reliance on the "body count." The measure helped fuel a perverse incentive structure (Daddis 2011: 89). As units (and individuals) reaped rewards for number of kills, the counterinsurgency campaign suffered in consequence. American commanders insisted that an ever-growing body count spoke to a reduced enemy capability to fight. Yet what did those figures mean if the body count included a large number of civilian casualties; combat destroyed civilian homes and property and uprooted populations; and enemy kills included the sons and daughters of the peasantry, whose fealty was ultimately required to establish government control? Rather than building popular support, US forces often went out of their way to alienate the populace; they hit villages hard with bombs and artillery despite the potential collateral effects on local populations. Then, after engaging the Vietcong, they evacuated areas (Hamilton 1998: 6–7, 109). The Vietcong returned to renew operations and punish those who had cooperated with the enemy.

For their part, US civilian officials—especially in the State Department and the Agency for International Development (USAID)—feared losing their prerogatives in a combined US government force, especially one controlled by the military. Across the US government, pacification languished from neglect; competing agendas; resource deprivation; and poor coordination, planning, and execution. Many US civilian and military officials had an understandable philosophical aversion to a US-led counterinsurgency effort. Taking the lead in counterinsurgency was counterproductive if it reaffirmed the weakness of the Saigon government, encouraged it to shirk (by doing for it what it should be doing for itself), and allowed it to engage in self-indulgent practices that undercut effective domestic institutions. In this view, the Saigon government had to take ownership of pacification if it were to succeed.[47] Yet that was unlikely. Its personnel were unenthusiastic about living and working among the villagers, especially in dangerous regions of the country. The South Vietnamese military, in turn, routinely flouted counterinsurgency principles. It often served as an agent of wealthy landlords, stole from the villagers, or simply communicated its indifference to civilian lives by firing indiscriminately at the Vietcong from a distance (Lebovic 2010: 35, 91).

The point is that Westmoreland would have faced an exhausting pacification challenge—absent a number of favorable developments (discussed later in the chapter)—even had he decisively defeated adversary main units. The United States would have fought hard, achieved victories, and yet ended up in the same place—confronting the military and political demands of the war—though now with diminished US resolve.

At no point, however, did the president and his advisers seriously consider altering the US ground strategy or fundamentally reassessing its utility. They focused instead on augmenting the US military force so that it could better conduct its existing missions.[48] When, toward the end of 1966, the US command came to recognize that it had underprojected enemy strength—that the Vietcong and North Vietnam were continuing to build up their forces in the South—it "solved" the problem simply by asking for more US troops (Cosmas 2006: 254). The number of US troops in South Vietnam increased with each passing month and dramatically over the ensuing years. By the end of 1965 the numbers stood at 184,000; by the end of 1966 they had more than doubled (385,000); by the end of 1967 they were approaching half a million (486,000); and by the end of 1968, the high point of US ground engagement, the US combat force in Vietnam stood at 536,000 troops—a year in which US troops suffered around three hundred deaths a week.[49]

In sum, the administration's qualms about the ground war centered generally on numbers of troops, not their usage or likely impact, given Hanoi's options and dedication to the fight. The administration allowed the US military to fight its war, and it did so persistently, on its own terms. When McNamara finally concluded that the "answer" to the US challenge in Vietnam was not more US troops, he did not question Westmoreland's strategy or troop allocations (Cosmas 2006: 489). Once Johnson had sent US combat troops to Vietnam, the policy "debate" narrowed considerably.

Stage III, Limitation: Constriction

Years into the effort, Johnson reluctantly conceded that he could not foresee victory in Vietnam at an acceptable level of investment. Pressure was mounting for policy change, from outside and within the administration. Johnson essentially responded by freezing the war in place. He did not aim for a more cost-effective strategy; rather, he sought to avoid the cost of escalation or defeat.

The Decisional Context

When pressed by the military command to break the will of the adversary, destroy its war-fighting capabilities, and ultimately "win" the war, Johnson relied on McNamara to "dicker" with Westmoreland to get the requested numbers down to the lowest levels that the general would support publicly (Bator 2008: 318, 322; McMaster 1997: 308). Johnson preferred to test the political waters and avoid dissent by doing what he believed was minimally necessary to improve the military outcome (Gelb and Betts 1979: 25). In early 1967 Westmoreland requested an increase in US forces to 670,000 troops to assemble an "optimum" force, setting 565,000 troops as the essential minimum (Gelb and Betts 1979: 155). Seeking to hold the line, McNamara obtained a compromise—force levels were set at 525,000 troops—and pushed the military, unsuccessfully, to get more production out of available troops by increasing the combat-to-support personnel ratio and raising the South Vietnamese combat profile (Cosmas 2006: 426–427).[50]

However, McNamara, who had once championed the commitment of US combat forces to the fighting, had grown leery of Westmoreland's troop requests. Raising US force levels in Vietnam would require mobilizing standby reserve units (Gelb and Betts 1979: 173). McNamara also feared it would boost US defense spending dramatically and generate pressure to extend the ground war into Cambodia and Laos, and even into North Vietnam, presumably to justify—and ultimately end—the large expenditure and huge force commitment (Warner 2005: 196).[51] McNamara had tired of the familiar pattern; granting the military's troop request would inevitably invite another.

McNamara was now deeply skeptical that the United States would move closer to victory in Vietnam by adding troops to the US fighting force. His doubts about the war had been building. By 1967 they increasingly spilled over into his off-the-record conversations with journalists, friends, and others (Halberstam 1969: 632–633; Hoopes 1969: 86). In August of that year his reservations about the war burst into the open when he challenged the military's desire for reduced bombing restrictions. He testified before Congress that nothing short of depopulating North Vietnam would affect its behavior: Quite simply, Hanoi could not be "bombed to the negotiating table" (Hoopes 1969: 87). His trepidations apparently cost him his job, or would have done so, had he stayed. His show before Congress—a very public questioning of US strategy—left the president unamused (Halberstam 1969: 644). Indeed, McNamara later believed that he had permanently ruptured his relationship with Johnson in November 1967 when he wrote the president a memo restating his own "belief that continuation of our present action in Southeast Asia would be dangerous, costly in lives, and unsatisfactory to the American people."[52] A few weeks later, Johnson announced that McNamara was to become the new president of the World Bank: McNamara later confessed that he was not sure whether he quit or was fired (McNamara 1995: 311). For the next three months he languished in a political purgatory—neither dissenter nor dispassionate adviser—having lost his influence with the president.

McNamara's departure at the end of February 1968 did not inject a fresh dose of optimism at the top; his successor, Clark Clifford, also became a *former* Vietnam hawk.[53] Nor did McNamara's departure end the military's appeal for more troops. When the military continued its push for over 200,000 additional troops[54]— perhaps in the absence of McNamara's traditional constraining influence (Hoopes 1969: 163–165)—Clifford pushed back (Warner 2005: 210), having come to the conclusion that Vietnam was a "bottomless pit."[55] The enemy's surprise Tet Offensive in early 1968 (discussed later in the chapter) greatly shook his confidence that the United States could achieve its military objectives (Acacia 2009: 257). Clifford was not convinced that the proposed force increase would substantially improve the US military position in Vietnam, even years hence, and recognized its detrimental consequences: "The more we continued to do in South Vietnam, the less likely the South Vietnamese were to shoulder their own burden" (Clifford 1969: 613). He warned that Westmoreland would return in a year to ask for a similar force increase (Acacia 2009: 266).

Political and military conditions now looked bleak for Johnson. He had tried, through back channels, to open dialogue with Hanoi. He had paused the bombing to signal to domestic and international audiences that the United States was willing to back peaceful talk with action. He soured on talks when Hanoi failed to reciprocate; Hanoi insisted on an unconditional bombing halt, dismissed talks except to arrange a US exit from Vietnam, and showed no evidence of slowing its support to the Vietcong. The war had also lost critical support within Johnson's formal and informal advisory circles; indeed, it was under challenge throughout the US government. The intensified bombing in 1966 and 1967, hitting all targets on the administration's expanded list, had not produced visible returns; from the early months of the Rolling Thunder bombing campaign, various intelligence and civilian Pentagon assessments had revealed that the bombing was not only cost ineffective but also had failed to stem the southward flow of war materials (Gelb and Betts 1979: 147, 168; Warner 2005: 197). Civilian analysts at the Department of Defense argued that proposed force increases would make the US effort more difficult to sustain, not end the conflict (Cosmas 2007: 97–98; Gelb and Betts 1979: 175). Naysayers in the CIA and State Department, now bastions of dissent, looked askance even at "good news" in the ground war (Cosmas 2007: 142). Even hawks in Congress had lost their appetite for troop increases (Acacia 2009: 268–269).

For Johnson, a large troop increase was at its core a hard pill to swallow. It would invite inflation, domestic budget cuts, and a revenue-enhancing war tax. It would also extend the domestic reach of the war; calling up the military reserves risked politically damaging protests from a responsive and influential segment of the US population, given the demographics of military reserve and National Guard units. Inasmuch as a mobilization of the reserves required congressional action, it would also invite unwanted legislative scrutiny and damaging criticism of the administration's war policies. Johnson recognized the implication: he would have less influence to press for his preferred programs, and pressure would build on him to do what was necessary—escalate, at great risk—to end the conflict, sooner rather than later.

Slammed now by the military's request for a 40 percent increase in US force levels, Johnson ordered a reassessment of US strategy (Cosmos 2007: 88–98; Gelb and Betts 1979: 173–174). On one level, it involved his "Wise Men," an experienced and prestigious group of current and former high-level government officials (including former secretary of state Dean Acheson, Ambassador Averell Harriman, and General Omar Bradley) from whom he had previously sought advice. On another level, it involved a special task force, under Clifford's direction, that included various policy heavyweights: Secretary of State Rusk, CIA director Richard Helms, JCS chair Earle Wheeler, Maxwell Taylor (former JCS chair and US ambassador to South Vietnam), National Security Advisor Walt Rostow, former ambassador to South Vietnam Henry Cabot Lodge, and Deputy Secretary of Defense Paul Nitze, among others.

The result, for Johnson, was bracing. Although the task force interpreted its charge narrowly—"how to give Westmoreland what he said he needed, with acceptable domestic consequences" (Hoopes 1969: 172)—it was torn by the "big issues." Rusk, Wheeler, Rostow, and Taylor supported the troop increase and a hard-line military strategy; Clifford, Nitze, and others expressed their dissent. Although the task force's recommendations "in all essential respects confirmed existing policy" (Hoopes 1969: 177), Clifford shared his contrarian views with the president, as his predecessor had—again, to Johnson's chagrin (Hoopes 1969: 181). Johnson was particularly upset—shocked, in fact—by the defection of his Wise Men (Gelb and Betts 1979: 176). In a joint meeting with Johnson in late March 1968, Bundy delivered the news. "There is a very significant shift in our position," he said. "When we last met [in November 1967] we saw reasons for hope."[56] A majority now favored de-escalation.

A Decision of Sorts: Staying the Course

Johnson, as always, tried to navigate the opinions of his military and civilian advisers. With some pushing for escalation, others pulling for de-escalation, and still others looking to stay the current course, Johnson chose (again) to split the difference. The problem, however, was that these conflicting recommendations once more rested on divergent assumptions about the adversary's capabilities and intentions.

Johnson placed himself in the middle of the debate without reconciling the divergent points of view. Those who wanted more troops and an expanding war effort believed that (a) superior US capabilities would permit the United States to prevail eventually; (b) political, not military, impediments were preventing a US victory; (c) Hanoi's foreign allies were not fully committed to the fight and were unlikely to join North Vietnam in its (ultimately) losing effort; (d) Hanoi and its allies were tempted, even emboldened, by US equivocation and unwillingness to escalate; and (e) the consequences of a US defeat in Vietnam would resonate widely. Those who wanted to disengage from Vietnam believed that (a) the United States had given what it could give to the war; (b) pouring additional resources into the country was unlikely to improve the US position and more likely to provoke the adversary to mobilize additional labor and resources to compensate; (c) widening the war geographically would further strain US resources and create overwhelming military challenges, should Russia or China intervene; and (d) the consequences of a US withdrawal from Vietnam would be mitigated by a host of political forces and paled in comparison to the consequences of maintaining the existing posture, postponing the inevitable, and forcing the United States to face the same stark choices from a weaker position at some point in the future.[57] Those who wanted to stay the course essentially accepted the negative consequences that de-escalation advocates predicted for escalation and that escalation advocates predicted for de-escalation. Although some of Johnson's advisers, especially McNamara, had argued in late 1967 for persevering at some sustainable level to convince Hanoi that it could not outlast the United States,[58] those who wanted to stick to the current strategy were swayed less by the promise than by the pitfalls of escalating or withdrawing.[59]

In splitting the difference in the policy recommendations, by choosing a middle option, Johnson avoided the risks of an expanding war, the domestic political costs of expanding the military labor pool, and the alleged US national security (and domestic-political) costs of "losing" South Vietnam to Communism. But Johnson's middle course stemmed not from a deliberative consideration of net benefits, short versus long-term gains, attendant trade-offs, or levels of uncertainty. Instead, Johnson's decision to enforce a troop ceiling and pursue the war within geographical and targeting limits amounted to a short-term gamble that staying the current course while extending an olive branch to Hanoi—a bombing pause—might bring North Vietnam to the conference table. His focus was on tactics, not on strategy: "Johnson limited his queries to a framework of *techniques* rather than *basic issues*" (Sellen 1973: 227).

Settling for the lower costs of the middle option, with its potential short-term benefits, Johnson avoided finding answers to essential questions. Would Hanoi ultimately concede its seemingly intractable positions? If so, how, and when? If not, how long could the United States persevere, and could Saigon carry the load without direct US support? When Johnson finally dug in his heels to resist further increases, he acted in response to the costs of expanding and intensifying the war, not to a reassessment of strategy and goals in light of these costs. To Johnson, the all-important question was unfortunately not, "Is continuing along the current course worth the price given available resources?" In the end, his strategy was at best a desperate bet on the future. Escalating the war had failed to deliver hoped-for gains. Now the administration "was set on stabilizing the American effort in the hope of holding on long enough to negotiate an acceptable compromise with the Communists or, failing that, to prepare the South Vietnamese to take over the fighting" (Cosmas 2006: 469).

Stage IV, Disengagement: Extrication

In 1967 the door was closing for increasing the US war commitment; by 1968 the door had slammed shut. The momentum for a policy shift was building well before the shock of the Tet Offensive, when the Vietcong jettisoned insurgent tactics and occupied provincial capitals and major cities throughout the country.

True, the offensive was a *military* disaster for the Vietcong; US and South Vietnamese forces beat them back, inflicting many thousands of enemy casualties. Hanoi had also failed to deliver on its political promise that attacking cities throughout South Vietnam would trigger a public uprising. Short on personnel and public support, the Vietcong thereafter had to adopt more aggressive tactics to obtain recruits, raise revenue, and achieve popular compliance, with the effect of alienating their popular base. They were unable to re-establish their strong political and military hold in the South Vietnamese countryside or field main force units (Talmadge 2015: 85). From the US military's vantage point, Tet was at worst a momentary setback with a substantial upside: it brought the enemy out of hiding to fight US military strengths.[60]

The offensive was nonetheless a political triumph for Hanoi. From the US public's vantage point, the offensive exposed the emptiness of the administration's claim that a US victory in Vietnam was in sight. Public confidence that the United States was making progress in Vietnam plummeted—taking along, with it, public approval of Johnson's war management (Johnson and Tierney 2006: 135). Johnson felt he was out of options when, in March 1968, he addressed the nation. He announced a halt to the US bombing of much of North Vietnam; his readiness "to send [US] representatives to any forum, at any time, to discuss the means of bringing this ugly war to an end"; and the shocking withdrawal of his presidential candidacy so that politics ("personal partisan causes") would not hamper his quest for peace.

The 1968 election brought a change in the guard—from a Democratic to a Republican administration—and thus new personnel to US war strategy and planning. The election itself was not a war "referendum" in the conventional sense of the term. The Vietnam War was not yet the polarizing issue that it would become in the 1972 election (Berinsky 2007, 2009). Indeed, the public did not perceive major differences between the positions of the two candidates: Nixon was circumspect about his war strategy (touting a "secret plan" to end the war), and Hubert Humphrey, the Democratic challenger, was saddled—rightly or wrongly—with Johnson's war legacy, having served loyally as Johnson's vice president. The public overall, despite growing dissent and protests, did not look to the election as a referendum on a war exit. Even Eugene McCarthy's strong showing in the New Hampshire primary was largely attributable to his support among hawkish Democrats, who presumably were "looking for a change." And Johnson—as a write-in candidate—still won a plurality of votes.

To its successor, the Johnson administration bequeathed ironic wartime conditions. The United States had actually improved its position throughout much of South Vietnam, though it had ostensibly fought the "wrong war" by targeting main units rather than countering the insurgency. By the time Hanoi shifted its strategy—and actually played more to US strengths—most Americans, including their leaders, had tired of the war, with large factions ready to leave.

The US election brought new thinking from a leadership team that was less invested in past policies. It arrived somewhat confident that it knew how prior US policies had failed. Yet the Nixon administration soon sought to depart from the conflict, on less-than-ideal terms. It began a slow but deliberate march toward the exit.

Backdrop: The (Ironic) State of the Conflict

General Creighton Abrams is often credited with improving the overall US position throughout much of South Vietnam when, in 1968, he assumed command and showed greater deference toward counterinsurgency principles. Indeed, Lewis Sorley (1999), a prominent Vietnam War historian, argues that by the end of 1971 the United States had won its war in South Vietnam. Appearances aside, the differences between the commands resided less in war strategy (in fact, Abrams had served as Westmoreland's deputy commander) than in the conditions of battle.

As we have seen, "pacification" was not alien to the US military under Westmoreland's command. The point of contention was not *whether* pacification mattered. Instead, it was *how much* population control should matter in US strategy relative to attritional objectives. In 1967, under Westmoreland's command, the United States had established the US Civilian Operations and Revolutionary Development Support (CORDS) program, a centralized civilian pacification program. It combined thousands of US military and civilian personnel at all levels with their South Vietnamese counterparts to build security and satisfy popular needs in villages throughout the country. The US military command also engaged in prolific data gathering, drawing from a multitude of measures of peasant attitudes and experiences through the Hamlet Evaluation System, assessments from US military advisers related to the performance of individual South Vietnamese military units (covering "topics ranging from leadership and unit discipline to training and equipment" (Daddis 2011: 171), and so forth. Conversely, under Abrams's command, US forces still gave primacy to attacking Communist main units and base areas and relied on massive artillery barrages and heavy bombing in the South (Birtle 2008: 1234–1235; Cosmas 2007: 132, 134, 255). Abrams's goal, as relayed initially to his military commanders, was to find and kill the enemy. Put more discreetly, "putting pressure on the enemy remained fundamental to Abrams's operational guidance and 'one war' approach," which ostensibly bridged the divide between attrition and counterinsurgency (Daddis 2011: 164). Indeed, by imposing limits on bombing North Vietnam, the Johnson administration permitted the US military command under Abrams to use air power to serve the ground campaign more directly, by hitting supply lines into, and military targets within, South Vietnam (Cosmas 2007: 109).

Although the Johnson administration pushed its preference for securing territorial gains ("stabilizing" the war) rather than escalating to achieve (seemingly elusive) victory (Cosmas 2007: 119), the evidence does not suggest that a change in US military strategy per se improved the US position on the ground. The improving combat environment in South Vietnam was actually due to other factors. First, more of the population fell under the Saigon government's control as villagers fled Vietcong-controlled areas to get away from the fighting. Second, the Vietcong, having already suffered enormously in the 1968 offensive, were targeted directly by the US intelligence led Phoenix program. Forged to destroy the Vietcong infrastructure by "neutralizing" (capturing or killing) its leadership, the program is credited with inflicting over ten thousand deaths between 1968 and 1972, mostly low-level agents and innocent civilians who were falsely implicated and could not buy themselves out of their predicament (Kalyvas and Kocher 2007: 194, 201; Prados 2009: 327–328; Thayer 1985: 208). Controversial (to say the least) for its purported use of torture, extrajudicial detention, and assassination, the program arguably uprooted the Vietcong infrastructure in the country.[61] Third, and most significant, US forces gained ground when the Vietcong lost territory and personnel in the Tet Offensive. After Tet, the Vietcong compensated for their weakened position by relying on coercive tactics that alienated the local populace, filling their ranks with North Vietnamese personnel, and laying low to avoid US forces.

Thus, General Abrams is frequently lauded for moving toward "One War, One Strategy," thereby bridging the divide between attrition and pacification (Kimball 1998: 96) with a more cohesive and effective military effort. Yet the credit belongs in no small part to political and military conditions that allowed a change in US tactics. The US military had the resources, and now the capability, to pacify the countryside, with the depletion and evacuation of Vietcong main forces (Birtle 2004: 1230–1231; Cosmas 2007: 133): "Stronger allied forces, a relatively stable Saigon government, and a weakened enemy permitted Abrams, for the first time in the war, to mount the balanced military and pacification offensive which Americans had envisioned since the early 1960s" (Cosmas 2007: 139).

Hanoi's change in strategy, however, muted the impact of these seemingly favorable developments. Following the principles of General Vo Nguyen Giap, North Vietnam's legendary defense minister (and hero of Dien Bien Phu), Hanoi now adopted a more conventional war plan. When the time was right, it planned to seize ground, take the cities, and bring down the government in the South (Wirtz 1991: 56–57). Although Hanoi was readying to fight, ostensibly on US terms, the issue for the United States was now not capability, but rather perseverance and will.

Nixon's Initial Plans to Turn the War Around

President Nixon entered office having rejected Johnson administration policies (Johns 1999); indeed, Nixon had interceded (through an intermediary) with Nguyen Van Thieu, the South Vietnamese president, to convince him not to participate in impending negotiations with North Vietnam. Nixon feared that negotiations would give Hubert Humphrey a late electoral boost (a much-feared "October surprise") in the November presidential contest.[62] Although Nixon arrived in office with far less than the "secret plan" to end the war that he claimed to possess (the absence of a plan was the "secret," according to Nixon's opponents), Nixon and his national security adviser, Henry Kissinger, drew from a set of general principles to end the war on favorable terms—in Nixon's words, to achieve "peace with honor."[63]

First, Nixon and Kissinger planned to employ trilateral diplomacy—indeed, to leverage the hostility in Sino-Soviet relations—to get Russia and China to pressure Hanoi into making critical concessions. In their view, Chinese intransigence and support for North Vietnam was neither limitless nor inevitable. Although Nixon and Kissinger were responsible for the opening to China, placing US-Chinese relations and US-Soviet relations on a new footing, their hopes to leverage big-power relations to bring Hanoi to heel were ultimately disappointed. Neither Russia nor China exercised sufficient influence over Hanoi to soften Hanoi's long-held positions significantly, despite US threats, probing, and prodding. At the very least, Nixon and Kissinger had misjudged how much incentives for cooperation with the United States (e.g., for the Soviet Union on the issue of strategic nuclear arms control) would motivate one or the other of the two rival powers to press Hanoi harder when that could strengthen Hanoi's bond with the less-demanding power.

Second, Nixon and Kissinger believed that they could play hardball to advantage—that is, renounce prior restraints to weaken the enemy militarily and, if necessary, escalate the conflict precipitously to coerce the enemy to back down. These goals were achievable presumably by expanding military action into neighboring states and curtailing Johnson-era bombing restrictions. In Nixon's second full month in office, the United States commenced a massive, secret bombing campaign in Cambodia and greatly increased the tonnages dropped over Laos (Kimball 2004: 21). The military intention was to ease the task of defending South Vietnam by destroying North Vietnamese bases and staging areas and disrupting the flow of personnel and supplies into South Vietnam; the political intention was to convince the adversary that further resistance would be costly.

In the summer of the same year, the administration initiated planning for an intense aerial bombing and port-mining campaign against North Vietnam, codenamed Duck Hook. Following Nixon and Kissinger's implicit (and perhaps explicit) guidance, planning documents testify to a "no-holds-barred" approach, a bombing campaign of explosive bursts that could last for months but would break the war's traditional (politically imposed) barriers. The nuclear option was not taken off the table.[64] As Kissinger outlined to Nixon in a contingency planning document, the "action must be brutal"—underlined, for effect, in the original document—and continue along its course until it achieved its objectives: "We should not allow ourselves to be deterred by vague, conciliatory gestures by Hanoi."[65] Although the administration called off the operation in October, due largely to internal administration resistance and anticipated public dissent,[66] Nixon and Kissinger had not conceded their desire to escalate the conflict for political effect. They channeled the spirit of Duck Hook into a less violent, yet still risky, gambit.

Nixon and Kissinger—inspired by the strategic thought of the period—pushed coercive escalation to new heights, in a futile attempt to obtain Soviet concessions from Hanoi. Assuming no one would fool with a "madman," Nixon thought it wise to appear angrily risk prone, responding disproportionately to any offense (Kimball 1998: 76), to communicate to the Soviets that they could not count on the president's "rational" restraint. On Nixon's command, eighteen B-52 bombers were loaded with nuclear weapons—the reason kept even from the Strategic Air Command (Kimball 2004: 111)—and then flown toward the Soviet Union and back in an orbiting pattern (Sagan and Suri 2003; Suri 2008). To ensure that the Soviets got "the message," US strategic bombers remained on alert for three weeks, US tactical forces and nuclear missile submarines took actions to increase their combat readiness, and US naval forces engaged in maneuvers around the globe.[67] The US military monitored accordingly for signs of an active Soviet military response, relaying indications that the Soviet navy had repositioned in apparent response to the US naval maneuvers.[68] Unfortunately—perhaps fortunately—the Soviets were unmoved by Nixon's frightening gambit. They presumably dismissed it as a gimmick and might well have perceived it as a feeble effort to end a conflict from which the United States wanted desperately to disengage.

Third, Nixon and Kissinger believed that the United States could gradually turn the war over to South Vietnam. The accompanying policy, initiated by the president in his first months in office (Cosmas 2007: 149), came to be known as "Vietnamization." In current parlance, "*they* will stand up as *we* stand down"; that is, South Vietnamese troops would take charge once US troops left the battlefield. Departing from its predecessor, the Nixon administration assumed that US troops would leave South Vietnam with enemy units still active in the country. Yet the underlying thinking was actually more complicated and controversial than it appeared. The accompanying issue for Nixon and Kissinger was how much to push the "de-Americanization" of the war. De-Americanization could signal to Hanoi that the United States was reducing its troop commitment to sustainable levels and to the US public that an end to US involvement was in sight. But de-Americanization could also encourage the US public to expect a speedier than possible end to the war and leaders on all sides of the Vietnamese conflict to assume that the United States had abandoned South Vietnam, complicating US relations with both Saigon and Hanoi.

The administration struggled to stay on message. For instance, in 1969 Kissinger warned Nixon in a memo that "a too rapid withdrawal might seriously shake the Thieu government, particularly if coupled with pressure on Thieu for a political settlement"; it might "create excessive optimism in the United States and make the withdrawal irreversible." Hanoi would certainly get the message: "Hanoi's reading of the domestic U.S. political implications of an accelerated U.S. withdrawal is likely to be quite accurate" (reprinted in Kimball 2004: 88). Believing that "we have to impress Hanoi with our staying power,"[69] Kissinger feared that domestic pressure would "lock" the administration into the withdrawal process (Kissinger 1979: 1329). The US public would become addicted to troop withdrawals like "salted peanuts"; "the more US troops come home, the more will be demanded."[70] Kissinger expressed his displeasure when Secretary of State William Rogers stated publicly that US plans for withdrawal were "irrevocable" (Kimball 1998: 183).

The problem, however, ran deeper than messaging. Kissinger acknowledged that whether the president signaled right or left—that is, placated hawks or doves—Hanoi would see validation, "to confirm it in its course of waiting us out." Hanoi's leaders, it seems, were "the last people we will be able to fool about the ability of the South Vietnamese to take over from us."[71] It appears that even in 1969 Kissinger had recognized that Hanoi, not Washington or Saigon, held the stronger hand.

Nixon's War: Moving Toward Exit

Nixon and Kissinger were not always on the same page. In fall 1970 Kissinger prevailed when Nixon seriously considered pulling US troops out of Vietnam (while intensifying the bombing and blockading North Vietnam) in response to growing domestic antiwar protests and Hanoi's persistent intransigence. Hanoi continued to insist on a unilateral US withdrawal and change in the Saigon regime. Although Kissinger successfully argued for staying the current course (Kimball 2004: 27), Nixon wavered between a hard line—"settle or else" (Dallek 2007: 382)—and a softer resolution that would speed the US exit from the conflict. The two principals nonetheless had much in common. Both Nixon and Kissinger saw escalation as useful for improving the US bargaining position. Conversely, both were soon "entertaining" the idea of a settlement that would allow the United States to claim victory—over a period of some unspecified length, before the Saigon government collapsed—but "had not yet embraced it" (Kimball 1998: 233). That idea, in the lore of the period, is known as the "decent interval."[72]

A bigger divide separated Nixon and Kissinger from others in the administration who sought a quicker exit. Secretary of Defense William Laird's priorities were Vietnamization and lowering the US military profile in Southeast Asia (Randolph 2007: 114–115, 169). Along with Secretary of State Rogers, Laird pushed against escalating the war, which he believed would increase US troop casualties and inflame domestic political opposition (Hunt 2015: 98), favoring a more deliberate

US withdrawal. The two secretaries influenced some major decisions. Over their opposition, Kissinger argued unsuccessfully for the Duck Hook operation (Kimball 2004: 22).[73] Yet Nixon and Kissinger—with their confidence in their own decisional capabilities, penchant for secrecy, distaste for the give and take of group strategy sessions (on Nixon, see Glad and Link 1996: 13, 15), and desire for control—frequently left others in the presidential advisory circle out of the loop and on the losing side of the issue. Laird and Rogers learned of the Duck Hook operation from a newspaper column (Dallek 2007: 155), and—to their dismay—of Nixon's decision to invade Cambodia—an operation they had opposed (Dallek 2007: 196–197)—only once the decision was made, and then within days of the invasion. They opposed the 1972 US bombing campaigns against North Vietnam, to no avail (Kimball 2004: 218). However, Laird used his position as secretary of defense to lobby the administration and constrain the latitude of the US military command. He often (albeit not consistently) opposed requests to expand the number, nature, and scope of US bombing operations (e.g., see Cosmas 2007: 313–314, 342), and he imposed budget and troop ceilings that forced the services to defend their actual priorities. He eventually realized success when the military accepted a speedy and unconditional withdrawal of US troops from Vietnam (Cosmas 2007: 141–178).[74]

In the end, these differences in viewpoint within the administration mattered little. They determined the style and timing, but not the reality, of the US exit from Vietnam. In various ways Nixon and Kissinger signaled—even facilitated—US steps out of the conflict, though critics at the time believed that the administration was taking the United States in the opposite direction.

First, de-Americanization of the war proceeded apart from its Vietnamization. Through de-Americanization, Nixon tried to quell domestic protests over the war's social and economic costs by ending US reliance on the draft. His objectives in moving toward an all-volunteer army were unmistakably political, not confessions of faith in the professional US military (or Saigon's capability to fight on its own). As Nixon confided to Kissinger, "Ending the draft gives us breathing space in Vietnam. We'll restore the draft later, but goddamn it, the military, they're a bunch of greedy bastards that want more officers clubs and more men to shine their shoes. The sons of bitches are not interested in this country" (quoted in Zelizer 2010: 225). At best, then, the de-Americanization of the war rested on the poorly grounded hope that withdrawing US troops from Vietnam would pressure Saigon to carry the load. It was indeed a risky bet that the South Vietnamese military could at least contain an adversary that the US military could not defeat.

Although Nixon initially tied US troop withdrawals to the state of negotiations with Hanoi, permissive combat conditions on the ground, and Saigon's ability to carry the load (Hunt 2015: 104–105), de-Americanization of the war eventually outpaced Vietnamization. The administration held to the troop withdrawal schedule proposed in 1969: within two years, the US military would remain capable only of supporting South Vietnamese operations, and in the following two years, the US military in Vietnam would possess capabilities equivalent to those of "a large assistance and advisory group" (Cosmas 2007: 179). Still, the US military, under Abrams's command, had neither prepared nor equipped Saigon's military to assume the US role in battle. On the contrary, it consistently took the lead in offensive operations; managed the withdrawal schedule to preserve US combat strength in Vietnam where US forces were needed; and deflected Saigon's requests for the heavy arms that would help make the South Vietnamese army more than a light force, for counterinsurgency or territorial defense. Although the US command cautioned against turning the war over to Saigon prematurely (Cosmas 2007: 141–178, 277), even General Abrams recognized, early in his command, that the United States would eventually withdraw from the conflict. He obliged himself to ensure that "the United States disengaged in an orderly fashion" (Cosmas 2007: 180) and concluded that there was little to gain from negotiating the size of the US force that would be left in Vietnam after 1971, since it would lack the capability to affect combat realities on the ground (Cosmas 2007: 166).

By 1971 US civilian and military leaders agreed that US forces would adopt a more defensive stance and not conduct large-scale offensive operations (Cosmas 2007: 259). The burden would pass to a deficient South Vietnamese force that would take control of the fighting. Whether it was up to the challenge was not the main issue. The withdrawal schedule simply assumed a "best-case" scenario with a US departure—that is, that the South Vietnamese military would contend only with the guerrilla threat that it could plausibly defeat (Cosmas 2007: 159).

Second, the administration defined "peace" and "honor" to serve its growing desire to exit the conflict. Kissinger implicitly lowered the stakes for America in Vietnam by seeking a resolution that would permit the United States to spin success from failure politically.

Confirmatory evidence in this regard emerged in Kissinger's early dealings with Moscow, Beijing, and Hanoi. In May 1969 Kissinger told Soviet ambassador Anatoly Dobrynin that "Nixon is even prepared to accept any political system in South Vietnam, 'provided there is a fairly *reasonable interval* between conclusion of an agreement and [the establishment of] such a system.'"[75] In the fall of 1970, Kissinger signaled to Hanoi's negotiators that the United States had finally relaxed its long-standing commitment to South Vietnamese sovereignty and no longer required that North Vietnam remove its forces from South Vietnam as a condition for US withdrawal. Early the following year he made his position official. He offered to hold US forces to a withdrawal deadline while allowing North Vietnam to keep its forces in place (Kimball 2004: 27, 29). Weeks later, on his first visit to China, Kissinger confided his hopes to Premier Zhou Enlai that some time would pass between a US exodus and a South Vietnamese defeat, to ensure the credibility of US commitments. Although Kissinger might not have used the exact phrase "decent interval" in his negotiations, the implication was clear when he told Zhou of the need for "a transition period between the military withdrawal and the political evolution" (quoted in Kimball 2004: 187).[76] Toward that end, he proposed an unconditional US troop withdrawal to North Vietnamese negotiators, Ambassador Dobrynin, and the Chinese premier, on different occasions, that would leave things for the Vietnamese to work out (Kimball 2004: 134). The US position, as expressed by Kissinger to Zhou, was that it would "not interfere" (Kimball 2004: 191); that is, the United States "would not be looking for excuses to re-enter Indochina" (Lewis 2014: 49).[77]

By early 1971, however, Nixon and Kissinger had come to doubt whether the South Vietnamese government could survive absent direct US support (Kimball 2004: 28). Kissinger, for his part, took exception to Laird's optimistic assessments of Saigon's capacity to handle the Communist military threat (Hunt 2015: 129-131).[78] As late as January 1972, Nixon pushed back against Laird's rosy depictions of South Vietnamese capabilities, concerned that the United States had not prepared or equipped Saigon sufficiently to withstand a North Vietnamese attack (Hunt 2015: 212–213). Nevertheless, Nixon and Kissinger generally opted to move forward. They frequently disagreed over required next steps, such as whether negotiating or bombing would be the proper course (Kimball 1998: 338–371). Their disagreements were small, though, given their shared desire to exit the conflict sooner rather than later. Nixon himself put it in "cold-blooded" terms when, in August 1972, he confided his "candid" thoughts to Kissinger that "South Vietnam probably is never gonna survive anyway" (quoted in Hughes 2010: 500–501). Their exit strategy assumed that the United States could distance itself, and its reputation, from the conflict and then blame Saigon—*after* the US presidential election, to avoid political fallout—for not having capitalized on long-standing US support (Hughes 2010: 500). Kissinger could not have been more transparent about these plans than when, in March 1971, he confided to Nixon, "So we've got to find some formula that holds the thing together a year or two, after which—after a year, Mr. President, Vietnam will be a backwater. If we settle it, say, this October, by January '74 no one will give a damn" (quoted in Hughes 2010: 501). For Kissinger, leaving Vietnam was essentially a political optics problem. With real victory proving elusive, the administration would settle for "the next best thing" in the form of a ceasefire: "If Hanoi were to accept our offer of a cease-fire, we would not be able to respond with an open-ended commitment to continue the war in pursuit of unconditional victory" (Kissinger 1979: 1324).

Third, the administration escalated (and expanded) the war to set Hanoi's war effort back, to enable a US exit. Victory, it realized, was not in the cards, but it could buy time for Saigon to rise to the challenge. At the very least, the administration hoped to lengthen the period before Saigon fell (increasing the "decency" of the interval) while loudly signaling its support for Saigon to mask the fact of a US retreat. Nixon had periodically entertained the option of exiting the conflict with a "bang." If all else failed, his plan was to pair the withdrawal of US forces with a massive bombing campaign directed at North Vietnam's war-making infrastructure. The administration's military efforts on these fronts did little, however, to improve the final outcome. Escalations of the war brought additional political pressure on the administration to end US involvement in the conflict. Regardless, the upswings in the war amounted to brief departures that hid an increasingly obvious truth: the Nixon administration was slowly extricating the United States from a conflict in which victory had proven elusive.

American troops invaded Cambodia in 1970 to destroy North Vietnamese supply lines, base camps, and command centers. The administration claimed that the Cambodia "incursion" inflicted more than ten thousand enemy deaths and captured vast stores of weapons and ammunition. But the military impact of the operation must also be measured against its sizable negative political impact at home. Despite majority public support for the 1970 invasion (Katz 1997: 500), the Cambodia operation represented the Vietnam War's high-water mark for public protest and legislative efforts to curtail the president's war-making powers. College campuses throughout the country erupted in protest (spurred on by the killing by National Guard units of four students on the Kent State campus in Ohio), and many universities were forced to close down. Congress, too, was moved to take action. Although it proved unwilling to terminate a US military operation in progress, it sought to prevent a repeat performance when, in January 1971, it passed a modified version of the Cooper-Church Amendment, disallowing the use of defense funds to reintroduce US troops into Cambodia.[79] It also rescinded the Gulf of Tonkin Resolution, in December 1970, after Nixon used it to justify the US invasion of Cambodia.[80]

In 1971 US forces backed the invasion of Laos by South Vietnamese troops. The Nixon administration encouraged the South Vietnamese offensive—again, to weaken North Vietnamese forces, destroy their bases, and sever their supply lines—but also to demonstrate, and facilitate, the Vietnamization of the war. The Laos offensive was a last opportunity for US ground forces to assist such an operation, given dwindling US troop levels in Vietnam (Cosmas 2007: 321). Despite direct US aerial and logistical support, the South Vietnamese military proved no match for the defending North Vietnamese troops. Having anticipated the assault, they sent South Vietnamese troops into retreat. The offensive exposed South Vietnamese military weaknesses that would eventually prove fatal: a failure in basic tactical skills, poor coordination among military units, unwillingness to engage the enemy, overly centralized command, a lack of military leadership, and quixotic instructions from South Vietnam's president to his command on the ground (Talmadge 2015: 97–106). The Nixon administration suffered the effects of these shortcoming, politically when the media circulated pictures of fleeing South Vietnamese soldiers hanging from the skids of departing helicopters. Even the military gains from the offensive proved temporary at best. In spring 1972 North Vietnam, having re-established its supply lines and basing areas in Laos and Cambodia, launched its Easter Offensive. It seized large swaths of South Vietnamese territory and might have dealt a decisive blow to the Saigon regime but for the massive assistance of US air power.

In 1972 the Nixon administration lifted bombing restrictions on North Vietnam in two successive aerial campaigns (dubbed Linebacker I and II). To cut off foreign supplies, it also mined Haiphong Harbor. The US Linebacker I bombing raids (May to October 1972) on strategic and interdiction targets followed on the heels of the Easter Offensive. In turn, Linebacker II—the "Christmas bombing" campaign— brought US B-52 bombers fully into the conflict, and with them the heaviest strategic bombing of the war. The campaign targeted the North Vietnamese infrastructure: "eleven nights of air strikes highlighted by B-52 attacks on rail yards, power plans, and airfields in Hanoi and Haiphong Harbor" (Haun and Jackson 2015/2016: 172). The military effects of both campaigns are open to question.[81] Linebacker I and II, like the incursions into Cambodia or Laos, failed to change the fundamental balance of forces or compel Hanoi to renounce its goals. The Linebacker II sorties, however, did accomplish their goal: with negotiations stalled, they helped bridge an impasse (discussed later in the chapter) to expedite the US retreat from the conflict.

Fourth, the administration accepted terms in early October 1972 for an agreement with Hanoi that placed South Vietnam at a political and military disadvantage. The "breakthrough," as Kissinger (1979: 1341) termed it, came when he secured an important concession: Hanoi agreed that the Thieu government could remain in power. Neither Nixon nor Kissinger wanted to appear complicit in the demise of the Saigon government. Yet Saigon remained unconvinced of US support, with good reason. Kissinger had consistently tried to delink the war's military and political issues (Kissinger 1979: 1345), separating the matter of US-North Vietnamese force deployments from questions concerning South Vietnam's future governance. Indeed, Kissinger appeared amenable to terms (including a potential coalition government in Saigon) that did not bode well for South Vietnam's (or Thieu's) political future (Kimball 1998: 318). Now the United States had finally accepted terms that undercut South Vietnam's sovereignty and threatened its future. Specifically, the agreement (a) accepted the presence of Hanoi's forces on South Vietnamese territory (by allowing North Vietnamese troops to remain in place), (b) legitimized the Vietcong through formal acceptance of the provisional revolutionary government as a legal party to the conflict (Herring 1986: 250–255), (c) acknowledged the 17th parallel as a "provisional" boundary (separating North from South Vietnam), and (d) referenced Vietnam's "unification" as an end goal (of a political process). In other words, the United States had come around to accepting negotiating terms that North Vietnam might well have accepted years earlier.[82] It had done so knowing that the Saigon government was probably unable to hold its own should the fighting continue.

Thieu let the negotiations play out as long as they remained deadlocked on critical issues. The US refusal to accept a coalition government was for him a "safe haven from the risks of the negotiations" (Kissinger 1979: 1311). Kissinger had previously tried to cajole Thieu by minimizing the impact of US concessions and promising an upswing in the US bombing campaign after the November election (Prados 2009: 503–505). Yet promises and denials, at this critical juncture, could not overcome Saigon's resistance. Thieu understood his predicament no less than Kissinger did (1979: 1310): "A compromise would be the beginning, not the end, of massive problems in South Vietnam." Thus, Thieu picked at the negotiating terms with endless questions, "opposed whatever aspect appeared close to a solution," and ultimately rejected terms that he had previously accepted.[83] When US sweeteners, and sweet talk, proved insufficient, coercion was tried. Nixon and Kissinger explicitly warned of a cutoff in all US support if Saigon failed to accept the negotiated terms. Nixon even wrote to Thieu in early October reminding him of Diem's uncooperativeness; he "should be careful not to create conditions that 'could lead to events similar to those which we abhorred in 1963' " (Kimball 2004: 247), a thinly veiled reference to the chain of events that had led to Diem's assassination. An angry Thieu nonetheless confronted Kissinger when he traveled to Saigon late in October to gain the former's adherence to the agreement. Thieu's message was clear: he would not sign the agreement (Kimball 2004: 255; Kalb 2013: 164–174).

Kissinger (1979: 1317) recognized the consequences of publicly abandoning an ally, not least one who could undercut the agreement. Nixon saw a recalcitrant Thieu—just weeks before the 1972 election—as a potentially damaging political issue (Dallek 2007: 424). So Kissinger looked to Hanoi for a better deal. Hanoi figured it, too, could play that game and retracted its prior concessions (Kissinger 1979: 1418). With negotiations at an impasse, Kissinger cabled Nixon that "the president now had only two options: to cut off the talks and resume heavy bombing, or to accept an imperfect document, knowing in advance that Thieu would likely sabotage the deal" (Kalb 2013: 178). The administration thus answered Hanoi's defiance—that is, Saigon's intransigence—by launching the Linebacker II bombing campaign. The administration continued to battle on multiple fronts, bombing Hanoi and threatening Saigon with a loss in all support should it remain defiant. Nixon personally drafted the last sentence of a letter to be delivered to Thieu: "The time has come for us to present a united front in negotiating with our enemies, and you must decide now whether you desire to continue our alliance or whether you want me to seek a settlement with the enemy which serves U.S. interests alone" (Kissinger 1979: 1459–1460).

Hanoi, not Saigon—or the United States—was holding the cards. Although the bombing inflicted thousands of civilian casualties in the North, Hanoi's bargaining position barely budged.[84] Thieu pressed the Nixon administration, almost to the end, for additional concessions (Kalb 2013: 193; Kissinger 1979: 1469), to no avail. The administration would not press Hanoi further; it would only *promise* "continued assistance to Saigon" and a US response "with full force" should Hanoi violate the terms of the agreement (Kissinger 1979: 1462). On January 27, 1973, with Saigon's acquiescence, Kissinger formally accepted the terms that the United States and North Vietnam had essentially negotiated early in October.

Congress finalized the US exit, first when it passed the Case-Church Amendment—as of August 1973, it ended all US combat in Southeast Asia—and then, in 1974, when it cut military aid to the Saigon government.[85] Nixon might have had the votes to prevent an override if he had vetoed the Case-Church Amendment.[86] That he let it stand and conceded to the will of Congress by default is telling. That Nixon planned the US withdrawal from Vietnam believing that once US troops had departed, Congress might slam the door on further aid to Saigon (Kimball 2004: 150, 152), is even more revealing.

Final Resolution: Accepting a Perhaps Inevitable Loss in the South

North Vietnamese and South Vietnamese troops skirmished for territorial control as the war continued into 1975. When Hanoi thought the time was right, it went in for the kill; South Vietnamese forces, absent US aerial and logistic support, failed their final test.

The weaknesses that had long bedeviled the Army of the Republic of Vietnam conspired to produce a calamitous outcome. The South Vietnamese military proved no match for a more professionalized (and indeed, smaller) North Vietnamese force. South Vietnamese units dissolved in hasty retreat; senior officers abandoned their troops; and defending forces received, at best, poorly conceived presidential instructions. Command failures, deficient military communications, outright panic as soldiers and civilians sought to save themselves and their families, and bottlenecks on main transit routes doomed efforts to reposition South Vietnamese forces to defend the capital and other portions of the country (see Talmadge 2015: 118–129). In a matter of weeks, South Vietnam was no more.

Whether Kissinger had procured a "decent" interval—at reasonable cost—must certainly be judged by the speed with which the South Vietnamese military disintegrated, the divisive politics of the US withdrawal, the enormous toll in Vietnamese lives in the months between the US withdrawal and South Vietnam's defeat, the lives and resources invested in achieving the negotiated agreement, and the muted effects of South Vietnam's inglorious defeat on the US reputation for commitment. Ironically, in lamenting the reputational effects of an early US departure from Vietnam, the Nixon administration was no more attentive to cause and effect than the Johnson administration had been when preparing, years earlier, for US military intervention.

Conclusions

The legacy of the Vietnam War survives the generation that fought it in the cities, villages, and countryside of Southeast Asia—and that supported or opposed it at home. It stands as a virtual symbol of bad decision-making. The war reminds some of the costs of exceptional civilian meddling and, ultimately, a politically motivated, no-win policy. For others, the war serves as a model of misguided policy, anchored in false optimism or the failings of incremental decision-making. These views are incomplete, however, when they fail to acknowledge the biases of means-driven decision-making.

Stage I, Engagement: Fixation

The Johnson administration went to war after committing early to using military force—first by hitting North Vietnamese targets through the air and then by pursuing a full-blown air and ground campaign. Yet it failed to reconcile the divergent views that administration officials held over how the US military might produce a favorable outcome. The administration hoped that Hanoi would concede to growing US military might; when it did not, the administration followed, unreflectively, its existing course.

For Johnson, the decision to engage in Vietnam was painfully difficult but not thoughtful or rigorously grounded. Consequently, the administration extended its short-term policies without assessing their long-term implications. It emphasized tactics over strategy and showed insufficient regard for how preferred options might facilitate the adoption of less-desired options. It adopted policies without fully committing to a view of the conflict (as an international war, civil war, or some hybrid of the two). Moreover, it failed to consider the requirements of fighting the war to a successful conclusion. The administration had allowed the military "solution" to prevail over diagnostics of the problem.

Stage II, Extension: Disjunction

The Johnson administration failed to adhere to the requirements of either a political or a military strategy. Its efforts to harness bombing for political effect suffered accordingly. It bombed within somewhat arbitrary limits out of fear of provoking

Soviet or Chinese intervention. The administration hit targets in and around North Vietnam for coercive effect without questioning whether the damage that the bombing could realistically inflict could ever get Hanoi to concede. It selected targets for their location, war contribution, and infrastructural importance, to send Hanoi clear messages under conditions that would nonetheless obscure and distort all messages. Any message that the administration intended to send competed at a disadvantage with the unintended messages sent by military and practical constraints on bombing, rising political discontent at home, and the trials and tribulations of the US war on the ground.

In fighting on the ground, by contrast, the Johnson administration paid little heed to political requisites. Following the military's strategy, it surrendered the initiative to the enemy by ignoring a fundamental political truth: the enemy was playing for time, knowing that the United States would tire first. The enemy chose to avoid decisive clashes; to accept high losses, if necessary; and to multiply its effectiveness, in the short and long terms, through a dual-war strategy. The neglected political dimension of the war would ultimately prove decisive.

Stage III, Limitation: Constriction

With roughly half a million US soldiers in country, a rising death toll, growing public protest, and no signs of the conflict abating, the Johnson administration reached its limit: it conceded that a victory in Vietnam was out of reach at an acceptable level of investment. Johnson ruled out a troop increase and an escalation or expansion of the conflict, despite military claims that the increased US investment would accelerate an end to the war. At the same time, Johnson never deliberatively weighed the benefits against the costs of a precipitous US withdrawal. Instead, he locked into the "middle" option, neither escalating nor withdrawing.

Staying the course allowed Johnson to avoid the risks and domestic political costs of an expanding war at one extreme and the alleged US national security and potential political costs of "losing" South Vietnam at the other. Johnson nevertheless chose an option primarily for its cost, not its payoff. He constrained US force levels, hoping that a US strategy, which had not yet pushed Hanoi to negotiate, would convince it to concede to US terms.

Stage IV, Disengagement: Extrication

The Nixon administration jettisoned some Johnson-era limitations. It escalated US involvement in the Vietnam conflict by invading Cambodia and supporting a South Vietnamese invasion of Laos and then by expanding the air war over North Vietnam. Its intention, however, was only to *weaken* Hanoi to facilitate a US exit from the conflict. Its underlying purpose became apparent when the administration pursued de-Americanization apart from the progress of Vietnamization of the war effort; defined *peace* and *honor* to serve its growing desire to leave the conflict; and escalated (and expanded) the war only to set Hanoi's war effort back and, ultimately, to cover a US retreat. It was most obvious, finally, when the administration negotiated an agreement with Hanoi that left Saigon at a political and military disadvantage.

The Nixon administration allowed the US exit from Vietnam to proceed along its own course. Leaving became the US objective, no matter how US leaders framed their fateful decisions at the time.

3

The Iraq War, 2003–2011

In the decade that followed the 1991 Gulf War, Iraq refused to open its territory to international inspections to establish indisputably that it had dismantled its weapons of mass destruction (WMD) programs. In 2003 the George W. Bush administration answered Iraq's defiance by forcefully removing Saddam Hussein's regime from power. The administration had concluded that US restraint was no longer necessary, given favorable military conditions. Yet before and after its invasion of Iraq, the administration showed all the signs of means-driven decision-making. First, it focused narrowly on bringing down the Baghdad regime and failed to plan for the aftermath of war (*fixation*). With the fall of Baghdad, it increased its occupational challenges by expanding US objectives, even though America lacked the resources and organizational capabilities to pursue them, and by continuing to rely on an undersized and underprepared US military force (*disjunction*). The administration adjusted course in 2007, sending additional US forces into Iraq to implement a counterinsurgency strategy. Still, its new strategy had the US military pursuing modest goals to suit "available" capabilities (*constriction*). The administration then benefited unexpectedly from a fortuitous break in the ranks of the Sunni insurgency and the stand-down of the principal Shiite militia opposing US forces. The US "strategy" subsequently amounted to staying the course through 2011, the negotiated end of US combat involvement in Iraq. As the 2011 departure deadline approached and renegotiations continued, the Obama administration did not offer much to make a deal. It chose to leave Iraq rather than compromise (*extrication*).

Stage I, Engagement: Fixation

In US planning for the Iraq War, the proposed solution fit the problem—*as defined*. US policy makers concluded that the regime in Baghdad was the main culprit; US military officials answered with a relevant but flawed military strategy. Time would expose serious deficits in the administration's Iraq War decision-making: the administration never truly settled on a justification for the war, it focused prematurely on regime change, and it failed to prepare adequately for the consequences once the regime fell.

Failing to Establish a Justification for Intervention

The Bush administration largely pinned its public case for war with Iraq on the latter's alleged WMD holdings; that Saddam Hussein possessed these weapons meant that he (or someone else) might use them. On September 8, 2002, National Security Advisor Condoleezza Rice made the case most memorably when she challenged skeptics in a CNN broadcast, warning that the "smoking gun" evidence they sought might appear, too late, as a "mushroom cloud." Congress was convinced; on October 11, 2002, the Senate (in a 77–23 vote) and the House (in a 296–133 vote) passed a resolution authorizing the president to use force against Iraq. The Bush administration then made its case before the UN Security Council. On February 5, 2003, Secretary of State Colin Powell presented evidence, in exhaustive detail, of illicit Iraqi weapons holdings. He spoke with authority and urgency. "Every statement I make today is backed up by sources, solid sources. These are not assertions. What we're giving you are facts and conclusions based on solid intelligence." His appeal was nonetheless insufficient to win over the more skeptical international audience; the United States failed to garner UN support for a resolution authorizing military action against Iraq.

After the US invasion, as evidence emerged that Iraq did not possess WMD, administration officials (and supporters) nevertheless insisted that the United States had acted appropriately to protect US security in the lead-up to the attack. In their view, the administration had more than enough reason for war. It simply could not afford to delay a decisive response in the post-9/11 environment; the unprovoked al-Qaeda assaults on the US Trade Center in New York and the Pentagon outside Washington, D.C., had established that the United States now faced an enemy that would go anywhere and do anything to accomplish its destructive goals. Since Saddam Hussein's motives and actions were suspect, many officials could not help but subscribe to him a role in that attack or in potential acts of malign destructiveness should he use his WMD or pass them to some terrorist group. Regardless, the United States had no reason to wait; the implicating intelligence information was strong, and Iraq had failed to disarm *transparently*, as required under the terms of multiple UN Security Council resolutions.[1] Absent transparency, uncertainty would always remain about Iraq's actual weapons stocks and future weapons holdings.

For that reason, Douglas Feith, undersecretary of defense for policy in the Bush administration, insists that US officials should have made a public case that Iraqi intent and weapons know-how posed a threat to US national security interests.[2] His point is well taken. Saddam Hussein might eventually have rearmed; even the CIA's authoritative postwar report on Iraqi WMD concluded that Saddam Hussein planned to resuscitate his WMD programs once sanctions had ended (Iraq Survey

Group 2004). Certainly the United States could have guarded against that possibility by maintaining sanctions, actively monitoring Iraqi programs, disrupting suspicious Iraqi activities, and destroying suspect Iraqi sites. Yet these actions came with costs: across the US government, civilian and military officials had to devote significant time and resources to sanctions enforcement and monitoring and containing Iraqi weapons programs. These actions also might have been ineffective. They might have done little to deplete Iraqi WMD holdings or production capabilities and then lost effectiveness as countries scrambled to secure access to Iraqi oil or withdrew sanctions out of concern for their deleterious humanitarian impact.

These claims did not keep administration officials and their supporters from trying to shift blame. Vice President Richard Cheney, for one, went on the offensive when he attributed the US decision to go to war to a purported statement by then CIA director George Tenet that the case that Iraq had illicit weapons was a "slam dunk."[3] Cheney's was certainly a viable political strategy. After all, the intelligence community had produced the now infamous October 2002 US National Intelligence Estimate (NIE), *Iraq's Continuing Programs for Weapons of Mass Destruction*,[4] which the administration used to make the public case for war. It asserted, without the administration's direct intervention, that Iraq had substantial biological and chemical weapons holdings and was reconstituting its nuclear program.[5]

That belief proved difficult to contest given Iraq's past and present behavior; Iraq had previously deceived the outside world, continued to act furtively, and behaved as if it were hiding something. Post-mortem investigations, however, established that the US intelligence community had uncritically held to the belief that Iraq had illicit weaponry and production capabilities (on this, see US Senate 2004). Intelligence analysts discounted exculpatory evidence as subterfuge. They treated the lack of evidence that Iraq had illicit weapons as evidence that it *did* possess these weapons.[6] They viewed implicating evidence as more compelling than its absence where it should exist if Iraq actually possessed active WMD programs. Moreover, they ignored or discounted alternative explanations for evidence that confirmed preferred explanations (Jervis 2010).

For critics of the administration, its blame-the-intelligence-community defense rang hollow. As they saw it, the *best* that could be said of the administration was that it too readily accepted the intelligence agencies' judgments. Most critics blamed the administration not for its passivity, but for trumpeting the impugning evidence and dismissing all caution. For many, faulting the administration for negligence simply did not go far enough. They insisted that the administration had intentionally twisted the facts: members of the administration, who had long desired the downfall of Saddam Hussein, constructed a fraudulent case for war, maligned doubters to weaken and intimidate the opposition, and then attacked Iraq with haste to preempt dissent. Skepticism over the official justification for war grew when invading Coalition troops made the securing of potential WMD sites a lesser priority. The fact that President Bush himself later acknowledged that he would have gone to war even had he known that Iraq did not possess WMD, when the administration had justified the war based on the existence of those weapons, fueled doubts about the administration's veracity.

The critics are indeed correct. Despite prewar justifications—and postattack recriminations over who was to blame for the bad intelligence that was used to make the public case for war—the evidence is now overwhelming that alleged Iraqi weapons holdings did not drive the administration's decisions. Paul Pillar (2014: 13–95, 140–174), who served as the national intelligence officer for the Near East and South Asia in the prewar (and early war) years, offers a spirited—and convincing—indictment of the administration's performance in the lead-up to the Iraq War.[7] He has issued multiple challenges to administration claims that Iraqi WMD led the United States to war.

First, at the war's onset, the administration's policy preceded evidence gathering. The administration decided to attack Iraq with limited input from the US intelligence establishment, well before the release of the 2002 NIE. The plan to attack Iraq gained traction in the earliest days of the Bush administration, when the US intelligence community did not judge Iraqi WMD to be a primary US threat; in its view, Iraq was unlikely to turn these weapons over to terrorists or use them, except under dire conditions. The exact date when war "plans" became more than that is elusive, of course, given the diffuse and indefinite planning process. Candidate months abound, however, in the 2001 calendar year. These include January, when the Bush administration entered office (Clarke 2004: 264) and then asked the Pentagon to examine military options for Iraq (Suskind 2004: 75); February, when Paul Wolfowitz was pitching the idea of arming and defending Iraqi opposition groups (Suskind 2004: 96–97); July, when Wolfowitz appealed to the NSC Deputies Committee (the second-in-command in various departments and agencies) to provide support to the opposition groups and establish a provisional government in portions of Iraq, as steps toward Iraqi regime change (Feith 2008: 208); the summer months, when General Tommy Franks, the US Central Command (CENTCOM) commander, began "dusting off plans" for a full-scale invasion of Iraq (9/11 Commission 2004: 336); September, when Bush directed the Pentagon to commence planning for an attack on Iraq as part of the administration's broader war on terrorism;[8] October, when the State Department's Future of Iraq Project initiated transitional planning for Iraq; and November, when Rumsfeld, acting on Bush's orders (Graham 2009: 327), directed General Franks to start planning a decapitation strike on the Iraqi government.[9]

The competing dates, varied participants, and operational focus provide little specific guidance for judging exactly when war with Iraq became a foregone conclusion. At some point, however, those who would know seemed to know the war was coming. Richard Haass (2009: 213), the State Department's director of policy planning, for instance, wrote that his sense that "something was up" increased when his staff, back from meetings, reported that their counterparts in government, who were known for their war advocacy, "appeared too cocky for comfort." George Tenet (2007: 309), then CIA director, recalls hearing stories of government meetings that would start with *if* and then transition to *when* we "went to war." He also reports the sense of senior CIA officials "from early in the Bush administration" that war was "inevitable." Such anecdotal evidence suggests that the war was on track before—perhaps well before—the arrival of a conclusive US intelligence community assessment.

Second, the administration eschewed neutral fact finding; seeking material from the intelligence community to help "sell" the war, it found in Iraqi WMD "a convenient consensus selling point" (Pillar 2014: 30). Consequently, administration officials pressed the intelligence community to focus on Iraq to uncover *implicating* evidence; they pushed back—hard—against exculpatory evidence (such as that belying claims that Iraq had attempted to purchase uranium from Niger), and they ignored the equivocations and actual guardedness of the conclusions in the intelligence assessments. Vice President Cheney "was perhaps the leading practitioner ... of referring to uncertain and ambiguous intelligence reporting as if it were fact" (Pillar 2014: 142). Indeed, US officials carefully coordinated with their British counterparts to offer consistent, even if invalid, claims to strengthen the case for war.[10]

Third, the administration would likely have made its argument for war absent implicating evidence; it could easily have dismissed the lack of such evidence by citing historical intelligence failures or the *possible* Iraqi acquisition of WMD. Feith was not alone in arguing that Iraqi *intentions* to acquire, transfer, or use WMD were an overriding threat to the United States; "the view of most of [the Bush administration's] top officials was that, if anything, the intelligence agencies might have understated the threat posed by Saddam." Cheney was unconvinced that US intelligence agencies, given their understating of Iraqi nuclear progress before the first Gulf War, would detect illicit Iraqi activities (Gordon and Trainor 2006: 126). Indeed, the fact remains that the administration had committed to Iraqi regime change before it had committed to the specific reason for such a change. When meeting with General Franks in November 2001, Rumsfeld offered an Iraqi 9/11 link, unrequited weapons inspection demands, and an Iraqi attack on the Kurds as candidate war triggers.[11]

Fourth, the administration sought input from the intelligence community when that suited its purposes. Bush administration officials persistently pressed the intelligence community to explore—that is, *expose*—the link between Saddam Hussein and the 9/11 attacks (Isikoff and Corn 2006: 114). Yet they did *not* seek the community's evaluation of conditions that the United States might encounter in Iraq. On the contrary, they ignored the intelligence community's warnings about dangers that might greet US troops and confound US nation-building efforts in that country.

Fifth, the administration imposed an implicit standard of proof that inhibited intelligence professionals from challenging its conclusions (on this, see also Rovner 2011: 137–184). The professionals could read the writing on the wall. They knew what the administration wanted; they also knew that raising doubts about administration claims was a losing proposition. What would it take to establish that Iraq did *not* have, was *not* seeking, and would *not* eventually seek WMD? Put simply, how can you prove the negative? With their professional futures on the line, intelligence personnel chose instead to qualify judgments—smooth some of the edges—yet produce a document that the administration could still employ to make its case.

Yet why, then, did the administration move against Iraq?[12] Administration officials confounded discovering an easy answer by hurling an arsenal of justifications, apparently hoping to find one or more that would resonate with the public: Saddam Hussein was brutal, a serial aggressor, a terror sympathizer and supporter, and so forth (Shimko 2017: 5–13). Academics rose to the explanatory challenge. They routinely scorned Bush administration officials for their dogmatic championing of unsound "neoconservative" principles, the belief that US-engineered democratic change would create a stable and peaceful Iraq that would catalyze democratic reforms throughout the Middle East. They criticized the administration further for its ideological adherence to the dangerously naive view that certain states, with bad leaders, were immune from the logic of self-interest and self-preservation (see Lebovic 2007). In banishing certain states—Iraq, Iran, and North Korea—to "rogue state" status, administration officials had wrongly depicted US adversaries in monolithic terms (much as their Cold War predecessors had done), united for a singular destructive purpose. For some critics, the administration's view stemmed from causal forces deep within the US political system. Their focus was on the excessive influence of "special interests." These included the large corporations (on whose boards prominent Republicans had served) that would reap huge profits from wartime sales and services; the oil industry (which reputedly eyed Iraq's healthy oil reserves); and the "Israel lobby," which had pushed for war (especially within Congress) in part to end Iraqi support for radical Palestinian groups (see Lake 2010/2011: 40–43).

Popular versions of events highlighted the flawed actions of key participants, based on rival accounts of those who had left the administration. The spotlight shown on officials—Vice President Cheney, Secretary of Defense Rumsfeld, Deputy Secretary of Defense Wolfowitz, Undersecretary of Defense for Policy Feith, and others—who had acted reputedly with peculiar exuberance or ineptitude. Indeed, popular accounts drew snippets from psychology to explain the invasion decision. In these accounts, holdovers from the first Bush administration (most notably, Cheney and Wolfowitz) sought to finish what they had started in the 1991 war with Iraq. A young president sought to outdo (or honor) his father by completing the job that the elder Bush had begun. Or a vengeful president sought to punish Saddam Hussein for the assassination attempt against his father (in 1993, in Kuwait).

Most of the explanations for US intervention contain some grain of truth, but none is complete. Blaming neoconservatives only gets us so far; Rice, Rumsfeld, and Powell actually showed little fealty to neoconservative ideas. Blaming the intelligence community ignores the administration's uncritical acceptance of the community's views, early commitment to a military course, and decision to act sooner rather than later (or even to rely on deterrence as an instrument of policy). Blaming lobbying groups confuses cause with correlation, insofar as the evidence points only to a convergence in viewpoints and raises the question, who was lobbying whom? Blaming particular individuals ignores the wide consensus that appears to have formed early in the administration on the need to move against Iraq.

Thus, the Bush administration's ideological proclivities, connection to special interest groups, and obsessions and peculiarities are ultimately unsatisfying explanations for the events that unfolded in the prelude to the attack on Iraq. They appear to fare no better than the Iraqi WMD argument in accounting for the Bush administration's march to war.

Focusing Prematurely on Regime Change

It is tempting to conclude that no single explanation accounts for the US invasion of Iraq; that is, that no one condition, had it been absent, would have kept the United States from war.[13] That conclusion does not hold up, however, for two reasons.

First, even if no condition is *sufficient* to explain the administration's decision for war, the presence of a single condition—a belief that the United States could defeat Iraq quickly and efficiently—was arguably *necessary* to explain that outcome. Despite their various differences in opinion, high-level officials do not appear to have feared the military consequences of taking on Iraq. Ken Adelman likely spoke for many when he infamously predicted in an op-ed piece that "demolishing Hussein's military power and liberating Iraq would be a cakewalk."[14] The compelling evidence included the quick and resounding Coalition victory over Iraq in the 1991 Desert Storm operation; the continued weakening of the Iraqi military and rising Iraqi discontent (Wright et al. 2008: 10); and the relative ease with which US forces, in 2001–2002, defeated the Taliban regime in Afghanistan. That view converged nicely with Rumsfeld's strongly held belief that with light, mobile forces, superior technology, and appropriate strategies, the United States could prevail in war against numerically superior forces.

Had US officials believed that a war with Iraq would prove unsuccessful or costly, they would have acted with caution. With just that concern, the George H. W. Bush administration had spent six months preparing to confront Iraq in Operation Desert Storm, assembling forces in the Gulf and constructing a global military and political coalition.[15]

Second, senior administration officials concurred that "the problem" and "the solution" resided in Baghdad, which (given the US capability to overthrow the

Iraqi regime by force) was *sufficient* cause to act. In this, they did not break entirely new ground. In 1998 Iraqi regime change had become formal US government policy when President Bill Clinton (albeit under political duress) signed the Iraq Liberation Act—a fact that the Bush administration was not hesitant to note. What was new was that regime change had become an urgent priority. Opinion differed on the specific benefits that would accrue from occupying Iraq, but a consensus formed early in the Bush administration that it should act militarily to bring down the Iraqi government. Administration officials directed the military to fine-tune its plans for attacking Iraq; supported working groups to prepare for a change in Iraqi governance; and hungrily eyed 9/11 evidence, hoping to implicate Iraq to strengthen the case for war. The prioritization of regime change was apparent in the administration's willingness to contemplate a war with Iraq despite the ongoing demands of the Afghanistan War and the US war on terrorism.

With an implicit consensus, the decision to invade Iraq amounted to a non-decision, that is, a decision by default. The shared diagnostics and comfortable fit between problem and solution freed US leaders from having to probe potential war ends, assess trade-offs, refine objectives, and reconcile policy differences. No one "in the know" at the time has gone on record as saying they participated in a meeting, or even knew of a meeting, in which the key decision to invade Iraq was made. Tenet (2007: 308) states that neither he nor his associates can recall a meeting in which there was "a discussion of the central questions. Was it wise to go to war? Was it the right thing to do?" Richard Armitage, who served at the time as deputy secretary of state, echoes that conclusion: "Never to my knowledge, and I'm pretty sure I'm right on this, did the President ever sit around with his advisors and say, 'Should we do this or not?' He never did it (Armitage 2009: 104)."

That rather staggering conclusion deserves explication. Neither the NSC nor the president's inner circle of principal foreign and national security advisers— Rice, Rumsfeld, Powell, and Cheney—met as a group with, or without, the president to decide whether to invade Iraq and for what goals and duration. They simply *understood*—through various directives, assorted conversations, and actual planning—that a war with Iraq was forthcoming. Even Powell, who would later voice his regret for his UN speech, was more a voice of caution than of opposition to the war.[16] Powell made his concerns known to the president (Woodward 2004: 150–151), but he finally reconciled himself to the seemingly inevitable and stayed with the team. The decision for war that was "in the air" after the Bush inauguration was essentially a done deal—perhaps for a year or more—before its execution. Thus, when Richard Haass (2009: 213) asked Condoleezza Rice, in July 2002, if they should assess the pros and cons of taking on Iraq, she responded dismissively; the president "had made up his mind."

The point here is simple. Administration officials knew where the train was heading and jumped on board or stoked the engines. Along the way, some officials eyed the tracks, wary of political hazards that might derail the express before it reached its destination. Although US policy makers took different intellectual routes to Baghdad, their aspirations converged, freeing them from debate and hard choices. Why quibble about policy goals, costs, and policy trade-offs when regime change promised something for everyone?

Unspoken agreement can mask a fragile consensus, however, that exists only because the participants fail to recognize their important disagreements. Diagnosing the Iraqi regime as the "problem" still left a full range of available alternatives, from simply decapitating the government and withdrawing quickly from Iraq, to preparing for the long-term US occupation of Iraq because its governance was rotten *beyond* the leadership core. Indeed, the worth of any alternative depended on the assumed nature of the problem, and on that there was no agreement. Whereas US policy makers acted as if the single policy on which they all agreed—a quick takedown of the Iraqi government—would serve various beneficial purposes, the opposite was the case.

For example, the assumption that Iraq threatened US interests because it possessed WMD should have provoked a critical question: How might Iraq employ them in time of war or its aftermath? Possible answers provided reasons for exercising restraint, or at least caution. Oddly, US policy makers were not overly concerned that Saddam Hussein would use his WMD against advancing US troops, nor did they make securing alleged WMD sites a military priority to prevent illicit transfers to terrorist groups (Gordon and Trainor 2006: 80–82). They assumed implicitly that Hussein would exercise restraint—and that these weapons were secure—at the very moment when he would most need to use or transfer them.[17] Had he not exercised restraint (and actually possessed WMD), the US effort to impose regime change would have produced the horrendous consequences that administration officials were seeking, through regime change, to avoid.

Likewise, the assumption that regime change would provide a necessary boost to democratization in the Middle East required scrutiny. What would happen, for example, if regime change failed to foster democratization and instead provoked indigenous conflict, unleashing forces that would threaten Iraqi stability? Might not such developments unwittingly demonstrate the advantages—and necessity—of authoritarian rule to excuse repression throughout the Middle East? One lesson from the Arab Spring uprisings of 2011–2012 is certainly that steps toward democracy within the Middle East can provoke reactions that further and reinforce authoritarian rule.

Thus, early decision-making on Iraq spoke to the dangers of illusory agreement. A policy that seemingly offers "all things to all people" is often ill suited to serve any one goal. Perversely, it remains a viable option because proponents who share the same bottom line have no reason to probe their potentially divergent assumptions. Indeed, any such probing—when it is at best superficial—might serve only to reinforce existing judgments. Policy proponents might take comfort in knowing that despite their disagreements, they have reached the same conclusion, or that a policy that failed to deliver as they had hoped could still yield various benefits. Thus, even an airing of disagreements, absent a deliberative effort to understand and reconcile thinking about ends-means relationships, might fall short of producing a viable set of operative mission goals.

In sum, administration officials effectively cast underlying goals aside when preparing for regime change. That officials chose to ignore their differences in opinion—treating them as complementary, not competing, views—imperiled the US mission.

Failing to Consider the Consequences of Regime Change

The US preparation for the aftermath of war suffered in multiple respects: US officials paid too little attention to postwar security requirements in military planning, incorrectly assumed that Iraqis would welcome a US occupation, and downplayed or ignored the challenges of a postwar transition to full Iraqi governance. These early deficiencies would haunt the US occupation of Iraq.

Military Planning: Postwar Security

Administration officials prepared for war to accomplish a military objective: bringing down Saddam Hussein's regime. In focusing on the plan of attack, not on its aftermath, they were "blind to the war's political objectives" (Shimko 2010: 162). In essence, US policy makers wrongly assumed that the security challenges in Iraq would end with the fall of Baghdad.

Donald Rumsfeld came to the Pentagon seeking dramatic reforms in US warfighting strategy. Like other enthusiasts, he insisted that the United States must capitalize on the so-called revolution in military affairs. Technological advances in sensors, communication links, imaging software, information processing, precision-guided weapons, and light, agile weapon platforms endowed US forces with superior firepower, mobility, and situational awareness, which could produce quick, easy victories when paired with appropriate strategies. Indeed, *quick* action—in preparing and executing an attack—was key to the military's combat success. It would allow US forces to take the adversary by surprise through the coordinated action of US air-, land-, and sea-based assets; capitalize on the adversary's confused, flat-footed response; and move finally against the opponent's center of gravity. For Rumsfeld and others, the rapid US victory over Afghan forces (in 2001–2002) convincingly showed that a new age of warfare was upon us: US aircraft, armed with precision-guided weapons, deployed quickly against the Taliban and its al-Qaeda affiliates and, through pinpoint delivery, left them vulnerable on defense and incapable of massing for offense. With the decisive US contribution, the Taliban proved no match on the ground for the primitively armed and poorly equipped Afghan opposition.

Rumsfeld chafed at US military reliance on preliminary plans for an Iraqi invasion that drew from the 1991 Gulf War playbook. He dismissed suggestions that a Desert Storm–sized force, requiring half a year to prepare and pre-position, was necessary to defeat Iraq. He thus rejected a US military plan that called for a force of nearly half a million US troops and then a succession of progressively more modest plans that would still demand an invasion force hundreds of thousands strong. The military, in his view, remained trapped in the past, unaware that its new capabilities freed it from traditional fears of being undermanned or overextended. A revolution in its thinking was necessary: a small US military force, reliant on speed, firepower, awareness, and agility, could rush to the Iraqi capital and take down the Hussein regime. Once the adversary's jugular was severed, the remnants of the Iraqi military would soon collapse—spasmodically, perhaps, but inevitably.

Rumsfeld and other Pentagon officials took this stand because they believed that the requisites of warfare had changed, but also because they assumed that the United States would encounter a generally benign postwar environment. Law and order would prevail, and US forces would go unchallenged. Their thinking reflected their view that Iraqis would greet US troops as "liberators" and Iraqi governing institutions would continue to function, relieving the United States of much of the burden of governing, enforcing laws, and assuring economic well-being in Iraq. Believing that "liberators are welcomed and unchallenged," US officials "assumed away any major security problems or popular resistance in postwar Iraq" (Bensahel 2006: 457). Believing in turn that Iraqi institutions would continue to operate, US officials presumed that Iraqi security forces would keep the peace. They assumed moreover that a light and inoffensive US presence gave Iraqis little reason for discontent; after all, the United States had freed the country of the "negatives" of rule by the Hussein regime and left the "positives" of a functioning bureaucratic structure.[18]

Their thinking about the necessary size of the US force drew also from an odd contortion of logic, which resulted in US officials scaling the US force to the size of the existing Iraqi *military* threat, such as when Rumsfeld and Wolfowitz strenuously rejected Chief of Staff Eric Shinseki's testimony, before Congress, that a US invasion of Iraq would require around 400,000 troops. Wolfowitz testified, in response, "It is hard to conceive that it would take more forces to provide stability in post-Saddam Iraq than it would take to conduct the war itself and to secure the surrender of Saddam's security forces and his army."[19] To him, it defied reason that providing public security would require more manpower than attacking and defeating a hostile military force. Yet the logical connection between the two missions begged for scrutiny. Even if the United States could capitalize on a small, mobile force to defeat a military and bring down a regime, public security is labor intensive and meant to deter and assure as much as to compel. It requires an active personnel presence in populated areas to combat criminal action, allay public fears, prevent breaches of the peace, and instill law-abiding behavior. The appropriate standard for scaling the force was not the military threat but the occupied country's population density, as extrapolated from prior occupations and adjusted for geography, demographics, and ongoing or potential levels of conflict (Gordon and Trainor 2006: 103–104).[20] Simply put, the Iraqi public was *not* the Iraqi military; it was not a *coherent* entity, vulnerable to defeat through targeting its leadership and command and control capabilities. Ironically, as the opposition formed against the US occupation, Rumsfeld and Wolfowitz were loath to accept its "coherence"—as an *organized* resistance—for that would require admitting it was an "insurgency." Of course their thinking "evolved." By the summer of 2003 Wolfowitz had conceded that prevailing assumptions "turned out to underestimate the problem." He nonetheless remained optimistic about "progress" in Iraq and attributed the ongoing violence there to political and military remnants of the Saddam Hussein era—"dead-enders," as Rumsfeld called them (Graham 2009: 425)—diehard supporters of a bygone regime.[21] The basic message had not changed: US war strategy was correct; the war was ending, not beginning.

In the short term at least, Rumsfeld was right. The two US divisions that moved from Kuwait in the south to Baghdad circumvented much of Iraq's military strength; capitalized on devastating air power and combined-force tactics to destroy Iraqi forces that stood in the way; took down hard-fighting Republican Guard units in the gateway to the capital; and once inside, encountered little resistance. Iraq's governing elite fled, leaving the US military in charge. In sum, the war for the United States went as well as anyone had expected. Yet this is not the whole story. It is one thing to say that the US military strategy worked in defeating Iraqi military forces and quite another to insist the strategy was well conceived.

On the contrary, the strategy failed in critical respects. It had not prepared US forces to take the initiative, should Iraqi security forces or their remnants retreat to urban warfare, or to secure Iraqi military sites to prevent the theft of Iraqi weaponry, move aggressively to seize the potential WMD sites that had troubled US leaders, or provide public security against lawlessness and social unrest. As would eventually become painfully clear, governance and reconstruction were impossible without security; personnel, buildings, and material stocks all required protection. Indeed, a failure to provide security from the start only compromised Iraq's future; the looting of the Iraqi public infrastructure—down to the copper pipes in buildings—increased the challenges of governance and reconstruction and the demands for security.

The problem, quite simply, was that administration officials could not think beyond Iraq's malign leadership to imagine that the problems of Iraq ran deep, if only because of that leadership, and that the administration's plans might ultimately fail due to the pervasive ills of Iraqi governance and society. Such an awareness led senior State Department officials initially to argue that "invading Iraq and replacing its totalitarian regime would require a U.S. commitment of enormous scope, carried out over a period of years" (SIGIR 2010: 3). It also led a high-level intelligence assessment to conclude that building "an Iraqi democracy would be a long, difficult and probably turbulent process, with potential backsliding into Iraq's tradition of authoritarianism."[22]

Postinvasion Security: Liberation versus Occupation

Assuming that a quick and easy US military victory in Iraq was assured, the questions "who will govern and for how long?" fueled an intragovernmental debate. US policy makers disagreed implicitly over the political, financial, and institutional resources that were required and available to remake that country. In the end, they went to war lacking a clear sense of what regime change would bring or the role that the United States would play in determining Iraq's political future.

US officials recognized that an Iraqi government they could control would lack the *legitimacy* to govern with necessary Iraqi support. Any effort to hand over the leadership of the country to a single person, one group, or groups would paint the resulting leadership as a US puppet and damn it to irrelevance or impotence. Conversely, allowing Iraqis to plot their own political course from the outset might not produce a peaceful, democratic Iraq. An early dispute pitted top civilian officials in the Department of Defense (specifically Wolfowitz and Feith), who favored a quick handover of power to anointed members of the Iraqi exile community, against the State Department. State Department officials pushed for a transitional civil authority—perhaps under UN auspices—that would provide tutelage, guidance, and resources to prepare Iraq for self-governance (Dyson 2013: 462). In this they gave voice to well-grounded concerns among policy experts and academic researchers that a premature transition from authoritarian to democratic rule could empower venal or sectarian individuals or groups and produce ongoing instability (see Mansfield and Snyder 2005).

The protagonists did not debate transition philosophy in a political vacuum. Participants were divided sharply in their assessments of—more like visceral responses to—Ahmad Chalabi, a leading candidate for the future leadership of Iraq within its exile community. He had strong backing from Bush administration officials within the Pentagon,[23] but he provoked deep mistrust within the State Department and CIA for his slick charm,[24] reputed financial shenanigans, and political wheeling and dealing—with good reason on all counts, as the administration discovered when he was finally ensconced in Iraq.[25] US officials agreed, however, that the United States should not try to duplicate the (successful) US experience in the postwar occupation of Japan, when the Allied powers had supervised the writing of Japan's constitution and steered that country's political development under General Douglas MacArthur's absolute authority.

Absent backing from Bush and Rumsfeld for installing a new Iraqi leader, the middle option of supporting an Iraqi Interim Authority won out (Dyson 2013: 469–472; Feith 2008: 401–411). The United States would select its membership for broad representation by dividing leadership between the exile and internal Iraqi political communities, initially giving members limited authority over the affairs of state expecting to increase their authority over critical ministries—including defense— while moving ultimately to an elected government that would oversee the writing of Iraq's new constitution. The thinking about that option never amounted to a fixed plan. Indeed, everything changed after the US occupation began, when Paul Bremer took control of the newly formed Coalition Provisional Authority (CPA), intended to govern Iraq, replacing the Office of Reconstruction and Humanitarian Assistance (ORHA), the Pentagon-based, civilian unit that oversaw the transition to Iraqi governance. Whereas ORHA had formally defined its goal ("the universally agreed end-state") for the country as "a stable Iraq, with its territorial integrity intact, and a broad-based government that renounces WMD development and use and no longer supports terrorism or threatens its neighbors," the CPA officially targeted a more far-reaching and ambitious end state. As the "ultimate goal" it sought "a durable peace for a unified and stable, democratic Iraq that: provides effective and representative government for and by the Iraqi people; is underpinned by new and protected freedoms and a growing market economy; and no longer poses a threat to its neighbors or international security and is able to defend itself."[26] With the implicit support of the president and secretary of defense, Bremer decided to limit the authority of the interim government and prepare for an extended stay in Iraq to promote a far-reaching, transformative agenda.[27]

Preparing for the Civil Aftermath of the Invasion

Of all the charges leveled at the Bush administration for its mishandling of the Iraq War, its alleged failure to prepare for the political, economic, and social aftermath of the war deserves the most scrutiny. This accusation deserves attention if only because it stems from a half-truth. Contrary to the popular view, various offices and individuals within government *did* invest considerable effort in trying to anticipate postinvasion problems and craft viable solutions. The issue is not whether qualified people thought about the challenges of a US occupation; they did. The issue, instead, is whether these challenges received the attention they deserved. They *did not*. Given the mission focus of planning—an emphasis on regime *change*—US policy makers prepared inadequately for the civil aftermath of the invasion. What would come next was essentially a nonissue to US policy makers, in various respects.

First, preparation for a US occupation started belatedly. The US military had developed contingency plans for an Iraqi invasion and of course had active experience from Desert Storm and years of action against Iraq on which to draw. In contrast, reconstituting local governance was largely uncharted territory for US institutions. Accordingly, planning was inhibited by a lack of ready-made US government agencies to lead the operation, political reticence to push the effort when the United States had not irrevocably committed to an invasion (Rudd 2011: 53), and a lack of clarity about exactly what the United States would do in Iraq and how long it would stay there. When the Pentagon inherited the lead in planning for a postinvasion Iraq, Department of Defense officials and military commanders largely sidelined relevant preparations and interagency planning and effectively reduced postwar issues to a matter of providing humanitarian assistance (Rudd 2011: 57, 60). They served their preference for avoiding post-occupation commitments by giving "Phase IV"—to follow Phase III, the invasion of Iraq—a somewhat nebulous standing. Phase IV was "originally defined as Transition, then as Post Hostilities, and by spring [2003] as Post-Conflict" (Rudd 2011: 152). Its practical implications remained intentionally unspecified. Jay Garner assumed the leadership of ORHA—the lead US organization for postinvasion humanitarian assistance and civil administration in Iraq— only months before the US invasion, "with no staff, no workspace, no funding, no knowledge of what planning had been done, and little insight of the situation in Iraq" (Rudd 2011: 94).

Second, preparation for a US occupation progressed without clear and consistent direction. Although interagency working groups were formed in 2002 to address the challenges of regime change in Iraq, their efforts were not closely monitored or coordinated, and their primary contribution appears to have been in preparing for a humanitarian crisis that never materialized (Rudd 2011: 92–93). Preparation for a US occupation progressed—without coordination—on multiple fronts, resulting in waste, duplication, and lack of effort across government. The planning process suffered from a plethora of deficiencies, including (a) the sheer number of participating agencies with divergent traditions and orientations; (b) the general absence of a common analytical framework, which meant that organizational products differed in emphasis, historical reference points, issue coverage, and policy orientation; (c) a disconnect across government that left Iraq working groups unfamiliar with the work of other groups that had formed or disbanded; (d) a lack of cooperation among government agencies (Rudd 2011: 98, 128); (e) the Defense Department's resistance to input and support from other departments and agencies, preoccupation with invasion planning, tendency to think of "post-hostilities" as someone else's problem, and preference to leave Iraq quickly (SIGIR 2010: 16; Wright et al. 2008: 71, 76–77); (f) the impracticality of civilian-based postwar planning when the US military was to run the postwar effort; (g) personality clashes, political suspicions, and ideological concerns (Bensahel et al. 2008: 30–31);[28] (h) the changing and irregular representation of agencies at planning meetings and the failure of agencies within the same department to coordinate their positions (Bensahel et al. 2008: 23, 30); (i) attempts by Defense Secretary Rumsfeld to stifle the interagency process so that the principals (not deputies) of the NSC would make critical decisions (Dyson 2013: 485); (j) the marginalization (and eventual dissolution) of the US military's Phase IV task force due to its competitive, distrustful, and distant relationship with ORHA and those charged with preparing and executing Phases I–III (Bensahel et al. 2008: 47–52); and (k) ORHA's dependence on the US military command. ORHA was left out of the decisional loop and was late on arrival in Baghdad, where it discovered that circumstances required a new set of plans (Bensahel et al. 2008: 67). Consequently, the planning process did not yield a useful synthesis that could command the attention of US officials or integrate governmental resources in pursuit of a shared set of goals.

Third, preparation for a US occupation was impaired by lack of support from a strong, dedicated, and coherent US bureaucratic infrastructure to support national reconstruction. Programs for development, reconstruction, and humanitarian assistance were (and still are) spread throughout the US government bureaucracy, reducing their available resources, hampering their performance in the field, and ultimately weakening their claims to future resources. Whereas the military had a unified structure, a large and active constituency, and a generous budget, foreign assistance was managed by a variety of civilian offices and funded reluctantly by US legislators. They viewed these programs as wasteful and unnecessary, even an outright giveaway of scarce US resources. "Nation-building" itself was dismissed as a noxious enterprise when George W. Bush argued, during the 2000 presidential election, that such operations deplete scarce US resources (which presumably are better used in pursuit of clear and limited goals in direct support of US national interests).[29] US governmental institutions that could serve a civilian reconstruction effort were also hampered by their own strong mission orientations, which impeded interagency cooperation. The State Department, for one, lacked a strong operational commitment—that is, a tradition of recruiting and training policy, planning, and management specialists. That orientation placed it at odds in Iraq war planning with USAID, an institution under nominal State Department control that actively promoted national development programs.[30]

Fourth, US preparation for the occupation occurred without due reference to US operations of the Cold War or post–Cold War periods. The lessons of Lebanon in the Reagan administration, Somalia in the Clinton administration, and a multitude of other operations—big and small, more and less successful—were effectively left on the shelf; "few members of the Bush administration had shared those experiences, and they did not want to undertake nation building on their watch" (Rudd 2011: 383). Indeed, US preparation failed to employ the lessons acquired from CENTCOM's own war game exercises, which had yielded prescient warnings of potential instability and conflict ensuing from a US invasion of Iraq.[31]

Fifth, US preparations for the occupation of Iraq did not cohere—anywhere in government—in operational plans. The Future of Iraq Project covered a full spectrum of issues and emerged as exhibit A when critics charged that the Bush administration had ignored the State Department's plans for the "next stage" of operations. Still, the project's intent was to generate ideas and to involve a wide range of people—including Iraqis who would help run Iraq—in planning (Bensahel et al. 2008: 32–33). Under State Department sponsorship, the project encompassed over a dozen working groups—with hundreds of participants, including members of the Iraqi exile community, academic experts, regional specialists, and government personnel—and eventually produced an impressive product, over a thousand pages covering the diverse challenges of transforming Iraq. It did not, however, strive for a final synthesis or policy recommendations that could guide postinvasion planning. "The working groups were given vague instructions, and only a moderate effort, at inception or at the conclusion of the project, was made to tie together the working groups, to prioritize their ideas, to attach a budget to the plans, and to render the concepts into a useable form" (Dyson 2013: 459). Even so, it received scant attention within the broader network of officials and specialists working on postinvasion planning. Garner himself only learned of the project many weeks after he had assumed his new position (Rudd 2011: 123). "No one at the top level of the State Department oversaw or championed the project, which remained the province of a few mid level officials in State's Near East Bureau, and was administered from a closet sized office near the Foggy Bottom cafeteria" (Dyson 2013: 459).

Sixth, US military officials saw the invasion almost strictly as a military problem, though postwar planning remained nominally the Defense Department's responsibility. Military officials were content to sidestep or sideline the "nonmilitary" responsibilities to avoid distraction, protect military resources, and reduce operational risk. Indeed, US military commanders recognized that placing US forces in position for Phase III missions would compromise their availability for Phase IV and chose to accept the costs and risks at the far end rather than jeopardize the "military" phase of the operation (Bensahel et al. 2008: 12–13). To be sure, ORHA officials addressed issues of postinvasion Iraqi leadership, civil administration, and humanitarian assistance. Still, they found it difficult to plan without a funding commitment from the administration or competent personnel on hand to staff the effort. Other departments and agencies jealously clung to their personnel and resources.

Top US officials, positioned to recognize and account for these tendencies, instead chose to prioritize the military effort, expecting to manage problems successfully as they arose. They conveniently relied on best-case scenarios. They presumed that Iraqi oil monies would cover the costs, that the Iraqi infrastructure (especially electricity) would function properly (it was not to be targeted), and that Iraqi institutions would continue to function to carry the load for such things as internal security. In their view, anticipating the worst case would surely produce a self-fulfilling prophesy; a large force of civilian personnel would only waste resources and slow the US exit from Iraq and was politically unwise. It could raise red flags and give war opponents and skeptics leverage to slow the movement toward war.

Admittedly, Rumsfeld took the initiative to compile a long, ever-growing list of what might go wrong in invading Iraq.[32] The "Parade of Horribles," as it was known, might actually have immunized the administration's commitment to military force from serious scrutiny. Rather than instilling caution, a numbered list of dozens of potential problems minimizes the severity of any one ("just one in the parade") and instills false confidence (e.g., manifested in the mockery implicit in the list's nickname) that those involved have thought through the problems. Indeed, Rumsfeld was careful to note that he could compile a similar list for the opposite choice of leaving Saddam Hussein in power (Feith 2008: 332fn). Regardless, a "list" will have limited impact unless it becomes what in this case it was not: a springboard for rigorous assessment. The list circulated only among high-level Pentagon officials and the NSC principals; neglected the dangers posed by instability and conflict in post-occupation Iraq; and failed to prioritize the Horribles, assess their likelihood and severity, or provide much specific detail. Just as important, it arrived shorn of remedies, except for one that played—not coincidentally—to the predetermined solution. Rumsfeld offered that a quick military victory, as planned, would help mitigate the problems. In Feith's (2008: 335) words, "The list of dangers sharpened our appreciation of the value of tactical surprise and of maximizing the speed of major combat operations. A number of the potential calamities—humanitarian crises, Saddam's destruction of Iraq's oil fields, regional instability, and terrorism by Iraqi agents against the United States, for example—were likelier to happen, and to be more severe, if the fighting to overthrow Saddam were prolonged."

In the end, the military mission reigned supreme in Iraq war planning. As Gordon W. Rudd (2011: 29), a historian assigned to ORHA, put it, "The military planning covered removal and replacement, although it was heavily weighted on removal. Military planners assumed that other agencies would work closely with them and focus on regime replacement, an assumption that would not be well validated." Phase III retained its privileged status even with the triumph over Baghdad. As the capital fell, Secretary Rumsfeld and General Franks chose to halt the deployment of US troops to the combat zone, without regard for even the troop numbers that military planners had assumed would be available to manage the next phase of the war effort (Bensahel et al. 2008: 15).

Stage II, Extension: Disjunction

Defense Secretary Rumsfeld appeared to prove doubters wrong with the rapid US victory over Iraqi forces. Some Iraqi units avoided battle, others fought hard, but the US military arrived in Baghdad in quick order, where it encountered little resistance. Within a few short weeks of the US invasion, Bush had announced the end of major combat operations (to his later regret) on board the USS *Abraham Lincoln* in front of a banner that read "Mission Accomplished." US military officials, for their part, sought a quick handover of responsibilities to civilian authorities and planned to withdraw US forces from Iraq.

Of course a US force withdrawal was not forthcoming. The ingredients of success in the first stage of the war—a relatively small, armored force, aimed directly at Baghdad (and the heart of the Iraqi regime)—proved a recipe for disaster, with violence to come. Conditions only worsened when US officials expanded their goals for Iraq. The US mission in Iraq hinged on the administration's success in pursuing a set of overambitious goals, formulated apart from realities on the ground; available US capabilities and resources; and the potential demands on US military forces. All aspects of the US mission would thus suffer—grievously, in fact—once US forces had to maintain order in a country spiraling out of control.

Expanding the Mission: Liberation Becomes Occupation

US officials "planned" to leave Iraq a far better place—that is, more liberal and democratic—when US forces eventually departed. They assumed, moreover, that the "hard work" would cease with the occupation of Iraq and that its government would largely cover the costs of transforming the country. That was not quite correct. US officials, under Paul Bremer's direction, immediately unveiled an ambitious agenda for transforming Iraqi governance. Critics thought his plans and edicts unwise—in fact, draconian.

What led to the policy shift? Most immediately, the answer rests in the deference that national security principals showed Bremer, the man in charge in Iraq. More generally, the problem lay in the failure of US officials at all levels to come to grips with the nature and severity of the challenges of the Iraqi occupation. US mission goals never cohered; actually worked at cross-purposes with one another; and lacked necessary support in any case in planning, organizational capacities, and resourcing. The result was that the US mission encountered problems that became substantially worse.

Thus, Bremer deserves blame for the yawning failures in the early occupation period. Still, his story is usefully understood by shifting the focus to those higher in the chain of command. It then becomes a story of deference and detachment of US leaders, who either cared too little or presumed too much about the likely and pressing challenges of a "liberated" Iraq.

Disjuncture Through Deference

Who was responsible for the abrupt policy shift? One answer is that US leaders contracted out important decisions. By default, a small group of individuals in country—in isolation from much of the US policy establishment—redefined and extended the US mission in Iraq. As Feith (2008: 437) concludes, "Bremer's views were crucial. As the man in the field, he was given great latitude to gauge the situation and craft his response." Rumsfeld (2011: 506) later lamented that he had not recognized that Bremer had "a robust definition of the term 'latitude.' "

Appointed by the president on a recommendation, Bremer took control of the US civilian operation in Iraq in April 2003 as an unknown to most high-level Bush administration officials. A former foreign service officer, he had not participated in prewar deliberations and had limited experience for the mission that he would head. He did not consider this a disadvantage; he was generally unconcerned with preexisting understandings about the transition to Iraqi sovereignty. He assumed the position of presidential envoy—exclusively, as he demanded—and insisted that as head of the CPA he report directly to the secretary of defense, not to the military command in Iraq. Indeed, Bremer—to Rumsfeld's chagrin—chose to go around him and directly to the president. Bremer declared subsequently that he answered neither to Powell nor to Rumsfeld (Bremer 2006: 12): "I was the President's man."

Now empowered, Bremer would be "ruling by decree" (Dyson 2013: 480). In his capacity as CPA head, he reversed US plans to transfer authority to Iraqis sooner rather than later. He shelved plans for the Iraqi Interim Authority, replacing it with an advisory body, the Iraqi Governing Council, and initiated a far-reaching transformation of Iraqi institutions. Under Bremer's guidance, the United States moved rapidly from "liberating" to "occupying" Iraq, a transformation that was quickly felt throughout that country.

The story is fuzzy on exactly how Bremer acquired the authority to reverse course. The evidence indicates that he operated with the "understanding" that he would oversee a now lengthier transition to Iraqi rule. Bremer quotes the president as saying, "We'll stay until the job is done."[33] Still, he describes neither the "job" nor the standards by which he would know it was "done." Elsewhere, he provides a lengthier explanation. "Sometime after March 10—I've been told by various participants it was early April—Bush decided the idea of a short occupation and a quick handover wasn't going to work.... But the problem was, I don't think it was ever documented. No one ever put a piece of paper in front of him and said, 'Here's the new guidance,' and so there was a lot of confusion" (quoted in Graham 2009: 404). That quotation strongly suggests that the president's views on the subject were not only undocumented, they were not firmly set. It suggests further that the president did not convey these views directly to Bremer. Another quotation usefully highlights the murky origins of Bremer's understanding about his new role. "But the President's instructions to me ... when I had lunch with him alone on May 6th, were that we're going to take our time to get it right.... The President had effectively, though perhaps not formally, changed his position on the question of a short or long occupation, having before the war been in favor of a short occupation. By the time I came in, that was gone" (SIGIR 2009: 69). That quotation is revealingly ambiguous. Stating that the president had "effectively," not "formally" changed his position is quite different from saying the president "directed me." "That was gone" is quite different from "he had decided." Perhaps most telling, however, is that Rumsfeld cites that very quotation—an excerpt from an interview, conducted five years after the fact—as his authoritative source of how things went down at a critical juncture. Rumsfeld's (2011: 510) response is no less telling. "That would have been news to me, and I suspect it would also have come as news to the President." The clear implication is that Rumsfeld and Bush had not discussed Bremer's formal charge.

Armed with his understanding, Bremer postponed the creation of an Iraqi interim government and national elections and placed Iraq under US control for the foreseeable future. Just as ominously, he announced two edicts, CPA orders no. 1 and 2, removing former Baath Party officials from government and disbanding the Iraqi military, respectively.

What went into the making of these two orders? Although the extent and specifics of both orders took many US officials, including the president, by surprise (Gordon and Trainor 2012: 13, 15; Dobbins et al. 2009: xxvi; Woodward 2008: 49), the principle behind order no. 1, de-Baathification, was discussed and accepted across the government (Dobbins et al. 2009: xxvi, 112–119). Following the model of the de-Nazification of Germany after World War II, US officials recognized the need to remove the elements of the prewar governing party from power. By contrast, CPA order no. 2, disbanding the Iraqi military, came with exceedingly narrow decisional input; the president, National Security Advisor Rice, and Defense Secretary Rumsfeld deferred to Bremer's judgment on the wisdom of the plan.

Rice, Powell, and Garner were among many top US policy makers who nonetheless were taken aback by the order (SIGIR 2010: 75–76; Gordon and Trainor 2012: 15; Rudd 2011: 332, 366).[34] For their part, the chair and vice chair of the JCS and the military service chiefs were "'blindsided' by the edict" (Graham 2009: 402). Like US military commanders and Defense Secretary Rumsfeld (2011: 516), they had assumed that the Iraqi army would take charge of Iraqi security after Saddam Hussein's defeat (Wright et al. 2008: 79). Indeed, Rumsfeld had accepted Garner's recommendation to reform, not reconstitute, the Iraqi army (Feith 2008: 368). Garner tried unsuccessfully to block the new policies, troubled deeply by the underlying failure to think beyond immediate consequences to appreciate the full—negative—societal and political impacts of these policy changes.

Although history has not entirely settled the debate over which officials were in, or out, of the loop, the more critical issue is *why* they were out of the loop. The most prominent answer is that US officials deferred to the "man on the scene" because he presumably knew best and had the president's trust. Yet that answer is unsatisfying, for it lets the principals off the hook. It ignores the haphazardly structured chain of command—a product of poor prewar and postwar planning—that allowed the principals to defer to Bremer. If Bremer answered to no one but the president—and the president was deferential—who in authority could say to Bremer, "No, that just won't work?" More fundamentally, the answer is insufficient because it fails to account for the laxity of the participants, shown in their willingness to defer. Asking "what did they know, and when did they know it?" is useful to get at the facts. So is asking "why exactly did they not know it?"

A claim by Rumsfeld is useful to make that point. Rumsfeld maintains that he first learned of Bremer's plans for Iraqi governance in September 2003, with the rest of Washington, from Bremer's opinion piece in the *Washington Post*.[35] Bremer, however, claims that he forwarded memos and reports on these plans to Rumsfeld and took "silence" as a form of "guidance" (Graham 2009: 405–406). Assuming that Bremer's version is correct, why would a defense secretary who found no detail too small for his attention and no one's job beyond the bounds of his scrutiny[36] have allowed Bremer to progress without significant pushback? Even if Rumsfeld was inclined to let Bremer "do his job," Rumsfeld did not want that job, and he was happy to defer on these matters. His important work was on the military side; he "was eager to lose the mantle of the one in charge of what he regarded as essentially nonmilitary activities" (Graham 2009: 437).

Fully six months into the flailing war effort, when much had already transpired under Bremer's management, the White House formally exerted its authority. Recognizing a need for more direct White House control, Bush transferred authority for Iraqi reconstruction and stabilization to Rice (and the newly created Iraq Stabilization Group within the NSC). That Bremer took charge for as long as he did reflects a simple truth. The exercising of US military force against Iraq was long choreographed and rehearsed; conversely, the exercising of US political power in that country—in nature, extent, and duration—was always left for a "future someone" to manage, leaving it susceptible to individual preferences and happenstance, even whim. With high-level officials deferring on critical transitional issues, Bremer was able to decide the fate of Iraq by default.[37]

Disjuncture Through Detachment

By neglect or default, US civilian officials made broad policy decisions—expanding US goals in Iraq—without fully grasping the practical implications or the trade-offs involved. Their failings, which greatly confounded the accomplishing of US objectives, were apparent in multiple respects.

First, US leaders lacked a clear sense of how deeply they must cut to remove the vestiges of Saddam Hussein's regime from Iraqi governance; removing Baathists was a matter of prewar consensus, but how many and how deep in the party hierarchy were not (Rapport 2015: 110–113). Indeed, US leaders appear to have relied, explicitly or effectively, on irreconcilable assumptions. The belief that Iraqi governing institutions would continue to function once Saddam Hussein and his cronies had been removed from power suggests that the problems of Iraqi governance were confined to Iraq's top leadership. With that assumption, US policy makers sought to place these institutions under new management, get officials back to work, and return Iraq to some normalcy. By contrast, the belief that extensive de-Baathification was necessary in a postwar Iraq implied that the political evils of the Hussein regime ran deep. Excising them was essential to place Iraq on its new track. True, a somewhat surgical approach was implicit in the de-Baathification order, as drafted by Pentagon officials: it aimed to target only 1 percent of party members, in the top tier of party leadership (Graham 2009: 402). Yet both Garner and the CIA station chief in Baghdad warned that the edict cut too deeply and would have prohibitive negative effects (Graham 2009: 402).[38] Then US officials abdicated. They allowed de-Baathification to become far more extensive when they looked to Iraqi expatriates, with Chalabi in charge, to implement the program. By Rumsfeld's (2011: 515) admission, under Chalabi's direction "de-Baathification gained a reputation for score settling."

Second, US leaders failed to anticipate the potential costs of the two CPA orders. With order no. 1 they denied former Baath Party officials their positions in government, stripping it of its knowledgeable elite. The casualties included managers, professionals, technicians, and teachers, many of whom—primarily Sunnis—had joined the party for professional gain, not political reasons. Worse, the order convinced Sunnis that it targeted them as Sunnis. The expatriates in charge had little appetite for the flexibility and judiciousness required to ameliorate the program's harsh effects (Chandrasekaran 2007: 83; Dobbins et al. 2009: 117–119; Wright et al. 2008: 97). With order no. 2 US officials lost hope of using the Iraqi military to establish security. The Iraqi military was admittedly in sorry shape (Wright et al. 2008: 95); its infrastructure was gutted and troops had deserted. Still, the United States delivered a death blow with that order (though it softened the blow a bit with belated adjustments that included extending payments to career officers and enlisted soldiers). The United States had thereby lost the ability to reconstitute the security force or exert leverage over senior military ranks by paying salaries (Boyle 2014: 274). Instead, it created a potent enemy, both by depriving influential Sunnis of their livelihood, social and political positions, and honor (Mansoor 2013: 9) and by putting hundreds of thousands of jobless, military-trained personnel—who kept their weapons and knowledge of arsenal locations—on the streets of Iraq. There they could nurture, and express, their strong grievance against US forces and the US-supported Shiite government (Wright et al. 2008: 96–98).

Third, US leaders failed to consider the challenges of moving Iraq *slowly* toward self-rule. They failed to appreciate that empowering Iraqi expatriates early, through the appointment of the Iraqi Governing Council, would alienate Sunnis and position members to lock in their control of an Iraqi government. They also ignored the frictions that could arise from empowering Iraqi's Shiite majority, disempowering Iraq's Sunni minority, and stoking the independence aspirations of Iraq's Kurdish minority. Just as important, US officials failed to anticipate the strong local resistance to a US occupation force that would determine the nature and pace of the transition to Iraqi sovereignty. Indeed, US officials were slow to appreciate that the US presence in Iraq would become a focal point for Iraqi grievances when a "liberated" population, that was free to act, acted freely in the aftermath of the US invasion. In the weeks and months that followed, widespread looting damaged much of the country's (already dilapidated) infrastructure, troops and police were out of work and off the job, government managers and professionals had left (when not denied) their positions, sectarian violence was on the upswing, electricity was in short supply (with rising heat), and the oil industry (with bottlenecks and looting) could not even satisfy Iraq's energy needs. The US presence became an easy target.

Having failed to anticipate events, US leaders had to respond to them. They shelved plans for a slow transition to an elected Iraqi government under a transitional constitution when Ayatollah Ali al-Sistani, the top Shiite cleric in Iraq, expressed his opposition. Under the new plan, US long-term efforts to build Iraqi institutions would simply cease, with the transfer of authority to a sovereign Iraqi government in mid-2004. "The time constraint left [individuals in CPA] with little choice but to find short-term answers that would enable the transfer of sovereignty, rather than long-term approaches that might in the end have been more effective" (Bensahel et al. 2008: 114). The CPA had assumed that the Ministry of Defense, under reconstruction, would be the last to transfer to full Iraqi government control. It found itself well behind schedule, even in staffing, when left with a handful of months to "finish" the job. Having largely excluded Iraqis from the formative decision-making, the CPA had little recourse when officials it had recruited were unwelcome after Iraqis took charge (Rathmell 2005: 27–32).

Fourth, US leaders failed to anticipate the requirements for Iraq's "transformation." They sought to remake Iraqi government institutions with the country's condition deteriorating and lacking the necessary organization, staff, and resources. They made do with a convoluted decisional structure and had far too few personnel on hand with the requisite training, authority, local knowledge, local experience, and links to their home agencies to manage the behemoth that the US occupation of Iraq had become (Dobbins et al. 2009: 243–264). US management suffered, specifically, in that (a) the centralized decision structure under Bremer, and his own micromanagement (Bensahel et al. 2008: 109), created decisional bottlenecks and impaired follow-through to ensure implementation; (b) the CPA's ad hoc structure provoked disputes with Washington over lines of responsibility and budgetary control; (c) a shortage of staff with relevant skills and experience impeded necessary outreach to government ministries and each of Iraq's eighteen provinces (Dobbins et al. 2009: 27); (d) the crushing onslaught of immediate problems inhibited broad consultation, policy coordination, and the addressing of longer-term problems (Bensahel et al. 2008: 111; Rathmell 2005: 18); (e) Defense Department rules and practices restricted the flow of reports and information to other departments and outside agencies that were involved in the US rebuilding effort; and (f) the Defense Department prevented nondepartmental staff from soliciting and obtaining support from their home agencies, leaving relationships with these entities to vary across individuals and units (Bensahel et al. 2008: 112; Dobbins et al. 2009: xviii–xix, 18–19). Scuffles with Washington over political control of the occupation further compounded CPA's organizational and resource challenges. Bremer's efforts to deal directly with the White House provoked the ire of Donald Rumsfeld, to whom the CPA nominally reported, and the Defense Department's (at least) nominal control over the enterprise left Condoleezza Rice, as national security adviser, feeling out of the loop (SIGIR 2010: 120; Dobbins et al. 2009: xvii, 16).

US officials had focused inordinately on regime change in Iraq and failed to foresee the political, economic, social, and security military challenges that would await the United States thereafter. The US arrival in Iraq did not force a change in course. US officials made their decisions (and non-decisions) to expand US objectives with little regard for available organizational, financial, and military resources or potential consequences, given political, social, economic, governmental, and religious realities in Iraq. They failed to recognize the limits to what the underprepared US government could deliver, in a challenging environment, in pursuit of poorly reconciled immediate goals.

The Downward Slide: Security Consumes the Mission

In the months after the CPA took charge, Bush administration officials were slow to appreciate the growing threat to the US mission. That was clear when Donald Rumsfeld famously quipped that "freedom's untidy," as if tumult and lawlessness were routine forms of political expression or a standard phase in a democratic transition. Yet US officials in Iraq could not ignore the growing threat from Sunni insurgents and Shiite militia groups that organized to defend, and lead, the Shiite majority. The US military, which had planned for a quick, relatively low-cost mission, now had to carry the burden of rescuing the US mission. It floundered, in multiple respects.

First, US military officials, with local and national police units off the job, had the wrong forces available—in the wrong places—to quell the violence and preserve the peace. Thus, US forces were a no-show, or a "distant" presence, throughout much of the country in the early occupation period. US military commanders shied from using US troops, who were untrained, unprepared, and in insufficient numbers for standard police operations. US patrolled urban areas in armored vehicles by day and returned to forward operating bases at night, conceding the streets around the clock to criminal behavior. Their limited, ineffective, but visible presence—armored and armed—made them unwanted symbols of the US occupation.

Second, US military commanders had insufficient numbers of US troops in country to confront Iraqi security problems. The deficiency reflected the insufficient handling of multiple uncertainties: the role of the US military in promoting Iraqi security, the usefulness of extrapolating force requirements from prior conflicts (given their divergent histories and demographics), the future capabilities of Iraqi security forces, and the likelihood of a strong and sustained insurgency. The deficiency also reflected serious misgivings in some quarters about doing for Iraqis what they could do themselves. US officials feared this would slow the US departure and create a dependent relationship (Wright et al. 2008: 167). By mid- to late 2003, however, US commanders knew they had insufficient forces on hand to deal with the insurgency (Wright et al. 2008: 171). The personnel shortage forced the US military to shift the war's burden to US military professionals (and their families). Those currently in uniform had to serve multiple and extended tours in Iraq. Then they were targeted by stop-loss orders, keeping them in uniform after their formal service commitment had ended. The burden sapped service morale, hurt retention and recruitment, and added the psychologically wounded to the ranks of the physically disabled as (uncounted) casualties of the Iraq War.

Third, the US military worked at a disadvantage in confronting an insurgency. It had limited success fighting an adversary increasingly adept at hit-and-run tactics: avoiding direct confrontations with US troops, planting improvised explosive devices (IEDs) on roads, employing booby traps, using car bombs and suicide bombers to strike vulnerable targets (including civilian gatherings, public buildings, and security force recruitment centers), and adopting countermeasures to offset changing US defensive measures. The adversary learned through experience, requiring constant changes in US tactics and equipment (including additional armor on vehicles), slowing troop movements, and distracting US forces from their own offensive operations.

Fourth, US military officials struggled to develop a command structure that would serve the military's expanding role. US commanders had assumed that Phase IV would commence with the fall of Baghdad: US military forces would provide some security, get the Iraqi army functioning again, hand off responsibilities to civilian authorities, and exit the country (Wright et al. 2008: 141). Instead, they found themselves lost in the twilight between Phase III and Phase IV (Wright et al. 2008: 162–164); the war had *somewhat* ended and "stability operations" had *somewhat* begun, leaving US civilian and military officials in Iraq uncertain about their respective responsibilities. The civilian authority (ORHA) and the military command (the Combined Forces Land Component Command, or CFLCC) in Iraq both answered formally to the Department of Defense. Further confusing matters, ORHA, understaffed and resourced, was hard pressed to manage civilian governance in Iraq under the best of conditions. Coordination challenges persisted with the transition to CPA authority. The US military sought to build up Iraqi security forces quickly to address a growing internal security threat. By contrast, the CPA sought to create an externally directed Iraqi military that was broadly representative of Iraq's demography, mindful of the legacy of Iraqi security forces as an oppressive arm of Saddam Hussein's regime. The CPA resisted US military efforts to control Iraqi police and military training and to form Iraqi paramilitary units that were drawn from their regions of operation and were therefore not necessarily representative of the country's demography (Wright 2008: 427–485).

The US military command in Iraq was itself in flux. Within months of the US occupation, CFLCC (under the command of Lieutenant General David McKiernan) was replaced by V Corps (under the command of Major General Ricardo Sanchez) as the senior military headquarters in Iraq, which would become Combined Joint

Task Force-7 (CJTF-7). V Corps had just arrived in Iraq, had "focused solely on the tactical level of war," did not have enough experienced senior officers to handle the emerging challenges in the country, and nonetheless assumed command in the country when control over civilian operations was shifting from ORHA to the CPA (Wright et al. 2008: 145–148, 157). The transition further lengthened the US military's adjustment period. It also required General Sanchez and General John P. Abizaid, commander of CENTCOM, to press for a higher-level joint command—which would become Multi-National Force-Iraq (MNF-I)—to handle expanding US military responsibilities in the country, including the training of Iraqi forces, the building of Iraqi security institutions, and the conduct of military operations. The problematic transition was complicated further by force rotations, the disruptive effects of larger-scale US combat operations (in 2004), and preparations (including safeguarding the elections) for the sooner-than-expected transition (in June 2004) to a sovereign Iraqi government (Wright et al. 2008: 173, 178–180).

Fifth, the US military adopted harsh, sometimes indiscriminate, but ultimately ineffective tactics to quell the violence. Caught between Phases III and IV of prewar military planning, commanders puzzled over whether new rules of engagement were in order or the old rules of combat applied. US commanders assumed the latter; at least implicitly, they shared Rumsfeld's attribution of the violence to Iraq's "dead-enders," irreconcilable remnants of Saddam Hussein's regime (Wright et al. 2008: 162). In targeting regime holdouts, they took the battle to the insurgents and militias. US troops raided private homes, held families at gunpoint, and conducted mass sweeps in attempts to kill or capture militants and obtain "actionable intelligence." These tactics did little, however, to weaken these groups; quite the opposite occurred. US troops often "got their man" when crashing through doors, taking neighborhoods by storm, and rounding up Iraqis to obtain tactical intelligence. Yet they also obtained a poor return on their investment because they did not possess the translators, trained interrogators, and cultural sensitivities needed to obtain information in time to put it to good use. US troops lost significant ground in the battle of public opinion when Iraqis were transferred by the thousands to detention sites—effectively, incubators for radicalism—where they were hardened further against the US occupation. Revelations in 2004 that some of the thousands of suspects held by the United States at Abu Ghraib prison (a notorious prison used by Saddam Hussein, no less) endured harsh interrogation methods, mock executions, and dehumanizing abuse fueled the common conception in Iraq that the United States opposed the interests of the Iraqi people (Wright et al. 2008: 191–239).

Although US military commanders pulled back from large-scale sweep operations after the first few months, once they recognized that these were weakening public support for US goals and driving Iraqis into the insurgency (Wright et al. 2008: 322), they continued to confront Shiite and Sunni militants in places where they sought to establish control. By the spring and summer of 2004 the US military had engaged in substantial combat operations. In Najaf, Karbala, and Al Kut, it challenged the Mahdi army of Moqtada al-Sadr, a radical Shiite firebrand who, following his (assassinated) father, became cleric to the Shiite poor and dispossessed. It also assailed Sunni insurgents in Anbar province, most conspicuously in Fallujah in April 2004, responding to the gruesome killing of four US contractors there. In the end, US forces crushed the Sadrist militia in cities where it sought control and ultimately (in November 2004) pushed the insurgents out of Fallujah. The high profile of the US military—and its negative actions—nonetheless fueled popular grievances (especially among Sunnis) against the US occupation.

Sixth, the US military ended up *moving*—that is, relocating—rather than weakening the insurgency by pursuing a strategy that observers likened to "whack-a-mole." In this game, once a staple on beach boardwalks, players hammer a mole as it emerges from a hole, only to see it emerge from another. In a similar manner, insurgents fled an area when under attack by US forces only to return when these forces had evacuated. US troops left local residents, suspected of cooperating with them, at the mercy of the insurgents. Without troops in place to hold ground to protect these people, the US military could not improve security conditions in any part of the country, let alone inspire public support for US military operations through ongoing contacts.

Seventh, the US military worked with unrealistic manpower targets, trying to build an Iraqi army that could fill the personnel void. The initial results were disappointing. With early emphasis on getting large numbers of personnel into uniform, poorly vetted and inadequately trained military and police recruits were thrown into the line of fire, sapping unit strength, morale, and professionalism. In consequence, even the numbers on paper exaggerated Iraqi security force capabilities. Within the Iraqi military, absenteeism was rampant (especially outside usual deployment zones), troops wilted under attack, a high annual attrition rate required constant unit replenishment and rebuilding, and putting a name on the payroll was simply a gimmick for siphoning off government funds.

Eighth, the US military promoted a dangerous redirection in Iraqi police operations to support the US military effort.[39] The United States pursued ambitious plans to expand the size of the Iraqi police force under the control of the Iraq Interior Ministry, once it was purged of mid- to senior-level officials. But the violence outpaced the increase in capability of the Iraqi police force. Recruits died in large numbers and quit in droves, severely overmatched and outgunned on the streets of Iraq. Pressed by the growing security threat, the administration transferred authority for police training to the Defense Department from the US Department of State and Department of Justice. Whereas these departments had preferred a decentralized force for community policing, the US military prioritized the creation of a military-style counterinsurgency force—"police" in name only—to address the deficiencies of the current force. The new battalions were equipped and trained to perform in high-risk, high-conflict environments.

The new units acquitted themselves in battle despite concerns about their loyalty. They were recruited heavily from the skilled labor pool of Sunnis who had served in

Republican Guard and special forces units under Saddam Hussein. Their problems, however, were yet to come. In 2005 the Interior Ministry—now operating with the authority of the Iraqi Transitional Government—fell under the control of the former leader of the Badr Organization (a militia linked to the dominant Shiite party in Iraq), with the approval of the elected Iraqi national assembly (in which Sunnis were underrepresented). The interior minister placed militia members in key official positions, and the ministry staffed the counterinsurgency units with militia personnel who then moved, with the sanctity and assets of the "state," against the Sunni population. Even the Sadrist militia had a strong personnel presence within the ministry's "police" units (Gordon and Trainor 2012: 146).

Much of the violence and abuse occurred outside the purview of US officials. In 2005, for example, they were shocked to discover a secret prison, run by the Interior Ministry, in which (mostly) Sunnis were interred, starved, and tortured.[40] Yet US officials deserved at least some of the blame for the violence and abuse committed by the police, which was due in part to a counterinsurgency emphasis and, on the local level, to inadequate vetting and training. "The attention that the military could give to local police was rudimentary, sporadic, and underfunded" (Rathmell et al. 2005: 51). More egregiously, the US military trained, armed, and otherwise supported the notorious Wolf Brigade, an elite commando unit numbering in the thousands, which was implicated in mass killings, torture, and disappearances. US military officials repeatedly encountered evidence of the brutality of the commando units but were "slow to acknowledge the problem" (Gordon and Trainor 2012: 148). Indeed, US troops who accompanied the Wolf Brigade allegedly turned prisoners over to these units for interrogation, aware of their likely fate.[41]

US support contributed to the violence even when offered with the "best of intentions." With US approval, the Facilities Protection Service was created to provide security guards for government buildings (to free up US security personnel). Instead, its 150,000 personnel were divided among ministries as private armies. They were used by various ministries (which had been horse-traded among dueling factions) to promote their sectarian goals, in league, moreover, with the organized militia. The Mahdi army, well represented among its ranks, could thereby employ the cover and resources of the state to pursue a sectarian agenda (Jones 2007: 30: Perito 2008b). Through the Health Ministry, for example, the Mahdi army used ambulances to deliver weapons and target enemies in hospital facilities.[42] In sum, "in its desire to empower the new Iraqi state and bring democracy to the country, the United States had built up the capabilities of the Shiite-dominated government and security forces and had willy-nilly taken sides in a brewing civil war" (Gordon and Trainor 2012: 356).

To their credit, US officials sought to correct their prior neglect and misjudgments. Notably, they lent their support to a new interior minister. Appointed in mid-2006, he strove to clean up and change the ethos of the ministry by purging the staff from top to bottom (of almost all commanders, at all levels, and many hundred uniformed police), by changing unit names and uniforms, and so forth. The US military (with European support) assisted in training and retraining the Iraqi police and paired up in the field with National Police units to monitor their behavior. The correctives were insufficient to compensate, however, for earlier US neglect and actions.

US forces had gone on the offensive against militia groups to achieve military goals, but in doing so had compromised US political objectives: Shiites were empowered, Sunnis were alienated, violence and sectarian strife were increasing, US rebuilding efforts were sidetracked, and Iraqi institutions that US officials had hoped would increasingly carry the load were now part of the problem. Whether through shortsightedness or neglect, US policy makers had allowed the ill-conceived security effort to consume all other goals for Iraq. The security mission absorbed available resources, exacerbated tensions, and empowered groups in Iraq, making the US challenge—stabilizing the country—considerably worse.

Stage III, Limitation: Constriction

Conditions in Iraq now looked exceedingly bleak. In February 2006 the Sunni destruction of the al-Askari mosque in Samarra, north of Baghdad, sparked dissent into chaos. The attack on one of Shiite Islam's holiest shrines galvanized Shiite resistance, boosted the ranks of Shiite militia, and brought Shiites fully into the conflict. The violence now crossed a critical threshold: Iraq was in a state of civil war. Thousands of Iraqi civilians were dying violently each month, victims of sectarian murders and suicide bombings. Kidnapping and gruesome torture were commonplace. Worse still, the US military proved unable to quell the violence. Although the administration rose to the occasion, when President Bush chose to send additional forces to Iraq, these forces would serve a constricted US mission ostensibly pursuant to a counterinsurgency strategy.

The Decisional Context: The Pitch for a Troop "Surge" and Counterinsurgency Strategy

By summer 2006 conditions in Iraq—and Rumsfeld's failures in leading the Pentagon—had rattled White House officials (Woodward 2008: 57). An early summer offensive (Together Forward, in Baghdad), with Iraqi security forces in the lead, never coalesced. Round two of the effort, in August, failed when Iraqi troops proved incapable—in number and qualifications—of holding neighborhoods cleared of insurgents (Ricks 2009: 44–51). General George W. Casey, who had taken command of the MNF-I from General Sanchez, wanted time for his strategy to succeed.[43]

Casey opposed a troop increase, as did Defense Secretary Rumsfeld, John Abizaid (the CENTCOM commander), and various members of the JCS.

Opponents generally argued that deploying more US troops would fuel popular discontent (at home and in Iraq), invite insurgent attacks, and still not solve Iraq's bigger problems. Indeed, by carrying the burden, US forces were a "crutch." They shielded Iraqis from the negative consequences of their own irresponsible behavior and gave them little incentive to carry the load. Thus, US forces must either accept an interminable burden or leave Iraq at some point, knowing that security improvements could not outlast the US exit (Ricks 2009: 53, 215). Opponents further argued that a US force increase was unsustainable. Service officials insisted that the US military had reached its breaking point and could not increase US troops in Iraq while maintaining other US global security commitments. Military officials were not alone in voicing resistance to enlarging the US force in Iraq. A decision to send additional US forces to Iraq was unpopular; a clear majority of the American public opposed that option,[44] as did much of Congress. Indeed, the report of the Iraq Study Group,[45] mandated by Congress and presented to the president on December 6, recommended, by consensus, that the United States redeploy its forces in Iraq to expedite the training of Iraqi security forces. Echoing the sentiment of much of the US military command, it stated that the US commitment to Iraq was not "open-ended," and that by "doing for" Iraqis, the United States kept them from doing for themselves.

The late summer and early fall saw the beginnings of a significant policy shift. Multiple efforts were now under way to wrest control of Iraq strategy from the existing US military chain of command. Although constrained by available resources, these various efforts increased, not decreased, the administration's investment in Iraq.

First, the president's national security adviser, Stephen Hadley, initiated reviews of Iraq strategy, adding to a host of others conducted by the government, including independent assessments conducted by the State Department and ordered by Peter Pace, chair of the JCS.[46] One NSC-initiated review found, importantly, that five combat brigades were available to support a troop increase (Woodward 2008: 288). Hadley himself served as a critical point person, and perhaps the singular linchpin, in forging the president's eventual strategy decision.[47]

Second, from behind the scenes at the Pentagon, Jack Keane (a retired four-star general) directed efforts to devise a strategy drawing from counterinsurgency principles. He maintained contact with Hadley (Woodward 2008: 299) and consulted closely with General Raymond Odierno, the second-in-command in Iraq, who was now "conspiring" to overturn a strategy that his immediate superior in Iraq, General Casey, insisted *was* working (Woodward 2008: 296, 309–310). Keane eventually coauthored an outside (American Enterprise Institute) study that validated the troop surge option.[48]

Third, in November 2006 Bush ordered a deputy-level (senior subcabinet) interagency review (Feaver 2011: 104).[49] The participants, deliberating into early January 2007, considered a range of options. They were divided over whether to emphasize a population-centric strategy, drawing from counterinsurgency principles, or Iraqi troop training to expedite a security handoff to local forces. They were divided as well on the contentious issue of whether to send additional troops to Iraq. These would remain matters for the NSC—which itself remained split (Secretary of State Rice voiced her dissent)—and thus ultimately the president to decide (Feaver 2011: 106).

Fourth, the president's advisers on the NSC staff sought to persuade a president who had proven resistant to overruling his military commanders that a change in war leadership was required.[50] In June 2006 the NSC staff arranged for the president to meet at Camp David with outside security experts, who voiced concerns over the war's mismanagement. By late fall the president was obviously listening. Although Bush stood by his defense secretary through the November election,[51] he fired Rumsfeld soon afterward,[52] a reluctant public concession that US military strategy had failed and required change. Holding Rumsfeld to his own quote, Bush lamented, "Iraq is not working well enough, fast enough."[53] Indeed, in November the president had accepted the key elements of a new, population-centric strategy (Woodward 2008: 246–247), though he had yet to embrace the troop increase that Casey still opposed (Feaver 2011: 107). The president's advisers continued their efforts to expose him to outside opinions. Thus, on December 11 Bush met at the White House, in the presence of the NSC staff, with a group of distinguished experts—three four-star generals (including Keane) and two academic security specialists—selected by his national security assistants for a range of views. The experts tilted three to two toward a troop increase (Gordon and Trainor 2012: 302–303; Woodward 2008: 279–281), yet all agreed that a change in military leadership was required.[54] Noting that *even generals* disagree over policy, Eliot Cohen told the president, "civilian leaders need to discover these disagreements, force them to the surface, and probe them" (quoted in Ricks 2009: 99).

These efforts should not distract from Bush's own influence in the decision process. Despite his long-standing deference to his commanders and first-term willingness to concede significant decisional responsibilities to his principal advisers, a chastened Bush pressed cautiously for a consensus option that might save the Iraq mission.[55] It appears that by November he was leaning toward a US troop surge in Iraq. Fearing that a US defeat in Iraq would sap US military morale and embolden terror groups, he all but ruled out "doing nothing" as an option. Yet neither a top-down model, with leaders imposing their preferences on subordinates, nor a model with subordinates constraining leaders by tailoring advice and controlling information, is entirely appropriate here. Indeed, whether influence flowed more in one direction than in the other—and which direction predominated—remains an open question. Did Hadley probe the surge alternative to influence Bush's preferences? To respond to the president's own preferences? Or simply to serve the president by exploring a potentially viable option? Relatedly, when exactly did Bush commit to the surge option? Parsing reality is difficult when influence flows are sometimes directional, are often reciprocal, and might reflect a convergence of views. It is more difficult in the case here, given the secretiveness and compartmentalization of the decision process and Bush's close consultative relationship with his national security adviser.

Yet such questioning should not bury the lead: the president's NSC staff, with strong presidential backing, engineered a re-escalation of the war effort by exerting (civilian) control over a recalcitrant military. On January 10, 2007, Bush announced his decision in a national address. He planned to send five additional combat brigades—a number that would swell to around thirty thousand troops—to support a population-centric strategy. It would be centered in Baghdad, the epicenter of the violence. The president's "surge strategy" received strong backing from his NSC staff, JCS chair Pace, and General Odierno[56] and eventually acquired support from the other JCS members (Feaver 2011: 112). Of course it received support from General David Petraeus, an articulate proponent of a population-centric strategy. Bush selected him to replace General Casey to implement the new strategy.

A New Strategy, under New Management

General Petraeus had emerged as the leading candidate to become the US force commander in Iraq. He was an obvious choice. He had advised administration officials in the lead-up to the surge decision,[57] taken charge of Iraqi troop training (as commander of the Multi-National Security Transition Command-Iraq), and coauthored the revised *US Army/Marine Corps Counterinsurgency Manual*.[58] When he took command of the MNF-I in early 2007, he introduced a fundamental shift in the US war strategy.[59]

Public security became the centerpiece of US strategy. Rather than allow insurgents to flee combat only to return once US forces had evacuated and to punish those who had cooperated with the US forces, the strategy now was to clear areas of combatants, hold territory that had been cleared, and move into new areas, leaving insurgents with ever-fewer places to retreat and hide (Ricks 2009; Robinson 2008). Civilian protection was also to receive priority over countercombatant operations (Kahl 2007). Under the prior focus on lethal force or "kinetic operations"—including large-scale "cordon-and-sweep" operations (Wright et al. 2008: 122)—US forces had attempted to deplete adversary ranks in battle. Reminiscent of the Vietnam War, the strategy had failed to kill insurgents faster than the enemy could replace them and might well have drawn recruits into the insurgency. By going after the enemy and inflicting a heavy body count, the US military (and its allies) had produced collateral damage—in property and civilian lives—that inflamed the public, rallied support to the insurgency, and reduced the public's desire to cooperate with the US military. In Iraq, the latter proved to be a particular liability. The strategy had failed to capitalize on popular grievances against al-Qaeda-linked groups. Many Sunnis had tired of the excesses and false promises (of a return to glory) of these groups and, it turns out, were willing to switch sides, with a promise of support.[60]

The new strategy was rooted in counterinsurgency doctrine: the power of an insurgency—its resources, low profile, and recruits—stems from a conditionally supportive population (Kilcullen 2009; Nagl 2005; Thompson 1966),[61] whose complicity remains decisive. If the counterinsurgents can protect the population from retaliatory violence—eventually providing political, economic, and judicial benefits of governance—the population will shift its loyalties, leaving the insurgency to starve and wither. Thus, population-centric principles informed a key change in US practices: whereas US forces had previously addressed the security challenges of Iraq essentially as a "day job"—traveling in heavily armed vehicles from forward operating bases to patrol population centers, only to return to those bases at night—soldiers were now required to maintain a continuous presence within those areas.

Consequently, the US command immediately established dozens of small outposts and joint security stations, mostly in Baghdad. Presumably, an around-the-clock presence would permit them to develop rapport with the local population to earn its trust, obtain leads on militant activity, and respond quickly and adeptly to plots and threats to public security. After establishing some measure of security, the US military would look to Iraqi security personnel to hold ground to prevent insurgents from returning.

The Limits of the Surge Strategy

In making his surge decision, the president pushed back against political and military constraints on US action in important respects. He moved against the political tide; he increased the US investment in prestige, lives, resources, and (personal) political futures in the conflict; and he offered a broad-based approach that combined military and nonmilitary elements. Yet the surge decision was bound by these constraints. The immediate gains possible from (more readily) available capabilities shaped thinking about the policy problem. In multiple respects, what the United States *could* do to reduce the violence, with these capabilities, influenced policy concerning what it *should* do in Iraq.

First, proponents were betting on *slowly* bringing US troops (by fall 2007) to peak levels roughly achieved earlier in the conflict; the force was still undersized when considering the density and spread of the Iraqi population. The resulting force was too small to clear areas of combatants, hold territory to prevent those same combatants from returning, and then move on to new ground to extend the clear-and-hold process.[62] To achieve its goals, the US military had to perform far more effectively than it had in the past. It also would have to rely heavily on support from untested Iraqi troops—they would have to take the lead, according to Bush in his national address—and cope with a Sunni public that had not warmed to a US troop presence.

Second, proponents placed their bets on what they *hoped* a somewhat larger US force could deliver, militarily and politically. US officials at all levels had not yet embraced a key opportunity available to a relatively small US force: Sunnis once allied, tacitly and otherwise, with al-Qaeda-linked groups had now turned against them. That was a critical deficiency; the evidence is unconvincing that by themselves either the surge per se or the Sunni Awakening movement—a crude alliance of Sunni tribes and insurgents that arose to combat al-Qaeda-linked groups—could have turned the tide against the insurgency (Biddle et al. 2012).[63] More correctly, the US operation benefited from a "'perfect storm' of trends and conditions (Metz 2010: 38), working in vital "interaction" (Feaver 2011/2012: 194). These conditions included a fortuitous decision by Moqtada al-Sadr to stand down his Shiite forces. US forces thereby avoided a fight against militia on both sides of the religious divide.

Even these benefits were insufficient. Were US forces to help quell the violence, lasting progress could be made only if the reduction in violence prodded the obstreperous Baghdad government to reform. The strategy left unclear how positive results might last and lead somehow to a more inclusive government or reconciliation among warring factions. Indeed, a reduction in violence might actually free the government to strengthen its position in the country, at the opposition's expense. The administration was well aware of the shortcomings of the Iraqi government. Hadley, upon his return from Iraq, wrote a secret memo to the NSC principals,[64] detailing the government's sectarian behavior: "The reality on the streets of Baghdad suggests Maliki is either ignorant of what is going on, misrepresenting his intentions, or that his capabilities are not yet sufficient to turn his good intentions into action."[65] The November 2006 memo proposed actions that the United States could take to support Maliki, predicated largely on the assumption that the challenges lay in his capabilities rather than his intentions. But what if his intentions were bad, or if he was so weak that no amount of US backing would make a difference and could hurt him politically by making him (and his allies) appear beholden to the United States?

President Bush, in announcing the surge, had stated that the Iraqi government had to stand up—that the United States would monitor the government's performance as measured by defined benchmarks. Less clear was how the United States could hold the government to these benchmarks. The White House had to push Maliki hard to accept an augmented US force—and therefore could not easily acquire leverage from threatening a US force reduction—and Iraqi leaders had reason to conclude that the United States was in the war for the long haul. After all, by sending additional troops to Iraq to carry the load of the fighting, the United States had communicated that its stakes in Iraq were too great to risk abandoning the government. Indeed, Bush delivered that very message by stressing the high US stakes in the conflict. As he stated in his January 11 address, "The changes I have outlined tonight are aimed at ensuring the survival of a young democracy that is fighting for its life in a part of the world of enormous importance to American security."

Third, placing tactics first, proponents did not yet have a fully developed strategy. What they offered was "more of a concept than a fully developed plan" (Gordon and Trainor 2012: 313)—more a broad philosophy for applying various military, economic, and political tools than a set of guidelines indicating which, when, and where tools would work best. Specific implications of these basic principles, moreover, were far from transparent, for the principles amounted to a set of paradoxes: using force could make US troops less secure and effective; doing nothing is sometimes better than doing something (that might place local populations at risk); having locals do something poorly is sometimes better than having US forces do it well; learning what works in one context could hamper adaptation in another; and so forth (see Cohen et al. 2006). Yet under some conditions, employing force, taking charge, and drawing lessons from experience are, in fact, the better alternatives. So how would the military know how to respond when ambiguous principles required action in one or another direction, depending on a nonspecific context? The answer is that they would need to "feel their way" through the operation: a general philosophy of warfare would need to become strategy largely on the fly.[66]

Fourth, proponents offered a strategy that *would not and could not* drive resource decisions. One problem was that counterinsurgency doctrine did not "scale down" well. It might work with unlimited time and resources; its success in Iraq was hampered, however, by a scarcity of political, economic, and military resources; severe time constraints; skepticism across the military command; a distrustful and unforgiving Congress; and limited US public support for the war. More significantly, counterinsurgency principles were arguably inappropriate in the immediate context. Knowledgeable observers rightly questioned whether a "counterinsurgency" strategy could work in Iraq, given the sectarian nature of the country's conflict (Biddle 2008). In such conflicts, the participants view outcomes in "zero-sum" terms. They keep their guard up so as not to render themselves vulnerable to attack, seek to capitalize on vulnerabilities that opposing groups create should they try to cooperate, and treat the resources of the state—especially its security forces—as a "prize" to use for political and military advantage. The outlook was not good, then, if winning the population over to the central government was the US goal. As violence subsided in Iraq, the country's Sunnis continued to express hostility toward the "Persians" (as many Sunnis viewed Shiites) who controlled the Iraqi central government.

Finally, the strategy emerged as a compromise of sorts, over strong resistance. The strategy required hard probing to find additional forces; secretiveness to avoid premature disclosures that might provoke organized resistance; support for Pentagon elements willing to consider alternative strategies; some dealmaking; and considerable persuasion to overcome resistance, package the elements, and make the strategy a viable option. The "final strategy emerged somewhat piecemeal, with logrolled hybrids from originally divergent proposals and even the occasional compromise bargain" (Feaver 2011: 112). The policy challenge was clear from General Pace's less-than-successful efforts to push internally for independent reassessments of US strategy. He pressed the CENTCOM and Iraq commanders (Generals Abizaid and Casey) individually for reviews of US strategy; he also turned to the Council of Colonels—a task force of senior officers—for a report that would come directly to him. That report alone emerged from the Pentagon. When first briefed to the NSC staff, as the "Council of Colonels" study, it examined the pros and cons of various options, without promoting any one. The options included "Go Big" with a sizable troop increase, "Go Long" (with a smaller troop increase, followed by a smaller, long-term US military presence in Iraq), and "Go Home" (Ricks 2009: 103). When briefed subsequently to the NSC staff as the "JCS" study—having been circulated among the JCS, the military command in Iraq, and CENTCOM—it now presented only one option, with a single recommendation: essentially, do what Casey had been doing—but quicker.[67] The solution played to existing practice and the military's desire to leave Iraq as soon as possible. Although the JCS joined the consensus favoring the surge strategy, they did so slowly through a process of give and take, and fully, only once the president had made his decision. Indeed, in the process they received two important concessions: a State Department commitment to bring its personnel more fully into the effort (with Provisional Reconstruction Teams, discussed later in the chapter) and a presidential commitment to pursue an increase in the size of the active duty US Army and Marines (Feaver 2011: 112; Woodward 2008: 286–287).

Of course the "right" decisions can arise from logrolling and intragovernmental politicking. For that matter, rational decisions can result if central participants have a strong sense of the direction that policy must move and the capability to push it in that direction. Yet in this instance, rationality was impugned by the absence of answers to critical questions. If the goal of stabilizing Iraq was important, why not reshuffle global military commitments, engage domestic opponents, and tap the resources necessary to mobilize more fully for the fight? If it was not, given the limited benefits and high risks, why increase the US investment in the conflict? In lieu of answers, reassessment centered—despite the US force increase—on "doing with what we have."

In sum, US officials, both in Washington and Iraq, hoped that a reduction in violence would create some breathing space that would permit the combatants to resolve their political differences (see, e.g., Petraeus 2013: x). However, their efforts centered on the immediate problem and a solution that catered to the (limited) resources they thought they could devote—or wanted to devote—to the problem.

The selected strategy certainly had a rational basis. Policy makers understandably sought—above all else—to stop the bleeding. The continuing violence promised to swallow up any gains the United States had made in the country and make conditions there considerably worse. It could even bring Iran, through its support for militia groups, more squarely into the conflict and raise tensions throughout the region. As a solution, an ongoing US troop presence positioned the US military to move against the violence, armed with a new strategy and additional forces. The president's surge strategy also constituted a logical challenge to surge opponents, who viewed indigenous force training as an "exit strategy." Their "low-cost" alternative ignored the potential detrimental consequences of an early US departure for Iraqi security forces (Dubik 2009: 2). US troops were needed to provide ancillary support, conduct joint operations so that Iraqis could learn through experience, keep Iraqi forces fighting within their capability, safeguard against catastrophic Iraqi military failure (reverberating widely through a loss in morale, desertions, and destruction of critical forces), and prevent Iraqi security forces from fracturing along sectarian lines to become active participants on one or both sides of the conflict (Biddle et al. 2008; Mansoor 2013: 51). Given these dangerous possibilities, US troops were not a crutch but a loose-fitting "splint" that kept the parties from employing the resources of the state in all-out conflict.

That said, US policy makers nonetheless defined their mission to serve an "available" option: a repositioning of the current US force, augmented somewhat modestly, and temporarily. Thus, surge critics had a point when they insisted the United States now do *less* in Iraq, boisterously backing the case for an exit. After all, the larger US forces could have tried and failed to reduce the violence, leaving the US military, and Iraq, in worse shape with fewer options. Had US troops proved successful in reducing the violence, Iraq would still be a tinderbox and dependent on US troops to solve its problems. What role would US forces play should the Iraqi government, and its security forces, prove partisan, venal, incompetent, and unwilling to reform?

For the purposes of this discussion, the more revealing question is: Why did the administration, given its presumed stakes, not strive harder to do *more*? After all, the United States had roughly one million personnel attached to the Army, Marines, and National Guard that were available for national emergencies, even if the draft was a political nonstarter and new recruits could not train fast enough to address the immediate challenge. The answer is that the limits to available resources—whether imposed or accepted—would simply not allow it.

The Surge in Implementation: "Counterinsurgency Light"

US officials in Iraq *sought* a cohesive, broad-based approach to stabilizing the country. In implementation, however, they strayed from the principles of counterinsurgency, as commonly understood, with a strategy that relied—opportunistically—on winning over *key elements* (mobilized portions) of the population, not the Iraqi public per se. The strategy offered an immediate "fix," and it profited, even then, from sheer luck. Thus, any success that the mission achieved in the short term should not mask its limited immediate security purposes.

The Military Front

To be sure, the US military strategy, as first implemented in the Iraqi capital, drew from basic counterinsurgency principles. The US military slowly and methodically cleared Baghdad neighborhoods of hostile groups. To protect these areas, it then established an ongoing neighborhood presence, set up blast walls to keep warring neighborhoods apart, and compiled biometric data sets (which included fingerprints lifted from unexploded bombs) to monitor residents and capture suspects. By offering security to local residents, it gained public confidence and valuable information for targeting militants. With time, it projected power into the surrounding "belts"—areas in concentric circles around the capital—to stop hostile traffic into the city and force the enemy to move and communicate to avoid US targeting (Mansoor 2013: 65–82).

The US strategy succeeded in quelling the violence in Iraq in no small part because the al-Qaeda-linked militants had laid the groundwork for the strategy. In areas under their control, al-Qaeda-linked groups had failed to deliver on their promise of returning Sunnis to their "rightful place" in the country and had alienated local Sunni populations with heavy-handed tactics—killing tribal leaders, banning certain product sales, confiscating property, and generally throwing their weight around—ostensibly to build conformity with fundamentalist Islamic practices. The US military benefited unexpectedly when Sunni militia groups simply switched sides. Sparked by the Anbar Awakening movement (Eisenstadt 2007), these Sunnis rebelled when their situation became untenable; they could not compete militarily with the Shiite militia and were suffering the zealotry, whims, excesses, and harsh practices of al-Qaeda-linked militants.

In Baghdad and the surrounding provinces, Sunnis who broke from the insurgency—eventually dubbed the "Sons of Iraq" (SOI)—provided eyes and ears on the adversary that US forces had lacked, helping the latter to identify al-Qaeda targets, dismantle the terror infrastructure, locate IEDs, and disrupt attacks and plots (Lebovic 2010: 66–67). With the backing of a now larger force, the US military successfully reduced levels of violence in the country. What it did not do, however, was win the "hearts and minds" of the local population. Iraqi public opinion data provide little reason to suppose that the Sunni population—especially in Anbar province to the west of Baghdad—was "won over" *by* the US military, much less *to* the Shiite-dominated Iraqi government. The majority of Sunnis continued to back attacks on Coalition troops, demand their speedy exit from the country, and view the central government in Baghdad with great suspicion (see Lebovic 2010: 97–100).

The US military benefited further from the prior actions of Shiite militia groups. Their push against the Sunni community had driven Sunnis out of much of Baghdad; violence subsided because in these areas, these groups had essentially "won." The US military benefited in particular from the contemporaneous, albeit tacit, cooperation of Moqtada al-Sadr's Mahdi army, which had violently confronted US troops. By standing down his Shiite militia, al-Sadr aided the US targeting of so-called special groups (offshoots supported by Iran) within his ranks.

The Political-Economic Front

Building capacity at the local level, codified as doctrine in the counterinsurgency manual, was also an important part of the new strategy. As a core mission, "stability operations" (nation-building by another name) required a comprehensive and coordinated approach. Ideally, it would combine resources across the US government, allied governments, and nongovernmental and intergovernmental organizations to establish the rule of law, support governance and economic development, and provide security to create conditions favorable to a stable and lasting peace. With General Petraeus and Ambassador Ryan Crocker now in the lead, US military and civilian officials sought, with the surge, to coordinate the many programs nominally under US oversight. They also promoted an integrated—albeit still limited—US government effort, designed for *immediate* impact at the provincial and local levels.

Main vehicles in this regard were the Commander's Emergency Response Program (CERP) and provincial reconstruction teams (PRTs).[68] CERP monies were available to the military for quick disbursement in small amounts for a wide variety of purposes: paying salaries for Sunnis who had switched sides, compensating families for combat losses, starting businesses, building schools, and so forth. Low-level military officers had the authority to distribute these monies, bypassing traditional contracting and management hurdles.[69] The PRTs also proved to be a flexible device for building community capacity and public support for the US mission. PRTs offered a model for stability operations; they aimed to improve local governance (as it pertained to popular participation, agriculture, law enforcement, and the like) by combining hundreds of personnel (from across government and beyond) under the lead of a State Department official. With the 2007 surge, the number of PRTs expanded—from ten to twenty-five—to include smaller teams of eight to twelve personnel that were embedded (ePRTs) in brigade combat teams under the lead of a brigade commander. Unlike the traditional PRTs, the ePRTs directly served the US security plan as military-led efforts to build bridges to local residents in Iraq's most violent provinces.[70] Although initially hampered by the violence,[71] ePRTs proved useful vehicles for resolving conflicts among groups, increasing political participation, improving governance, and distributing funds (including CERP monies) rapidly in communities (Perito 2008a).

Yet the assistance effort was limited in execution, by design. Its goal was to serve a pressing, proximate objective: the near-term stabilization of the country. The US military distributed cash and supported local programs on the fly to buy some local goodwill and build some local capacity. The US government could not, however, contend with the far-reaching challenges of promoting sustainable Iraqi development (as discussed later in the chapter)—especially in a combat environment—much less compensate for the failure of the Iraqi central government to reform.

Assessing the Gains from the Surge

Without question, the strategy succeeded—resoundingly, in fact—in reducing violence in Iraq. Those who facilitated and ultimately made the decision to change the strategy, increasing the US troop investment in the conflict, deserve credit in that regard. Yet their thoughtful efforts do not override some underlying truths.

First, absent facilitative conditions, the US military was unlikely to have met even its modest objectives. The US military accepted the severe limits of a population-centric approach that in key respects turned traditional thinking about counterinsurgency on its head: US forces did not win over a local population by establishing a security presence, building indigenous security capabilities, and satisfying local needs. Instead, US forces capitalized on the fact of a ready-made indigenous force when much of the insurgency switched sides, to defeat the *immediate* threat. The switch in alliances simultaneously weakened the ranks of the Sunni insurgency and multiplied the military effectiveness of US troops.

Second, the surge, though lessening the violence, offered limited gains. Iraq remained in an uneasy peace; al-Qaeda-linked groups were now weaker, and the Iraqi army was now stronger, but the country's social and political problems remained unresolved. The success of the surge was far more beholden to the "clear-and-hold" than to the "build" portion of the new "clear, hold, and build" strategy—and even then, the "hold" portion proved fragile. The decreased violence did not prod the Iraqi government toward greater inclusiveness; ultimately, it emboldened the government, reduced its incentive to broaden its base, and gave it new opportunities to punish even those Sunnis who had not joined the violent opposition. Skeptics had good reason to question whether the Iraqi government could sustain any gains the surge delivered.

In the end, the Bush administration had to accept these hard realities, despite the success of the surge. These realities set the stage for the next phase of the conflict with its problems and challenges for the Obama administration to address.

Stage IV, Disengagement: Extrication

The surge placed harsh demands on the US military. US troops had to endure multiple and extended tours in Iraq; military budgets, supplies, and stocks were stressed by the war's demands. The surge itself enjoyed little public support. Republicans, like Democrats (who as of early 2007 controlled both the US House and Senate), now wanted out of Iraq. They were not alone. Admiral William Fallon, the head of CENTCOM, with JCS backing, sought to pull US troops from Iraq (Gordon and

Trainor 2014: 413–415; Mansoor 2013: 53). In spring 2007 Fallon tried to block Petraeus's requests for troops to support the surge and even formed a fact-finding team that traveled around Iraq, apparently in search of incriminating information. General Casey, now a JCS member, continued to lobby for a reduced US military presence in Iraq to force its government to accept a larger share of the security burden (Mansoor 2013: 183).[72]

US military officials in Iraq successfully deflected the withdrawal pressure by warning of the dangers of extracting US troops too quickly: societal tensions were still up; the insurgency was down, not out; and the Iraqi army was not yet capable of dampening the flames should tensions reignite the insurgency. Petraeus relied on direct presidential access to safeguard the new US military strategy (Mansoor 2013: 94, 178–179). The political balance eventually shifted against a relatively large US military presence. Whereas President Bush had remained sympathetic to the concerns of his commanders in Iraq (Gordon and Trainor 2012: 427), President Obama sought a significant US force reduction in the country, leaving Iraqi leaders with little incentive to accept the US negotiating conditions. The priority for Obama, in Iraq, was to leave it behind.

Negotiating an Exit

Under Prime Minister al-Maliki, the Iraqi government initiated discussions with the United States for a broad understanding. The "Declaration of Principles," signed in November 2007, was to govern the US-Iraq relationship, with UN authorization set to expire at the end of 2008. It led, in turn, to contentious negotiations to flesh out the details in a "status of forces agreement" (SOFA). The Iraqi government sought, through the negotiations, to exert its sovereignty, constrain the activities of US forces in Iraq, and speed the US exit from the country. Pressed by strong domestic opposition, the Iraqi government would not accept an enduring US troop presence or permanent US bases in Iraq. Moqtada al-Sadr and Ayatollah al-Sistani insisted that any such agreement have broad public backing. In turn, US negotiators wanted to retain US legal control over US troops in Iraq, maintain their operating autonomy, and tie a US withdrawal to security improvements within the country. Thus, US negotiators initially sought the retention of fifty-eight long-term bases in Iraq, control over Iraqi airspace, and protection of US military personnel from Iraqi legal jurisdiction. The Iraqis held the stronger hand. Despite their strong opening position, US negotiators consistently gave ground over the ensuing months before finally relenting. They accepted a fixed departure date for US combat troops and conceded to al-Maliki's deployment demands: the United States had to redeploy its forces to combat bases outside of Iraqi cities by June 2009 and then remove all US forces from Iraq by the end of 2011.[73]

In January 2009 US forces formally lost their power to arrest Iraqis without court approval and had to coordinate all missions with Iraqi security forces.[74]

The reduction in US authority after June 2009 significantly constrained US operations. US troops could not operate in Iraqi cities; moreover, they had to obtain arrest warrants from Iraqi authorities, rely on Iraqi sources for useful intelligence, and conduct operations jointly with Iraqi forces. Under the new relationship, the Iraqi government took bold actions over US objections. These included forcibly occupying an Iranian opposition group encampment that US forces had protected; removing blast walls from around Baghdad (which snarled traffic and presumably gave residents a "false" sense of danger); extracting US-trained personnel from Iraqi defense and intelligence positions; and resisting calls to integrate tens of thousands of Sons of Iraq members who had hoped to obtain security jobs with the government.[75] The administration had no recourse, given Iraqi domestic opinion. When the SOFA was approved by Iraq's Parliament, all members of al-Sadr's voting bloc nonetheless opposed the agreement, and al-Sistani used the less-than-resounding affirmative vote as reason to support a public referendum on the agreement.[76]

Although the SOFA, as negotiated by the Bush administration, set a firm date for the US withdrawal of combat forces from Iraq, the Obama administration still hoped that negotiations with the Iraqi government would allow the United States to prolong its combat presence in the country. The administration was torn between its desires to (a) retain a force sufficient to back the fledgling Iraqi military and government and (b) limit the US military role in Iraq to serve President Obama's desire to shift resources to the Afghanistan War and honor his pledge to end US involvement in Iraq. Top US military commanders—the chair of the JCS, the head of CENTCOM, and the US commander in Iraq—wanted to maintain a relatively robust force of sixteen thousand personnel in Iraq. With it they could ostensibly train Iraqi forces, provide auxiliary support, and retain a presence sufficient to influence the Iraqi government and manage ethnic and sectarian tensions. The White House favored a smaller US force, set at ten thousand troops in initial deliberations, and then thirty-five hundred troops (with a smaller rotating force, capped at fifteen hundred) in later proposals (Gordon and Trainor 2012: 657, 669–670).

In a replay of history, civilian officials pushed the US military command to somehow make do with lower numbers. Getting the numbers down now, however, appeared less a means to accomplish some end in Iraq than a means to end involvement there. In opting for "a minimal force that would train the Iraqi military, support counterterrorism operations, and control Iraq's airspace with half a dozen F-16s" (Gordon and Trainor 2012: 670), the administration accepted only a feeble US presence in that country. The remaining force could not keep hostile elements of Iraqi society apart, monitor Iraqi security forces closely, or provide support—to give or to withhold—for leverage. The administration had essentially concluded that any success the United States could achieve in Iraq was largely insensitive to the size of the residual US force. Simply put, exit had become the objective.

Although both the US and Iraqi governments had expected to negotiate a resolution permitting US forces to stay in Iraq, the chances of reaching a mutually acceptable agreement were increasingly bleak. As the end of 2011 approached, the Iraqi government's unwillingness to yield on a critical issue—exempting US military personnel from Iraqi legal jurisdiction—proved decisive. It triggered a US decision to withdraw all US military forces from Iraq (as scheduled under the 2009 agreement) once US officials had rejected al-Maliki's final offer: an executive agreement granting immunity to US troops (which would not require parliamentary approval). That was less protection than US troops currently enjoyed under a parliament-approved agreement.[77]

The US position proved controversial over time. The administration had offered Iraq relatively paltry benefits—a very limited US troop presence—to sign the agreement. The Iraqi government apparently would have looked more kindly on a deal that retained a larger US troop presence (Brands and Feaver 2017: 24). Moreover, Maliki's terms for a deal were not fundamentally unacceptable; the Obama administration eventually accepted protection for US troops in 2014—under just such an executive agreement—when it reintroduced US troops into Iraq. Yet lost in the debate over whether the United States could have sweetened the deal—and whether a residual US force could have averted Iraq's subsequent polarization or the rise of the Islamic State (Brands and Feaver 2017: 25–30)—is a fundamental truth: the administration—and the public in general—had tired of the war.

Early in his administration Obama conceded the costs and the obstacles of pushing for progress in Iraq against the al-Maliki government. The Iraqi prime minister was strengthening his domestic power base, persecuting the opposition, and relying on all means at his disposal to stay in office.[78] In a word, Obama acknowledged "limits" to what the United States could accomplish in Iraq and was unwilling to give much to its government to get a deal.

The Abrupt US Departure

With the end of 2011 approaching, the US military was fighting the clock. In the spring and summer of 2011, US secretary of defense Leon Panetta and JCS chair Mike Mullen were among those who traveled to Iraq to appeal to its leaders to allow US troops to remain in the country beyond the existing deadline (Cordesman and Khazai 2014: 8).[79] Absent an agreement on an extension, the US military would soon have to start withdrawing from Iraq to ensure a safe and orderly exodus by year's end. For that very reason, President Obama announced in October that all US troops would leave Iraq at the end of 2011, per prior agreement.

Obama had perhaps telegraphed his intention to leave Iraq in the near future from the start of his administration. He had announced, in February 2009, that the US combat mission in Iraq would terminate at the end of August 2010.[80] The military sought to manage the taxingly swift transition to Iraqi control by planning around the concept of "minimum essential capabilities," which military leaders resolved (after considerable debate) would leave Iraqi security forces "capable of providing internal security and the minimum foundational capabilities to defend against external threat" (Hoffman 2017: 347). The transition was complicated, however, by the Iraqi government's budgetary distress, the Defense Ministry's unrealistic aspirations to build a strong force to defend against external threats, and the vast areas needing improvement to establish such "essential capabilities" (Hoffman 2017: 346–347). What these capabilities meant in practical terms was thus another matter. As one extensive RAND study (Brennan et al. 2013: xxxviii) of US end-of-war planning concluded, "instead of striving to develop requirement-based competencies, US officials worked to develop the minimum capabilities that would permit US forces to depart, defined in practice as *whatever was possible* [italics added] by the end of the time-constrained U.S. military presence." The capabilities instilled were "never viewed as anything more than an interim step along the path of development capabilities necessary to fulfill critical security missions" (Brennan et al. 2013: 201).

Only when the US withdrawal decision was announced in 2011 were the parties clear that the United States Force-Iraq (USF-I, which in January 2010 merged the prior commands) would hand over mission control, as planned, to the Office of Security Cooperation in Iraq (OSC-I), under State Department control. OSC-I itself suffered in the planning for the transition, separated as it was from both the military command and the civilian offices that would run the Iraq mission. "Operating under less than clear guidance, OSC-I forged ahead with establishing its plan, believing it was consistent with the latest guidance from CENTCOM and that CENTCOM was in sync with the Embassy and the State Department" (Hoffman 2017: 350). Unfortunately, neither assumption would prove correct.

As of January 2012 the State Department—still underprepared, understaffed, and underfunded—had to carry the load, despite a slow start and an uncertain role. It had to contend earlier in planning and budgeting with an unclear departure date and mission, given the possibility that some US troops would remain in Iraq. It had to contend now with the diverse challenges of the "revised" US-Iraq relationship, from getting permits, obtaining visas, and managing imports and exports to maintaining and acquiring influence with Iraqi leaders.

Ultimately, tightening US resource constraints proved decisive, dashing hopes for a smooth transition. The State Department had initially assumed that it could oversee a vast array of programs, a third of the thirteen hundred then run by the US military. It curtailed its ambitions sharply, over US military objections, as various factors conspired against prior planning. One such factor was Iraqi government resistance to maintaining, or acquiring, various US-sponsored programs (intelligence gathering, military training, etc.) that al-Maliki thought infringed on national prerogatives.[81] These factors also included pressure from Congress and the White House to cut costs, a contagious loss in governmental program support, a realization that programs could not survive absent US troops to provide protection in the field, shortages in State Department resources and staffing, resistance from other US government agencies to burden sharing, and the Pentagon's imposition of across-the-board budget cuts to meet target figures. US PRTs and an extensive police training program (Brennan 2013: 311–314; SIGIR 2012) were among the casualties. With these cuts, $1.6 billion previously appropriated for use in Iraq was redirected to programs in other countries.[82]

In sum, the Obama administration sought, above all else, to end US military involvement in Iraq. It sought neither to condition US withdrawal on achieving some critical set of military or political goals nor to prioritize some critical set of goals in the expectation that US military involvement in Iraq might precipitously end. The effects of this approach were predictable. In finally recognizing that US forces would soon leave Iraq, US military officials tried to finish what they could, pursuing tasks that they could complete, at some level, before the clock ran out. When time expired, the US military, much like the US civilian leadership, simply moved on.

Hitting the Wall: Iraqi Institutional Failings

Iraq was still a divided country. It remained fragmented among Shiites to the south, Sunnis to the west, and Kurds to the north, with a large zone of contention along the fault lines of the rival communities and a sovereign Iraqi government that remained suspicious and loath to compromise.[83] US officials chose to work sometimes with, sometimes around, the Iraqi police units, military forces, and governing institutions that they themselves had helped to create. They employed leverage to bridge divides, encourage reforms, and impede partisan encroachments, but in the end chose to accept Iraq with its deficiencies.

Politics

Under Prime Minister al-Maliki, Iraqi governance became increasingly hierarchic. He had come to power in 2006, at the height of Iraq's civil war. He sought to extend his power as US forces were battling insurgents with the surge and to consolidate his hold thereafter. He tightened his grip over governing institutions, including the Integrity Commission, which investigates government corruption, and the judiciary, which he relied on for favorable rulings to deflect legislative and electoral challenges. He capitalized on the de-Baathification commission's efforts to strip his opponents of power and employed the resources of the state to reward loyalists with positions throughout government.

To take direct control of national security institutions, he devised a parallel power structure in 2007, concentrating military command responsibilities within the Office of the Commander in Chief, which he had created outside the constitution. He used his position to select and retain politically loyal commanders, bypass the formal military command, work through provincial-level commands that he had established and staffed throughout the country, and direct security forces that he placed under the command of his office.[84] These units included thousands of elite Iraqi special forces in two brigades (under the immediate control of the Counter-Terrorism Bureau), an intelligence unit (the Office of Information and Security), two army brigades (including the Baghdad Brigade, which protected the Green Zone in the capital), and two presidential brigades (which operated as an executive guard force).[85] Al-Maliki relied on the Baghdad Brigade, like the other forces at his disposal, to conduct special missions, including the arrest of political opponents, *outside* of Baghdad. Likewise, he employed the provincial-level commands—funded and supported by the US military to improve command, control, and coordination of Iraqi security forces in the field (ICG 2010a: 7; Sullivan 2013)—to engage in operations including those targeting dissent (Sullivan 2013). When Maliki retained the position of prime minister after a controversial 2010 election in which hundreds of Sunnis candidates were banned (as Baathists), he also claimed the portfolios of defense minister, interior minister, and minister of state for national security to extend his formal grip.

Al-Maliki was not hesitant to use his growing capabilities to serve his political agenda. It took strong US resistance—drawing from an active US presence—to counter his efforts. During the surge, General Petraeus deflected al-Maliki's attempts to circumvent the formal chain of command, to keep US troops away from Shiite militia tied somehow to the ruling government, and to appoint less-than-competent loyalists to key military posts. Indeed, Petraeus answered al-Maliki's appointments—sometimes over successive iterations—with threats to withhold US support to Iraqi commands entrusted by al-Maliki to his loyalists.[86]

Once firmly in power, al-Maliki bypassed the formal chain of command to pursue sectarian policies. By 2009 his forces were arresting Awakening leaders and newly elected provincial council members (ICB 2010: 15), as his government more generally targeted members of the Sunni community. In 2010 a secret prison under al-Maliki's control was discovered that housed, under deplorable conditions, hundreds of Sunnis, many apparently tortured (by members of the Baghdad Brigade).[87] In the same year the Interior Ministry issued an ultimatum to hundreds of Sunnis that the United States had pulled from the Awakening movement to hold police positions in Anbar province: quit or accept a demotion.[88] Al-Maliki's government also fired hundreds of intelligence officers—mostly Sunnis—from their positions and replaced experienced officers with inexperienced party loyalists.[89] The effects were broadly felt. With the loss of Sunni intelligence officers and their capability to identify and locate terrorist suspects among the Sunni populous, the Iraqi military turned its US-supplied counterterror equipment and tactics against Sunnis: the new targets were those of military age, supposed friends and relatives of "terrorists," and tribal leaders.[90] The eventual US exodus from Iraq only worsened the Sunnis' plight.[91]

Of course al-Maliki might never have been able to satisfy Sunni demands or ameliorate growing Sunni discontent. Sunni groups—some Baathist remnants—

organized against him, capitalized on his missteps, and viewed all actions by the Baghdad government as stemming from its ties to Shiite interests. Yet al-Maliki treated Shiite officials with dark connections and pasts differently than he did Sunnis with suspect backgrounds; and he never seriously tried to assuage dissent or build an Iraq that was mindful of the interests and concerns of the Sunni minority.[92]

Thus, the good news was that Iraq had achieved some stability; violence was down and Prime Minister al-Maliki had managed to hold his position longer than his predecessors had. The bad news was that he was increasingly strong *and* nonconciliatory. Alleging a Baathist threat, he distanced his government from the Awakening movement, resisted calls to incorporate the Sons of Iraq into Iraqi security forces, worked within and outside the Iraqi Constitution to consolidate his institutional power,[93] centralized his control over Iraqi security forces, sought loyalty and sectarian ties over competence in staffing, and allied with influential Shiite politicians (including Chalabi) to undercut Sunni representation in elected and governmental positions. Unfortunately, Sunnis were left to believe that their future lay in fighting, not joining, the government. US officials, in turn, were left to contemplate their own absence of leverage to thwart al-Maliki's ambitions: "Likeminded leaders were too weak to push the US agenda, and the rest were too strong for the US to challenge given the absence of useful leadership alternatives" (Lebovic 2010: 172–173). US influence for bridging divides and bringing about reforms inevitably waned as Iraqi security forces acquired operational autonomy and US troops assumed a lower (and narrower) profile throughout the country. With a diminished profile, US forces could not influence events or even know when and where such influence was required.

Economics

The United States provided billions of dollars and tapped Iraqi and international funding to assist Iraqi reconstruction and development. The Iraqi beneficiaries were large and small. Considerable sums were invested, for example, in rebuilding Iraq's dilapidated petroleum, power, sanitation, and water infrastructure; building civil society; promoting local governance; and assisting small businesses. The US military had contributed to this effort even when it meant working outside the military's traditional areas of competence. It fixed power plants, built schools, and engaged in "tasks well beyond the usual military reconstruction tasks, such as establishing city councils, justice procedures, and local budgets and spending priorities" (Bensahel 2006: 465). Even with the surge, however, the US government simply lacked the capacity to organize, coordinate, and manage the full set of civilian and military programs that proliferated within Iraq. The ongoing challenges included (a) the profusion of funding agencies and contractors, which impeded centralized planning and control; (b) deficient checks on financial expenditures and quality of workmanship; (c) cost inflation, corrupt networks, and patronage systems, owing to the free flow of money into the Iraqi economy; (d) a preference for "large, over-ambitious projects that would take years to complete" (Mansoor 2013: 11); (e) the lack of local "buy-in" that feeds long-term project success; and (f) the inexperience, diverging priorities, turnover, and uneven integrity of individuals involved in assistance, reconstruction, and development (see, e.g., Bowen 2009: 295–319).

Put simply, the US government could not expect to build the Iraqi nation under the best of circumstances, much less under the worst that Iraq seemed to offer. Iraq stood near the very top of global rankings in corruption[94] and toward the bottom in rankings in rule of law, regulatory quality, and political stability.[95] Even with its oil revenues, Iraq remained economically challenged, because these rankings serve as bellwethers for foreign investment and economic growth.

Security

Government institutions—as instruments of power and sources of largess—cannot survive untainted in a corrupting environment. The Iraqi police and military were not exceptions to the rule.

Despite purges and reform efforts, sectarianism and corruption continued to undercut the professionalism of Iraqi governing institutions, including the Iraqi police under the control of the Interior Ministry.[96] A 2007 congressionally authorized investigatory commission—the Independent Commission on the Security Forces of Iraq, or Jones Commission (Jones 2007)—concluded that Iraq's vast Interior Ministry force was sectarian and corrupt to its core. The National Police still committed acts of violence against the Sunni population (Perito 2011)—targeting Sunnis in Baghdad, even with the surge—which forced the US military to ban them from certain neighborhoods and limit them to joint operations with US troops (Gordon and Trainor 2012: 340).

Within the Interior Ministry, as throughout the Iraqi government, sectarianism and corruption remained severe—indeed, interdependent—problems. Political loyalty shielded corrupt individuals (sometimes through the direct intervention of the prime minister's office),[97] and sectarians used the corrupt, from top officials down to the local policeman who was bribed to "look the other way." Inspectors general tasked with investigating corruption were outmatched, unable to prosecute cases because of a weak and overburdened Iraqi judicial system and fearful for their lives, especially, it seems, when investigating personnel within the Interior Ministry.[98] Professionals were purged for their professionalism (Robinson 2008: 336);[99] investigations were stymied; and correctives became part of the problem. Investigators themselves became targets of bogus corruption charges, aimed at neutralizing investigations.[100] Shiite militia continued to operate through the Interior Ministry, and graft and thievery continued to claim ministry resources (Perito 2008b).

The burden of addressing major security threats, however, fell largely on Iraqi military forces. Their military performance improved with time. By the end of 2008, the Iraqi army was hundreds of thousands strong. It operated now under more professional command, teamed with US forces while taking most of the casualties, and maintained stability in previously violent regions of the country (on the force improvements, see Biddle et al. 2008; Dubik 2009). With the pullback of US forces from Iraqi cities in June 2009, the Iraqi army was establishing some competency as a counterinsurgency force. Yet the military continued to suffer the maladies of Iraqi politics and society. Commands and resources were distributed to reward friends, keep political enemies at bay, and safeguard the regime from coup attempts. Corruption continued to drain resources, create security breaches, place the venal and incompetent in ("purchased") positions of responsibility, damage performance through substandard equipment procurement, and hinder the efficient disbursement of resources out of fear of theft (Cordesman and Khazai 2014: 232; ICG 2010a: 31–32). Sectarianism and political loyalty still drove out professionalism—in staff purges and discrimination—and conspired with corrupt officials in a protective huddle. Consequently, investigations of misdeeds were quashed, the wrong people were punished, and being the best and the brightest was too often a professional liability.

The United States had sought to build a traditional army for Iraq to defend against external, not internal, threats.[101] It remained critically dependent on US air support, logistical capability, intelligence, training, and a full spectrum of support functions, from maintaining supply stocks and ensuring delivery to equipment maintenance and repair. The Iraqi army had not cohered as a fighting force. Nor could it, given the enormous social, economic, and governmental impediments in the country.[102] Signs of distress remained visible. In early 2008 the US military had to rescue Iraqi security forces after al-Maliki attacked Sadrist militia in Basra (against the advice of US commanders). In 2009 high-casualty bombings around Baghdad—targeting embassies and various government ministries and installations—impugned the integrity and capability of Iraqi forces simply to staff checkpoints; suspicions were rampant that holes in security were not due to simple negligence or incompetence.[103] In the final analysis, the US military simply lacked the necessary access, information, and influence to impose its will or overcome political, cultural, and organizational impediments, as required to build an effective, professionalized Iraqi security force.

A Final Resolution: Accepting Iraq's Dangerously Precarious Future

The passage of time would only prove corrosive. Absent a strong professional ethos and requisite supportive structures, institutions fall into decay when time breeds complacency, indifference, and neglect. The personnel who guide and staff these institutions come and go and often stagnate in place; good practices that are not deeply imbedded, scrupulously maintained, and consistently observed do not survive; and divisions of labor that allow complex institutions to function efficiently come to impede performance by fostering redundancies, lapses in coverage and communication, and poor coordination of effort. In consequence, institutions that were difficult to create prove easy to destroy.

In 2014 the Iraqi military unceremoniously collapsed when fighting the lesser-armed, numerically inferior, but highly motivated fighters of the Islamic State of Iraq and Syria (ISIS). ISIS fighters built on their territorial gains in Syria, drawing recruits from within and outside Iraq, to capture much of the western and northern parts of Iraq—a third of the country—and threaten Baghdad and the Kurdish provinces. The Iraqi army crumbled in battle from the top down, as Iraqi commanders fled in advance of their troops, leaving hundreds of millions of dollars in US military equipment—armored vehicles, guns, and ammunition—to the insurgents. Even Lieutenant General Michael D. Barbero, who had led the US military's transition effort (training, organizing, developing, and equipping Iraqi security forces) in the years preceding the US withdrawal, observed disparagingly after the rout that the Iraqi military was still a "checkpoint Army." Despite a huge US investment in Iraq's military infrastructure, Iraqi commanders favored cell phones to coordinate military operations over US-constructed high-tech command and control centers and allowed training centers to fall into disuse; in Barbero's words, "our Army continuously trains; that wasn't in their DNA."[104] The 400,000-strong army that the United States helped build, at a cost of over $25 billion, had atrophied through corruption, dissipation, and neglect to around half its original size—even before the Islamic State offensive.

After the initial fighting in the summer of 2014, Iraq's active combat force stood at eighty-five thousand troops.[105] By the first month of 2015, the Iraqi army had fallen in size to a force of forty-eight thousand troops, eclipsed now in the fighting by numerically superior, well-motivated Shiite militias. The militia groups included the Badr organization and Asaib Ahl al-Haq, the very groups that the United States had sought, only a few years earlier, to contain or neutralize to forestall Iraq's descent into all-out conflict.[106] Unfortunately the militias returned to their old ways, using mass killing, torture, forced detention, and assassination in areas of the country, including the capital, under their control. For the January 2013–October 2015 period, the United Nations reported a grisly toll: around nineteen thousand civilians killed, thirty-six thousand civilians wounded, and over a million people internally displaced from sectarian fighting in the country.[107]

The collapse of the Iraqi army ultimately exposed the limits of foreign-led institution-building. Prime Minister al-Maliki was gone (for now), but not his partisan legacy or the circles of influence, security fears, and practices that benefited Shiite groups. Under the new leadership of Prime Minister Haider al-Abadi, Shiite militia leaders assumed command of Iraq army units. Iraq's deputy national security adviser, who was a top Iraqi commander in Iran's Revolutionary Guards Corp, was appointed to coordinate Shiite militia activities in Iraq.[108] In 2016 the "popular mobilization units"—militia units, now 100,000 strong—became a formal part of Iraq's security structure (answering nominally to the prime minister).[109] Consequently, the fragile future of inclusive Iraqi governance hinged, again, on the restraint of Iraq's majority.

US leaders had lost their taste for devoting significant US political and material resources in Iraq to exert a restraining influence or push for progressive changes. When the Obama administration was pressed by events to return US forces to Iraq, it did so in pursuit of finite goals (to defeat ISIS), in short-term assistance for a sovereign nation whose problems had worsened considerably with the US departure. A decline in oil prices, a deteriorating security environment, and the need to rebuild what violence had destroyed only added to Iraq's economic woes.[110]

Despite the rather abrupt US departure, the beginning—not the end—of the war is the biggest part of the story. In choosing to rebuild Iraq on the fly, the US government locked itself in an uphill battle against stiff political, societal, and cultural resistance. Whether better preparation would have produced better results remains unclear. A large and visible US presence might have made US forces an easy target for Iraqi dissent. A less draconian de-Baathification policy might have guaranteed a stalemated government that would eventually implode. The retention of the Iraqi military, in turn, might have left it open to the corrupt and sectarian influences that pervaded the Interior Ministry. In other words, a US invasion, short of minimalist objectives, would likely have placed the United States back in the middle of an expensive, perilous occupation. The US mission would have remained at risk as long as its success hinged on the finite willingness and ability of Iraq's new leaders to bridge political differences, forge compromises to broaden participation in government, form a stable government, and overcome the significant failings of Iraqi society.

Conclusions

In December 2004 Defense Secretary Rumsfeld famously quipped, "You go to war with the Army you have. They're not the Army you might want or wish to have at a later time."[111] He was responding to visible dissension in the ranks about the practice of sending US troops into battle without necessary equipment and armor. His comment said much— more than he intended—about the US approach to the conflict. The United States had gone to war with the army that it had *and* a plan that played to its peculiar comparative advantages. US plans and capabilities, however, proved to have blinding deficiencies.

Stage I, Engagement: Fixation

Administration officials allowed their primary goal—bringing down Saddam Hussein's regime—to subsume or crowd out all other goals. Administration officials offered various explanations for why the Iraqi regime had to go but spent no time reconciling their differences; getting rid of Saddam Hussein appeared to offer something for everyone. They acted as if the single policy on which they all agreed—a quick takedown of the Iraqi government—would serve various beneficial purposes, when in fact the opposite was true.

Resolving these differences in viewpoint would have usefully placed the focus on the aftermath of a US occupation. Absent that focus, the US government was left woefully unprepared to address political, economic, and military challenges in Iraq once the regime fell. In preparing militarily for a war *with Iraq*, administration officials put too little emphasis on a potential war *in Iraq* to follow. It assumed, instead, that security challenges would end with the fall of Baghdad. Preparatory deficiencies registered in the administration's failure to plan promptly and deliberately, for the US occupation; provide strong and consistent direction to such efforts; recognize a need for dedicated and coherent support within the US government to anticipate and address post-occupational challenges; draw lessons in planning from prior Cold War and post–Cold War operations; acknowledge that occupation, like other military operations, requires a plan; and accept that giving civilian responsibilities to a military department will likely reduce their operational profile.

In short, absent clear and emphatic direction from civilian leaders, the military did what it does—fight wars—and left other tasks for the future, and for others to accomplish. As a result, no well-funded and staffed organization in government could pick up the slack; top US officials failed to assign clear organizational roles and responsibilities; and across the government, officials, agencies, and departments resisted cooperation with other officials, agencies, and departments. The twist to this familiar story of bureaucratic politics and organizational dynamics is the wholesale indifference, at the highest levels of government, to "what comes next," the follow-on phase that would determine the success of US war policies.

Stage II, Extension: Disjunction

With the fall of Saddam Hussein, US civilian leaders expanded the US mission in Iraq. In practice, however, the mission was reduced to a haphazard, poorly resourced, and disjointed effort that failed to keep pace with political, economic, and security challenges in the country. US civilian leaders assumed they could do all things in Iraq, remaking the country and its government in the US image. Such thinking proved fancifully far removed from what the US government could realistically accomplish.

Through their consequences, early US decisions—including those to assume control of Iraqi governance, postpone elections, appoint expatriate Shiites to the

Iraqi Governing Council, engage in a far-reaching de-Baathification program, keep the Interior Ministry intact, and dismantle the Iraqi military—severely taxed US organizational, financial, human, material, and intellectual resources. US leaders assumed, however, that all was on course. They thus failed to realize how deeply they must cut to remove the vestiges of Saddam Hussein from Iraqi governance; examine the political and social consequences of excising Baathists from government positions or dismantling the Iraqi military; reconsider plans for Iraqi self-rule in light of popular pressures in Iraq; or scale US ambitions to transform Iraq to available time, personnel, and resources.

American civilian leaders looked to the US military to address the most pressing challenge, establishing security in the country, while dismissing the growing threat from the insurgency. US forces were neither trained, equipped, staffed, nor predisposed to deal with the country's lawlessness and violence, stem the rise of sectarian fighting, or quash resistance to the US occupation. The military had prepared diligently for Phase III of the war effort, leaving Phase IV for the future. Now, caught in the twilight between phases, it confronted a growing militia threat and insurgency by falling back on what it knew, taking the battle to the militia and insurgents without the capacity to hold ground to prevent their return once US forces had departed. All the while, the US military struggled to build an Iraqi security force that could take control of the effort. Its attempts to dampen violent dissent appeared only to inflame Sunni opposition. Its efforts to build up Iraqi security forces, in turn, compromised force competency and professionalism. Indeed, it empowered a sectarian police force that would turn on rival communities.

Stage III, Limitation: Constriction

In 2007 the Bush administration changed course in Iraq with a troop surge and counterinsurgency strategy. Yet the "strategy" amounted to less than might appear. The administration settled on a modest strategy, aided by a relatively small, short-term increase in US troop levels. That the decision was designed to serve the less costly option is found in evidence that surge proponents bet on the success of a US military force built up slightly, and then slowly, over many months; opted for a troop increase, unable to assess the likely impact of the Awakening movement, a key ingredient of the surge's success; committed to deployment plans absent a fully developed strategy; and drew from counterinsurgency principles that poorly fit Iraqi circumstances in key respects.

Stage IV, Disengagement: Extrication

The Bush administration sought to safeguard security gains in Iraq by staying the course, capitalizing on the surge's success and the growing self-reliance of Iraqi forces. By contrast, the Obama administration sought to reduce US involvement in Iraq. The administration had tired of the war; was reluctantly accepting a residual

US presence in Iraq; and was unwilling to concede much, if anything, to the Iraqi government to get a deal. For the Obama administration, the overarching goal was to "get the numbers down," a White House directive that oddly mimicked the prewar injunction to the Rumsfeld-led Defense Department. The administration was unwilling to maintain US troops at higher levels in Iraq, which could well have given the Iraqi government an incentive to soften its terms, or to accept the terms (covering judicial authority over US troops) that it willingly accepted years later when US troops were reintroduced into Iraq. Through its negotiating terms, then, the Obama administration expressed its desire to exit the conflict.

With the clock running out, the US mission effectively ended. Once it became clear, toward the end of 2011, that US combat forces would leave Iraq as scheduled, the US military plan for Iraq amounted finally to an orderly retreat. US civilian operations soon followed.

4

The Afghanistan War, 2001–?

The war in Afghanistan stands apart from other US conflicts of the post–World War II years. It remains the longest US war of the period; in fact, it is the longest war in American history. But it deserves analysis for another reason.

Policy makers believed that prosecuting the war in Afghanistan was vital to US national security interests, yet nevertheless succumbed to the four stages of decisional bias that had afflicted US policy in Vietnam and Iraq. The Bush administration committed early to a US-imposed military solution without duly assessing the implications of a Taliban defeat or how US goals in Afghanistan might serve the administration's "global war on terrorism" (*fixation*). Once engaged, the administration defined the US mission in Afghanistan broadly to include military training, stabilization, and development, by intention and by default, and it remained detached from harsh realities that impeded the realization of these goals (*disjunction*). The Obama administration soon capped US involvement in Afghanistan. By increasing US force levels in country—modestly and temporarily—it pursued only the limited goal of "reversing" the Taliban's momentum (*constriction*). Then it planned a troop exit from Afghanistan, despite the ongoing violence and instability there. The president stuck to his plan, slowing, but not reversing, the withdrawal as security conditions worsened in the country (*extrication*).

Backdrop to the War

The US war in Afghanistan had its origins in the fight by Islamic groups (the mujahideen) against Soviet forces. The Soviets had entered Afghanistan in December 1979 to quell the rebellion threatening the country's Communist leadership. The Soviet military employed force brutally in major offensives. It inflicted many hundreds of thousands, perhaps more than a million, Afghan fatalities and caused many more Afghans to flee to safer ground.

US policy makers were not content to watch these developments from the sidelines. Perceiving a Soviet threat to US regional (if not global) interests, the Jimmy Carter administration—which in 1977 had cut aid to Pakistan over concerns about its nuclear program, autocratic turns, and rights abuses—abruptly changed course. It now sought to aid Pakistan directly[1] and to use it as a conduit for assisting the anti-Soviet efforts in Afghanistan. Through Pakistan, the administration first provided non-lethal aid to the Afghan rebels; then, in December 1979, the president authorized the CIA to arm the mujahideen to teach the Soviets a lesson (Coll 2004: 58). The Ronald Reagan administration doubled down on its predecessor's policies. It increased US aid to the insurgents, joining with key allies (including Great Britain and Saudi Arabia) to press the Soviets to withdraw. It also tightened the US embrace of neighboring Pakistan, which had rejected Carter's offer of hundreds of millions of dollars in aid ("peanuts" in the Pakistani president's view).[2] Pakistan was "rewarded with a $3.2 billion proposal from the Reagan administration plus permission to buy F-16 fighter jets, previously available only to NATO [the North Atlantic Treaty Organization] allies and Japan" (Coll 2004: 62). Like its predecessor, the Reagan administration failed to look beyond the immediate problem to envision how boosting the insurgency might influence the trajectory of Afghanistan's future governance, affect stability and competition within the region, or eventually blow back to endanger US security.

The Reagan administration channeled hundreds of millions of dollars in US aid annually to the insurgents, along with a generous supply of arms. These weapons eventually included state-of-the-art, shoulder-fired (Stinger) antiaircraft missiles (Ballard et al. 2012: 16–17). Their introduction into the war provoked dissent within the administration, not because of concerns about insurgent ideology, but rather about the global political and military consequences of supplying the missiles. The CIA feared blowing its covert operation's cover by supplying weapons that had obvious US origins. Indeed, the United States was then paying for arms supplied *by other countries* to keep US involvement a secret. The CIA feared as well that the Soviets would retaliate by escalating their involvement in Afghanistan, attacking Pakistan, or supplying antiaircraft missiles to rebels in Central America (Kuperman 1999: 223–224). The US JCS feared that releasing Stingers to Pakistan or the insurgents would deplete the US arms stockpile; create new threats should the weapons flow to radical states or terrorist groups (who could use the missiles to shoot down commercial aircraft); and reduce the US military edge, in particular, for fighting in Europe. Should the Soviets acquire the missiles or experience in defeating them, they could then develop effective technological or operational countermeasures (Kuperman 1999: 230–232).

Simply put, Reagan-era civilian and military officials voiced reasons to limit support to the Afghan insurgents; a potential mujahideen threat to US interests, however, was not among them. Strong evidence in this regard is that US aid to the insurgents also included direct and indirect support for Islamic radicalism. USAID, for example, funded the publication of millions of textbooks for Afghan schools that celebrated violent resistance and Islamic militancy (indeed, Afghanistan retained the books under Taliban rule).[3] More significantly, the United States granted Pakistan effective control over the distribution and employment of US military resources when its government insisted that it alone channel US aid to the Afghan guerrillas (Coll 2004: 63–64). The result was to empower Pakistan's primary military intelligence organization, the Inter-Services Intelligence (ISI) directorate, which would back the mujahideen resistance but also the Taliban's eventual seizure of the country (Jones 2013: 18). The motives and activities of the ISI, for one, subsequently raised concerns in the George W. Bush administration about the duplicity of the Pakistani government, an ostensible US ally in the global war on terrorism.

With covert US support, the Afghan insurgents did what insurgents do: they avoided direct military encounters, operated in small groups, imposed what costs they could on Soviet troops, accepted casualties, and ultimately outlasted the foreign occupation. In 1987 Soviet president Mikhail Gorbachev announced that Soviet troops would start withdrawing from Afghanistan. With the departure of the last of its soldiers in early 1989, the Soviet Union left behind a country wracked by death and destruction, impoverished by any standards, and locked in a seemingly perpetual state of war.

The Soviet exodus created new threats and opportunities for rival insurgent groups; they had fought Soviet troops but not as a coherent, united fighting force. Mullah Mohammed Omar, the eventual leader of the Taliban and government of Afghanistan, emerged from the anti-Soviet resistance—as a fighter for a CIA-favored commander, no less[4]—to become a potent political and military force in the country. He built his militia, in his home base of Kandahar, by channeling grievances and religious zeal within the large Pashtun community on both sides of the Pakistani border.[5] The Taliban seized control of Kandahar, attracting a bounty of fresh recruits, and then gained control of surrounding provinces by pummeling, coercing, co-opting, or simply buying off the opposition. Within two years of its emergence in 1994, the Taliban controlled twenty-two of the thirty-four provinces in Afghanistan, including Kabul, the capital (CNA 2014: 50–51). A complete Taliban victory was thwarted, however, by rival warlords (Tajiks, Uzbeks, and Hazara), who maintained fiefdoms in the northern portion (constituting 10 percent) of the country.

The Taliban's rigid Islamist practices and restrictions sparked international condemnation, but its embrace of al-Qaeda (as a non-Afghan ideological and military partner) made Afghanistan a priority US security issue. During the Clinton administration, the Taliban leadership placed Afghanistan in the crosshairs of successive UN Security Council resolutions—and a 1998 US cruise-missile strike—by giving al-Qaeda leader Osama bin Laden a safe haven and allowing him to use Afghanistan as a base for recruiting, training, and planning attacks on US interests. After September 11, 2001 (9/11), the tight relationship between al-Qaeda and the Taliban was the latter's undoing.

Stage I, Engagement: Fixation

The Bush administration prepared for war within days of the 9/11 al-Qaeda terror attacks on the World Trade Center in New York and the Pentagon, outside Washington, D.C. The administration pursued a novel strategy, little aided by pre-existing plans, target sets, country knowledge, or indigenous intelligence assets. Innovativeness paid off—sooner than expected—when US-led forces drove the Taliban from power and al-Qaeda from Afghanistan. The success of Operation Enduring Freedom (OEF), which began on October 7, 2001, nevertheless proved short-lived, given the limited US war planning. It had centered on the immediate goal of driving the Taliban out of power, not on future governance and stability in Afghanistan or the conflict's ongoing demands on US resources once the Taliban government fell. That a US intervention force, devised intentionally to avoid the stigma of a foreign occupation army, would nonetheless find itself challenged over the years that followed by a Taliban-led insurgency was not a prospect worth much high-level discussion. As an official US army history conceded, "What would come after that victory never really came into clear focus" (Wright et al. 2010: 61). The "end of the war," however, was only the end of the beginning.

The Decisional Context

The deadly al-Qaeda attacks made war *almost* inevitable. President Bush later claimed that he knew from the moment the second plane struck the South Tower of the World Trade Center that the United States was at war.[6] Indeed, within days of the attack, Bush had authorized the call-up of tens of thousands of reservists; US strategic bombers were preparing for a long-distance bombing campaign; and US supplies, carrier groups, and bombers were pre-positioning closer to the combat zone (Ballard et al. 2012: 37). Comparisons were soon drawn between the 9/11 attacks—surprise, costly, unprovoked—and the attack, sixty years earlier, by Japan on the US Pacific Fleet at Pearl Harbor.[7] Like December 7, 1941, September 11, 2001, became a moment of "infamy." The symbolic floodgates opened. The kamikaze pilots of World War II became the aircraft-borne terrorists of 9/11, the ground zero of Hiroshima and Nagasaki became the ground zero of the World Trade Center, the World War II Axis alliance became the "axis of evil," the Munich appeasement became a failure to stand up to terrorists, and so forth.[8] US leaders, no less than the American public, were impressed by the similarities: Bush himself alluded to Pearl Harbor in his personal diary entry on the day of the attack.[9] The implication was clear: having failed, as before, to rise to a challenge, the United States now had to right a wrong—indeed, to eradicate an evil.

Mainstream opinion offered few dissenting voices to the call to arms. This was not the lead-up to the Iraq War, when the president had to make a case for war at home and abroad (with Secretary of State Colin Powell appearing before the UN Security Council), nor the prelude to full-scale US intervention in Vietnam, when the president kept growing US war preparations from the public to avoid resistance. The facts seemed unassailable to all: al-Qaeda had repeatedly attacked US interests abroad, at the cost of hundreds of lives, and had just killed thousands of Americans on US soil. It had thus exposed its will and capability to commit unspeakable crimes against US citizens. US security personnel now stood on high alert to protect large gatherings, transportation hubs, national monuments, critical buildings, and entire cities. Worried Americans spread rumors, avoided shopping malls, and spurned air travel, fearing that they, too, would become terrorist victims.

On September 14, 2001, the US Congress passed (through a joint resolution) the Authorization for Use of Military Force against Terrorists. Signed four days later by the president, it authorized the president to take action "against those responsible for the recent attacks launched against the United States." It amounted to a declaration of war that would give legislative cover to a war in Afghanistan and an open-ended, legal basis for Bush and his successor, Obama, to target terror groups around the world.

The Bush administration had every reason to discount the effectiveness of lesser military action. The Clinton administration had hit al-Qaeda training sites in Afghanistan with cruise missiles; the missiles arrived hours after bin Laden, his operatives, and members of other terror groups had met there.[10] The president, in his own words, did not want to "pound sand with millions of dollars in weapons" for the sake of doing something and believed, much like his secretary of defense, Donald Rumsfeld, that Clinton's ineffectual response had only emboldened the enemy.[11] Pulling a response from the Clinton playbook would likely produce no better result. Al-Qaeda and the Taliban were apparently evacuating their bases and camps, anticipating a US airstrike.[12] Limited strikes on Afghanistan's primitive infrastructure was not a promising alternative. Rumsfeld, for one, believed that the Taliban government was unlikely to yield to US attacks on the country's electric power grid or ministry buildings.[13]

The Bush administration thus had strong justification for going to war, especially once the Afghan government proved unwilling to compromise. The president outlined US demands in a speech before a September 20, 2001, joint session of Congress. There, he insisted that the Taliban "deliver to United States authorities all of the leaders of Al Qaeda who hide in your land," "close immediately and permanently every terrorist training camp in Afghanistan," and "hand over every terrorist and every person and their support structure to appropriate authorities."[14] Not surprisingly, Taliban leaders remained defiant: the Taliban was implacably hostile to the West, willing to accept isolation over global engagement, tightly linked to the al-Qaeda leadership, dependent on al-Qaeda as a professionalized security force, and quite unlikely under any conditions to break with the group. Moreover, the administration—with its strong, firm, and open-ended demands, stated publicly no less—did not make it easy for the Taliban to shed its resistance.[15] Mullah Omar had initially denied bin Laden's involvement in the attacks. After meetings with a high-level Pakistani military delegation, including members of the ISI, the position of the Taliban changed only slightly; among its new demands,[16] it insisted on documentary proof of bin Laden's involvement, judged by a tribunal of Islamic legal scholars, before it would hand him over.[17] Taliban leaders subsequently claimed ignorance of bin Laden's whereabouts; according to them, he had "gone missing."[18]

The administration's case for war appears less compelling, however, in light of what we know from early deliberations of Bush's war cabinet. Composed of national security principals, it included the president, vice president, secretary of defense, secretary of state, national security adviser, and CIA director. Disclosures from these discussions support claims that the administration was inattentive from the start to the challenges of fighting and winning in Afghanistan. The discussions reveal multiple signs of (non-rational) mission-based thinking.

First, the administration gave little thought to the implications of regime change for the future stability of Afghanistan or its neighbors. Yes, the administration appreciated that deposing the Taliban invited some costs and risks. After all, it demonstrated *some* initial reluctance to take on the Taliban. Despite Bush's early vow to punish terrorists and those who "harbor" them alike,[19] the administration did try to leverage a split between the Taliban and al-Qaeda, hoping (albeit without much optimism) that the Afghan government would surrender the terror group's leaders.[20] In addition, participants expressed some misgivings about US military action in Afghanistan. For example, Vice President Cheney and National Security Advisor Rice voiced concerns that potential instability might spread to Pakistan;[21] Rice also acknowledged the danger of the United States becoming entrapped in Afghanistan, much as Britain and the Soviet Union once had.[22] Still, decisional participants treated these concerns as potential reasons to strike some other country, for an easier win,[23] not as reasons to explore—and address—the potential complications of an Afghan operation.

An all-important question would arise *with time*. A full month after the 9/11 attacks, with the start of US military operations, Bush supposedly asked the principals, "Who will run the country?" At *that point*, Rice apparently "*was beginning* to understand that that was the critical question [emphasis added]" (Woodward 2002: 195). The focus in the early discussions had been on taking down states because they presumably *fall* easily. For example, Cheney observed, "It's easier to find them than it is to find bin Laden."[24] Likewise, Defense Secretary Rumsfeld noted that terrorists "don't have armies and navies and air forces that one can go battle against. They don't have capital cities with high-value assets that they're reluctant to lose."[25] Yet no one was seriously asking, "What happens when states *break*?" The principals failed, then, to grasp an opposing reality: state targeting might distract attention and draw critical resources from the fight against terrorism. For one thing, the unseating of a "terror-supporting" government might spark an insurgency that would impede

US efforts to battle terrorists on other international fronts. Administration officials had good reason, then, to fear that any such war would become a quagmire, but it nevertheless downplayed or ignored them.

Some insights into Rumsfeld's thinking emerge from a memo he wrote on October 16, 2001, to Douglas Feith, undersecretary of defense for policy, with copies requested for other national security principals. The memo made the destruction of al-Qaeda and the Taliban the clear priority. In Rumsfeld's view, considerations of governance in a post-Taliban Afghanistan should not determine the progress of the war; the United States "should not agonize over post-Taliban arrangements to the point that it delays success over Al Qaida and the Taliban." Moreover, the United States should head for the exit with the accomplishing of that goal: "The U.S. should not commit to any post-Taliban military involvement since the U.S. will be heavily engaged in the anti-terrorism effort worldwide."[26] In Rumsfeld's defense, the destruction of the Taliban and al-Qaeda was just that: with their demise, the United States would have little reason to dawdle in Afghanistan, with US military forces needed elsewhere. Yet why would Rumsfeld assume that the complete destruction of the Taliban was in the offing, or that the "destruction" of the Taliban would preclude its return? He disregarded or downplayed those possibilities because he had two apparent priorities in Afghanistan: (a) vanquishing the adversary and (b) not getting stuck. Once the US military was engaged, he wanted to move quickly to destroy the enemy, then leave.

Indeed, the second of these priorities loomed heavily in Rumsfeld's thinking. In an earlier memo to the president (dated September 30), Rumsfeld had expressed his desire to avoid bold, precipitous action. He proposed instead that the United States opt for a slow buildup of forces, aid to indigenous opposition groups, selective leadership targeting, and a reduced US profile to avoid antagonizing Muslim populations. To quote Rumsfeld, "It would instead be surprising and impressive if we built our forces up patiently, took some early action outside of Afghanistan, perhaps in multiple locations, and began not exclusively or primarily with military strikes but with equip-and-train activities with local opposition forces coupled with humanitarian aid and intense information operations."[27]

Second, the principals defined the adversary expansively—indeed, indiscriminately. Envisioning the enemy in global terms, it had to see any long-term strategy for Afghanistan as an encumbrance. In the president's view, as articulated in his September 20 speech, the United States was now engaged in a war against *global terrorism*: "Our war on terror begins with Al Qaeda, but it does not end there. It will not end until every terrorist group of global reach has been found, stopped and defeated." Indeed, the president rejected a less grandiose draft statement from his National Security Council Deputies Committee[28] that limited the US war effort to groups that threatened "our way of life."[29] In doing so, Bush defined the terrorist enemy implicitly by its tactics and capabilities, not its goals or grievances. The war that Bush outlined took inadequate account of the enormity of the task; its counterproductiveness, should it spread or galvanize opposition to the West; and the support that it would render to oppressive governments that could then cloak their brutality against dissidents and separatists in the rhetoric and symbolism of Bush's global fight.

Beyond this, Bush gave state supporters of terrorism standing equal to terrorists in the US global campaign, with little regard to their levels of culpability or threat to US interests. A war with Iraq loomed ominously in the discussions. True, Bush and his advisers gave priority to targeting al-Qaeda *in Afghanistan*; they acknowledged that with a US focus on other priorities, public support would dwindle, the US effort might lose focus, and the global coalition might crumble. Indeed, Secretary of State Powell and JCS chair Henry Shelton were among those who, in early deliberations,[30] challenged Paul Wolfowitz's case for invading Iraq in response to the 9/11 attacks.[31] Opinion coalesced eventually around forgoing an attack on Iraq;[32] in Powell's view, going after Saddam Hussein would "'wreck' the coalition."[33] Yet the challenge only kicked the issue into the future. Bush ended the Iraq-first discussion by giving his blessing to war planning for an eventual war with Iraq.[34] He and his advisers viewed the 9/11 attacks—unanimously, it seems—as requiring an ever-expanding mission against a broadly defined adversary.[35]

Third, the administration was unjustifiably optimistic that (in Afghanistan and elsewhere) other states would yield to US preferences in the war on terror. Administration officials took note of the unprecedented outpouring of international sympathy and support for the United States in the wake of the 9/11 attacks. NATO—for the first time in its history—invoked article V of the North Atlantic Treaty. Accordingly, members considered the "armed attack" against the United States "an attack against them all" (requiring that each member take actions that "it deems necessary"). Thus, Bush expressed the view that the United States now had the opportunity to seek common cause with Russia and China and place US relations with these countries on an entirely new footing.[36] The administration even reached out (unsuccessfully) to Iran (requesting access to its airspace), hoping to leverage its antipathy toward the Taliban and al-Qaeda.[37] From the president's standpoint, the global battle lines were clearly drawn. They amounted to a war between good and evil: "Either you are with us, or you are with the terrorists," as Bush put it in his post-9/11 address to Congress. Whether or not the other principals shared the president's view, they nonetheless gave significant weight to the depth of the US grievance, the rightness of the US cause, and the newfound US commitment to it—and a likely demonstration effect. That is, by acting with force, quickly and emphatically, the United States could convince doubters not to tempt US power. The principals generally assumed, then, that victories in the war on terror would only become easier, as the United States capitalized on momentum to disrupt and destroy the global terror network.

Admittedly, administration officials recognized challenges to building broad-based support for US post-9/11 goals.[38] Secretary of State Powell, in particular, appeared concerned that the United States might lack coalition partners, fearing the consequences should the United States end up "going it alone" (Woodward 2002: 81). He expressed surprise then when Pakistan accepted the full set of US demands (Woodward 2002: 59). These included that Pakistan allow US ground troops and special forces to operate from its territory, provide the United States with basing and overflight privileges, curtail the Taliban's access to money and supplies, and share the government's knowledge about bin Laden and his support network.[39] The challenges were certainly on display in tough-minded discussions with critical countries, including Uzbekistan, for military access and privileges to assist a US war in Afghanistan.[40] Testifying to the perceived challenges of alliance building, President Bush was determined to go it alone if necessary, and his advisers recognized that alliances would change with the US target. Secretary of Defense Rumsfeld famously captured this sentiment: "The mission will define the coalition—not the other way around,"[41] a view shared by Vice President Cheney.[42]

Still, the administration understated the challenges of obtaining active and ongoing international support. Administration officials assumed, in general, that the United States could deal effectively with reticent partners, including Pakistan, a nettlesome linchpin in the US antiterrorism effort.

The president's war cabinet seemed impressed by their blunt challenge to Pakistan's leaders. On September 12, Deputy Secretary of State Richard Armitage met with Pakistan's ISI chief, Mahmoud Ahmed, to convey an unequivocal message: "Pakistan must either stand with the United States in its fight against terrorism or stand against us. There was no maneuvering room."[43] The following day US ambassador to Pakistan Wendy Chamberlin, referencing that conversation, informed Pakistan's president, Pervez Musharraf, that US relations with his country were "at a turning point"; Pakistan "was either with us or not with us." "Action now is the only language that matters."[44] The message was reinforced that day when Powell told Musharraf, "The American people would not understand if Pakistan was not in this fight with the U.S."[45] This strong and unwavering US stance—communicated in many voices—would surely show Pakistan that it could no longer play the United States for a fool.[46]

The administration nonetheless had good reason to remain wary of the Pakistani government. President Musharraf had backed down before in the face of Islamic protests;[47] now he and his generals engaged in long and intense debate over whether to comply with US demands.[48] Moreover, Pakistan's ISI had a long history of association with Islamic elements in Afghanistan—a fact that Ahmed tellingly denied when Armitage confronted him: he said he wanted to dispel the "misperception" of his country "'being in bed' with those threatening U.S. interests." Pakistan, on the contrary, had always viewed the issue as "black and white." President Musharraf also defended his country, telling the US ambassador that Pakistan had always been and would be a "front line state" in the fight (presumably, from the context of the remarks) with the Taliban. For the US intelligence community, however, the reality was equally clear: the ISI had a long history of entanglement with nefarious Islamic groups, including the Taliban. Ironically, when the Clinton administration launched cruise missiles against terrorist camps in Afghanistan, the camps were being used by Pakistan's ISI to train Islamic guerrillas for action against India (in particular in Kashmir).[49]

Of course the Pakistani government conceded—officially—to US demands. Still, Pakistan's leaders also gained a critical US concession: the Bush administration lifted economic and arms sanctions that had been imposed on Pakistan for its 1998 nuclear test. The administration was also now acting under duress. Would the Pakistan government continue to cooperate once the shock of 9/11 had subsided? When it faced internal pressure to resist US demands (including that it end its long-standing support to Islamic groups opposed to India)? When it recognized that it could credibly deny the Pakistani military's ongoing support for the Taliban? When it believed that the Afghan government threatened Pakistan's interests? Or for that matter, when the United States at some point sought to reduce its profile in Afghanistan, leaving Pakistan to fend for itself and protect its interests?[50]

The Bush administration was confronting an unfortunate reality, appreciated or not: Pakistani officials could not separate their support for the Taliban from other critical strategic concerns.[51] The former head of Pakistan's ISI was among those who remained openly defiant: "Afghans defeated one superpower, and by the grace of God they will defeat another if the United States decides to attack Afghanistan."[52] While President Musharraf conceded to the US ultimatum, Pakistan was left in "an increasingly difficult and contradictory position" (Kagan 2012: 104).

Fourth, the administration had not set its priorities to determine the share of resources that it would, and should, devote to the war effort in Afghanistan. For that purpose, administration officials could have planned around the *limits* of the terrorist threat. After all, the 9/11 hijackers had relied on tactics that could work *once*: they depended on an open cockpit door and compliant passengers (who chose not to confront men armed only with box cutters). The policy makers might also have considered the merits of a defensive over an offensive strategy. For example, the administration could have prioritized homeland defense, stressing border security, increased vigilance, and protection of vulnerable and lucrative targets. Instead, the policy makers (much like the US public) envisioned a boundless terror threat to the United States: terrorists, thriving with sponsorship from so-called rogue states (an axis of evil connecting Iran, North Korea, and Iraq) and armed with the world's most odious weapons, threatened entire cities. In consequence, the administration assumed that to succeed the United States must do all things well. It took the offense and defense, at home and abroad (for a critique, see Lebovic 2007). That is, it mobilized the US government broadly to disrupt and destroy the terrorists' financial, intelligence, logistical, and military networks, assuming that the threat required an intensive and wide-ranging global response. The resulting profusion of policies on multiple fronts stretched available resources and begged the question, "Did the administration actually have a *strategy*?"

Members of Bush's war cabinet all shared the opinion that the new US adversary—immoral, devious, and relentless—remained unbound by the rules of the past and must be stopped at all cost. That view explains why the administration chose to employ decisive force against al-Qaeda and its Taliban supporters in Afghanistan. But it cannot explain why the administration neglected the requirements of *long-term* success in its desire to oust the Taliban and al-Qaeda from Afghanistan. A fuller explanation requires a recognition that administration officials focused inordinately on immediate mission purposes and failed to ask essential questions. What goals would the operation serve? Which alternatives might better serve them, given accompanying benefits, costs, and risks?

The War, 2001–2002: Success, Early but Incomplete

The president and Secretary of Defense Rumsfeld—the administration's point man on Afghanistan (Auerswald and Saideman 2014: 87)—tasked CENTCOM to develop a full range of military options for Afghanistan, from air and missile attacks to an all-out ground invasion. The NSC had initially presented President Bush with two alternatives. The JCS favored deploying multiple US divisions in Afghanistan for action against the Taliban, months into the future; the CIA favored a plan to bring US air power, US special forces, and local militia to bear more quickly, in lethal combination, to purge the country of the Taliban. The CIA plan won out.

Rumsfeld clearly favored the "unconventional" approach. He ardently believed that US advantages in command, control, communications, and intelligence, and edges in mobility, firepower, and precision, allowed the United States to win wars—quickly and efficiently—and depart, with similar haste, to avoid the burdens of occupation. His thinking found a home in the administration (O'Hanlon and Sherjan 2010: 23). George Bush, as early as the 2000 presidential campaign, made his aversion to (postwar) nation-building clear; he did so again, to his advisers, early in the Afghan operation (Woodward 2002: 237).

The resulting plan was a historical first: the CIA, not the US military, would take the lead in US war planning. George Tenet, the CIA director, and Cofer Black, his counterterrorism chief, outlined the basic plan to the president and NSC two days after the 9/11 attacks (Woodward 2002: 50–51). With Rumsfeld's support, CENTCOM (under the command of General Tommy Franks) responded with option packages of increasing strength: (a) cruise missile attacks; b) cruise missile attacks in association with strategic bombing sorties; and (c) some mix of a and b, paired with air controllers (for target designation) and special operations forces to obtain intelligence and otherwise assist the Northern Alliance. CENTCOM favored the latter approach, as did President Bush. The president approved the overall plan ten days after the 9/11 attacks (Wright et al. 2010: 46).[53]

Around two weeks after the 9/11 attacks, the first team of CIA operatives, capitalizing on long-standing CIA links to the Afghan opposition, entered Afghanistan to gather intelligence, build local alliances, and lay the groundwork for the US-led operation.[54] US special operations forces followed, though with some delay. When finally assembled in Afghanistan, a team of one hundred CIA operatives and three hundred special operations forces personnel paired with around fifteen thousand local militiamen to assail a numerically superior Taliban force. The Pentagon prepared to bring US military force more fully into the conflict. On September 20 it announced the start of a military buildup involving ground troops and aerial assets for striking Afghanistan.[55]

Two pressing considerations challenged these preparations. First, a war in landlocked Afghanistan was a logistical nightmare. Its neighbors, uniformly led by authoritarian leaders, were either hostile to a US presence (Iran) or only willing to offer their help at a high price. Although the US military acquired basing and transport privileges within bordering countries—importantly in Pakistan, to the east, and Uzbekistan, to the north—it had to contend nonetheless with enormous bottlenecks imposed by sheer distance, harsh terrain, and the exceedingly poor Afghan transportation infrastructure. All of these factors conspired to impede the expeditious movement of US personnel and material to the war zone. Second, a war in Afghanistan, fought with a large US occupation force, could easily become counterproductive. Geography and topography, and an agile and scattered opposition, worked against classic American advantages in scale and heavy armament: "The country's size and dispersed population required a mobile force to provide effective security, . . . [one] that could conduct operations and be inserted, supplied, supported, and evacuated by helicopter" (Neumann et al. 2013: 8–9). Furthermore, a heavy US footprint would offend local and nationalist sensitivities (Wright et al. 2010: 58)—as a Soviet presence once had—and perhaps galvanize opposition to the US presence throughout the Islamic world.[56] The US military preferred, then, to maintain a low profile. It would rely on US air power, US special operations forces, and local militia to destroy the adversary's military capability, but it would depend on the local units to seize ground and hold territory. Simply put, the US military chose not to become an occupying force.

Despite the major obstacles, the war unfolded generally as planned. In the first days of operations, US aircraft and cruise missiles targeted the Taliban's limited air-defense network, training bases, and other military sites. Within the first week of air strikes, US aircraft—having achieved air superiority and destroyed preexisting military targets—concentrated their fire on Taliban forces (Wright et al. 2010: 78). But the Taliban fielded a "nontraditional" army; it was neither centrally directed nor a cohesive fighting force. It was more a disparate conglomerate of local militia and foreign fighters that included al-Qaeda-linked militants. US and allied forces could not defeat it by targeting command centers or seizing the Afghan capital. Indeed, the country offered few critical targets, like energy plants or bridges, for US aircraft to strike. Thus, "the only preplanned targets were a few buildings used by al-Qaeda and Taliban leadership, some al-Qaeda training bases, and a few tactical aircraft and antiaircraft batteries" (Wright 2010: 62–63). The United States had little option but to assault Taliban concentrations around the country.

On November 10, 2001, CIA paramilitary officers and Northern Alliance militia joined US Army special forces operators in the north of the country to assail Taliban positions protecting Mazar-e Sharif. When the city fell, the so-called Afghanistan model was established. A small US ground presence—special operations forces to coordinate ground operations and air force spotters to target aerial strikes—would soften or destroy enemy positions, opening them to primitive assaults by local militia (in Mazar-e Sharif, on horseback, carrying Soviet-era weapons). The Northern Alliance, composed largely of Tajiks, Uzbeks, and Hazara, moved methodically to establish control over cities and territory in the north of the country, and Kabul, the capital. The Taliban oddly played to US military strengths by concentrating forces in vulnerable positions outside the major cities (O'Hanlon 2002). Pinpoint air strikes and powerful bombs exacted their toll on Taliban fighters, whether they hid in trenches, mobilized for offense, or ran from attacks.

With the defeat of the Taliban in the north, the US military turned its attention to the less-hospitable south and east of the country, where the Taliban reigned and ethnic hostilities precluded US reliance on a force of Tajiks and Uzbeks. The US military benefited enormously when it received backing from Pashtun leaders—most significantly Hamid Karzai, who would become the first president of Afghanistan in the post-Taliban period. In December, Kandahar—where Mullah Omar had built his base—surrendered to Karzai and those who had rallied around him.

The US military shifted focus to the east, for the major battles of the Afghan war. In March 2002, in the Shahi Kowt Valley, Operation ANACONDA sent US forces into the heaviest fighting of the war. Despite logistical challenges, the neutralization of US aerial weapons by unfavorable mountain topography, and unanticipated resistance, they emerged victorious (Ballard et al. 2012: 68–72). US troops killed or captured hundreds of insurgents and scattered the remainder. It was the prior operation, in December 2001, at the al-Qaeda redoubt at Tora Bora, however, that became the centerpiece—fairly or unfairly—of popular analyses of the administration's war strategy.

Critics claim that the US military had "outsourced" the mission of hunting down bin Laden—and along with him, perhaps over a thousand al-Qaeda fighters—to venal and incompetent local militiamen. Short on initiative and commitment, they made their own deal with the al-Qaeda suspects, allowing them to slip across the border and take refuge in the tribal regions of western Pakistan. The criticism is not without merit. The US military command refused to put boots on the ground to block an escape, despite the entreaties of Henry Crumpton, the CIA coordinator for Afghanistan. He appealed directly to President Bush and Vice President Cheney, to no avail (Ballard et al. 2012: 61–62; US Senate 2009). Critics claim that the administration lost a critical opportunity to deliver a potentially decisive blow. They argue that US special forces personnel had successfully traversed the forbidding terrain to call in air strikes against entrenched al-Qaeda positions, and that US forces had the tenacity and capability to prevail, as they would soon demonstrate on a similar battleground in the Shahi Kowt Valley (Krause 2008; O'Hanlon 2002: 58; US Senate 2009).

These arguments deserve some scrutiny. If the critics are right, US ground forces could have advanced, with necessary haste, through the steep mountain passes and rugged terrain of Tora Bora. They could have moved against fixed enemy positions and avoided ambushes, coping with high altitudes and extreme weather. They could then have found and searched the extensive cave networks that housed al-Qaeda remnants while blocking (from the opposing direction) their short retreat across the border into Pakistan. But the case for the mission was apparently not decided on its specific merits. Secretary of Defense Rumsfeld and General Franks refused to approve the mission, drawing from the logic of the US war plan, which advised making a light US footprint in the country (Rumsfeld 2011: 402–403).[57] The preference to avoid entanglements, casualties, and local pushback from a large conventional force overrode the thinking of US military commanders in Afghanistan that "the risks were worth the reward" (US Senate 2009). In this important sense, Tora Bora offers a view of the US war strategy, and its *deficiencies*, in microcosm. The war supported a military strategy divorced from considerations of overall benefits and costs.

The US military nonetheless had delivered on its promise, and with unexpected speed; it had capitalized on its mobility, firepower, and arsenal of smart weapons—with assistance from a vast and responsive US intelligence, communication, and command network—to overwhelm the opposition.[58] The Taliban abandoned Kabul without a fight. Unsurprisingly, Rumsfeld would see vindication in the quick "victory" that the small US force had achieved. The speedy result reinforced his (already strongly held) belief that US technological advantages had changed how the United States should fight wars. Still, a quick, relatively painless victory—no less one in which the US military largely *enabled* local ground units—should have provoked critical questioning. Were combat conditions unique? Was the victory actually complete?

US policy makers had not looked beyond any immediate success in Afghanistan to anticipate the challenges ahead or longer-term costs of US intervention, much less to consider whether overarching US goals necessitated those costs. Planning for a humanitarian crisis in the aftermath of US military intervention did occur, "but in the fall of 2001 and winter of 2002, neither [General Franks, the CENTCOM commander] nor his staff offered any detailed concept of how the Coalition would move Afghanistan from Taliban rule to a stable state that no longer harbored terrorist organizations" (Wright et al. 2010: 333). The Taliban—currently feeble, disorganized, and fighting from exposed positions—would prove a formidable and elusive adversary when it shifted to an insurgency strategy.

Stage II, Extension: Disjunction

The Taliban was now in disarray, severely weakened, and left to engage US forces mainly through low-level harassment. The US military continued its operations, targeting pockets of residual Taliban and al-Qaeda strength, especially in the southern and eastern portions of the country. In spring 2002, with its reorganization of the command structure in Afghanistan (under the command of General Dan K. McNeill), CENTCOM continued to assume that the military "would turn over responsibility for security, civil-military operations, and humanitarian assistance to the Afghans within twelve to eighteen months" (Neumann et al. 2013: 13). In 2002–2003, as the first phase of the US war in Afghanistan was winding down, Secretary of Defense Rumsfeld and CENTCOM commander Franks turned their attention to the impending war with Iraq (Auerswald and Saideman 2014: 89).

Rumsfeld essentially put the Afghan War on hold. That war was ending, he believed, and the United States could soon hand off responsibilities to US allies and (newly minted) Afghan security forces. Consequently, he left US commanders in Afghanistan much to their own devices. The US command in Afghanistan persevered, even innovated, with the limited resources available, mindful that success in the country was fragile. With such delegation—and more decidedly, the detachment of US civilian officials from challenges and requirements on the ground—US policy suffered. US forces attempted to do too much, with too few resources and an ever-increasing security challenge. Although Rumsfeld eventually tried to get the US mission back "on course," US officials still failed to confront (and fully grasp) the impediments in Afghanistan that blocked the accomplishment of even his more limited goals. Their failings were apparent in (a) the under-resourcing of Afghan stabilization and development, (b) the underestimation of the challenges to building an Afghan security force, (c) undue optimism concerning Afghan government capabilities, (d) the overestimation of the military contribution of US allies, and (e) the underestimation of the Taliban challenge.

Under-Resourcing Stabilization and Development

The US military had gone to war in Afghanistan under a civilian and military leadership that rejected nation-building as a prohibitively burdensome mission: " 'nation-building' was explicitly *not* part of the formula" and "unit commanders were forbidden from using the word 'counterinsurgency' in describing their operations" (Barno 2007: 33, 34). Despite these aversions at the top, the US military command in Afghanistan recognized a need to consolidate gains in the country by building support and allaying the grievances that had once set the country on its disastrous course. With the routing of the Taliban, the command took steps to address the humanitarian needs of the Afghani population and facilitate local stability and development (Neumann et al. 2013: 33–34). Increasingly apparent, however, was that US civilian (and military) leaders in Washington, and the US command in Afghanistan, were not on the same page.

The stabilization effort was strained from the start as the Pentagon struggled to come up with funds—and work around restrictions on the use of monies—for various local purposes (Feith 2008: 150–152). Notwithstanding President Bush's 2002 pledge for a "Marshall Plan" in Afghanistan, per capita outlays fell short of levels that the United States provided to other postconflict and poor countries and remained well behind US funding levels in Iraq. Indeed, in 2002 the United States deployed eight thousand US troops to Afghanistan to combat the Taliban and al-Qaeda, with orders that they not engage in peacekeeping or reconstruction operations. Well over a year after the president's speech, USAID had only seven full-time staffers in Afghanistan.[59] In consequence, the stability and development mission was severely under-resourced. As Dov Zakheim, appointed by Rumsfeld as the Pentagon's coordinator for Afghan reconstruction, later surmised, "The U.S. government did not engage, anywhere in any of its various departments and agencies, in extensive planning for a post-Taliban Afghanistan." Instead, "the assumption was that the international community would pick up the pieces after the Taliban regime was displaced" (Zakheim 2011: 8). The US government would remain unable to organize a coherent reconstruction effort. In this regard, one story is especially telling. Rumsfeld initially appointed Zakheim to serve as the *US government's* coordinator for Afghan reconstruction, unaware that Richard Haass (director of policy planning in the US State Department) was heading that effort as coordinator for the future of Afghanistan. Indeed, Zakheim only learned of Haass's role—and the existence of the coordinator position—after Haass had *left* the government (Zakheim 2011: 173).[60]

To be sure, the United States received support from other donor governments, the United Nations, and hundreds of NGOs in a vast array of activities. But the US military could not coordinate (per its usual role) the large and rapid inflow of resources. The military ended up at odds with other providers of services and assistance, who viewed the US military, with its logistical and protective advantages, as a competitor in the field (Wright et al. 2010: 239). Whereas the earlier departure of nongovernmental organizations from Afghanistan had created a vacuum that the US military alone could fill, the returning NGOs proved loath to coordinate activities with the US military. They feared losing control of their operations, tainting their own good work by association with the military, and endangering their own security (Perito 2005: 9–10). Yet the military command was also conflicted. Support for reconstruction and development had to compete with the (operational, tactical, and strategic) demands of improving the country's security environment. These demands included working effectively with the fledging Afghan government, building an indigenous security force, and coordinating the efforts of US allies working within the broad coalition. Thus, military commanders struggled to engage in nation-building while combating Taliban fighters who remained in the country (Wright et al. 2010: 251).

The US-military-led reconstruction effort obtained direction in late 2002 when the military turned to PRTs to combine (and protect) the efforts of various US civilian agencies across the provinces of Afghanistan.[61] These innovative organizations came to invest hundreds of millions of dollars a year in districts across Afghanistan, in a wide assortment of projects such as building roads and bridges, constructing schoolhouses, and training and equipping local police. The US PRTs embraced a distinctive US model: they were overwhelmingly staffed by US military personnel, co-located with combat units, outfitted to provide security for PRT personnel, and designed to favor quick-impact projects to promote goodwill and local governance. In other words, the US PRTs served US military goals: their intent was to improve the security situation in less stable parts of the country. But the PRTs faced enormous challenges. These included supply shortages; a lack of trained specialists to provide services; insufficient knowledge of local needs and resources; low US civilian participation rates; the initially sluggish release of monies to fund projects; constant rotation of personnel; a lack of oversight and accountability for money spent; and limited outreach to parts of the country due to their geographical remoteness, poor roads, and security threats and the diverting of security personnel to competing military operations.[62] The proliferation of programs also strained their management. Despite the monies spent, PRTs initiated projects without due regard for their sustainability, synergy with other projects, or fit with an overarching national plan. These programs sometimes produced mixed blessings, yielding progress that amounted, in some respects, to regression. By working with provincial governors and police chiefs, PRTs helped build goodwill and institutional capacity but also helped to empower corrupt, abusive warlords and power brokers, who contributed to the country's problems (Perito 2005: 6).[63]

The PRTs received significant support from US NATO allies. In December 2001 the International Security Assistance Force (ISAF) was formed (under the direction of the UN Security Council) to secure the areas in and around Kabul.[64] The Northern Alliance had previously taken control of Kabul, though the Bush administration (and the Pakistani government) had feared that it might establish itself there—and in power—and thereby alienate the Pashtun south (Dobbins 2008: 7, 56). In August 2003, when ISAF officially became a NATO-led force, the UN Security Council expanded its mandate. With NATO in the lead, ISAF soon took over the German-led PRT in Konduz and then moved to lead PRTs around the country, as provinces transitioned to ISAF control. By mid-2005, ISAF led nine of twenty-two PRTs in Afghanistan (Perito 2005: 1). Through PRTs, ISAF contributors could place their own national stamps on Afghan stability and development and gain political cover for involvement in a ("Bush administration–led") military operation.

Philosophical conflicts and operational inefficiencies nevertheless encumbered the stabilization and development efforts. US allies imposed geographical and performance restrictions (so-called caveats)—limiting PRT operations, for example, to daylight hours—to keep their nationals out of the fighting. Non-US PRTs also rejected the US model. For example, the German PRTs employed considerably larger, overwhelmingly civilian staffs and distanced themselves—physically and otherwise—from military operations (Perito 2005: 3–4). Their performance followed the German government's prioritization of development assistance for infrastructure projects that would yield longer-term benefits such as clean drinking water, primary education, and rural development (Behr 2012: 43). In consequence, the US- and ISAF-led efforts worked independently in the early years. Even devising a unified development and stabilization plan for the country proved problematic; US allies disagreed over how they could contribute and ran their PRTs as national enclaves.

In fall 2003, with most of the roughly ten thousand US troops in Afghanistan concentrated in central bases outside Kandahar and Kabul, the US-led coalition established a new headquarters in country (Combined Forces Command-Afghanistan). General David Barno, its first commander, assumed responsibility for handling political-military affairs—working with the Afghan government, the US embassy in Afghanistan (partnered with Ambassador Zalmay Khalilzad), and (as of August 2003) the NATO-led ISAF. Under Barno's command, stabilization and reconstruction received new impetus. After initiating a comprehensive reassessment of US policy in Afghanistan, Barno introduced a new strategy, based in counterinsurgency principles. With the shift, the US military command oversaw an increase in the size, scope, and function of the US-led coalition as attention turned to training Afghan security forces, developing the country's infrastructure, and guiding the Afghan government toward institutional reform (Wright et al. 2010: 18, 251, 254).

Two aspects of the counterinsurgency campaign were central to its activities in the field. First, US forces moved from their main bases to establish security in assigned "areas of operation," though continuing larger operations (out of forward operating bases) aimed at Taliban concentrations (Wright et al. 2010: 264). Although the country's geographical expanse and low US troop numbers kept US forces from establishing a continuous security presence in much of the country, these areas of operation allowed US forces to acquire knowledge of the terrain, people, and challenges to provide assurance to the local population and better identify and target enemy elements (Wright et al. 2010: 260–261). Second, PRTs expanded in size, number, and operations. With funds acquired through CERP and other sources (especially for larger projects), US-directed teams sought to promote local stability and development by building up the vital civil infrastructure throughout the country. They engaged in a full range of activities, from managing local conflicts to providing aid, constructing a public service infrastructure, and fostering local governance. Coordination between these two aspects of the campaign would presumably work increasingly in tandem to win popular support (Wright et al. 2010: 261).[65] Thus, the US command was now focusing on winning the peace to secure a stable transition to Afghan government control.[66]

Civilian leaders in Washington assumed, however, that the US military was primarily engaged in counterterrorist operations (against the Taliban and al-Qaeda) and in training the Afghan security force. Word of Barno's strategy shift in Afghanistan apparently arrived at the Pentagon via the media, not the chain of command (Auerswald and Saideman 2014: 92). The upshot was that the US military command and civilian leadership were moving in opposing directions, as the Pentagon was now preparing for a war in Iraq. The result was an under-resourced policy in Afghanistan that was strained by the competing demands of its various purposes.

Of course the tension could have been resolved with additional resources for Afghanistan stabilization and reconstruction and a more expansive vision of the US role in the country. Rumsfeld's hope, however, was to speed the transition to Afghan control of the war effort. He pressed General Barno's military superiors—including Richard Myers, chair of the JCS, and General John Abizaid, now commander of CENTCOM—to accelerate the training of the Afghan military (Auerswald and Saideman 2014: 91), and he pushed General Barno directly to focus on training the Afghan military (Graham 2009: 501–504). He also increased oversight of Barno's actions and war management and pressed Pentagon officials to develop their own strategy for Afghanistan (Auerswald and Saideman 2014: 92–93).

In May 2005 General Karl Eikenberry replaced General Barno as US military commander in Afghanistan. The command change better aligned US practices in Afghanistan with Rumsfeld's own preferences; Eikenberry, among his various accomplishments, had been responsible for building and training the Afghan National Army. Other changes further undercut the counterinsurgency strategy. Barno's political partner in the effort, Ambassador Khalilzad, became US ambassador to Iraq (befitting its increased importance to the administration). Moreover, US aid to Afghan was reduced by 38 percent, from $4.3 billion in 2005 to $3.1 billion in 2006.[67]

Under Eikenberry's command (through February 2007), Rumsfeld relaxed his war oversight. Although the intensifying war in Iraq had grabbed his attention, the civilian leadership and military command were also now working in greater harmony. Eikenberry shifted the military focus from counterinsurgency to counterterror operations (Auerswald and Saideman 2014: 93–95); ordered US units to partner with Afghan units (Grenier 2015: 54); and ended high-level coordination with US civilian agencies, which Barno had engineered via the US embassy in Kabul (Ballard et al. 2012: 133).

Underestimating the Challenges to Building an Afghan Security Force

US civilian leaders mistakenly assumed that the US military could meet ambitious goals for building up the Afghan army and police. At a donor country meeting in Geneva in April 2002, the United States agreed to lead the army reform effort as part of a five-pillar security plan. Under the plan, Germany, Italy, Britain, and Japan would lead police reform; justice reform; counternarcotics; and disarmament, demilitarization, and reintegration, respectively. Rumsfeld (2011: 483), with good reason, later lamented this attempt to create a division of labor among US allies "without any realistic assessment of their ability to deliver." In his words, it yielded "a series of unfulfilled pledges by well-intentioned but poorly equipped coalition partners."

Rumsfeld was not anxious to join the effort. He grudgingly accepted the lead in building an Afghan security force: Rumsfeld "gradually came to believe that the best way out of Afghanistan was to train the ANA [Afghan National Army] as quickly as possible" (Auerswald and Saideman 2014: 89). Throughout its tenure, the Bush administration pressed the US military to meet ambitious goals for building and extending the deployment of the Afghan army (Auerswald and Saideman 2014: 91).

To field indigenous troops quickly, the US military initially relied on tens of thousands of local troops—operating as the Afghan Militia Force (AMF)—drawn largely from Northern Alliance militia. But US special operations forces and the CIA were soon forced to curtail the funding and training of the AMF, which was beholden to warlord patrons and infringing on the ANA by grabbing available recruits.[68] The curtailment did little good. The US-led training effort suffered from insufficient recruitment and retention, a lack of qualified US military trainers, and equipment shortages (US GAO 2005). It also suffered as a fractionated effort. Responsibility for Afghan military training was spread thin among national contingents (with differing traditions and priorities) and was relegated by the US military to National Guard units and other available personnel (Neumann et al. 2013: 26–30). In its first years, then, the ANA, "a patchwork of command structures and little coordination between ISAF, U.S. forces and the Afghan [Ministry of Defense], made ... only incremental and stuttering progress" (Barley 2015: 2).[69]

The US military did establish successive commands to train the Afghan military. It started with the Office of Military Cooperation-Afghanistan (OMC-A). It then passed control to the Office of Security Cooperation-Afghanistan (OSC-A), when the United States also took charge of the (lagging) police training mission from Germany[70] and, in 2005, to the Combined Security Transition Command-Afghanistan (CSTC-A), when the command assumed responsibility for staffing, equipping, and training the ANA and the Afghan National Police (ANP). Yet the alphabetic profusion hid an essential fact. Not until November 2009, with the creation of the NATO Training Mission-Afghanistan (NTM-A) as a three-star command, did constructing the ANA become a dedicated, coherent effort (Barley 2015: 1–3).[71]

Even for a dedicated, organized effort, constructing an Afghan army from scratch would have presented a daunting challenge. Stifling impediments in Afghanistan included the absence of a basic military infrastructure; widespread illiteracy; low pay and difficult working and living conditions; limited troop dedication (leading to desertions, long absences from units, and low retention rates); a shortage of foreign personnel to assist the effort; the divergent military practices (including restrictions on involvement in combat) of foreign nationals charged with training; military factionalism based on ethnic divisions; favoritism, patronage, and little incentive for professionalism; graft, theft, and propriety holds on available military resources; a top-heavy Afghan command system that created bottlenecks and inefficiencies and stifled initiative; strong Afghan government resistance to reforms that would compromise existing influence relationships and disrupt patronage networks; and the persistent ties of military units to the country's warlords and their militia (on this, see ICG 2010b).[72] Pressure from the administration to get troop numbers up only exacerbated the challenges. Troop quality was lost, and long-term force capabilities suffered with the favoring of "infantry as opposed to logistics, medical, and other support personnel" (Zimmerman 2015: 21).

Having expected US allies to take charge once the US combat mission in Afghanistan concluded, US officials were now stuck. Their aspirations to build up Afghan security forces clashed repeatedly—indeed, inevitably—with conditions in country that blocked a US exit.

Undue Optimism Concerning Afghan Government Capabilities

US civilian leaders assumed too readily that the Afghan government would unify, reform, and build sufficient capacity to assist the foreign-led effort. In actuality, the US military, US civilian offices, and the global donor community lacked a capable governing partner.

The Bonn agreement (signed on December 5, 2001) laid the foundation for the government of Afghanistan. It set a six-month term for an interim authority (the sovereign government of the country as of December 22, 2001). It further required establishing an emergency Loya Jirga ("grand assembly") within those six months to determine the role and composition of a "broad-based" transitional authority to rule for the next two years; a constitutional Loya Jirga, to convene within a year and a half of the establishment of the transitional authority; and national elections for the president and legislature to follow. The identities of the prominent Afghanis who participated in the conference—warlords and power brokers, divided by ethnicity, geography, and sectarian affiliations—largely explain the government's dysfunctionality under the agreement. For decades Afghanistan had essentially lacked a central government; now its government was effectively reduced to fiefdoms controlled by feuding factions.

The Bonn participants proved unwilling to compromise their own interests to serve the common good. They settled instead for a "division of the spoils." With the Northern Alliance insisting that it hold the three key ministries—defense, foreign affairs, and interior—and three-quarters of ministries overall, the parties accepted a compromise, enabled by an increase in the number of ministries (Dobbins 2008: 95). The conference selected Hamid Karzai to chair the interim authority and divided its roles among the conference participants. Ministries within the government were apportioned among the membership so that everyone received their "fair share" (or, from the agreement's text: "Each member, except the Chairman, may head a department of the Interim Administration"). "For the next six months an Interim Administration comprised of twenty-nine department heads plus a chairman would govern Afghanistan" (Dobbins 2008: 96).

The proliferation of departments under this agreement had two critical political purposes. First, it kept a fragile coalition together: "Departments were to be distributed as rewards to the various factions that took part in the conference, and there had to be enough rewards to go around" (Maley 2015: 20). Second, it reiterated, and reinforced, the existing balance of power among the country's rival mujahideen commands: over half of the key positions went to the Northern Alliance, including all the major ministries such as defense and interior (Sharan 2011: 1110, 1117; Sharan 2015: 100). Indeed, even the distribution of top-level positions understates the position in government—and in the country—of the Northern Alliance and its key factions. Tajiks were vastly overrepresented in the upper-tier positions of the main ministries (Sharan 2011: 1120), and various leaders controlled their own militia and provinces to boot.

The result was perhaps inevitable: "With different factions in control of departments, with considerable ostensible overlap in the responsibilities of different agencies, and with incoming donor money as a stake over which to struggle, the scene was set for a state that would be weakened by administrative complexity and by bitter rivalry between different ministers, ministries, and officials" (Maley 2015: 20). By 2004 Karzai, as the country's elected president, was tasked with keeping the government—and country—together. He did this by building and maintaining alliances, keeping some public distance from his foreign benefactors, suborning the corrupt and self-interested, and employing the heavy-handed practices that permeated—indeed, perpetuated—the system. He extended his power base by appointing loyal provincial and district officials; co-opting potential rivals and favoring the Pashtun technocratic elite; pushing Tajik and Uzbek leaders out of their government positions; and unabashedly buying votes to obtain parliamentary support (Sharan 2011: 1111, 2015: 100–101, 105).

US officials had mistakenly assumed that a competent Afghan government would arise quickly to help carry the load. Ironically, the US government now chose, when possible, to work around Afghanistan's ineffective and corrupt governing institutions. For example, they sought to rely on various international parties or engage in reconstruction efforts and build up local security forces directly, to avoid the inefficiencies, unresponsiveness, and theft that would result from making the Afghan government an intermediary. In the words of one analyst, "Positions in government are routinely sold to the highest bidder, who then sells subordinate positions—and the process ends with Afghan citizens having to pay bribes for virtually all government services" (O'Hanlon 2010: 73). Corruption of that magnitude undercuts all efforts to build governmental capacity through the diversion of public resources, distortion of government policies, and rewarding of official venality and incompetence. Indeed, building the capacity of a corrupt Afghan government, even if possible, would create additional problems by allowing the corrupt to extend their reach, further alienating the citizenry.

The Bush administration, however, sought to nurture its relationship with the Karzai government. It held weekly videoconferences and avoided actions that might delegitimize the Afghan leadership.[73] It turned a blind eye to President Karzai's corrupt practices; thwarting of corrective action; and refusal to fire, and appointment of, corrupt officials.[74] For example, despite efforts beginning in late 2005 to reform the police and the Ministry of Interior, Karzai overruled the selections for provincial police chiefs by an independent committee and named his own personnel for the slots. Fourteen of them had failed the police entrance exam, while others had been implicated in human rights abuses and assorted criminal activities (Zimmerman 2015: 22).

US officials knew all the while that the Afghan government must eventually take charge. Thus, a paradoxical tension in policy remained. In doing for Afghanis what they must eventually do for themselves, would the United States ultimately leave them incapable of doing so? Yet in encouraging Afghanis to do for themselves—and turning responsibilities over to local institutions—might those institutions not surrender to the maladies of the Afghan government and society?[75]

Overestimating Allied Military Contributions

US civilian leaders wrongly assumed that NATO allies in ISAF in Afghanistan could assist the US-led OEF force, *as needed*, to establish security. Whereas the United Nations authorized ISAF, in 2001, to provide security in and around Kabul, the Bush administration initially opposed extending control of the ISAF force outside of Kabul (Dobbins 2008: 103), seeking freedom from multilateral constraints (Rynning 2012: 76, 87). But the administration soon looked to ISAF and its diverse (largely) NATO participants to take charge of military training, reconstruction, and security efforts in the country.

ISAF slowly extended its national reach and involvement in military combat. It eventually assumed control of all five of Afghanistan's "regions," starting in Kabul and then moving in a counterclockwise direction, with a different NATO country taking the lead in each region (see Auerswald and Saideman 2014: 33). ISAF first took charge in the north (2004), and then the west (2005). In July 2006 ISAF extended its presence into the south of Afghanistan to cover six additional provinces, including Helmand and Kandahar (adding four PRTs to its holdings). ISAF completed the integration process in October 2006, when it acquired responsibility for the troubled eastern portion of the country from the US-led coalition.[76]

Although US forces partnered with allied countries—foreign troops joined US forces as part of OEF, US troops joined the ISAF force under NATO command,[77] and OEF and ISAF forces coordinated their nominally separate efforts—OEF and ISAF nonetheless worked along separate tracks. For much of the war, OEF troops focused mainly on counterterrorism operations, while ISAF contributors focused more on (the typically less violent missions of) counterinsurgency and peacekeeping. The operational independence sometimes bred conflict, for example, when the nighttime raids of US special forces units undermined the local-outreach efforts of ISAF contingents (Auerswald and Saideman 2014: 45). No less significantly, ISAF itself was a loose-knit group. "ISAF was hobbled by an ad hoc patchwork of objectives without a clear consensus on a common strategy when confronted with the dual missions of nation-building and counterinsurgency" (Nagl and Weitz 2015: 170).

The coordination challenge was no greater than in the provision of military security. Largely for political reasons, NATO contributors shied away from supplying troops for active combat, using "caveats" to exempt their own troops from the fighting. Initially German troops were limited to daytime patrols in armored vehicles, could fire only in self-defense after repeated warnings, had to disengage under attack, and could not pursue their attackers (Behr 2012: 50; Nagl and Weitz 2015: 175). For that matter, German caveats proscribed the use of intelligence information, gathered by German military forces, for purposes of capturing or killing insurgents (Mattox 2015: 94). ISAF performance undoubtedly suffered from these varied, and changing, restrictions. Caveats aside, ISAF lacked the equipment and personnel to project power in hostile portions of the country;[78] it was further impaired as a coherent fighting force by a diffuse, fragmented command structure. High-level NATO decisions required unanimity among members but left them to contribute resources and to fight as *national* entities. The result was that members often failed to follow through on their troop commitments; regional command headquarters were not capable or authorized to serve effectively as operational headquarters; and regional operations were essentially "Balkanized" into national enclaves (Auerswald and Saideman 2014: 42–44, 47–48). In the end, ISAF contributors "struggled to implant a military footprint on the Afghan ground, and once there they became holding units" (Rynning 2012: 123).

As the war heated up in Bush's second term, ISAF nevertheless remained a collection of uneven burden sharers. The United States, Britain, Canada, and the

Netherlands were doing almost all the fighting,[79] while France, Germany, Spain, and Italy were refusing to send their forces into the volatile south of the country. Negotiations to resolve differences in preference and approach produced hard-fought yet limited concessions from the bigger potential contributors.[80] The Netherlands—as well as Romania, the Czech Republic, Slovenia, Denmark, Greece, Hungary, and Luxembourg—agreed to relax their exemptions.[81] France, Germany, Spain, and Italy stood firm; they refused to send their forces south except in extreme circumstances (Rynning 2012: 125).[82]

Defense Secretary Rumsfeld had hoped for a quick handoff of US military responsibilities to NATO. He had severely underestimated the ongoing—indeed, growing—military challenge and overestimated the capability and willingness of US allies to carry the military burden.

Underestimating the Taliban Challenge

US civilian leaders assumed incorrectly that the war had essentially ended. The word by early 2003 from Secretary of Defense Rumsfeld was that the country was now "secure" (Wright et al. 2010: 251). The explicit message was that the security environment had improved enough to allow the US military to engage in postcombat operations; the implicit message, however, was that US policy makers wanted to reduce the US military's profile in the country.

That message was reinforced when top US military commanders told the local command that US forces were not in Afghanistan to stay (Wright et al. 2010: 282, 333). Verbal cues in that regard were unnecessary, however. The message was conveyed quite effectively by ceilings on US troops in Afghanistan; the organization (and reorganization) of the command structure, in country, to make best use of available forces; the centralizing of operations (from key bases in the country) to maximize their geographical coverage; and the absence of a continuous US military presence throughout much of the country. The message was perhaps most clearly conveyed by the widespread assumption within the US military and intelligence communities that the war in Afghanistan was won and by the resulting shift in resources to the impending war in the Middle East (Neumann et al. 2013: 39; Wright et al. 2010: 252). With the Bush administration redirecting personnel, reconstruction, intelligence, and paramilitary assets—CIA teams, special forces units, and Predator spy planes—for operations in Iraq,[83] the US military did not conduct "significant military operations" in Afghanistan from the spring through the summer of 2003 (Ballard et al. 2012: 111).

As the administration was shifting its focus, and ISAF was nominally taking charge of the more violent and contested parts of the country, the Taliban was rebounding. The administration was slow to respond to the challenge.

In fall 2004 the Taliban started recruiting heavily from the Pashtun regions of Afghanistan and Pakistan (Ballard et al. 2012: 120), pulling profits from illicit dealings (including the opium trade) to finance operations and build a support base.[84] It slowly developed its offensive and defensive capabilities. The Taliban, which had once wilted before US firepower, was a different opponent when it adopted the strategy of the "weak." It relied on hit-and-run tactics and improvised explosive devices, employed indirect fire to concentrate US troops and then hit them with guns and grenades, broke off attacks before US aircraft arrived, and hid within (an actively, tacitly, or involuntarily) supportive local population (O'Hanlon and Sherjan 2010: 25).[85] By imposing costs on foreign troops and hitting soft government and public targets for heightened political effect (Wright et al. 2010: 253), the Taliban could raise the price of foreign intervention, weaken the Afghan government—and play for time. In its leaders' view, the outsiders would tire, leaving behind a government that would flail and soon fail.[86]

From 2004 to 2006 Afghan security conditions deteriorated significantly. During that period the number of security incidents increased many times over; coalition troop casualties more than tripled, to 191 deaths (Ballard et al. 2012: 137). In 2006 the Taliban launched a prolonged offensive with attacks throughout the south and (to a lesser extent) the east (CNA 2014: 53). The pace and targets varied by province, but the effects resonated far and wide. The Taliban took control of rural areas, attacked isolated security outposts, returned to areas to attack hold-and-build operations, ambushed convoys, launched massed attacks on district centers, cut roads and communication links, and engaged in suicide and car-bomb attacks against local officials and government targets (CNA 2014: 54–55). All the while, the Taliban gained new recruits.

Violence trends moved unmistakably upward. By 2007 the United States and its allies were confronting a full-blown insurgency; that year, 232 foreign troops were killed in Afghanistan, the highest annual toll since the US invasion. By the end of 2008 the annual toll had reached 295 foreign troops. The United Nations reported late that same year that on average, 740 "security incidents" had occurred monthly in Afghanistan, compared to 573 in 2007 and 428 in 2006 (UN Security Council 2008: 2). Admittedly, foreign troop fatalities were low compared to the enormous tolls of prior wars (by the end of 2008, foreign troop deaths in the Afghanistan War were only a quarter of the number for the Iraq War),[87] and certainly when compared to fatalities in Afghanistan from insurgent attacks on soft-civilian targets.[88] The adversary's strategy, however, was to bleed, not destroy, the opposition. For that purpose, high-profile attacks worked nicely. In July 2008, in the northeast of the country, over one hundred militants attacked a remote US outpost from multiple sides, killing nine US soldiers. In August ten suicide bombers, backed by one hundred fighters, hit Camp Salerno in eastern Afghanistan, wounding a number of US and Afghan soldiers. With its deadly attacks on non-US contingents, the Taliban could undermine support for the foreign-backed effort at its weaker political links. In August 2008 ten elite French paratroopers were killed just east of Kabul in an ambush, almost doubling France's entire war toll. By the same month, due mainly to roadside bombs,[89] the death rate in Afghanistan for British troops had exceeded their toll in the first six weeks of the 2003 Iraq War.[90] Efforts by US and allied forces to limit collateral civilian deaths by reducing reliance on firepower[91] only played to the Taliban strategy. The Taliban could effectively use civilians as hostages to reduce lethal enemy fire.

Despite the increasing violence, US troop levels in Afghanistan grew slowly. In 2006, with only around twenty thousand US troops in the country, the administration redirected its attention to the worsening situation in Iraq, and then to the surge to follow (Ballard et al. 2012: 173). From 2001 through 2009, when President Bush left office, these totals increased only by around a couple of thousand troops a year.

To be sure, time brought a change in mission. In November 2006 Bush fired Rumsfeld as defense secretary, albeit largely due to conditions on the Iraq front. Rumsfeld's departure brought with it a philosophical reversion of sorts. With Robert Gates installed as secretary of defense, General David Petraeus now commander of CENTCOM, and General David McKiernan commanding (concurrently) the NATO-led ISAF and US Forces-Afghanistan, the Pentagon and military command gave renewed voice to counterinsurgency principles (Auerswald and Saideman 2014: 98–100).

Still, with roughly thirty thousand US troops in Afghanistan, the US military lacked the personnel for a significant—let alone effective—change in mission. The administration had slowly upped the ante in the war, without an end game, a willingness to invest more fully in the conflict, or a sense of what it, or the US public, would realistically pay to reach a favorable outcome.

Stage III, Limitation: Constriction

The Bush administration seemed determined to exhaust the reservoir of support for the Afghan mission, which ensued from the 9/11 attacks. The administration had attacked Iraq without the international community's endorsement and then severely mismanaged the occupation that followed. Now, with violence on the rise in Afghanistan and its central government lacking a useful presence in much of the country, the administration expected its NATO allies to pick up the slack.

The Iraq War provided some impetus, however, for US re-engagement in Afghanistan. With deteriorating conditions in Afghanistan, the Iraq fiasco legitimized claims that the Bush administration had taken its "eye off the ball" in neglecting the Afghan War. Barack Obama used that very phrase to electoral advantage as the Democratic Party's nominee in the 2008 presidential election. By placing the focus on misshapen military *priorities*, he softened the impact of his rejection of the Iraq War. He could assuage the fears of those who thought he lacked the fortitude to act forcefully when necessary to address US national security challenges.

The new president soon soured on the Afghan mission, however, wary of the costs of pursuing the broad strategy for Afghanistan that he initially seemed to embrace. Belying his campaign rhetoric, he expressed trepidations early in his administration about the future direction of the war effort, such as when he met with prominent historians who had studied the decisional failings of the Vietnam era.[92] To Obama, a more ambitious strategy promised some vaguely defined outcome, at unknown cost, in a distant future. He was not alone in his concerns. His advisers were divided over the wisdom of backing such a strategy with additional troops and resources or instead accepting a narrow set of objectives that would require fewer US troops and reduce the US profile in the country. Obama essentially split the difference in opting to raise US troop levels in Afghanistan above the 100,000 mark for an abbreviated period. He made it clear, moreover, that US force levels—from that high point—would only go down.

The Decisional Backdrop

In his first months in office, President Obama *seemed* willing to engage fully in Afghanistan. Obama retained Robert Gates as secretary of defense and then appointed current and former military officials to high-level presidential advisory positions traditionally occupied by civilians. He appointed former general James Jones as his national security adviser and Lieutenant General Douglas Lute (who had served in the Bush White House as a senior adviser on Iraq and Afghanistan) as deputy national security adviser. In his first weeks on the job, the president accepted the military's recommendation to send seventeen thousand additional US troops to Afghanistan. In March 2009 Obama announced that he would send another four thousand US troops to train and advise the Afghan military. That would bring US force levels in Afghanistan to around sixty thousand and the entire NATO country contribution to roughly ninety thousand troops by late summer.[93] In May Obama dismissed General McKiernan. His secretary of defense and the chair of the JCS had concluded that McKiernan's traditional background and approach would not serve a mission that required new resources and drew more heavily from counterinsurgency principles.[94] Whether the president treated McKiernan fairly or unfairly remains a matter of contention (Grenier 2015: 58).[95] The case for retaining him was certainly not helped, however, by the downturn in security in the country, which begged for a "fresh" approach (Rothstein 2012: 63), or the availability of strong replacement candidates. Obama replaced McKiernan with General Stanley McChrystal, who had led the Joint Special Operations Command.

Signs of a potential retraction in administration policy were evident as early as March 2009. Whereas a high-level assessment team, appointed to advise the president on US war strategy, was nearly unanimous in its support for "executing and resourcing an integrated civilian-military counterinsurgency strategy in Afghanistan,"[96] its strategic emphasis was another matter. The Interagency Policy

Group's Report on US Policy toward Afghanistan and Pakistan stressed the importance of building up institutions at the *provincial and local levels*; recognized the need to monitor, and obtain leverage to deal with, a corrupt central government in Afghanistan; and gave priority—in building centralized institutions—not to a democratic and representative government in Kabul but instead to its security forces. Indeed, when the assessment team's chair, Bruce Riedel, briefed the president, he stressed that the US focus should be on Pakistan (Woodward 2010: 105). The assessment did not offer a specific recommendation on force levels; indeed, it was not clear to Riedel that the strategy required additional forces, beyond those previously authorized.[97]

When in March 2009 Obama announced his initial strategy (along with the sending of the four thousand additional troops to Afghanistan), the White House statement noted that the primary US goal was to "disrupt, dismantle, and defeat al Qaeda and its safe havens." Indeed, the statement noted pointedly that the goal was "clear, concise, attainable," suggesting a narrowing of US objectives absent reference to other US goals.[98] The Bush administration's aspirational phraseology was notably lacking from the document; gone were the references, for example, to building Afghanistan into a "flourishing democracy."[99]

The US military, by contrast, planned for a wide-ranging—and costly—upgrading of the US mission in Afghanistan. That was clear from the strategic assessment delivered by General McChrystal at the end of August 2009 in response to a June request from the secretary of defense. The "Commander's Initial Assessment"—a secret document[100] leaked to the *Washington Post*—grimly described the current US challenge in Afghanistan. Enemy attacks were increasing; portions of the country were back under Taliban control; the enemy operated with near impunity from within Pakistan; the Afghan central government was corrupt, distant, and ineffective; local power brokers were self-interested and abusive; and an impoverished, disillusioned populace was caught between these evils and the insurgency. The assessment warned that conditions for the US-led war effort would only worsen, even with a massive infusion of resources, absent a redirection of policy and fundamental change in the operative mindset. The assessment called for a "profoundly new strategy" based in the principles of counterinsurgency doctrine, warning that success would not come easily. In the general's words, "I do not underestimate the enormous challenges in executing this new strategy." General McChrystal assumed that the president would provide the resources to support the counterinsurgency strategy he believed he had been appointed to implement.

The additional US troops that Obama ordered to Afghanistan earlier in the year were most definitely insufficient to support a COIN campaign. Indeed, half of those forces—including a Marine brigade—were sent to Helmand province. There, the Taliban was active but the population was sparser than in Kandahar province, the Taliban's long-standing base of support, recruitment, and activity and the likely centerpiece of any Taliban effort to regain control of the country (O'Hanlon and

Sherjan 2010: 26). Even General McChrystal was disconcerted by the diversion of valuable labor to Helmand,[101] a decision that reflected Pentagon politics and organizational doctrine, not the requisites of a COIN strategy.[102]

The evidence on all fronts spoke increasingly to the tough, unforgiving slog ahead, with no promise of a favorable end. Afghan security forces were generally in sorry shape, "poorly led, ill equipped, overstretched, undersized, -trained, -educated, and—motivated" (Lebovic 2010: 215);[103] the Afghan police force was corrupt to the core;[104] and the central government of Afghanistan was, to put it mildly, "short on capacity." In 2008 Afghanistan ranked one from the bottom on the Brookings Institution's Index of State Weakness in the Developing World and near the bottom on the Foreign Policy/Fund for Peace Failed States Index.[105] Total US aid to Afghanistan in 2009 amounted to almost half the country's total gross domestic product (GDP) for 2008 and over ten times the country's annual tax revenue.[106] Although low in capacity, the Afghan government excelled in corruption. Befitting its status as a failed state, Afghanistan ranked near the bottom of countries surveyed on Transparency International's 2008 Corruption Perceptions Index.[107]

The United States lacked obvious levers to address these problems. The Bush administration's approach had not worked. The question then was whether the United States risked throwing good money after bad at these problems—or even making them worse—and sacrificing American lives to boot.

Moving Toward a Decision

The president knew that a request from McChrystal for additional forces was forthcoming. In September the general forwarded a request for another forty thousand troops to General David Petraeus, the commander of CENTCOM, and Admiral Michael Mullen, the chair of the JCS. His military commanders were only making it more difficult for the president to say "no." They had made their support for a troop increase public—Mullen, before Congress.[108] They had also embraced a counterinsurgency strategy that required more troops and suggested further that the troop increase sought was a down payment on the still larger force needed to implement the strategy.

Obama believed that the military had stacked the deck to deepen US involvement by closing ranks around a narrow set of options (Woodward 2010: 196).[109] He challenged the military to give him real options, not one option framed as many (Woodward 2010: 258, 278).[110] If the administration had planned initially to address the challenges of the Afghanistan War with a new sense of purpose, the enthusiasm had faded with events, a greater appreciation of the challenge, and growing dissent within the presidential advisory circle.

Some of the internal conflict stemmed, as usual, from an uncomfortable mix of personalities in high-level administrative positions. Tensions existed between the president's national security team—including his secretary of defense—and his close circle of political advisers.[111] In turn, these advisers battled over the control of regional policy with Richard Holbrooke, the president's Afghanistan-Pakistan tsar.[112] His experience alone had positioned Holbrooke to promote his grave misgivings about the likelihood of a US victory in Afghanistan and argue the case for negotiating with the Taliban. Holbrooke had brokered the Dayton accords on Bosnia in the Clinton administration and was a close associate of Secretary of State Hillary Clinton. Years earlier, he had served as a foreign service officer in Vietnam and joined the US delegation to the Paris peace talks. Although Holbrooke was not alone in his pessimism, his outsized personality, and competition for policy control and credit, were his undoing (in an administration led by a president who disdained "drama").

Conflicts also arose over policy preferences. Vice President Joseph Biden became a strong and consistent advocate for constricting US goals in Afghanistan. In his view, a counterinsurgency strategy was unworkable, prohibitively costly, and misdirected. Simply put, it conflated the two goals of defeating the Taliban and keeping Afghanistan free of al-Qaeda. Achieving the first goal was unnecessary, if even possible, because the Taliban was not a direct threat to the United States or its global interests. Indeed, any effort to defeat the Taliban would drain scarce resources (military, economic, and political) needed for achieving the more important, second goal and might well be counterproductive. By focusing the US war effort on the Taliban insurgency in Afghanistan, the United States was effectively letting the Afghan government off the hook; forgoing opportunities to negotiate a resolution with the Taliban; and pushing the Taliban into Pakistan, which would exacerbate its problems and distract its government from combating al-Qaeda. For Biden and his supporters, the United States was best off forgoing counterinsurgency and adopting a counterterrorism strategy. A small, residual US special operations force, paired with drone aircraft, could target terrorist elements to keep them under control. Indeed, by Biden's thinking, Pakistan—not Afghanistan—was the main theater for the alternative approach.[113] He eventually joined National Security Advisor James Jones and his deputies (Douglas Lute and Thomas Donilon) in backing a troop increase of between five thousand and ten thousand troops to support a "counterterrorism plus" strategy (Marsh 2014: 274).

Critics both in and outside the government assailed these arguments on practical grounds. Bruce Riedel (former chair of the president's assessment team) was among the skeptics.[114] In a September opinion piece, he argued that a counterterrorism strategy would not succeed because, above all else, an effective strategy requires an ability to obtain and protect intelligence sources through an active ground presence.[115] Gates (2014: 365) claims, in that regard, that he informed Obama that "counterterrorism plus" "had all the disadvantages of a counterterrorism strategy and not enough capability to reap any of the advantages of a counterinsurgency strategy." Even sympathetic experts acknowledged that a counterterrorism strategy might require surrendering a large portion of the country to Taliban control, reducing the US capability to target terrorism assets (Long 2010).

Sentiment among the president's advisers appeared stacked against a relatively large force infusion. Along with Jones and his deputies, White House chief of staff Rahm Emanuel and US ambassador to Afghanistan Karl Eikenberry (the former US force commander in Afghanistan) had lined up against it. Although Secretary of State Hillary Clinton broke civilian ranks to back the military's position, even Secretary of Defense Gates was not anxious to inject a generous flow of new US resources into the fight in Afghanistan. By Gates's thinking, his position fell somewhere between Biden's view of a counterterrorism strategy and the military's push for counterinsurgency; it amounted to a combination of the two approaches "to degrade the Taliban's capability to the point where larger and better trained Afghan security forces could maintain control of the country and prevent the return of al-Qaeda" (Gates 2014: 344). Gates did not endorse Biden's strategy and supported the supplying of additional US troops.[116] Still, he feared an open-ended commitment to Afghanistan and its current government, and he eventually helped bridge the distance between Biden's view and those of US military commanders—McChrystal, CENTCOM commander Petraeus, and Admiral Michael Mullen, the chair of the JCS—to build the policy consensus.[117]

The president's basic sympathy lay with the skeptics. He was haunted, it seems, by a fear of replaying US failings in Vietnam. Was the United States now stuck in a quagmire, and would his own decisions mire it ever more deeply in the sludge? The specter of Vietnam loomed over administration deliberations as Obama and his advisers recoiled from the military's pressure to engage further in Afghanistan.

The president grew increasingly wary of the war's direction as he came to recognize the high costs of achieving something approximating a victory over the Taliban. His advisers claim, in fact, that the August 2009 Afghan election was a watershed for the president.[118] The election produced widespread fraud: ballot stuffing, inaccurate counts, bribery, voter intimidation, and all the rest. Adding insult to injury, Karzai attempted to deflect charges of fraud by protesting outside interference in the election.[119] He even accused the United Nations of trying to manipulate the election to install a puppet government in Afghanistan.[120] The election dragged on for months—the results prompting endless charges and countercharges—before Karzai's opponent preempted a runoff by quitting the race in disgust.

Events would not ease Obama's doubts. In November 2009 he received bracing evaluations from Ambassador Eikenberry of malfeasance in the Afghan government and its prospects for change, transmitted to Washington in two classified cables (subsequently leaked to the *New York Times*). In Eikenberry's view, the Afghan government lacked essential capacities to partner effectively in the US-led war effort; a US counterinsurgency effort required the Afghan government to perform at levels in excess of its military, economic, and political capabilities. Under Karzai's leadership, it was loath to reform or carry its weight. Committing additional US military and economic resources to the fight would only encourage further malfeasance; indeed, it would reinforce Karzai's belief that the United States would persevere by shouldering the burden.[121]

So what could the United States do? Establishing a more "correct" relationship with Karzai had born little fruit and might actually have made matters worse. Obama's failure to reassure (or rather indulge) Karzai, and Karzai's frank interactions with US emissaries (including Eikenberry and Holbrooke), further reduced US influence over his actions. Now suspecting the worst of US motives, Karzai circled the wagons to resist: "The more Karzai felt endangered and undermined, the more he tightened his ties with his political supporters, many of whom were corrupt and the source of bad governance that gave so much support to the Taliban" (Neumann 2015: 12). But who could replace Karzai, and would another leader possess the power to assist the US-led mission?[122]

Obama had come to recognize that for one or more reasons—corruption, a self-interested aversion to reform, political rivalry, and low capacity—the Afghan government's performance would fall painfully short. These challenges reduced the likelihood of meaningful success in Afghanistan but also raised its price. Obama's budget office had estimated that an expanded US military presence in Afghanistan would cost the United States around a trillion dollars over the next ten years. The cost in lives of US troops would also escalate; Obama's advisers said that visits to Arlington Cemetery, and with hospitalized veterans, had moved and troubled the president.[123] The costs might mount politically as well, for the American public had largely left the fight. Only around half (51 percent) of Americans expressed the opinion in July 2009 that given the costs, the war in Afghanistan was "worth fighting," and somewhat fewer (46 percent) expressed the view that the United States was making "significant progress toward achieving success" in Afghanistan.[124] Public support for the US war was fading quickly; the percent of Americans who now advocated a US force reduction in Afghanistan had doubled (to 45 percent) since the start of the year.[125] Half the US public claimed to favor the Afghanistan War in May 2009, but only 39 percent (and less than a quarter of Democrats) expressed that view in September 2009.[126]

The good news for the president, should he want to do less in Afghanistan, was that the public was not demanding that he do more. The bad news was that the military was not on board, and he could not satisfy its requests without exceeding the resources that he wanted to invest in the war effort. Making things worse, relations between the White House and the military commanders had greatly deteriorated. The White House, the military believed, was asking it to perform without a workable strategy or resources; the military, the White House believed, was pressuring it, through leaks, public comments, and a premature request, to opt for a substantial force increase.[127]

The December 2009 Decision

The president recognized that he had to act. In the late summer and fall, over a three-month period, Obama joined his advisers in ten lengthy sessions for a thorough reassessment of war strategy (Petraeus 2017: 160).[128] By all available accounts, the deliberations were painstakingly rigorous, and the president remained highly engaged. He challenged his advisers to provide information and to express and support their opinions.[129] Under his direction, the discussions focused first on conditions in Afghanistan; the president wanted to understand "the problem" before entertaining solutions.[130] Opinions (including the president's) apparently changed over the ensuing months, testifying to the rigors of the deliberation.[131]

The US military command had not anticipated the White House's resistance and was surprised by the depth of the reassessment and concerns over the ambitiousness of the new US strategy. General McChrystal claimed that *he understood* the administration's strategy—the administration had outlined it in March—and was intent on implementing it.[132] Based on that strategy, he required additional forces to "protect the population," a key requirement of what was for him a *counterinsurgency* mission.[133] He was hardly alone in his reading. Riedel had publicly briefed his report as supporting a counterinsurgency approach, which he explicitly denied was "minimalist" in nature—a position that was backed, in the briefing, by Undersecretary of Defense for Policy Michèle Flournoy, who described the strategy as "stepping up to more fully resource a counterinsurgency strategy."[134] That interpretation registered in a NSC memo delivered to the Pentagon later that summer (Petraeus 2017: 161). A reading of the March text could not settle the debate. The "truth" was a matter of textual emphasis—and de-emphasis—and perhaps creative extrapolation about what the "mission," as conceived, would require in practice. As Defense Secretary Gates (2014: 342) surmised from the document, "far too much attention was paid to *what* should be done and far too little attention to *how* to get it done"— interestingly, a positon he attributes to Flournoy.

After months of deliberations, a compromise emerged. The administration would not endorse a major buildup or accept Biden's proposed shift to counterterrorist operations. The new policy was designed for "proof of concept," reflecting Biden's doubts that a COIN strategy would succeed.[135] The US military was to receive thirty thousand additional troops to implement the strategy, paired with a withdrawal of US forces from less-populated or hard-to-defend outposts in the north and east of Afghanistan.[136] A nationwide progress assessment (on all aspects of the mission) was mandated for December 2010; a decision on the ongoing mission was to follow in July 2011, as the United States commenced a drawdown of its forces.

The focus of US policy had shifted to achieving success at the provincial and local levels and training the Afghan military to permit a US handoff of security responsibilities.[137] The administration had concluded that security in Afghanistan would depend not on its central government, but rather on building cooperative relationships with provincial governors, tribal leaders, local militia, and perhaps even Taliban elements.[138] Counterinsurgency references were noticeably missing from the strategy, as outlined in a presidential memo. Indeed, the memo spoke to Biden's aversions: "This new approach is not fully resourced counterinsurgency or nation-building, but a narrower approach tied more tightly to the core goal of disrupting, dismantling and eventually defeating *al Qaeda* and preventing al Qaeda's return to safe haven in Afghanistan or Pakistan [emphasis added]" (quoted in Woodward 2010: 387).

Notwithstanding the rigors of the decision process, evidence abounds that the deliberations were designed above all else to contain the costs of the Afghan operation. The dutiful deliberations thus revealed symptoms of a cost-driven policy.

First, the president put the emphasis on less costly options. Can we "narrow the mission and tighten the timelines?," as his national security adviser put it.[139] Obama did not ask his advisers specifically for high-performance or cost-effective alternatives and instead sought goals that the US military could accomplish at a "reasonable" cost.[140] Indeed, the president chose to limit operational costs without much assurance of a sustainable, let alone contagiously positive, outcome. After all, projected US force levels—around 100,000 troops—fell short of the troop-population densities of successful counterinsurgencies (even with additional troop contributions from US allies).[141] The US military planned (over Afghan leaders' objections) to support the operation in densely populated areas by pulling US forces out of less-populated areas where the Taliban was active.[142] The strategy's success required support from local and provincial leaders, warlords and power brokers who undermined accountable and effective Afghan governance. Indeed, the Taliban remained among the key players in politics and society in the south of the country. The strategy also required that the Pakistani government move against Taliban enclaves in North Waziristan and Baluchistan, where the government was loath to go on the offensive.[143] It required further that (still unproven) Afghan security forces rise to the challenge, to ensure long-term mission success. The president himself appeared far more confident that the US military could succeed in the "clear and hold" portion of a COIN strategy than in the "build and transfer" portion.[144] As progress was difficult and eminently reversible, the president, it seems, was searching for a quick, lower-cost job that the military could "finish." In essence, he had reverse engineered the problem, selecting an option and then devising a goal to suit it.

Second, the president ultimately gave the US military fewer troops than it said it needed. General McChrystal had requested forty thousand troops and presented high and low options of eighty thousand (for a full-blown counterinsurgency effort) and ten thousand troops (for training the Afghan military). In setting his number, the president did not scale the force to meet some narrowing of objectives. Instead, he set the number as a compromise that was not true to any of the rival strategies. The number was too high to serve Biden's counterterrorism strategy and too low to serve the (more ambitious) counterinsurgency strategy that the military had envisioned (Jervis 2014: 327). The president, of course, had strong reason to suspect that the military's numbers were politically cooked: at least one of his advisers expressed that view.[145] The military had not presented an intermediate option between ten thousand and forty thousand troops and had presented a high-end figure, double the middle option, that could make the middle figure seem reasonable. But the president's ultimate figure did not come with a strong sense of which goals would be met, or how. Obama offered his number instead seemingly as a compromise. His decision to send thirty thousand additional troops to Afghanistan claimed the halfway point between McChrystal's request for forty thousand and Biden's proposal for twenty thousand (an option that Obama developed in cooperation with the vice chair of the JCS, General James Cartwright).[146] Indeed, Obama pushed back against proposals that would inch the final numbers closer to McChrystal's request, in part to deliver a political message. As Gates (2014: 382) described it, the numbers had to communicate to the general that "he was being given a different number and a different *mission*" [emphasis added].

Third, the president established mission goals that were not just modest, they were hard not to achieve. Gone were ambitious references to advancing "opportunity and justice," which had appeared in his March announcement.[147] Indeed, the US goal was no longer to defeat the Taliban, but instead to "reverse its momentum." By weakening the Taliban, the administration could presumably reduce the threat to the Afghan central government and buy time for its fledging security forces to take charge. Yet intentionally vague mission purposes left "success" in the eye of the beholder. As Ronald Neumann, the former US ambassador to Afghanistan, said that he remarked to General McChrystal in a 2010 trip to Afghanistan, "While everyone spoke of needing significant progress by 2011, there was no definition of what this meant or what would happen if it were achieved—or not achieved" (Neumann 2015: 6). The nettlesome question in all of this, then, was what "was the purpose of the surge?" (Paris 2013: 545). If based in "proof of concept," what exactly was it trying to prove?

Fourth, the president imposed a compressed timeline for the mission. Deliberations centered on a so-called bell curve that, over a multi-year period, had US force levels growing, plateauing, and then declining; the president's goal was to push that curve forward so that US forces arrived earlier and left sooner. Still, Obama had no military rationale for designing policy around an eighteen-month timeline; military officials believed, in fact, that a fixed withdrawal date was counterproductive.[148] As the president put it to his advisers when confronting McChrystal's unappealing forty-thousand-troop option, "What I'm looking for is a surge."[149] Once again, a finite resource commitment—now, an imposed time limit—drove presidential planning.[150] Paradoxically, the frequent administration refrain that July 2011 was merely a *start date* for withdrawal—that might affect only a "handful" of US personnel—implied as much. After all, why commit to a timeline when only a small number of troops might leave, much less when conditions in the country remained unsettled and, as critics were quick to point out, setting a timeline publicly gave valuable information to the enemy (which it could use to lay low until after a US troop exit)? For that matter, why set a broad-based, nationwide assessment of the US mission in Afghanistan a half year *before* US forces were set to depart under the presidential schedule? Although Secretary of Defense Gates won a concession—that conditions would determine the pace of withdrawal[151]—even he had strong reasons to think the president had set his sights on departure.

This is not to downplay the importance of the troop decision. It was very important *politically*; it allowed the president to establish and communicate the limits of the US force commitment. By controlling *what he could control*,[152] formally and otherwise, Obama sought to constrain future choices. He personally drafted the aforementioned (six-page, secret) memo outlining the decisional essentials, pressed each of his advisers to commit verbally to the plan, and then resisted efforts to "renegotiate" the agreement. He told Defense Secretary Gates that the conversation was over when Gates pressed him for wiggle room on the thirty-thousand-troop figure. He obviously sought to foreclose misunderstandings and opportunities to reopen debate.

For some, at least, the issue remained unsettled. General McChrystal could not hide his disdain for the principals who had opposed his counterinsurgency plans. His unguarded comments and tolerance for crude comments by his subordinates— aimed at Vice President Biden, Ambassador Eikenberry, and others in the presence of a (*Rolling Stone*) journalist—were inexcusably insubordinate, in the president's view. Thus, in June 2010 McChrystal's military career came to an unceremonious end. The events of 2010 created additional opportunities for the president's advisers to revisit their policy differences.

Neither McChrystal's departure nor Obama's efforts to nail down a consensus quashed disagreement over the force requirements of the announced strategy. General Petraeus, McChrystal's replacement as force commander, was among those who employed the language—and requirements—of counterinsurgency, when he described the US approach in Afghanistan to Congress.[153] Neither could the protagonists agree on how to proceed once the strategy was implemented. The president had detailed monitoring criteria but had not rank ordered them. Nor had he presented some mix of futures—perhaps as bundles of successes and failures— for determining the pace of the US withdrawal schedule. In consequence, the strategy had to yield ambiguous evidence for assessing operational effectiveness. Assessments would reduce inevitably to assumptions about the contribution, reproducibility, and sustainability of any apparent accomplishment. In other words, assessments would depend on judgments about whether the Afghan government and its military could maintain or build on progress that US forces had achieved. They would depend further on a host of specific judgments pertaining to tribal relationships, the Taliban's decision to operate in one area rather than another,

Taliban activities in Pakistan, the month of the year (whether the insurgents had returned temporarily to the poppy fields or closed down operations for the winter), and so forth.

President Obama expressed his frustration when the arduous deliberations failed to answer a fundamental question: "What are we trying to accomplish?" He secured at least a partial answer: "reversing the Taliban's momentum" in order "to deny the Taliban the ability to threaten to overthrow the Afghan state" (Woodward 2010: 269). But what did that mean, and how exactly were the pieces of the causal puzzle to come together to meet mission goals and serve US interests? The deliberations had not produced an answer: "There was no real plan for how segments of the Taliban were to be won over, how the border with Pakistan was to be sealed or the Pakistani government convinced to mend its ways, or how the government and security forces of Afghanistan were to be brought to a level where they could take over the areas that the American forces had cleared of insurgents" (Jervis 2010/2011: 698). The president's strategy promised to avoid a loss in Afghanistan, or at least to postpone it. Still, an Afghanistan in perpetual conflict hardly boded well for the country's future.

The logic, though fragile, nonetheless explains the administration's decision. The president was looking to the "surge" paradoxically to contain the US force commitment—and then ultimately to facilitate political movement in the opposite direction. His priorities were apparent in his directive to Secretary of Defense Gates: "I want an exit strategy" (Woodward 2010: 253).

The Decisional Aftermath

A change in US thinking and strategy, drawn nevertheless from counterinsurgency doctrine, would now guide the US military force in Afghanistan. With population centers the focus (O'Hanlon and Sherjan 2010: 40), under General McChrystal's command, US troops took position in the south of Afghanistan, including districts in Kandahar, to control roads and cities.[154] To avoid alienating local populations, US troops avoided actions such as night searches or strikes that might inflict civilian casualties (Rothstein 2012: 66–67). Yet the task was formidable, and time was fleeting. The Taliban had rebounded by late 2009 to its pre-9/11 levels, with an estimated force of twenty-five thousand full-time fighters (O'Hanlon and Sherjan 2010: 26). There were roughly ten thousand villages in the south and east of the country, and the undersized US force could not cover them all. Other US troops had to take the offensive. Thus, when General Petraeus assumed command he took a more direct approach against the insurgency, despite tightening restrictions on military action to safeguard civilian lives.[155] US special operations units engaged in kinetic operations, for example, against the Haqqani network in the east of Afghanistan.[156]

The president certainly hoped that by July 2011 US forces would have weakened the Taliban. That would buy time for Afghan forces to improve, to facilitate a US exit. Still, the president had not established markers—positive or negative—to pace the US departure. He had only constructed a "framework" for US action, then sought solutions outside the framework. By the summer of 2010 he was confiding hopes to his advisers for a negotiated resolution to the conflict. His aspirations implicitly challenged the thinking of his military commander, David Petraeus, the Iraq War's surge architect.[157] Negotiating with the adversary had never been part of Petraeus's plan for the Iraq War.

In December 2010, twelve months after his major policy decision, the president received, on schedule, his first major assessment of war progress.[158] The assessment implicitly spoke to the limits of US goals: "to deny safe haven to al-Qa'ida and to deny the Taliban the ability to overthrow the Afghan government." The assessment noted areas of progress, including the growing capacity of Afghan security forces and success achieved—through a larger US troop presence, special operations targeting, and village security efforts—in containing and reversing the influence of the Taliban in its heartland, the southern provinces of Helmand and Kandahar. The clear emphasis in the assessment was nonetheless on the "fragile and reversible" nature of progress; the significant threat to Afghanistan and the US mission posed by Pakistan as an insurgent supply conduit and safe haven; and the "uneven" US-Pakistan relationship. Despite massive infusions of US aid to that country, Pakistan remained unwilling to combat elements hostile to the Afghan government in the tribal areas of western Pakistan.

The administration planned to increase attacks, largely by drone aircraft, against Taliban insurgents, the al-Qaeda leadership, and the non-Taliban Afghan insurgency (the Haqqani network) in the tribal areas of North Waziristan.[159] It had pressed Pakistan to target Islamist groups behind the Afghan insurgency and had dramatically increased the number of US drone strikes in Pakistan against insurgent and al-Qaeda leaders.[160] But acquiring Pakistani cooperation was another matter.

The year 2011 proved exceptionally challenging for US relations with Pakistan, its government buffeted by public outrage at repeated US military breaches of the country's sovereignty. The shooting of two Pakistanis by a CIA contractor, followed by the surprise killing of Osama bin Laden by a Navy Seal team in Abbottabad a few months later, exacerbated the tension. The atmospherics worsened with US suspicions that the Pakistani military had given refuge to bin Laden (he was hiding virtually in plain sight) and the Pakistani public's suspicions that its government and military had backed US military actions. Relations deteriorated further with the killing, in a NATO strike, of dozens of Pakistani soldiers at a checkpoint that had been set up to control insurgent supply flows into Afghanistan.[161] Pakistan's leaders roundly condemned the attack (Pakistan's military head called it an unprovoked act of aggression), closed the border and other vital supply routes to NATO traffic, and clamped down on US drone operations from Pakistani territory.[162] Civilian deaths from the larger number of US drone attacks constrained the government's outward cooperation and fed (and excused) its unwillingness to act forcefully against Afghan insurgent groups.

The administration would thus have to work around Pakistan's sensitivities, like them or not. Even with an increase in US drone strikes in the tribal areas, the United States refrained, for example, from hitting Baluchistan Province, where the Taliban leadership, including Mullah Omar, resided (Jones 2013: 19). When the United States pushed the Pakistani government, it resisted. Despite sending billions of dollars in annual aid to Pakistan, US leaders could only try to persuade it to do more. When quiet diplomacy failed, US officials fell back on counterproductive public rhetoric. In September 2011 Admiral Mullen called out the ISI for its ties to the Haqqani network; Secretary of Defense Leon Panetta, Gates's replacement, publicly questioned whether Pakistan would follow through on its veiled promises to attack the network in North Waziristan (Markey 2013: 57). Although the Pakistani government was far more complicit in US drone attacks than it would, or could, publicly acknowledge,[163] US leaders chafed at the apparent duplicity of the Pakistani government and its reticence to take decisive action or accept a more active US military role in Pakistan.

Thus, the president had held the line on a troop increase and battled back against the US-military-supported strategy that would have necessitated one. President Obama had defined the objective for the surge: to reverse the momentum of the Taliban to prevent it from taking over the state. But what that meant in practical terms remained unclear, as Obama himself acknowledged when noting, two years hence, "We'll have to ask, is this good enough?" (Woodward 2010: 299). Two years later, the answer was not any clearer. "Progress" in Afghanistan would amount to a mixed bag of successes and failures. Which mattered most, however, would remain a matter of perspective. US military operations brought some stability to the south of the country, but the Taliban remained active in Afghanistan, especially to the east. The question remained, could US achievements in the country outlast a US exodus?

Obama's question would remain unanswered though it would lose its urgency. In the White House, State Department, and Pentagon, the phrase, "Afghan good enough" had come to express the increasingly modest US goals and expectations for Afghanistan.[164] Successive US administrations had never entirely warmed to the idea of remaking Afghanistan; their clear focus now was to establish security and prepare for a changing of the guard.

Stage IV, Disengagement: Extrication

The 9/11 attacks galvanized Americans across the political spectrum. Public commentators insisted that Americans had learned lessons from neglect, having failed to rise to the al-Qaeda challenge. Yet the public lost focus in the ensuing years, and the Afghanistan War faded from view. By 2012, after a decade of fighting, America's now longest war was effectively a non-issue in the presidential campaign. A Republican challenger—who in principle could have rallied a hawkish base for electoral gains—instead recognized the limited benefits, and the large downside risk, in making the war a campaign issue. A "must-win" war for the United States became a "forgotten war" to much of the US public.

The Obama administration persevered, with an eye to the exit. In setting—then resetting—withdrawal deadlines, the administration understood the United States would eventually leave Afghanistan an unfinished work.

The Obama Administration: Setting (and Resetting) a Withdrawal Deadline

Roughly a year after the surge decision, the administration had a plan for the phased withdrawal of US forces from Afghanistan. The United States would gradually turn provinces over to Afghan control, under the US military's mindful watch. It would postpone the transition of the least secure provinces, like Kandahar in the south, until the end of 2012. By the end of 2014, the United States would cede full responsibility for security in Afghanistan to its own security forces. The administration planned to facilitate the exit by increasing Afghan army and police personnel totals from their current level of 264,000 to 350,000, by 2013.[165]

In June 2011 President Obama announced, in a televised address, that the thirty-three-thousand-strong surge force would leave Afghanistan in phases over the next fifteen months, with a third of the additional force to be taken out of Afghanistan over the following six months. By September 2012, that would still leave seventy thousand US troops in the country.

President Obama's withdrawal plans incurred some resistance from the Pentagon. Outgoing secretary of defense Gates had reportedly pushed for a withdrawal of support personnel, not combat troops, and together with General Petraeus had pressed for an end-of-the-year withdrawal of a third to half the size that the president eventually ordered.[166] The president's announcement generated partisan backlash as well; while Democratic leaders encouraged a speedy withdrawal, Republicans advocated caution, accusing Obama of playing politics with an important military decision. The Afghanistan War, however, was not a polarizing public issue. A clear majority of the Republican public now favored at least some withdrawal of US troops, a ratio that had soared in late spring 2011 with the death of bin Laden in a US special forces raid.[167] The president thus had a strong domestic base from which to pursue an exit.

In May 2014 President Obama announced his exit plan: by the end of that year, the US combat role in Afghanistan would end. In the president's words, "the Afghans will be fully responsible for securing their country."[168] The United States would agree only to train Afghan forces and engage in counterterrorism operations. The president had officially accepted the "Biden model"[169] and once again resisted professional military opinion. His military commanders had recommended that the president leave at least ten thousand troops in Afghanistan, for several years. That would allow the US military to advise Afghan troops directly on the battlefield.[170]

The tone and substance of the president's announcement were telling, especially in the self-described "bottom line": it was "time to turn the page on a decade in which so much of our foreign policy was focused on the wars in Afghanistan and Iraq." Obama had started his term with "180,000 troops in harm's way"; the number, by year's end, was to be "less than 10,000." The linking of the two *long* wars was the message; this was not a presidential victory lap celebrating a job completed, or well done, but rather an attempt by the president to place these wars behind him and the nation. After all, Obama had taken office pledging to end one war, in Iraq, and hoping to finish another, in Afghanistan. With thirty-two thousand US troops currently in Afghanistan and a final departure date set for the end of 2016, three weeks before the next presidential inauguration, Obama could leave office having ended the long and exhausting war he had inherited. US forces would essentially have left the country, except for a small force guarding the US embassy in Kabul and providing security assistance to the Afghan government.[171]

Certainly the president spoke of wide-ranging progress in Afghanistan, the vanquishing of al-Qaeda and decimation of its leadership, and the United States "finishing the job" that it started. Obama had chosen, however, to end US involvement in a war that was unwinnable with available US resources. In the president's words, "this is how wars end in the 21st century." They do not end with "signing ceremonies," much less with unconditional surrender. They end, instead, "through decisive blows against our adversaries, transitions to elected governments, security forces who take the lead and ultimately full responsibility."[172] They end, perhaps, when one party determines it has accomplished enough, or simply has had enough, and chooses to leave.

Presidential aspirations clashed, however, with the realities of the battlefield and Afghan force capabilities. A smooth transition, with competent Afghan forces taking control of a manageable war effort, proved elusive as the Taliban recovered from its losses in Obama's troop "surge." In 2014 the Taliban launched a major offensive, concentrated mainly in Helmand province (Sedney 2015: 20–21). Its ambitious, yet apparently realizable, strategy was "to subvert, weaken and drive out institutions of state governance, isolate the Afghan security forces, and build parallel institutions with which to increase its influence across Afghanistan's periphery" (McNally and Bucala 2015: 11).

The effects of the offensive were felt far and wide. Insurgents struck provincial capitals; attacked targets in Kandahar, Jalalabad, and Kabul; seized territory, including district capitals; and used their forward positions to threaten further gains. They took charge in southern and eastern provinces and territories to the north, including the city of Konduz in September 2015,[173] marking the first takeover of a major Afghan city by the Taliban in the post-9/11 period (Katzman and Thomas

2017: 26–27). In areas under their control, the insurgents *acted* as if they were in control; they established shadow governance, collected taxes, and imposed laws (McNally and Bucala 2015: 11–12). Taliban gains in the north were especially problematic given the relative support for the central government and the weaker military, political, and ideological standing of the insurgents in that part of the country (McNally and Bucala 2015: 21). Although the Pakistani military did finally push the Taliban out of North Waziristan in a major offensive, the unwelcome consequence was injecting insurgents representing various Islamist groups into Afghanistan (Wilder 2015: 37).[174]

Afghan forces often held their ground. Yet their positions were frequently overrun; and they were generally incapable of taking the offensive. Without the backing of US troops and their logistical, intelligence, reconnaissance, and aerial support, the Afghanis often chose to remain at their bases or to staff checkpoints (McNally and Bucala 2015: 11). By October 2015 the untoward consequences of transitioning to Afghan control were clear: Taliban insurgents now held more territory in Afghanistan than at any time since 2001,[175] and Afghan forces were increasingly stressed. In the first seven months of 2015 alone, over four thousand Afghan security personnel were killed (and almost twice that number wounded), a steep increase in fatalities from the prior year. As a barometer of conflict, the civilian death toll stood at even higher levels (Wilder 2015: 36). In 2014 over ten thousand civilians died in the violence.[176] The numbers were an order of magnitude higher than five years earlier throughout the country—almost two times higher in the east, around two and a half times higher in the south, and over four times higher in the north (McNally and Bucala 2015: 12).

The president was pressed to stem the Taliban advances and prevent (or, at least forestall) an Afghan military collapse. In October 2015 Obama revised his withdrawal schedule after an intensive reassessment. He now expected to leave 5,500 US troops in Afghanistan after he left office. US troops would remain at bases in Bagram, Jalalabad, and Kandahar; continue to train Afghan troops; and conduct counterterrorism operations.[177]

Yet conditions in the country continued to spiral downward. By April 2016 at least 20 percent of the country, in large pockets throughout the north, south, east, and west, remained contested or under Taliban control.[178] Although the Taliban did not yet control major provincial cities, it maintained sanctuaries throughout the country from which to threaten those cities.[179] The increasing violence registered in internal civilian displacement. In the first six months of 2016 alone, around 150,000 people fled their homes to escape the violence.[180]

Obama now walked back his commitment to curtail the US combat role. US forces had not joined Afghan military forces in battle since 2014, when the United States had officially ended its combat operations in Afghanistan. Moreover, air strikes had been restricted to exceptional circumstances: defending against a direct threat to coalition or Afghan forces or forestalling an Afghan "strategic defeat." In June

2016, however, the president authorized US personnel to accompany Afghan forces in combat offensives, an implicit acknowledgment that the depleted US presence and the shift to counterterrorism operations had left Afghan security forces unable to prevent insurgent advances. US ground personnel could now call in air strikes, and commanders had greater latitude to authorize them.[181] Under the revised guidance, US air strikes could serve as enablers in Afghan offensive operations.[182]

The departure schedule also continued to slow. Whereas the US troop contribution to the ISAF mission, currently at 6,800 troops, was supposed to drop by half by the end of 2016,[183] with another 2,000 US troops engaged in counterterrorism operations, Obama now planned (as announced in July 2016) to keep around 8,400 troops in Afghanistan—maintaining six major bases—when he left office.[184]

Importantly, however, the president had only *slowed* the departure from Afghanistan of US troops, then at very low levels, and he held to the reduced numbers despite the demands of the battlefield. The military struggled to perform its tasks while staying *formally* within the imposed troop ceilings; it hired contractors to assume the traditional duties of uniformed personnel and imposed counting rules that understated the actual number of US troops present in country at any given time.[185] Moreover, doubts persisted over whether US forces were adequately scaled to fend off the Taliban. The current results were hardly cause for optimism.[186] By August the Taliban was again driving forward, threatening to overrun the provincial capital of Helmand province. Local officials complained that familiar problems continued to plague Afghan security forces: ghost payrolls, poor communication and coordination, dependence on US aerial support, poor leadership, and less than full dedication to the mission.[187]

Conditions continued to deteriorate. In September 2016 the Taliban sent Afghan forces reeling in a surprise attack on Tarin Kot, the capital of Uruzgan province.[188] In the adjacent weeks, armed attackers also struck high-profile targets (including CARE International and the American University of Afghanistan) in Kabul and tripped bombs around the capital (including one near the Defense Ministry). Dozens of people were killed, a number of top security officials among them.[189] By October security conditions in the country had substantially worsened, reversing the progress of the 2010 surge. Eighty-five percent of Helmand province was now under Taliban control, and the Taliban was launching brazen attacks against the provincial capital.[190]

The United States had undoubtedly scored permanent victories against the perpetrators of the 9/11 attacks; drone attacks had killed much of al-Qaeda's top leadership, including Osama bin Laden. Even Mullah Omar was now dead. But these deaths failed to temper the Taliban's resolve. Mullah Akhtar Mohammad Mansour replaced Mullah Omar, forging closer ties with the Haqqani network.[191] In turn, Mansour's death in May 2016 in a US drone attack—the first in Baluchistan—seems to have empowered a more implacable Taliban leader. Mansour's successor, Mullah Haibatullah Akhundzada, was known for his harsh religious edicts and was viewed by some experts as even more rigid than his predecessor.[192] Were he a "moderate," it might not have mattered. He would still need to manage a fragile coalition that included hardcore elements that could push him toward militancy and an increasingly defuse insurgency with a growing appetite for violent tactics. The depletion of the senior Taliban leadership (in part through drone strikes) and the globalization of Islamist tactics had empowered a new generation of insurgent commanders. Unbound by cultural norms or ties to local communities, they sought to extend their dominion through sheer brutality and barbaric acts of intimidation.[193]

Any Taliban leader who could control restive elements had little incentive to accommodate the United States or the existing Afghan government. Why should the Taliban seek talks?[194] It was gaining strength, and time was seemingly on its side. Indeed, with the rise of the Islamic State, the United States was feeling the heat on other global fronts.

Hitting the Wall: Afghanistan's Institutional Failings

By the end of Obama's second term, formidable obstacles remained to making progress in Afghanistan on the political, economic, and security fronts. The administration had to contend with an often resistant, and certainly incapable, government; woeful economic conditions; and an underperforming Afghan security force. The administration continued to address these deficiencies. More important, however, is that it largely accepted them now as beyond US control.

Some problems had gotten worse; others had marginally improved—for now. That the Obama administration plotted an exit, despite Afghanistan's poor prospects—indeed, *because of* the country's poor prospects—is, however, the main story. The administration had come to recognize that addressing the wide-ranging challenges of Afghanistan would continue to impose prohibitive costs. It would absorb budgetary and material resources, take American lives, strain relations among NATO allies, and distract from other US global commitments. In return, it would offer only a faint promise of a stable Afghanistan that would still depend on foreign resources. The Obama administration had finally accepted that Afghanistan would have to remain an unfinished work, politically, economically, and militarily.

Political

The Obama administration's relationship with Karzai, never good, consistently deteriorated. Karzai did what he thought necessary to secure his power base: he bought support, protected and promoted cronies, and suborned corrupt officials throughout his government. All the while, he sought to divert blame. He focused his criticism, to boot, on the United States and other foreign entities for their interference and contribution to the woes and ills of his country.[195] He assailed the US military in particular for its callous indifference to Afghan civilian lives and insisted, for instance, that US special forces units stop their night raids. In 2010, with the US troop surge, he demanded that the United States begin withdrawing its troops by the following year.[196] Then, in 2012, he insisted that foreign troops retreat to their bases within the next year and effectively hand over security to Afghan forces.[197] In 2013 he refused to sign a long-term security agreement with the United States covering US basing rights and protecting US military personnel who were alleged to have committed crimes from Afghan prosecution.

Under the US-Afghanistan Strategic Partnership Agreement (SPA), signed in May 2012, the United States and Afghanistan accepted fundamental understandings and commitments pertaining to US aid and Afghan governance. The SPA included a joint commitment to finalize a bilateral security agreement (BSA) to replace the 2003 status of forces agreement (Mason 2012). Under the SPA, the United States would have access to Afghan facilities; could engage in counterterrorism operations; and would advise, train, and assist Afghan security forces—in principle, through 2014 and beyond. The BSA, however, was to spell out the specifics: where the United States would have bases and the terms under which the US military would operate in Afghanistan. The BSA would therefore determine whether the United States and its NATO allies continued their military efforts in the country.

The Obama administration wanted to seal the deal. The absence of an agreement meant that it could become an issue in the upcoming 2014 Afghan presidential election. It also disrupted US force planning.[198] Karzai saw opportunity in the US dilemma. In 2013 he tried to commit the United States to protecting Afghanistan against external threats, a guarantee that could require US attacks on insurgent harborages in Pakistan.[199] He also tried to preserve his leverage. Fearing that the United States would sell him out after it had opened negotiations with the Taliban, Karzai suspended the negotiations with the United States over a long-term security deal until the Taliban agreed to meet directly with his government. His obstinacy that year prompted Obama to seriously consider the "zero option" of withdrawing US troops from Afghanistan—in full—by the end of the following year.[200]

The contentious US-Afghan negotiations did finally yield an agreement late in 2013 after Secretary of State John Kerry personally intervened. Still, Karzai did not make it easy. He insisted on a letter from President Obama assuring that US troops would not enter Afghan homes, barring exceptional circumstances (to save lives), and apologizing for the US role in the suffering of the Afghan people over the course of the war.[201] The plan was to read the letter to a special Loya Jirga—a gathering of thousands of elders—convened to decide the fate of the agreement.[202]

What Karzai got for his efforts, in the form of a presidential letter, was more a "tribute" than an apology and a reiteration of restrictions *under the agreement*: "Many of my countrymen and women have given their lives or been seriously wounded in the pursuit of protecting Afghans, and we honor the enormous sacrifices they have made, side by side with Afghans. As this new Agreement states, U.S. Forces shall not enter Afghan homes for the purposes of military operations, except under extraordinary circumstances involving urgent risk to life and limb of U.S. nationals."[203] After Karzai committed to abide by the decision of the Loya Jirga, he changed course when, after four days of deliberation, it voiced strong support for the immediate signing of the agreement. Karzai insisted on renegotiating the agreement to address his concerns; threatened to nullify the agreement if US forces raided one more Afghan home; and announced, much to the Obama administration's dismay, that he would leave the actual signing of the agreement to his successor.[204] Karzai seemed unmoved by thinly veiled White House threats, delivered, for example, by Susan Rice, President Obama's national security adviser, on a visit to Afghanistan: "Without a prompt signature, the U.S. would have no choice but to initiate planning for a post-2014 future in which there would be no U.S. or NATO troop presence in Afghanistan."[205] Still refusing to sign the agreement, Karzai sought negotiations with the Taliban, at the cost of further poisoning the US-Afghan relationship. In pursuing his failed initiative, he insisted that the United States release hardened Taliban prisoners and accused the United States of war crimes.[206] Karzai would not relent, though billions in US aid dollars and the security of his country (and government) were at stake. For whatever reason, ideological, political, or personal, it seems he could not bring himself to legitimate the extension of the US military presence.[207]

When Karzai left office in September 2014, as constitutionally required at the end of his second term, he was succeeded by Ashraf Ghani (a Columbia University PhD, former World Bank official, finance minister, and Pashtun). The transitional election earlier that year was, unsurprisingly, replete with controversy and drama. An April election, among eight candidates, had whittled the field to two: Ghani and Abdullah Abdullah (a former resistance fighter and foreign minister of mixed Tajik-Pashtun dissent, with a power base in the north of the country). The outcome of their June runoff election was tainted by widespread fraud involving perhaps millions of votes and accusations that Karzai himself had played a key role.[208] The candidates both declared victory, then feuded over the conduct of an independent audit, the terms of any power-sharing agreement, and the actual meaning of the agreed-upon terms (ICG 2014: 14–21). Confronting a debilitating stalemate, the Obama administration (through Secretary of State Kerry) brought heavy pressure on the candidates to compromise. In the end, the parties accepted a power-sharing agreement that made Abdullah an "executive prime minister," with the promise of future amendment to the Afghan constitution and—for now, by presidential decree—a "chief executive officer" ("with the functions of an Executive Prime Minister").[209] The agreement, with its vaguely defined division of responsibilities, nonetheless split appointment powers, promised electoral reforms, and gave Abdullah some role in policy decisions and implementation. Still, he would answer ultimately to the president (who retained exclusive powers; among his responsibilities, the president controlled the armed forces).[210]

The compromise had only changed the rules of the competition by moving it, formally, into (a divided) government. Indeed, divisive issues flared up again in early 2016, when Abdullah challenged plans for an October election for district council and parliamentary seats. He criticized the absence of necessary electoral reforms and the failure of a Loya Jirga to meet to create the position of "prime minister" for him to occupy, as required (within two years) under the 2014 power-sharing agreement.[211] In April 2016 Secretary of State Kerry flew to Afghanistan in an effort to extend his brokered compromise. Ghani's supporters insisted that the compromise agreement, which had no constitutional basis, was up for re-evaluation; Kerry insisted, in return, that the agreement applied for the full five years of the current president's term.[212] The result was an uneasy truce—a recipe for continuous competition and gridlock. As of May 2016, key positions in government, including that of defense minister, remained unfilled, as candidates failed to acquire parliamentary approval.[213] In August Abdullah played to his support base, quite publicly. He chastised Ghani for his unilateral decision-making, failure to consult with him on appointments, and lack of commitment to electoral reform, claiming Ghani was "not fit for the presidency."[214]

The Obama administration still got what it could reasonably hope to get from the compromise agreement. Under Ghani's presidency, relations with the United States greatly improved. Ghani immediately signed the BSA and a parallel agreement with NATO forces. He also lifted night-raid restrictions on US special operations forces; promised to take steps to build a more-inclusive, less-corrupt government; and appeared anxious to partner with the United States into the future.[215] Still, the Obama administration was not seeking a grand new bargain, permanent security arrangement, or reinvention of Afghan governance. It was settling, instead, for a commitment from the Afghan government to permit the administration to stay its existing course.

At this point, the administration was slowly leaving Afghanistan, having concluded that its problems were bigger than any one (or two) Afghan leader(s) could solve. The economy was in trouble, security conditions in the country were worsening, the Afghan leadership had all that it could do to prevent a governmental collapse, and endemic problems remained. Despite Ghani's pledge to prioritize the fight against corruption, the problem in Ghani's first year in office might actually have worsened.[216] Indeed, any success that Ghani had achieved, through his strong efforts, had come at the cost of his growing isolation and elite dissent, which together could undermine governmental stability.[217] Even as Ghani patched up his relationship with Abdullah, he faced a parliamentary revolt against his (ostensibly autocratic) leadership style and actions that had alienated various political constituencies; in November 2016, the parliament reacted resoundingly by impeaching seven cabinet ministers.[218] For the Obama administration, simply keeping the Afghan government together had become a challenging objective.

Economic

From 2001 to the present, the international donor committee has provided massive amounts of aid to fund projects around Afghanistan. The injection of monies and support helped build national institutions and, through a wide assortment of projects, positively affected local communities. The positive results were evident in aggregate statistics, which showed improvements, for example, in the country's GDP per capita, infant mortality, public health, and women's education. Aggregate statistics inevitably provoke questions, though, about the actual distribution of benefits: whether gains register more with some groups, in some areas, than with others. For instance, donors were most active in secure areas of the country, which creates a serious "selection problem" for analysis if monies and projects fail to flow to unstable parts of the country. The aggregate numbers also raise questions concerning the efficient use of resources; that is, whether alternative projects, funding, or policies might have yielded greater benefits. Indeed, the inflow of over a hundred billion dollars in aid to the Afghan economy had fostered an enormous and complex domestic patronage system.[219]

Yet concerns about the distribution and efficient use of resources provoke a bigger question: Are the gains sustainable? There are strong reasons to suspect, in fact, that the gains in Afghanistan will survive only if foreign benefactors infuse massive amounts of know-how, labor, and cash into the country, as they have for the now over a decade and a half of post-Taliban rule. Despite diverging donor priorities and different aid managers, a characteristic funding pattern has emerged. Donors have channeled huge amounts of aid directly into the field, with far too little concern for long-term benefits and far too much confidence that Western-influenced Afghan expats, who have held positions in government and in local affiliates of international funding agencies, could exert the control and oversight necessary to maintain program solvency. Afghan government officials too frequently had limited knowledge of the specifics or requirements of managing the country's programs, let alone the control of funds to support them; the United States, for one, had chosen to work around the government by dispensing aid through private contractors, the United Nations, and NGOs.[220]

The funding pattern has produced a disparate collection of poorly conceived, inappropriately designed, and partially finished projects undertaken with limited accountability, management, coordination, or concern for whether results would outlast the inflow of foreign resources. Indeed, CERP-funded projects typically emphasized a rapid impact with limited regard for strategic coherence, continuing oversight and management, and the overall contribution to development (ICG 2011: 18). Grand infrastructure projects (e.g., the refurbishing of the Kajaki hydroelectric dam in Helmand Province and construction of the Kabul power plant) offered huge returns for foreign companies but were impractical, as constructed, when assessed against actual need and the tax base, knowledge, and material resources necessary to support the projects, should they ever get finished.[221] Costs skyrocketed, schedules of completion repeatedly suffered, and projects remained idle when the insurgency threatened.

Much of the money spent has undoubtedly helped build Afghanistan's woefully inadequate infrastructure. With its billions of dollars in assistance, USAID alone accounted for well over a thousand miles of roads, many hundreds of schools and health clinics, and a quadrupling of the population on the electric power grid (SIGAR 2016: 7–8). With the curtailment of aid, these improvements can survive, however, only with the fresh resources, expertise, and support supplied by self-sustaining economic growth, which even massive infrastructural development could not guarantee. The indications of growth were hardly promising. By early 2016, the US special inspector general for Afghanistan reconstruction surmised, in its quarterly report to Congress, that security and economic challenges had left Afghanistan in poor shape: "Intractable insurgents, cutbacks in foreign military personnel, persistent emigration of people and capital, and a slowing global economy are shifting Afghanistan's economic prospects from troubling to bleak" (SIGAR 2016: 3). Insecurity, a retraction in donor funding, and a reticence to invest, or hold, money in the country all contributed to an economic contraction that tracked the US troop exodus.[222] The low growth rates were all the more ominous given Afghanistan's high level of poverty, the channeling of US aid overwhelmingly into the security sector (which fails to spur the growth returns of investments in human capital or the economy), and the country's standing as one of the most corrupt countries on earth.[223]

The only "good" news here perhaps was that Afghanistan had little room to fall. With its low literacy rates, health challenges, and extreme poverty, it remained one of the most challenging development projects on the planet.

Security

Whereas ISAF largely met its quantitative goals for building up the Afghan police and military, serious questions remained. In the short term, were these forces up to their tasks? In the long term, could these forces survive the corrosive effects of depletion in battle, a host of societal ills, and venal and incompetent Afghan governing institutions? That is, could they become the effective, self-reliant, professional, and legitimate force necessary to thwart, or reverse, Taliban gains? Their record of performance to date provides reasons for skepticism.

The Afghan Police
Under the nominal control of the Ministry of the Interior, the ANP and the Afghan Local Police (ALP) failed to acquire the effectiveness or legitimacy needed to build security in the country. The ANP remained undersized, even once the United

States took charge of police training. By the start of the Obama administration, the police-training mission was still short thousands of trainers and had limited ability to embed trainers in the field (O'Hanlon and Sherjan 2010: 28). Police training varied by trainer nationality (US training, for example, was directed more decidedly toward counterinsurgency), was generally rudimentary, halted once police officers were deployed, and was more the exception than the rule; most Afghan police officers received *no* training (O'Hanlon 2010: 70). But the problems of the force ran deeper than its limited skill set. Much of the Afghan population viewed the police as venal and self-interested, for good reason. The Afghan police were notorious for taking bribes, embezzling funds, thievery, and extortion (Bayley and Perito 2011: 2–3, 5). According to the US State Department's 2015 (annual) assessment of Afghan policy performance,[224] gross human rights violations remained rampant, justice remained "partial" at best, due process remained poorly followed or understood, and corruption remained a deeply rooted scourge at all levels of police practice. ANP officers paid for their promotions, corruption was rarely prosecuted, checkpoints were opportunities for police to collect "taxes," and bribes were paid to avoid arrest or obtain release from custody.

Unfortunately, getting rid of a few—or many—bad apples would not solve the problems of the Afghan police, which are embedded in its (informal) institutional structure. The ANP "began as a warlord-dominated institution and, with its district-level chiefs and beat cops, is extremely effective at reading and manipulating local dynamics." The police are "likely to act in service of local or familial interests above the laws and interests of the central government" and have proven capable of outwitting and outmaneuvering correctives. "In part, reforms to the police fail because politicians, warlords, businessmen, and ordinary citizens coordinate to some degree with police for protection and profit, and this gives police information and leverage enough to resist major organizational reform" (Zimmerman 2015: 22).

Building a professionalized police force is undoubtedly challenging—perhaps impossible—within a corrupt environment. Still, the United States and its allies deserve some blame for the persistent challenge, given the prevailing priorities in security-sector reform, that is, "the short-term imperatives of addressing the insurgency and creating security conditions conducive for international military disengagement" (Sedra 2015: 143).

The ALP offers a case in point. The ALP followed numerous prior unsuccessful US attempts to create viable local defense forces. Growing from the concept of village stability operations (VSO), with the support of General McChrystal and, later, General Petraeus, the program was placed under the control of the Ministry of Interior, with personnel answering to the local district chief of police to give the Afghan government a necessary sense of ownership (Hulslander and Spivey 2012: 128). The concept, from counterinsurgency doctrine, was to build local security from the bottom up, with local personnel; a high degree of local outreach and input; and support, training, and guidance from US military and special operations units. The program was intended to build security in areas of the country where Afghan security forces lacked an ongoing presence, and ultimately to foster good governance and development (Hulslander and Spivey 2012: 131, 134; Moyar 2014: 9).

Both President Karsai and US ambassador Eikenberry resisted General McChrystal's efforts to expand the program in 2010, fearing these units would exploit rather than serve their communities. Ironically, the program required arming the very men whom, in an effort to build national institutions, security, and stability, the United States and its allies had invested hundreds of millions of dollars to disarm.[225] Petraeus accepted Karzai's condition that the Ministry of the Interior control the ALP and blunted the remaining opposition (Moyar 2014: 11–12). The ALP was expanded in late 2013—after it showed initial promise—positioning tens of thousands of ALP personnel in districts around the country (Grenier 2015: 59–60). The United States sought a further expansion of the ALP, after the loss of Kunduz in September 2015, to thwart the Taliban advance.

One sympathetic military study (Moyar 2014: 1) concluded that even with active US stewardship, the VSO and ALP had "succeeded in some areas, failed in other areas, and encountered a mixture of success and failure in the remainder" (Moyar 2014: 1). A somewhat less sympathetic assessment of the ALP's "mixed record" estimated that "one-third of the ALP function correctly," noting that popular praise for the ALP's security efforts was exceeded by public complaints about ALP predation (ICG 2015: i, 25). The ALP's performance record—notably including allegations and evidence of corruption, human rights abuses, and ties to local strongmen—provoked US NATO partners to express severe reservations about the program.[226] That US military personnel had to go to great lengths to monitor, investigate, and punish abuses (Moyar 2014: 81) was obviously cause for concern when US monitoring, mentoring, and active support for the ALP lagged with the reduction in the US military presence in Afghanistan. Whether the ALP could stay true to its foundational principles remained in doubt. Its future was likely determined by the absence of program support in the Ministry of Defense and Interior; the temptations of predation and tribal and ethnic politics; Taliban penetration and threats; the withholding and pilfering of program resources by central government and police officials; and the corrosive influence of local police chiefs, warlords, and power brokers (Moyar 2014: 63–68).

Police ideally enforce laws and maintain the peace, and they can serve as a first line of defense against an insurgency. Yet they also serve a critical symbolic role: "The police are the most visible representatives of the state to most Afghans" (Sedra 2015: 136). As such, police corruption in Afghanistan constitutes a critical—and potentially decisive—national failing.

The Afghan National Army
Arresting troubling security trends was no small task for the ANA; it remained a work in progress. The NTM-A made great strides in Afghan military recruitment, training, and professionalization. It was involved at all levels in Afghan security: building the capacity of the Ministry of Defense; educating a wide range of military specialists; training commissioned officers, noncommissioned officers, and infantry; and developing the military's logistical, aerial, and intelligence capabilities. In partnership with the International Joint Command (ICJ), it also embedded ISAF trainers in battle, aiming to eventually push the Afghan military into the lead (Barley 2015: 6–8). Afghan military performance improved with time. It was now bigger, fielding a greater variety of skilled personnel, and taking casualties at ever-higher rates, indicating that it was not shying from battle. The military nevertheless remained beset by serious problems and deficiencies.

First, Afghan military casualties had risen to potentially unsustainable levels. In 2014 the Afghan military and police sustained 12,500 casualties (dead and wounded); in 2015, they sustained 16,000 casualties.[227] The death toll skyrocketed. Annual deaths of Afghan security personnel now greatly exceeded the number of fatalities of all foreign troops over the full fifteen years of the US-led war effort. By one set of estimates, the number of Afghan security personnel killed was approximately 925 in 2009, 1,950 in 2011, 4,700 in 2013, and 7,000 in 2015.[228] For the first ten months of 2016 alone, fatalities among these forces approximated the totals for the entire prior year (SIGAR 2017a: 98). Heavy casualties helped fuel a force annual attrition rate that stood at 35 percent (SIGAR 2017b: 106). The rising tide of casualties threatened to exceed replacement capacities and affect personnel retention, cohesion, and morale.

Second, the ANA had yet to develop critical logistical, intelligence, planning, maintenance, and aerial support capabilities. It had long depended on the US military to serve in these capacities as an "enabling" force. Indeed, it had long depended on US troops, when paired with local troops, to carry the burden in the fighting.[229] In battle, the ANA therefore had trouble obtaining and maintaining equipment; anticipating attacks and seizing the initiative; compensating (on the ground) for a lack of combat air support; and shifting forces, when required, to deflect attacks, take the offensive, or preserve unit strength. With the Taliban on the offensive in 2016, Afghan forces consistently reverted to form: they manned checkpoints rather than actively seeking to engage the adversary, abandoned their posts in large numbers, retreated to more defensible positions within and around main provincial cities, depended on well-trained commandos to do the work of regular troops, relied heavily on US air strikes to keep the adversary at bay, and proved unable to hold ground once it had been cleared.[230] The effects were apparent in ever-larger swaths of territory surrendered to Taliban control.

Third, the ANA suffered in command at all levels, as it weathered the maladies that beset Afghan governance. These included patronage and factionalism (with competing Tajik and Pashtun blocks within the defense establishment); a lack of transparency and accountability; shoddy and fraudulent record keeping that made it impossible to know the actual inventory or size of the Afghan military; proprietary holds on personnel and resources; and of course, pervasive corruption. The lack of good leadership (from noncommissioned officers on up) remained a critical deficiency, responsible for a host of ills, including troop attrition.[231] These problems conspired to drain military resources, drive out military professionalism, inhibit efficient military planning, and ultimately impair the military's ability to perform effectively and coherently as a combat force (on these deficiencies, see ICG 2010b).

Despite these problems, or because of them, the Afghan military and police were costly to build and maintain. For that reason, in 2012 NATO negotiated a force ceiling that would reduce the combined size of the Afghan military and police from 352,000 to 230,000 personnel. Inasmuch as the decision reflected donor budgetary concerns, not military conditions on the ground,[232] the United States and its NATO allies later reconsidered this action.[233] The US goal at the NATO summit in the summer of 2016 was to raise $15 billion to fund Afghan security forces through 2020 (in addition to the $68 billion already expended to fund the Afghan military and police forces). The US Defense Department had budgeted around $3.5 billion annually, with the Afghan government slated to provide an additional $420 million annually, to cover the expected annual budget of $5 billion. The summit brought the United States close—in pledges—to achieving its goal.[234]

The appeal for funds occurred against a bleak history of prior support and a recognition of declining donor leverage to bring about change. Billions of dollars in aid had been pilfered or squandered, concerns persisted over the functional size of the Afghan military, and the Afghan government had failed to meet military spending targets or stem corruption. Donor countries recognized that they could not hold the Afghan government to new benchmarks or corruption standards—especially with security conditions deteriorating in the country.[235] The United States and its allies nevertheless, concluded that they had no real options except to fund Afghan security forces. The unappealing alternatives were to (a) let these forces fail or (b) carry the physical load into the indefinite future themselves.

The risk, of course, was that Afghan security forces, despite the infusion of funds, would become a "work in regress." They could well disintegrate or collapse, perhaps in a slow yet accelerating downward spiral. As security conditions deteriorated, all involved might fend for themselves—by cutting and running, grabbing what benefits they could, or making deals—allowing the Taliban to press its advantages.[236] Pulling from its (now over two-decades-old) playbook, the Taliban could establish itself in the hospitable southern and eastern portions of the country and eventually move to envelop the rest.

Nearing a Final Resolution? The Trump Administration in Afghanistan

Donald Trump, of course, inherited the war that Obama had so much wanted to end. What Trump would do with it, however, remained a riddle. Trump's ever-changing policy positions and proposals surfaced, untethered to a consistent set of principles.

Trump had argued that his two predecessors had ensnared the United States in costly and unnecessary wars in Iraq and Afghanistan. When the Bush administration was negotiating the SOFA in 2008, Trump insisted that the United States should "get out of Iraq right now," a position he repeated in 2011 when Obama tried to negotiate an extension that would permit US forces to remain in Iraq.[237] Yet Trump also argued that Obama had pulled US forces out of Iraq prematurely, creating the Islamic State menace that the United States now confronts in Iraq and Syria. Trump held open the possibility, at least, that he would not repeat that mistake in Afghanistan.

In office, Trump challenged Washington with iconoclastic rhetoric. He complained that the United States had given away too much to the world and received too little in return. He surrounded himself with a coterie of "believers" drawn from the nationalist/isolationist fringe of American politics. With their counsel, Trump promised to "drain the swamp" of old Washington hands and pursue policies that place "America First." Although much of the Republican establishment expected Trump, once elected, to "pivot" from candidate to president—some even claimed Trump had risen to the challenge and requirements of the office by adopting a familiar foreign policy approach[238]—critics decried Trump's unconventional—even erratic—policy shifts and inattentiveness in governance.[239] They asked whether Trump's pursuit of what he dubbed "a different kind of presidency"[240] would involve a decreased US willingness and capability to confront global military challenges.

For much of his first year in office, Trump shunted aside the Afghanistan War, avoiding a decision on whether to stay or leave. His signals on that point were ambiguous and inconsistent. He railed at his national security advisers, complaining that US strategy, in a sixteen-year effort, had failed to deliver a win. Yet he suggested that the problems reduced simply to a matter of (bad) management when he demanded the firing of the widely respected ISAF commander (General John W. Nicholson Jr., whom he had yet to meet). He eventually delegated decisions for an incremental force increase to his secretary of defense, James Mattis, while failing to provide the strategic guidance for the force deployment that Mattis required to act on his delegated authority.

The Taliban would push ahead, with or without a White House strategy. Early in the Trump administration, US military commanders described the situation in Afghanistan as a "stalemate."[241] Yet high-profile attacks continued to enforce a "new reality." In April 2017, in the north of the country, ten Taliban fighters—dressed in army uniforms—breeched a military base and managed to kill 250 Afghan soldiers. In May 2017 a truck-bomb explosion near the presidential palace in Kabul killed 150 people and wounded many more. Aggregate statistics looked grim. Daily security incidents reached near-record levels. Civilian casualties topped five thousand in the first half of 2017 alone. In the first five months of the same year, Afghan security forces incurred around six thousand casualties.[242] Perhaps most ominously, 40 percent of Afghanistan's districts were under Taliban control, influence, or contestation (SIGAR 2017b: 83–88).

A harsh reality had set in. Security in the country depended on Afghan security forces that were still not up to their task, either offensively or defensively. Any progress achieved, with or without US military support, was clearly reversible.

White House signals became clearer six months into the administration, indirectly a product of abysmal presidential approval ratings,[243] poisonous White House feuds, and an endless turnover in advisory personnel. In the housecleaning that ensued, a triumvirate of Trump advisers—all (former and current) generals[244]— closed ranks to force the nationalists from advisory positions. Whereas many in Washington viewed the change in guard favorably, the ascendance of military leaders within the White House sparked concerns that civilians had ceded their responsibilities to the military.[245] The fear was that the administration would place military considerations and preferences above all else in US foreign and national security policies. On that count, Trump's own predilection—his affinity for having high-ranking military officers under *his* immediate command ("his generals," as he referred to them)—was not reassuring.

The effects of the new order registered almost immediately. Trump, in August 2017, met with his national security advisers at Camp David and accepted their recommendation that the United States re-engage in Afghanistan. After he reputedly "studied Afghanistan in great detail and from every conceivable angle" (quoted from a national address), he announced a strategy that amounted *vaguely* to staying the current course.[246] Indeed, the US decision, as announced, amounted to a non-decision, cloaked in the rhetoric of the presidential campaign. Trump had lambasted Obama for giving the enemy too much information about US deployments, sacrificing the element of surprise, failing to put due emphasis on the "radical Islamic terrorist" threat, and leaving Iraq prematurely. More generally, Trump had criticized past US attempts to engage in "nation-building." His new strategy, paired with a troop increase, would supposedly address these deficiencies while purportedly employing US troops specifically to fight terrorism. Yet fundamental tensions in policy remained.

Trump promoted the virtues of nontransparency, much as he had touted unpredictability during his presidential campaign. He had claimed, "We must as a nation be more unpredictable."[247] Trump would not commit to a mission deadline or even announce the number of US troops deployed to Afghanistan. Yet the secrecy that keeps valued information from adversaries becomes a liability if it strangles useful discourse. A lack of transparency can cloak deficiencies, limit useful policy inputs and criticism, and make it more difficult for policy makers to establish viable goals and policies.

Trump promised a "conditions-based" US troop withdrawal. Yet he failed to disclose what those "conditions" might be. He left unanswered whether US troops could solve problems that in the preceding administration a significantly larger US force could not. After all, the problems of Afghan governance and institutions remained. Opponents still chafed at President Ghani's remoteness, lack of inclusiveness, and dealmaking;[248] corruption still permeated interactions at all levels of governance; and Afghan institutions still lacked the capacity to provide for the country's essential economic, social, and security needs.

Trump promised to press Pakistan—hard—to engage the insurgency within its borders. Yet he failed to differentiate his approach from the Obama administration's in 2009,[249] which could not compel Pakistan to change its ways. True to form, the Pakistan government warned the United States against "scapegoating" its country (despite its cooperation and problems beyond its control),[250] and relations with Pakistan deteriorated from there.[251] Trump accused Pakistan of "lies and deceit" and voiced regret for the billions in dollars in US aid that previous administrations had "foolishly given" to that country.[252] Shortly thereafter, the United States announced the suspension of aid to Pakistan.[253] Yet the administration—still relying on Pakistan for intelligence and military support—could not push Pakistan to accept responsibility for harboring Afghan insurgent groups, much less renounce its use of the insurgency to maintain a controlling hand in Afghanistan.

Trump announced that his strategy would focus on killing terrorists, not nation-building; still, he also claimed it would forge the "integration of all instruments of American power—diplomatic, economic, and military—toward a successful outcome." Then he failed to answer the essential question: Can one kill terrorists without adopting some elements of a nation-building approach? Specifically, can one find terrorists, and preserve gains against them, absent the personnel and resources of a successful counterinsurgency operation? Can Afghan security forces strengthen their hold in the country without support for the kind of "nation-building" required to improve government efficiency, combat corruption, and build the infrastructure by which Afghan civilian and military institutions can extend their local reach? Conversely, can one lift restrictions on commanders in battle, as Trump promised to do, without inviting civilian casualties that would play into the hands of the insurgents?

No less important, Trump promised to combat al-Qaeda and stop the Taliban, but nonetheless waffled on the distinction between the two. With al-Qaeda no longer the threat within Afghanistan that had justified US intervention, how far would the administration go to achieve some accommodation with the Taliban?

With these nagging issues, Trump still promised a "win." Yet he implicitly defined a goal, however, that fell decidedly short of that—indeed, a goal that echoed the narrowed objectives of the Obama administration. He did not speak of defeating the insurgency but rather of preventing the Taliban from taking over the country. Presumably the administration, like its predecessor, hoped eventually to pass the burden to a fledgling Afghan military, which would rise to the challenge or create conditions for a negotiated settlement. In short, he offered less than a "win" and more a glimpse of the past, as he channeled the (dashed) hopes of the preceding administrations. Trump's "innovation," however, was in his claims that his strategy would do it all, do it well, and do it without requiring trade-offs. "Our troops will fight to win. We will fight to win. From now on, victory will have a clear definition. Attacking our enemies, obliterating ISIS, crushing Al Qaeda, preventing the Taliban from taking over Afghanistan and stopping mass terror attacks against America before they emerge." Yet critics could rightly ask, so what about the strategy is "new?" For that matter, what about the strategy is "strategy?"

Absent a clear strategy, it is impossible to know at this point whether, by merit of its actions, the Trump administration has "pulled free" of Obama's exit schedule by plotting a re-escalation of the conflict. The signs, however, do not suggest the administration plans a "breakout." Trump approved a "surge" force of four thousand troops that still kept US forces at a fraction of the peak (surge) levels of the Obama administration. Then the Trump administration adhered generally to the qualitative limits set by the Obama administration: US troops were set to train, advise, and support Afghan troops, not to fight on their behalf.

Trump took the understandable course of recommitting—*minimally*—to the fight. He had to do *something*, having sold himself to the public as an agent of change; blamed US security challenges on the oversights, ineptitude, and low commitment of the prior administration; and inherited two unappealing choices (maintaining the current course or leaving Afghanistan entirely). He pinned his hopes on a mix of upgrades to existing policy instruments. The United States would train more members of effective (yet overused) Afghan special operations units; advise and train Afghan soldiers; employ US air power; and back Afghan-government security reform efforts aimed at rooting out incompetence, fighting corruption, and improving coordination among security services.[254]

The first year of the new administration did not produce a significant upswing in US action. The United States planned to bring US force levels by 2018 to around fifteen thousand troops in the country and task advisory teams to work with Afghan troops at the battalion level.[255] True, it conducted air strikes at a ferocious pace, under more limited rules of engagement. Between August and December 2017 the United States and its Afghan ally conducted two thousand air strikes, nearing the total for all of 2015 and 2016 combined.[256] Yet the United States success ultimately depended on the capabilities of Afghan security forces and the Taliban's willingness to negotiate[257] when the number of Afghan soldiers and police in uniform declined dramatically in 2017[258] and the Afghan government was progressively losing its hold on the country. With the year ending, the Afghan government controlled just over half of the country's districts, a 16 percent drop from the levels in late 2015.[259]

Although the signs did not point to a reversal in fortune, the administration had neither the will, nor the practical latitude, to do much more than it did. Given Trump's limited affection for the Afghan mission, a largely indifferent public, and a war that had lasted too long, US re-engagement occurred loosely within constraints set by the preexisting exit schedule. The administration imposed an implicit troop ceiling at levels higher than the ceiling of the departing Obama administration; but it nonetheless set those levels in reference to the low prior levels. The Trump administration seemed inclined to constrict US forces at these *somewhat* higher levels before plotting its own exit. By the end of 2018, with the exiting of the team of military generals from his administration, Trump signaled his intent to order a substantial reduction in the US troop presence in Afghanistan.

The underlying reality here is simple. The Trump administration cannot reverse the history ("unring the bell") of prior US troop withdrawals. These withdrawals make the mass reassertion of US troops into Afghanistan unpalatable—psychologically, intellectually, and ideologically—for multiple political constituencies.[260] Indeed, much like its predecessor, the Trump administration paired a troop increase with movement toward disengagement. It pressed Afghan forces to withdraw from rural areas to defend more populated parts of the country, which would leave rural areas for the insurgents to control.[261] It also commenced direct negotiations with the Taliban, which had insisted for years on *bilateral* talks over US objections that any such talks should be "Afghan-owned and Afghan-led."[262] With the Afghan government sidelined in these negotiations, the "military issues" of the conflict had been separated from the less tractable "political issues" of the conflict. In that sense, the Trump chapter of US involvement in Afghanistan read much like the final chapter of US involvement in Vietnam. The United States had engaged an adversary diplomatically who viewed negotiations as a means to facilitate a US exit.

Conclusions

The Vietnam War sent hundreds of thousands of American protesters into the streets and fueled dissent across university campuses; the Iraq War soon brought recriminations, finger pointing, and charges of incompetence and deceit against some or all members of the Bush administration. The Afghanistan War was different in certain respects, yet strikingly similar in others. In all three conflicts, the United States weathered the four stages of means-driven policymaking. US leaders shifted their focus from immediate mission goals, to disjoined mission tasks, to cost constraints, and then to the exit schedule.[263]

Stage 1, Engagement: Fixation

The Afghanistan War was neither Vietnam nor Iraq in an important respect: US military leaders proved adept at innovating, early and repeatedly, to handle unconventional challenges. But the Bush administration went to war in Afghanistan with little sense of how the US effort in that country would serve, or undermine, the broad goals that US policy makers articulated for the new "global war on terrorism." The evidence in that regard is substantial. The principals devoted little thought to the future governance of the country, even though the politics and leadership of a post-Taliban Afghanistan and the spread of instability to neighboring Pakistan could make or break a US victory. The administration wrongly assumed that the United States could dispatch the Taliban quickly and move on to target other countries in a global antiterrorism campaign. It failed to recognize the challenges of acquiring international cooperation for a war in Afghanistan (and a global war on terrorism). More generally, it viewed the US struggle in Afghanistan as one small part of a global multifront effort that required the United States to do all things well without difficult trade-offs.

Stage II, Extension: Disjunction

The Bush administration left the US military to fight with severe constraints. It had failed to plan for a lengthy stay in Afghanistan; wanted to expedite a US exit from the country; and with its turn toward Iraq, left the US military to survive on dwindling resources.

The US mission in Afghanistan *expanded* as the US military took charge of training Afghan security forces, continued counterterrorism operations, and channeled resources into national stabilization and development. Yet US leaders left the military to define the Afghan mission through default. Delegation fostered wide gaps between what US civilian leaders sought to achieve, what the US military, more ambitiously, hoped to achieve, and what the US military could actually deliver given formidable challenges and limited resources. With this disconnect, US civilian officials mistakenly presumed that the US military could meet ambitious goals for enlarging the Afghan army and police; the Afghan government would unify, reform, and build its capacity sufficiently to assist the US-led effort; the regional handover of OEF responsibilities to ISAF would both follow and facilitate the geographical extension of security in the country; and the war was essentially over, requiring neither an injection of resources nor the administration's full attention.

Rumsfeld would eventually intervene to pull the military command in Afghanistan back into line. With the appointment of a new US military commander, Rumsfeld delivered a clear message: build up the Afghan military so that it could take charge. Still, Rumsfeld could not, through sheer force of will, mandate the

Afghan institutional development, alliance cohesion, and security improvements required for an easy US exit from the conflict.

Stage III, Limitation: Constriction

With the US mission floundering, the Obama administration opted for a US force "surge" into Afghanistan. It hoped to regain the initiative and turn the tide against the Taliban insurgency. But the president had grown wary of the direction of the war effort. He recognized—apparently early on—the high costs of scoring a win against the Taliban and the reality that the Afghan government would remain an unreliable and ineffective partner. His efforts to extend the US presence in Afghanistan, by borrowing a late-stage strategy from the Iraq playbook, provoked fractious debate among the president's advisers over war costs and priorities. When the president chose finally to send additional forces to Afghanistan, he sought to constrict the mission. His intentions were apparent when he pressed his advisers insistently for less-costly options; gave the US military fewer troops than it said it needed; imposed a compressed timeline for assessing the success of his surge; and established a modest (indeed, somewhat nebulous) mission for US forces, which they could not help but achieve. His goal was not to defeat the Taliban and build viable, transparent, and effective central government institutions, nor was it even to ensure that Afghan security forces could carry the load with a US departure. His goal was to weaken the Taliban—to "reverse its momentum"—in order to create an environment in which Afghan forces could hold their own. Missing from the extensive discussions leading to the president's surge decision was an overriding sense of what the infusion of US troops should, or could, accomplish.

Stage IV, Disengagement: Extrication

Obama eventually committed to a "fixed" withdrawal schedule before settling for what amounted to a "withdrawal in place" when Afghan forces proved unable to stem the Taliban resurgence. The retraction reduced the military exposure of US troops but also limited their military effectiveness. In consequence, US forces remained in limbo as the administration struggled, in its final months, to end its participation in the war by contracting troop levels and responsibilities, adopting restrictive rules of engagement, and pursuing openings (and partners) for negotiations with insurgent factions. Although the president had asked his advisers for an "exit *strategy*," which implies attentiveness to overriding goals, the question of US goals that "came up throughout the deliberations," "was never central to them, perhaps because it was too difficult and divisive" (Jervis 2010/2011: 698). The president settled for an exit *plan*, designed to reach milestones on the path to total withdrawal.

In May 2014 President Obama articulated the principles of exit with his troop withdrawal plans: "We have to recognize Afghanistan will not be a perfect place, and it is not America's responsibility to make it one."[264] Events repeatedly forced him to delay the US departure and to expand the US military role in that country. But even with deteriorating conditions on the ground, he did not retract his initial commitment, and he continued to work around his departure schedule. He did not reintroduce US forces into Afghanistan; instead, he *delayed* their exit from the country and *limited* US troops to an enabling and oversight role. Despite mounting evidence that Afghan forces—and the Afghan government—were ill-equipped to take the lead, he supplied only the support required to avoid imminent defeat. As Obama added in his 2014 announcement, "The future of Afghanistan must be decided by Afghans."[265]

5

Three Long and Costly Wars

What Can We Learn?

US decision makers fought on their own terms in Vietnam, Iraq, and Afghanistan; that was the problem. Their strategies played to immediate mission goals, disjoined tasks, cost constraints, and an exit schedule, not to deliberative thinking about ultimate goals and how best to achieve them. Decision makers had to contend with adversary forces, recalcitrant host governments, and unsupportive local populations in wars that played unwittingly to adversary strengths and resolve. US success remained partial, fragile, relative, and contingent; consistently fell short of initial promise; occurred astride a progressive narrowing of options; and proved insufficient, in the end, to convince US leaders to endure. At some point they had had enough and prepared to depart the conflict.

To be fair, chroniclers of the Vietnam, Iraq, and Afghanistan Wars, including military and civilian officials who orchestrated them, could contest this dismal portrayal of US wartime decision-making with a rival account of the US wartime record. With some justification, members of the Nixon and Ford administrations accused Congress of undermining what US forces had gained in combat by curtailing aid to the Saigon government before it fell to North Vietnamese forces—two years *after* the US exodus. The prosecutors of the Iraq and Afghanistan Wars can also claim successes. In Iraq, US forces quickly toppled Saddam Hussein's regime; and they eventually snatched a victory of sorts from seemingly imminent defeat with the 2007 troop surge back into Iraq and the accompanying turn toward counterinsurgency principles. The Bush administration thus created space, at least, for the Iraqi government to implement reforms that might stabilize the country. In Afghanistan, US special forces units teamed with Afghani irregulars to drive the Taliban and its al-Qaeda cohorts from power. The quick dispatching of the Taliban government validated claims that mobility, precision, and firepower gave the United States a critical edge against many a military contender.

Yet the facts belie a sanguine portrayal of these various US military efforts. The United States went to war in Vietnam without a clear sense of what it could accomplish through force; fought to US military strengths without due regard for enemy strategy; ultimately enforced a ceiling on the US troop investment to serve domestic political, not US strategic, goals; and finally left the conflict with little but a delayed defeat to show for its efforts. The idea that the United States achieved Nixon's stated goal of "peace with honor" in Vietnam is contravened by the terms of the 1973 peace accord, which left fundamental issues unsettled, and the outright collapse of the South Vietnamese army in 1975 against a smaller force of North Vietnamese regulars. In Iraq, the Bush administration was overwhelmed from the start by the political, economic, and military challenges of keeping the country functioning, even before it erupted in all-out civil war. Two years removed—again—from the US departure, even modest US goals for Iraq proved ambitious, as its political and military institutions, built with US support, verged on collapse. The Iraqi army was in tatters, Sunni Islamic militants controlled the northern third of the country, and the Iraqi government had turned for security to the same (Shiite) militia that had helped stoke civil war in the country. In Afghanistan, the United States fought the longest war in its history yet settled for exiting the country, on a fixed schedule, before Afghan institutions proved they could stand on their own. Afghan security forces had not shown they could provide security, nor had the Afghan government established that it could overcome corruption, resource deprivation, political squabbling, and warlordism to address the pressing needs of its citizens.

Policy failure was not preordained; none of the deleterious conflict phases followed inextricably from one another. Political leaders could have short-circuited the process by pursuing goals that suited US capabilities or avoiding no-win wars in the first place. They *did not do that*, however, and they thereafter allowed policy to run its (four-stage) course. Indeed, US policy makers were strikingly unwilling to re-evaluate current policies, much less change course. In Vietnam, it took a change in administration, then years of additional fighting, to move the United States—ever so slowly—toward an exit. In Iraq, it took a civil war and the prospect of a pending US defeat in the country to motivate the Bush administration to take action. Years into the Iraqi venture, the administration did what it should have done from the start: it convened experts, reviewed US options, thought realistically about the endgame, and made a deliberative choice. In Afghanistan, it once more took a change in administration, and its startling recognition that the problems of Afghanistan ran deep (its acknowledgment, in fact, that the United States was likely, with a US troop increase, to repeat the errors of Lyndon Johnson in Vietnam), to push the US leadership to take a long, hard look at the US mission and debate the consequences of escalating US involvement, persevering, and reducing the US footprint.

These moments of reckoning came late in part because policy makers resisted questioning and debate. Where sound policy requires openness, competition, a free flow of ideas, and a willingness to re-evaluate and reject arguments, politics often requires the opposite: secrecy, restrictive access to information, a closing of ranks, the creation of "realities" through definitive action, and a dogged determination to make past policies work. Leaders thus seek to foreclose discussion rather than derail a policy, undercut a consensus, or arm potential critics with compromising or embarrassing information that could sabotage the administration or its policies.

These moments of reckoning occurred all too infrequently, moreover, because the key decisional problem defies standard correctives. It cannot be solved merely by studying the problem, seeking alternatives, acquiring more information, or structuring decision-making to somehow allow for competing views. The reason lies in the problem's insidiousness: specifically, the generous availability of immediate goal substitutes that masquerade as overriding purposes. It is no wonder then that inflicting costs on the adversary in Vietnam, and regime change in Iraq and Afghanistan, became consensus policy choices; that staying the course became the intellectual path of least resistance once US policy makers had committed to a military solution; and that US policy makers, when they finally had had enough, headed for the exit.

Lessons from the Decisional Stages of War

Over a half century has passed since the start of the Vietnam War, but the US wars in Afghanistan and Iraq display similar markings, a decisional pattern rooted in the non-rational tendencies of a "means-driven" process. Critical lessons from these three long wars emerge from examining non-rational decision-making in the four stages of these conflicts.

Stage I: Fixation

Military missions loomed large in US decision-making during the Vietnam, Iraq, and Afghanistan Wars when policy makers failed to connect preferred actions to broader purposes. They thus failed to appreciate the costs and consequences of their actions or the potential benefits of policy alternatives. True, the first stage of these three wars differed in some respects. In Iraq and Afghanistan, the primary mission was adversary regime change; in Vietnam, the US targeted the allied Diem regime in Saigon as an outgrowth of an ongoing US commitment to an independent South Vietnam. These differences aside, the early actions of the Johnson and Bush administrations inspire several lessons.

First, *policy makers must recognize the danger of illusionary consensus*. Much is made of the problems of premature agreement in group-level decision-making. Members of cohesive groups eschew the careful consideration of options and consequences, avoid useful dialogue, quash dissent, and move too quickly toward resolution (Janis 1982). Far less is made of a tendency for policy makers to latch onto alternatives that represent a lowest common denominator of agreement, when those same policy makers diverge in their views of the problem or the workings of given alternatives. That tendency was on display in the early stages of the Vietnam, Iraq, and Afghanistan conflicts.

The Johnson administration inaugurated its Vietnam bombing campaign without reconciling conflicting assumptions about how bombing would produce desired ends; it then expanded the size and mandate of the US ground force without considering the purpose of the US military mission, the conditions that would make US policies succeed, or the confounding consequences of the growing US war investment. The administration could only hope that US military intervention would persuade Hanoi to end the fight; should Hanoi refuse to concede, it had no plan beyond upping the ante. In consequence, the administration could not answer basic questions. Was the war in Vietnam essentially an international or a civil conflict? What results would the United States accept short of victory, and what costs would the United States willingly pay to achieve them? Was the US strategy to punish the enemy to coerce concessions, to defeat the enemy, or to deny victory to the enemy to press it to reconsider its goals?

In Iraq, the Bush administration prepared for combat with a blinding objective: to bring down the Saddam Hussein regime. Accomplishing that goal would presumably disarm Iraq of its purported WMD, help spread democracy, aid the global fight against terrorism, and make a military point: the US military, with its enormous technological advantages, could bring down governments quickly through decapitation. What the administration did not do was acknowledge, let alone settle, vital issues: how long it planned to stay in Iraq; what it intended to accomplish there; and how deeply it planned to intrude, as an occupying force, in the ongoing governance of the country. The administration paid little heed to warnings of the political dangers ahead in Iraq that might challenge an undersized and underprepared US occupation force.

In Afghanistan, US forces routed the Taliban from the capital within the first weeks of the US-led operation. The Bush administration went to war, however, without probing how unseating the Taliban would facilitate—and maybe confound—the administration's ambitious global war on terrorism. Thus, it was unprepared to prevent the enemy's leadership from escaping, forestall its re-emergence as an insurgent threat in far-off reaches of the country (and the tribal areas of Pakistan), and fight a war in which success depended on the quality of Afghan governance. It failed to ask all-important questions. How could the United States assure a stable future for Afghanistan if the plan was to leave the country as soon as possible? How could the United States succeed, moreover, given the widespread poverty, conflict, and rivalry within Afghanistan that threatened its central governance; the woeful state of Afghan governmental institutions; and reliance on the uncoordinated military contributions of allies who were reticent to employ military force and disagreed over how the mission would contribute to Afghan nation-building?

In these wars, then, policy makers accepted solutions (bombing or regime change) that offered something for everyone—indeed, *because* they offered something for everyone. In Vietnam and Iraq, in particular, the policy makers ignored bright, shiny signs that their disagreements ran deep. Ironically, they would have stood on firmer ground had they disagreed outwardly over policy prescriptions but had shared views of the essential problem.

Second, *leaders must recognize, before they leap, that getting into war is a lot easier than getting out.* Military intervention is a costly entanglement of uncertain proportions and duration. Ironically, Richard Haass (2009) has done sound planning a disservice by distinguishing "wars of necessity" from "wars of choice" when arguing that the United States, with its "vital" oil interests at stake, *had* to act against Iraq in 1991 yet merely *chose* to act against Iraq in 2003. War is *always* a matter of choice. Threats to US interests always reduce to matters of quantity, not fundamental quality. After all, Saddam Hussein presumably planned to market Kuwaiti oil, and the United States would have retained options had it not gone to war, whatever Hussein's specific plans. Thus, the decision to intervene must always inspire a thoughtful weighing of the pros and cons—that is, a rejection of the belief that the United States has no recourse but to act. More fundamentally, making such a decision requires thoughtful answers to the fundamental question, "'How does it end?'" (Petraeus 2017: 162). The answer lies in the probing of mission goals and the costs and the likelihood of achieving those goals.

Third, *leaders must acknowledge, well before intervening, that preparedness for a post-occupation period is essential.* It is not enough for leaders to insist, for example, that they "won't do nation-building," will fight only to defend US interests, have a clear exit plan, and expect allies to pick up any slack. Secretary of State Powell was right when he offered some version of "you break it, you own it" to suggest that intervening countries have an obligation for, and likely a considerable interest in, rebuilding a country after dismantling its government (Gilsinan 2015). Such ownership, even if only recognized belatedly, brings with it unexpected challenges that reduce the chances of an early or easy departure. The key questions in today's wars are not "how do we win, or avoid defeat?" but rather "how do we define success?" and "how will we know it from failure?" Indeed, Haass (2009: xxi) again misses the point when noting that "somewhere along the way . . . Afghanistan changed from a war of necessity to one of choice." By placing the focus on the goals of the war, not on its planning, the false dichotomy relieves the war's orchestrators of responsibility for helping to create the conditions, through poor planning, that made perseverance a matter of "choice." Indeed, Haass (2009: xxii–xxiii) looks to Obama's lengthy planning for the 2009 surge, and then finite troop commitment, as evidence that the Afghanistan War became a matter of choice. What is the implication: that some wars are too important to require, or allow, the careful consideration of goals, costs, contingencies, or departure plans? The fact remains that non-conventional wars, like that in Afghanistan, *require* the dutiful evaluation of payoffs, timelines, and exit strategies.

Fourth, *leaders must recognize that preparations for postwar contingencies will fall short absent dedicated bureaucratic support.* As long as the government lacks strong organizational backing for post-conflict development and reconstruction, the mission will remain subordinate to military operations in planning. Government leaders will continue to push post-conflict contingencies into the distant future, forcing government agencies to invent a "postwar" mission on the fly that will inevitably suffer in planning, coordination, and resourcing. Most definitely, building dedicated support for the postwar mission will generate resistance, in the form of turf battles within government and fears among high-level officials of a self-fulfilling prophesy. They will worry that preparing for the "worst case"—a demanding, seemingly interminable, post-conflict mission in a far-off land—will give a green light to nation-building, and even to intervention for that purpose. These fears draw from the so-called law of the instrument, which suggests that capabilities motivate action: with a hammer in hand, all the world is a nail. Yet what is the alternative? By the same logic, the United States should dismantle its military to ensure that wars, like those in Vietnam and Iraq, never happen. In actuality, dutiful planning for post-conflict contingencies could inject realism into planning. Just as the US military frequently has served as a counterweight to civilians arguing for precipitous US intervention abroad (currently, in Syria), those schooled in the challenges of post-conflict environments can offer reasoned and informed assessments of likely traps and pitfalls, which could slow down the drive toward intervention. After all, the United States did not intervene in Vietnam, Iraq, or Afghanistan because the US military pushed a reluctant civilian leadership into war.

Stage II: Disjunction

In principle, civilian leaders set the parameters of war policy by outlining objectives, promoting a strategy, and allocating resources to serve the strategy; government organizations translate strategy, and the accompanying resources, into practice. Civilian leaders might envision a sharp divide between the making and implementing of policy. The US wars in Vietnam, Iraq, and Afghanistan show, however, that the dividing line between the two is fuzzy at best. Government organizations can effectively usurp leadership prerogatives when they turn a general mandate into implementation specifics, pull solutions from an existing repertoire, impose solutions based on organizational preferences, innovate with new strategies or tactics, or act in any number of other ways. Simply put, a lesson from all these wars is that *government organizations charged with implementing policy can effectively define (or redefine) it.* Yet the US problems in these three wars were not due just to the administrations' deference to these organizations. They resulted even more decidedly from the administrations' detachment. The elements of policy never fully developed, cohered, or fit tightly with conditions on the ground. More generally, then, a lesson of these wars is that *sound policy requires that leaders thoughtfully consider and integrate the dimensions of policy and ensure its integrity in practice.*

In Vietnam, the Johnson administration failed to determine what a political, as opposed to a military, strategy required; whether, how, and when the requirements of a political or military strategy worked in harmony or at cross-purposes with each other; or how the exigencies of combat affected the success of either strategy. The political prevailed in strategy when Johnson and Defense Secretary McNamara set the resource and geographical parameters for the war effort and micromanaged the air war to an unprecedented degree, through weekly target selection. They hoped to devise the right coercive package that would convey US resolve *and* restraint. Yet they failed to ask what coercion from the air would require to succeed or whether the messages that US leaders wanted to send could actually reach their targets. Indeed, any message that they sought to send to Hanoi was lost in the cacophony of signals, in the air and on the ground, that drowned out—even contravened—the intended message. Confused messaging was but one result when US civilian leaders conceded effective control of the war to the US military command. Fighting to its strengths and traditions, the military sought to target enemy main units, starve the enemy of resources from the North, and ultimately crush the enemy in the South through an attrition campaign. In that war, monitored by civilian leaders only from a distance, surrogate goals—the successful hitting of targets, the expansion of the target list, increasing the number of sorties flown, and upping the notorious enemy "body count"—effectively defined US strategy. Lost in the *military* effort were the requisites of competing successfully with the adversary's *political* strategy. By denying the United States its victory and playing for the long term, Hanoi planned a victory of its own.

In Iraq, the Bush administration—despite the reservations of key principals—deferred to the CPA's efforts to expand the US role in the country, without having ascertained the requisites of political stability or the costs and consequences of pursuing a broader agenda. The administration's deference and neglect produced disastrous results. The CPA sought to rid the government of Baathists without fully appreciating the detrimental effects of such a policy on national reconciliation and stability. It tried to build an inclusive government without recognizing that inclusion could breed exclusion by empowering new sets of actors. It attempted to transform Iraq politically and economically without the resources, expertise, and staffing to accomplish this objective. Yet the CPA was not alone in its shortsightedness. The US military attempted to quash the escalating violence in Iraq by imposing institutional changes and adopting tactics that exacerbated sectarian grievances. Indeed, at all levels of the US government, officials failed to foresee that deteriorating Iraqi security, due in no small part to bad US decisions, would come to consume the US agenda.

In Afghanistan, the Bush administration sought a quick US exit once it had driven the Taliban from power. In shifting its attention to Iraq, the administration simply assumed that the US mission in Afghanistan was phasing down and on track to succeed. Yet the US military command had greater ambitions; with the Taliban regime defeated, it turned to a resource-intensive, counterinsurgency strategy. The mission remained overly ambitious and severely under-resourced as it expanded to include stability, reconstruction, security force training, and institutional development. Despite the military's plans and mounting challenges, the Bush administration still pushed for a speedy exit from the country, with undue expectations and negative effects. It accelerated the training of Afghan security forces to get numbers in the field, sacrificing troop quality and force performance. It assumed incorrectly that fledgling Afghan institutions—political, economic, and military—would rise to the challenge to carry the load. It exaggerated the capability and will of US allies to relieve the United States of much of its economic and security burden. It remained unprepared, moreover, to thwart the Taliban resurgence militarily throughout much of the country.

Stage III: Constriction

In all three wars, US leaders eventually reached their limit. President Johnson reached his limit in Vietnam with a US military request for hundreds of thousands of additional troops (with half a million US troops already in Vietnam); to meet the request, the administration would have had to mobilize the US reserve force, extending the war's domestic reach. President Bush reached his limit in Iraq with the explosion of violence in the country, the Iraqi government being in a perpetual stalemate, the US public and most of the Democratic opposition pushing for withdrawal, and the US secretary of defense and much of the senior US military command favoring withdrawal. President Obama reached his limit in Afghanistan when he confronted a US military request for additional troops; the prospect of additional requests to follow; and the harsh reality that US success in Afghanistan would ultimately depend on its failing, incompetent, and venal governing institutions.

True, these three presidents acted differently, under different conditions. Johnson sought to avoid the domestic-political fallout of a troop increase in Vietnam. In *choosing not to change strategy*, Johnson responded to the military's request for more troops by imposing a troop freeze. For his part, Bush acted despite the potential domestic political fallout from a troop increase. In *choosing to change strategy* in Iraq, Bush responded to the military's preference for a speedy US troop exit by increasing US troop levels in country for the months that these troops were available. Obama, who was perhaps the least constrained politically, acted from his own sense that a large, long-term US investment in Afghanistan would involve high costs with low returns. In *choosing to avoid a strategy* (specifically, a full-blown counterinsurgency strategy), Obama gave the military fewer troops than it requested, and then only for an abbreviated period.

Notwithstanding these differences, all three presidents offered few clues to how the preferred option would serve broader purposes and had plenty of reasons to suspect that the proposed strategy, given its limits, would just not work. The Johnson administration froze US troops and the US bombing strategy at levels that had failed to persuade Hanoi to concede. The Bush administration settled for an undersized military force without anticipating the decisive contribution of the burgeoning Awakening movement to the impending US effort and knowing that success on the ground would still not solve Iraq's intractable governing problems. The Obama administration accepted a military solution that, if successful, would have served only a vague and limited goal—reversing the adversary's momentum—and have still required the Afghan government and its institutions to play against type and actually rise to the challenge.

These seemingly dissimilar policy conditions and responses thus support a common lesson: *selecting options by deferring to their costs might deliver the "worst of both worlds" in consequences*. The resulting policies might yield too little performance at an unsustainable cost, assessed politically, economically, or militarily.

Stage IV: Extrication

In all three conflicts, then, leaving became the US goal. In Vietnam and Afghanistan, the Nixon and Obama administrations set exit timelines and substantially stuck to them. In Iraq, the Obama administration sought to reduce the US military profile in the country in order to facilitate an eventual US departure, which gave the Iraq government limited incentive to accept US negotiating terms. Whereas the US leaders entered the Vietnam, Iraq, and Afghanistan conflicts to achieve grand (albeit amorphous) goals, they finally accepted a more modest US role in all three wars: supplying, training, and backing local forces. They thereby scaled the residual US footprint in country to the requirements of the exit plan, not the battlefield returns. Indeed, the host country's forces had not established that they could operate autonomously, let alone "win."

The lesson, then, is that *exit schedules assume a life of their own*. For Obama, at least, that *was* the plan. He recognized that setting the pace of withdrawal apart from conditions on the ground would create bureaucratic and political realities to facilitate an exit. Neither Nixon nor Obama sought to push back against these realities even when conditions in country worsened.

Coping with Bias, Imperfectly

How can policy makers ameliorate these biases? The answer seems simple enough. Policy makers constantly need to ask, "What do we want to achieve, what can we expect to achieve, and how do we expect to achieve it?" Yet these demanding questions can easily produce policy paralysis. In the spirit of cautions and guidelines, then, I propose a number of *imperfect* decisional strategies.

First, *policy makers must recognize that assessment is a continuous process*. Policy makers understandably seek to avoid difficult discussions and endless debate. The constant revisiting of issues feeds dissension in the ranks, creates uncertainty about future strategy, fuels suspicions that policies are not working, and hampers consistent policy implementation. Yet sound policy requires some—albeit difficult—compromise between openness and closure. As Robert Jervis (2014: 326) sagely put it, policy makers must address "the agonizing and unanswerable question of how to balance the need to sustain a policy with the requirement to question it, the need to finally come up with answers versus the need to keep questions open for consideration, and the need to prevent subordinates from undercutting policy and the simultaneous requirement to get people to provide honest doubt and to avoid a false consensus." Toward that end, policy can benefit substantially from bringing "new people," with "new ideas," into assessment and deliberations. Not coincidentally, US policies changed markedly in Vietnam, Iraq, and Afghanistan when an election brought the opposing party into power.[1] The alternative, postponing questioning until conditions demand it, can push the day of reckoning beyond the point where events have depleted the range of choices.

Second, *policy makers must guard against* ad hoc *argumentation*. In all three wars, policy makers rationalized their policy choices without concern for underlying assumptions or consistency with their prior positions. Deserving special attention in this regard is the tendency to "manufacture" interests that bind the nation to unsound policies. In the Vietnam War, policy makers relied on poorly grounded and infinitely malleable "credibility" arguments to make the case for intervention, perseverance, and withdrawal. By their reckoning, US credibility required the United States to intervene to win, to do just enough to say it had tried to win, to stick around until the bitter end, to depart the scene to show that it could act in its own interests, to fight until the conflict was viewed as "Saigon's war," or to fight regardless of whether the credibility of the United States initially required its intervention. Their loose handling of the concept thereby begged essential questions.[2] How easily does a reputation form? How broadly does it travel? When and how can a party overcome a bad reputation? Answers were not forthcoming.

Third, *policy makers must recognize that sound policy requires comprehensive assessment*. Policy makers must determine whether participants *at all levels of policy* are on the same page—that is, whether all involved understand what the policy is, how it is expected to work, and whether the operational aspects of policy align with its underlying principles. Missions "creep" in no small part due to a pervasive disjunction between policymaking and implementation that effectively turns practitioners into policy makers.

Fourth, *policy makers must guard against temporizing*. Policy makers justifiably seek to avoid major decisions to gain time, to acquire information to make better decisions, and to avoid the risks that come from leaping headlong into the unknown. The passage of time presumably allows events to run their course; and small policy changes presumably carry a lesser risk of catastrophic failure. Indeed, the allure of the "middle option"—option B, staying the course—lies in its *promise* of positive outcomes with the *certainty* of delivering them at a reduced price (with lower risk). Yet staying the course or taking actions that depart only incrementally from existing policy carries the less-appreciated risk of avoiding decisions until circumstances have reduced the latitude for choice. What policy makers might gain in information, they might lose in opportunities to use that knowledge effectively.

Fifth, *policy makers must recognize the value of dutifully preparing fallback options.* US leaders shy away from "planning for mission failure" out of fear that the plans will go public or somehow become reality. Domestic critics might take such planning to indicate that policies *have* failed, foreign adversaries might take these plans to suggest that the United States is conceding a loss, and government bureaucrats might take planning as a signal to retract or shelve program commitments. Regularized contingency planning across a spectrum of options, if recognized as such, could help offset the negative political consequences of preparing fallback options.

Sixth, *policy makers must recognize their limited capability to control military and nonmilitary outcomes.* They are advised, in particular, to recognize that the success of any intervention will likely hinge on the limited capability of US leaders to gain the host government's support for a US-led mission. Indeed, in all three wars US leaders were slow to acknowledge the paradox of trying to leverage a host government to gain its support. To leverage desirable outcomes, the United States must invest time, resources, and prestige and threaten or promise to invest more time, resources, and prestige, with the significant risk that US support and largess will be misused, misdirected, or taken for granted. The problem for the United States, quite simply, is that too great a US investment in the affairs of other governments shifts the balance in favor of those governments. They will pass on to the United States the burden (cost) of achieving some shared goal and grab the benefits—at additional cost to the United States—by pursuing self-interested agendas.[3] The United States can certainly try to avoid that trap with threats to reduce its commitment or to withdraw entirely as an intermediary or a party to a conflict. Yet the logic of the paradox blocks an easy exit. The effectiveness of threats to withdraw depends on the credibility of those threats, yet threats—if credible—spark fears of abandonment that can reinforce misbehavior, leaving the United States with little in reserve to secure influence with additional threats or promises.

Seventh, *policy makers must recognize the benefit of reverse engineering decisional problems when confronting threats and opportunities.* Rather than thinking first about abstract objectives, policy makers can focus their thinking on some basket of alternatives and their potential consequences (expressed perhaps in terms of "best," "worst," and "most likely" cases). Ideally, thinking about alternative futures will press policy makers to identify and evaluate the benefits and costs of plausible outcomes, recognize potential trade-offs, and explore potential means-ends relationships. Policy makers might recognize, then, that different alternatives can produce the same result at lower costs, discounted options might produce a positive result at an acceptable cost, favored alternatives might produce a result only at a prohibitive cost, and some alternatives might produce a result only under restrictive conditions. The underlying logic here is to turn the tables on decisional bias. If biased decisions are made because policy makers fail to see beyond immediate referents, assorted referents should be employed to push those policy makers to address bigger questions.

Finally, *policy makers must remain wary of the non-decision.* No one should expect decisions—let alone sound policy—to emerge necessarily when they are airing views, probing assumptions, and exchanging information. The complexity of problems and the diversity of opinion on the goals and values at stake likely preclude that. Yet the dangers of the alternative—the ever-present non-decision—are clear. These dangers appear in the tendency to believe that better opportunities to re-evaluate policy will arise, competent parties are running the show, too many agencies and policies are now engaged to risk mucking up the works, policies require time to succeed, events should run their course, and the decision has "already been made." The "moment for decision" too often becomes "the moment" many moments too late. At that point, options have withered and mission success, by any standard, is unlikely.

Whatever the correctives, daunting challenges will remain. The path ahead will remain dimly lit, alternative routes will hold only a faint promise of a better outcome, and all routes and alternative destinations will risk making matters worse. For policy makers in wartime, just doing their best, under these circumstances, is an ambitious aspiration.

NOTES

Chapter 1

1. Throughout this book, except when qualified, I use the terms *leaders* and *policy makers* interchangeably to refer to the president and his top civilian advisers.
2. In this sense, my argument subsumes Rapport's (2015) intriguing thesis that policy makers assess short-term goals by weighing their feasibility but assess temporally distant goals—abstract and devoid of context—by considering their desirability. I regard time as but one criterion determining the "distance" of goals, and I make no assumptions about whether the desirability (undesirability) inclines policy makers toward long-term optimism (pessimism).
3. President Johnson was bound to view the middle alternative favorably, then, when compared to "withdrawal" or "escalation." President Obama's advisers appreciated the psychology of choice when complaining, in the president's first year in office, that military commanders had cooked the options for Afghanistan: to get the president to the "comfortable" middle, they had wedged the alternative between an unacceptably large increase and a small one that would require a fundamental change in current US military strategy.
4. The challenge for researchers in applying any and all of these perspectives is the unavailability of data to back theoretical claims, an overabundance of explanations that fit the same evidence, and a widespread tendency to attribute favorable and unfavorable outcomes to good and bad thinking, respectively.
5. I assume that these influences predominate in decision-making despite variations in impact, owing, for instance, to leaders' levels of "experience" (Saunders 2017).
6. On whether and how democracies fight wars, see Downes (2009); Merom (2003); Reiter and Stam (2002); and Valentino, Huth, and Croco (2010).
7. On this see, for example, George and Stern (1972).
8. On US power in a unipolar world, see Wohlforth (1999); on the limits of US power under "unipolarity," see Lebovic (2017).
9. The "Vietnam syndrome"—an unwillingness to assume the burdens of power—became the Vietnam conflict's lasting legacy. US policy makers have shown a similar disinclination (shying from a direct combat role in Syria, for instance) in the aftermath of the Iraq and Afghanistan interventions. Whether the aversion toward employing US troops constitutes an unreasonable bias against foreign intervention is, however, a topic for another book.
10. On this point, Saunders (2012) argues that the incidence and nature of US military intervention depend on whether US presidents are externally or internally directed: Do presidents focus on threats that derive from other states or on those from forces internal to those countries?

11. The surge of UN forces across the thirty-eighth parallel into North Korea provoked Chinese intervention; hundreds of thousands of Chinese "volunteers" sent the UN forces into retreat back across the parallel and forced the parties into a punishing stalemate for years to come.
12. Gordon Adams and Shoon Murray (2014: 14) attribute this tendency to changes in the US military, which has more broadly defined its contribution and increasingly performed abroad in various humanitarian and "nation-building" capacities: "Over time, these expanded missions, programs, authorities, and the budgets that support them have become institutionalized in the structure, doctrine, and training of the military services."
13. As Bakich (2014: 29) observes, informational challenges vary depending on where one stands within the governmental hierarchy. "At lower levels, the greatest obstacle to effective performance is 'task uncertainty', or the vagaries associated with completing specific jobs under internally derived constraints. At higher levels, task uncertainty is replaced with 'environmental uncertainty', or the difficulties in determining how the organization's objectives are being affected by outside actors and influences."
14. Indeed, realists essentially ask, "Who knows, or cares, what any given policy maker thinks?" They thereby dismiss psychological influences by claiming that the beliefs of individual leaders have no, or only a small, influence on state behavior, or else they insist that these beliefs are too idiosyncratic, elusive, and variable to study effectively or efficiently.
15. This distinction is developed further in Bendor and Hammond (1992).
16. In Vietnam, the US Army relied on the notorious "body count" to assess whether the military was killing the enemy faster than it could replace its fallen personnel, and the US Air Force relied on a host of input measures—such as sorties flown and bomb tonnage dropped—to establish progress in the war effort.
17. Again, there is a rational component to this. Charles Lindblom (1959), in his famous discussion of "muddling through," recognized the value of taking small steps away from current policy to allow for useful feedback on the payoff from the altered course while avoiding the pitfalls of dramatic departures from the status quo that could fail, and fail "big."
18. See Lebovic (1996) for the early post–Cold War effects of this goal conflict on the US military services.
19. The literature often minimizes the disconnect between leaders and governmental organizations, depicting leaders as bureaucratic infighters or artful manipulators who know the game, its stakes, and its rules. These leaders use their power of recruitment and appointment to mobilize support for key policies, create new organizations, and fence off budgets to promote or safeguard cherished programs, distribute incentives, issue threats to bring hostile elements into line, and so forth.
20. Leaders often expect government agencies to do more with less by cutting the "fat" or resetting priorities in leaner times. There is some truth to their assumption; resource demands are politically inspired. Government agencies tend to ask for more than they need, expecting a beneficial compromise. Yet the belief that government organizations can survive, even thrive, on existing resources often persists in leadership circles absent a ground's-eye view of the challenges of translating policies into practice.
21. For a more elaborate view of how the wartime public processes information and elite cues, see Baum and Groeling (2010).
22. It declines, in fact, across various demographic groups (Lunch and Sperlich 1979: 38–43).
23. Indeed, a domestic push might operate universally to bring closure to costly foreign-military interventions. Popular discontent in the authoritarian Soviet state brought pressure on its new reform-minded leader, Mikhail Gorbachev, to extricate Russia from its costly Afghan venture.
24. Certainly the explanation in the Vietnam, Iraq, and Afghanistan wars was not negative electoral fortunes. Presidents Johnson and Bush were essentially lame-duck presidents when they chose a "middle" option in Vietnam and Iraq, respectively. President Obama, for his part, eventually sought disengagement in advance of his re-election bid.

25. Fearon (1995) also recognizes that some issues are potentially indivisible; that is, they are essentially "zero-sum" and do not allow for compromise. He also notes that compromise is often inhibited by a commitment problem: states might not lower their guard short of (impossible) guarantees that the opponent will not use the concession to unilateral advantage.
26. On this, see also Rathbun (2007).
27. For that very reason, competing lessons from Vietnam loomed heavily over the Iraq War, and the "lessons" from Iraq, in turn, fueled debate over the Afghanistan conflict.
28. For that matter, an adversary might feign willingness to compromise, as Hanoi did when tying its readiness to negotiate to an unconditional US bombing halt. The consistent raising and lowering of hopes for a settlement could undermine an opponent's leaders at home, who then receive blame for their unwillingness to compromise from an increasingly demoralized public.

Chapter 2

1. The Military Assistance Command, Vietnam or MACV.
2. In Goldstein's (2008: 68) words, "Despite the overwhelming pressure imposed on him by his senior counselors, the president's determination never wavered."
3. This is not to say that a decision to go to war "was made" by late 1964. On this point, see Logevall (1999: xvii). He insists that US leaders "always possessed real choice."
4. By July 1964, twenty thousand US advisers had been ordered to Vietnam (Warner 2003: 836).
5. McNamara had traveled to South Vietnam in December 1963.
6. Memorandum from the Secretary of Defense (McNamara) to the President, Washington, D.C., March 16, 1964. https://history.state.gov/historicaldocuments/frus1964-68v01/d84.
7. Draft Memorandum from the President's Special Assistant for National Security Affairs (Bundy) to the President, Washington, D.C. May 25, 1964. https://history.state.gov/historicaldocuments/frus1964-68v01/d173.
8. The recommendation was based on the premises that "the U.S. cannot tolerate the loss of Southeast Asia to Communism," the "present prospect is not hopeful, in South Vietnam or Laos," and a credible decision to use force ("backed by resolute and extensive deployment") might itself prove sufficient (to avoid force). (The document refers initially to South Vietnam and Laos and later to South Vietnam or Laos.)
9. Memorandum for the Record of a Meeting, White House Washington, [D.C.], November 19, 1964, 12:30 p.m. https://history.state.gov/historicaldocuments/frus1964-68v01/d417.
10. It did not arrive on Johnson's desk until February 1965 (Preston 2006: 159), where it apparently remained unread (Goldstein 2008: 132).
11. Paper Prepared by the Executive Committee. Washington, D.C., December 2, 1964. https://history.state.gov/historicaldocuments/frus1964-68v01/d433.
12. For the content and context of the memo, see Preston (2006: 165–167).
13. Maxwell Taylor, chair of the JCS, believed that the Marines could now take on a "'strike role'" within fifty miles of a US base (Cosmas 2006: 208).
14. Johnson apparently accepted the conclusions of an intelligence assessment of the consequences of a South Vietnamese defeat. Requested by Johnson in June 1964, it implicitly challenged the depiction of proximate countries falling like dominoes to Communism, viewed the effects of a Communist takeover as limited to Southeast Asia, and recognized that a unified Vietnam might actually become a divisive influence within the ranks of Communist states (Warner 2003: 834).
15. Indeed, the evidence also plausibly supports the exact opposite argument—albeit circumstantially, again—that Johnson pushed his domestic programs to placate liberals to buy breathing space to fight in Vietnam.
16. Such efforts soon gave birth to the "credibility gap," an ever-widening disconnect between the official spin on events and harsh realities and unpleasantness.

17. These friends included Senate Foreign Relations Committee chair J. William Fulbright (Barrett 1988/1989: 642–646).
18. Except where noted, these points are taken from Kaiser (2000: 331–337) and Hanyok (1998), a now declassified US National Security Agency study.
19. Summary Notes of the 538th Meeting of the National Security Council, Washington, D.C., August 4, 1964, 6:15–6:40 p.m. Gulf of Tonkin Attack. https://history.state.gov/historicaldocuments/frus1964-68v01/d278.
20. Draft Congressional Resolution Prepared in the Department of State, Washington, D.C. May 24, 1964. https://history.state.gov/historicaldocuments/frus1964-68v01/d169.
21. On the willful misrepresentation of the Tonkin events, see Logevall (1999: 196–200) and McMaster (1997: 120–136, 152–153).
22. Put somewhat euphemistically, Johnson was "impatient with involved explanations" (Seller 1973: 209).
23. In early April 1965, on the eve of the decision to introduce US ground troops and a few weeks before the first army brigade arrived in country, Taylor even thought he had successfully interceded to thwart the decision (Halberstam 1969: 570–572).
24. By the end of 1965, "the President was beginning to withdraw, to concentrate his interactions more and more with those people whom he felt he could trust and with whom he felt comfortable" (Best 1988: 543).
25. Johnson was nonetheless exposed to a full range of opinion in the critical decision period. On this see, Garofano (2002: 157).
26. Johnson had decided to prevent the loss of Vietnam through all available means. In March 1965, the president voiced that sentiment to key advisers and, later, to the Joint Chiefs of Staff (McMaster 1997: 248); in April, he conveyed a softer version of these sentiments in a televised speech to the American public.
27. These sentiments were widely shared in Johnson's advisory circle (see Logevall 1999: 234–235).
28. Even (second-tier) officials such as John McNaughton and William Bundy maintained that sending US ground forces to Vietnam could usefully boost Saigon's resolve and reduce Hanoi's inclination to fight (McMaster 1997: 202–207).
29. Expressed more cynically, "McNamara's strategy of graduated pressure seemed to 'solve' the president's problem of not losing Vietnam while maintaining the image that he was reluctant to escalate the war."
30. Unlike the Korean War, the issue was not whether to expand US aerial targeting to include China, but the Vietnam War nonetheless echoed its predecessor in debate.
31. New York Times, 1971. Bombing and a Pause. *New York Times* (July 2) https://www.nytimes.com/1971/07/02/archives/bombing-and-a-pause.html.
32. Special National Intelligence Estimate Washington, D.C., May 25, 1964. SNIE 50-2-64. https://history.state.gov/historicaldocuments/frus1964-68v01/d174
33. On the thinking behind China's backing of North Vietnam in the 1964–1965 period, see Bakich (2014: 100–105).
34. Even had Hanoi recognized any limits to the US bombing campaign, why should it view these limits as stemming from US "restraint" rather than US "fear" of a widening or intensification of the conflict?
35. On the bombing, see Thies (1980).
36. I would like to thank Doug Macdonald for his useful insights, and source materials, on this issue.
37. On the ever-increasing North Vietnamese military presence in the South, however, see Moise (2017). On the controversy over the numbers as it relates to his book, see H-Diplo Roundtable Review, Volume XIX, No. 44 (2018). http://www.tiny.cc/Roundtable-XIX-44. For a historical CIA assessment of the controversy, see 1967–1968: CIA, the Order-of-Battle Controversy, and the Tet Offensive. https://www.cia.gov/library/center-for-the-study-of-intelligence/

csi-publications/books-and-monographs/cia-and-the-vietnam-policymakers-three-episodes-1962-1968/epis3.html.
38. The effective size of the insurgency was, however, a matter of contention: CIA analysts challenged official military figures for understating the numbers of "home-grown" adversary personnel. Critics would later accuse the military of understating the enemy combat presence to boost the impression that the United States was winning the war in the South. These accusations would find their way into the courtroom when General Westmoreland sued CBS (for libel) for a 1982 documentary accusing him of falsifying the numbers. The misleading figures presumably left the US military unprepared for the adversary's 1968 Tet offensive. Still, the figures on all sides of the debate were beholden to (varying) assumptions (that is, categorization, extrapolation, source reliance, and evidentiary standards).
39. On this, see the CIA declassified study on the Sihanoukville Route at: https://www.cia.gov/library/readingroom/document/loc-hak-12-1-38-5
40. Caverley (2014) argues that US military strategy was influenced, over military resistance, by the civilian leadership's desire to substitute capital for manpower to avoid costs that would politically undercut the US mission. Although Caverley is correct that Johnson operated with manpower constraints—and ultimately balked at escalating US involvement when the war's manpower requirements became politically prohibitive—Johnson delegated the prosecution of the ground war to the military because its *preferred* attrition strategy played to ostensible US strengths and reduced the demands for US troops. To strengthen his case, Caverley argues (albeit unconvincingly) that the US military pushed for a less conventional approach over civilian resistance. At the very least, the evidence on the sources of US strategy is overdetermined: who influenced whom is unclear because civilian *and* military leaders pushed strategy in the same direction. Even this conclusion understates the military's push for a more aggressive conventional campaign (such as by using US airpower). From the beginning of the war, the Joint Chiefs of Staff insisted that "guerrillas were partisans who depended on the support of conventional armies, not insurgents who lived off the population, and that they could therefore be defeated only by attacking the conventional forces upon whom they relied and denying them secure bases." For his part, Westmoreland "not only took an almost purely military view of the problem the United States faced but also accepted the premise ... that North Vietnam directed the insurgency and could call it off at will" (Kaiser 2000: 301, 414). For a strong retort to Caverley, see McAllister (2010/2011).
41. Telegram from the Commander, Military Assistance Command, Vietnam (Westmoreland) to the Chairman of the Joint Chiefs of Staff (Wheeler) and the Commander in Chief, Pacific (Sharp), Saigon, February 9, 1968. https://history.state.gov/historicaldocuments/frus1964-68v06/d63. For Wheeler's concerns, see footnote 1. For Westmoreland's response, see footnote 4, Notes of Meeting, February 11, 1968, 4:25–6:15 p.m. https://history.state.gov/historicaldocuments/frus1964-68v06/d67.
42. Indeed, the Vietcong—or, more formally, People's Liberation Armed Forces—were divided among Main Force units, regional units, and village-level operatives; the Main Force units were led by North Vietnamese regulars and were organized, armed, trained, and performed much like their northern counterparts.
43. Regardless, the US army had good reason not to "reinvent" itself as a counterinsurgency force in Vietnam when a redirection in training and preparedness would weaken the US capability to respond to a conventional attack in Europe—for the United States, the primary global threat.
44. In that sense, "attrition" was less the operative US strategy under Westmoreland than a desirable outcome (Cosmas 2006: 399).
45. Westmoreland's thinking about pacification meshed to some degree with the thinking behind the PROVN study, which Westmoreland's critics read as an excoriating indictment of existing army strategy. It can be read instead for its emphasis on one (albeit critical) dimension of an

overall strategy, not as a critique of army priorities. The internal military debate between attrition and pacification largely reduced to a matter of *military* emphasis—whether to attack enemy main units or focus on the guerrillas and their infrastructure—and much was left to the discretion of local commanders (Cosmas 2006: 398–399).

46. On US counterinsurgency in Vietnam, see Long (2016: 105–138).
47. In Westmoreland's thinking, the US military would "provide the shield behind which the South Vietnamese could get their house in order" (Birtle 2008: 1223).
48. Under Westmoreland's direction, the military command set its force levels by deferring to crude algorithms: it estimated future enemy strength, accounted for the greater relative value of US troops, and tried then to maintain a necessary numerical personnel advantage (Cosmas 2006: 241).
49. The Gilder Lehrman Institute of American History. Infographic: The Vietnam War: Military Statistics. https://www.gilderlehrman.org/content/infographic-vietnam-war-military-statistics.
50. By the end of 1967, however, the push to improve the South Vietnamese military and to involve it significantly even in territorial security to facilitate pacification was consigned largely to "plans and rhetoric" (Cosmas 2006: 429–430).
51. See also, New York Times, 1971. The 200,000 Request. *New York Times* (July 3). https://www.nytimes.com/1971/07/03/archives/the-200000-request.html.
52. Draft Memorandum from Secretary of Defense McNamara to President Johnson, Washington, D.C., November 1, 1967. https://history.state.gov/historicaldocuments/frus1964-68v05/ch6. On the memo pushing the relationship between Johnson and McNamara to the "breaking point," see McNamara (1995: 311).
53. Whether Clifford was actually a hawk provoked some debate. Indeed, Clifford had expressed dovish views as a White House adviser early in the Johnson administration (Acacia 2009: 239–242, 254).
54. In February 1968, General Earle Wheeler, the chair of the JCS, requested these troops, planning to use them in part to build up the US central military reserve force to address potential needs on other global fronts. To Westmoreland's chagrin, Wheeler had prodded Westmoreland to push for more troops and then used that request to pursue his own goal of expanding the reserve force (Cosmas 2007: 97; Gelb and Betts 1979: 173–174).
55. Quoted in Barrett (1988/1989: 657).
56. Notes of Meeting, Washington, March 26, 1968. https://history.state.gov/historicaldocuments/frus1964-68v06/d158.
57. On these positions see, for example, Gelb and Betts (1979: 264–265).
58. By the end of 1966, McNamara argued for stabilizing US forces at 470,000 and signaling to Hanoi that the United States was preparing for a long stay (Gelb and Betts 1979: 147).
59. Dean Rusk maintained, for instance, that a cessation or pause in the US bombing would be dismissed by Hanoi and allow it to operate with impunity; others in Johnson's inner circle, such as Walt Rostow and Maxwell Taylor, dismissed McNamara's stabilizing plan (and bombing-halt proposal) as a palpable sign of weakness (Warner 2005: 207–208).
60. Indeed, the US military command had discounted intelligence suggesting that a major offensive against southern cities was imminent, based in part on accurate assessments that US forces in place, and the limits of the Communist political infrastructure in these areas, would prevent the adversary from holding territory (Cosmas 2007: 32).
61. For a more sober assessment of the net effects of the Phoenix program, see Rosenau and Long (2009).
62. The gambit so infuriated Johnson that he is heard in a telephone conversation with the (Republican) Senate minority leader (Everett Dirksen) charging Nixon with "treason." David Taylor, 2013. The Lyndon Johnson Tapes: Richard Nixon's Treason. BBC Magazine (March 22). http://www.bbc.com/news/magazine-21768668.
63. On these principles, see Kimball (2004: 53–86).

64. National Security Archive, 2006. Vietnam, Declassified Documents Reveal: Nuclear Weapons, the Vietnam War, and the "Nuclear Taboo." National Security Archive Electronic Briefing Book No. 195. http://nsarchive2.gwu.edu//NSAEBB/NSAEBB195/index.htm. See also Tannenwald, 2007: 232–236.
65. Henry Kissinger, Memorandum for the President, October 2, 1969. Contingency Military Operations Against North Vietnam. National Security Archive. http://nsarchive2.gwu.edu// NSAEBB/NSAEBB195/VN-2.pdf.
66. For relevant documentation on the administration's Duck Hook planning, see http:// nsarchive.gwu.edu/NSAEBB/NSAEBB195/.
67. On the alert or "readiness test," see National Security Archive, 2002. Nixon's Nuclear Ploy: The Vietnam Negotiations and the Joint Chiefs of Staff Readiness Test, October 1969. National Security Archive Electronic Briefing Book No. 81. http://nsarchive2.gwu.edu//NSAEBB/ NSAEBB81/index2.htm.
68. General Earle G. Wheeler, Chairman, Joint Chiefs of Staff, Memorandum for the Secretary of Defense: US Military Readiness Tests—Worldwide, October 21, 1969. National Security Archive. http://nsarchive2.gwu.edu//NSAEBB/NSAEBB81/nnp10.pdf.
69. Quoted in Kalb (2014: 114).
70. National Security Archive, 2006. Kissinger's "Salted Peanuts" and the Iraq War. http:// nsarchive2.gwu.edu//news/20061001/index.htm.
71. National Security Archive, 2006. Kissinger's "Salted Peanuts" and the Iraq War.
72. See Kadura (2016) for an unusual take on the "decent interval." He argues that Nixon and Kissinger looked to the interval to buy time, hoping that would help ensure the survival of the Saigon regime.
73. Kissinger himself "urged Nixon to defer the Duck Hook plan, because it could not attain the quick, decisive military action he thought was necessary" (Hunt 2015: 120).
74. Laird notably supported the 1971 South Vietnamese operation in Laos (Cosmas 2007: 327).
75. William Burr and Jeffrey P. Kimball. Nixon, Kissinger, and the Madman Strategy during Vietnam War. National Security Archive. http://nsarchive.gwu.edu/nukevault/ ebb517-Nixon-Kissinger-and-the-Madman-Strategy-during-Vietnam-War.
76. Kissinger did handwrite the phrase in the margin of his briefing book. See Lewis (2014: 49).
77. At the 1972 Moscow Summit, Leonid Brezhnev, reminded Nixon of Kissinger's noninterference pledge, which the Soviet leader claimed Kissinger made directly to him. In his telling, the United States would not interfere if peace lasted a mere 18 months (Dallek 2007: 396).
78. Laird's assessments often came with damning qualifications. In May 1971 he told Nixon that the South Vietnamese military "had the potential to cope with the projected threat from North Vietnamese and Viet Cong forces as long as they improved qualitatively and mustered sufficient will, leadership, and morale" (Hunt 2015: 208).
79. The original amendment, which would have cut off funding to US troops in Cambodia and Laos, lost in the House of Representatives.
80. Nixon maintained, regardless, that the commander in chief possessed the constitutional authority to prosecute the war.
81. For contrasting views, see Haun and Jackson (2015/2016) and Pape (1996).
82. For an even stronger statement—that Hanoi was willing to accept the final terms as early as 1967—see Herring (1986: 169).
83. See Kissinger (1979: 1323, 1339, 1412).
84. Hanoi's dependence on military supplies had waned with the end of the Easter Offensive.
85. Congress cut US aid, but the amounts remained substantial despite the myth of a termination of US aid that grew around the retraction. On this, see Ken Hughes, 2010. The Myth That Congress Cut Off Funding for South Vietnam. http://historynewsnetwork.org/article/ 126150.
86. Ken Hughes, 2011. Nixon's "Decent Interval" Vietnam Strategy Should Give Obama Pause on Afghanistan. http://historynewsnetwork.org/article/140712.

Chapter 3

1. Regardless, they would insist that the world, including Iraq, was better off without Saddam Hussein than with him.
2. See Feith (2008: 225). In the international politics literature on bargaining, the US challenge is depicted as a "commitment" problem: Iraq could not credibly commit not to create WMD, which meant that the United States was arguably pressed to act (on this, see Lake 2010/ 2011: 12, 23–25).
3. Scott Shane and Mark Mazzetti, 2007. Ex-C.I.A. Chief, in Book, Assails Cheney on Iraq. *New York Times* (April 27). https://www.nytimes.com/2007/04/27/washington/27intel.html.
4. The key judgments of the estimate are available in a declassified document at the National Security Archive, http://www.gwu.edu/~nsarchiv/NSAEBB/NSAEBB80/wmd15.pdf.
5. It reached this conclusion despite the conclusion by the International Atomic Energy Commission (based on its inspections through 1999) that there was "no indication that Iraq possesses nuclear weapons or any meaningful amounts of weapon-usable nuclear material, or that Iraq has retained any practical capability (facilities or hardware) for the production of such material." The skepticism was backed by the US State Department Bureau of Intelligence and Research (INR). It maintained that the evidence was "inadequate" to conclude that Iraq was pursuing an "integrated and comprehensive approach to acquire nuclear weapons." James Risen, David E. Sanger, and Thom Shanker, 2003. After the War: Weapons Intelligence; in Sketchy Data, Trying to Gauge Iraq Threat. *New York Times* (July 20). https://www.nytimes.com/2003/07/20/world/after-the-war-weapons-intelligence-in-sketchy-data-trying-to-gauge-iraq-threat.html
6. This tendency was expressed in Secretary of Defense Donald Rumsfeld's famous retort that "the absence of evidence is not evidence of absence."
7. As the representative for the Middle East on the National Intelligence Council, Pillar would have participated in the writing of the 2002 NIE on Iraq.
8. Rumsfeld (2011: 425); and Glenn Kessler, 2003. U.S. Decision on Iraq Has Puzzling Past; Opponents of War Wonder When, How Policy Was Set. *Washington Post* (January 12). A1.
9. National Security Archive, 2010. The Iraq War—Part I: The U.S. Prepares for Conflict, 2001. National Security Archive Electronic Briefing Book No. 326. Document 8, November 27, 2001. https://nsarchive2.gwu.edu/NSAEBB/NSAEBB326/
10. National Security Archive, 2010. The Iraq War—Part III: Shaping the Debate, National Security Archive Electronic Briefing Book No. 330. U.S. and British Documents Show Transatlantic Propaganda Cooperation. https://nsarchive2.gwu.edu/NSAEBB/NSAEBB330/index.htm
11. National Security Archive, 2010. The Iraq War—Part I.
12. For a provocative scholarly effort to validate the counterfactual argument that a Gore presidency would still have invaded Iraq, see Harvey (2012).
13. On the contrary, Harvey (2012) argues compellingly that, given a multitude of forces at work, a US attack on Iraq might well have occurred even had Al Gore won the presidency in the disputed 2000 election.
14. Ken Adelman, 2002. Cakewalk in Iraq. *Washington Post* (February 13). https://www.washingtonpost.com/archive/opinions/2002/02/13/cakewalk-in-iraq/cf09301c-c6c4-4f2e-8268-7c93017f5e93/?utm_term=.0748bbe244fb.
15. For that matter, with just that concern, the George W. Bush administration did not seriously consider an attack on North Korea despite its erratic leadership and well-developed nuclear weapons program.
16. Douglas Feith (2008: 245–250) excoriates Powell on this point. On Powell's regrets, see Steven R. Weisman, 2005. Powell Calls His U.N. Speech a Lasting Blot on His Record. *New York Times* (September 9). http://www.nytimes.com/2005/09/09/politics/powell-calls-his-un-speech-a-lasting-blot-on-his-record.html

17. Ironically, a scenario involving the leader who has nothing left to lose had concerned US policy hawks in the Cold War decades. They argued that under such dire conditions, leaders ignore costs and will act recklessly.
18. Although US military planners were less sanguine than top civilian defense officials were about the popular reception that would await US troops in Iraq, they did not believe that the threat of an insurgency was sufficiently great to justify an alternative US course of action (Bensahel et al. 2008: 13–14).
19. Peter Sleven and Dana Priest. Wolfowitz, 2003. Concedes Iraq Errors. *Washington Post* (July 24): A1.
20. For an assessment that establishes the relative benefits of a larger troop presence in Iraq, see Malkasian (2008).
21. Sleven and Priest, and Wolfowitz, Concedes Iraq Errors.
22. National Intelligence Council. 2003. Principal Challenges in Post-Saddam Iraq. *Intelligence Community Assessment.* https://www.cia.gov/library/readingroom/document/0005674817. For a summary assessment and supporting documents, see US Congress (2007).
23. Exactly how much Defense Department backing Chalabi had remains a subject of contention. Rumsfeld (2011: 489) and Feith (2008: 254–256) both push back against the "myth" that they were trying to install Chalabi as leader of Iraq. On this, see Graham (2009: 339–340).
24. As Martin Indyk, who as assistant secretary of state for the Middle East had dealings with Chalabi, surmised, "Of course, he was a con man. That was his charm" (quoted in Isikoff and Corn 2006: 49).
25. Scott Wilson, 2004. Chalabi Aides Suspected of Spying for Iran. *Washington Post* (May 22): A20. How much the Pentagon backed Chalabi per se as the new leader of Iraq is a matter of contention. For the "con" view, see Feith (2008: 255–256).
26. On this, see ORHA. A Unified Mission Plan for Post-Hostilities Iraq, http://www.pbs.org/wgbh/pages/frontline/yearinirag/documents/orha.html; and CPA. A Vision to Empower Iraqis. Reprinted in Talmon, 2013: 865.
27. Bremer's views of his mandate differ from those of other officials. Feith (2008: 440) insists that Bremer processed his instructions through his own "filter."
28. Tom Warrick, who headed the FIP, was unceremoniously dropped from the ORHA planning team, apparently at the insistence of the vice president's office (Rudd 2011: 129–131).
29. Those who would assume key national security positions in the Bush administration initially staked out similar positions. See, for instance, Rice (2000).
30. A similar fit issue within the State Department would arise with the creation in 2004 of the Office of the Coordinator for Reconstruction and Stabilization (S/CRS), formed expressly to address the kinds of challenges that the United States encountered in Iraq and Afghanistan. Perhaps predictably, even relations between these two organizations were strained: USAID resisted efforts to employ the agency as an auxiliary, follow-on, or mop-up force for US military operations and insisted that S/CRS not duplicate its own capabilities. In 2011, to address its problems, S/CRS was folded into a new Bureau for Conflict and Stabilization Operations within the State Department. For a good discussion of the bureaucratic challenges and turf battles that affected the civilian-led operation in Iraq, see Miles (2013). On the dizzying array of reforms to increase cross-government coordination in such operations, see SIGIR (2010).
31. National Security Archive, 2013. The Iraq War Ten Years After. National Security Archive Briefing Book No. 418. Document 1. U.S. Central Command, "Desert Crossing Seminar: After Action Report," June 28–30, 1999. https://nsarchive2.gwu.edu/NSAEBB/NSAEBB418/
32. National Security Archive, 2010. The Iraq War—Part I.
33. Bremer, as quoted by Gordon and Trainor (2012: 13).
34. Even Rumsfeld subsequently claimed that only on reading Bremer's (September 2003) op-ed piece in the *Washington Post* did he realize that Bremer was instituting a longer transition plan than was originally intended (SIGIR 2010: 119), whereupon Rumsfeld and other Bush

advisers started to push for a quicker transition to Iraqi sovereignty (Gordon and Trainor 2012: 28–30).
35. L. Paul Bremer III, 2003. Iraq's Path to Sovereignty. *Washington Post* (September 8). https://www.washingtonpost.com/archive/opinions/2003/09/08/iraqs-path-to-sovereignty/92ccd663-ab69-4a56-b85b-af5f8a5f0baf/
36. "In his own efforts to probe, he would often get down to a level of minutiae that struck some officials as inappropriate for a defense secretary" (Graham 2009: 681).
37. Rumsfeld (2011: 511) notes that Bremer "certainly never discussed with me his *perception* [italics added] that the President had decided on a significant reversal in his policy toward Iraq."
38. On such warnings, see also Chandrasekaran (2007: 80).
39. This discussion of the Iraq Interior Ministry draws heavily from Perito (2011).
40. The interior minister noted, however, that there were "no killings and no beheadings." John Daniszewski, 2005. "OK, There Were Signs of Torture," Iraqi Says. *Los Angeles Times* (November 18). http://articles.latimes.com/2005/nov/18/world/fg-abuse18.
41. David Leigh and Maggie O'Kane, 2010. Iraq War Logs: US Turned Over Captives to Iraqi Torture Squads. *The Guardian* (October 24). http://www.theguardian.com/world/2010/oct/24/iraq-war-logs-us-iraqi-torture.
42. Michael R. Gordon and Alissa J. Rubin, 2007. Shiite Ex-Officials Face Trial in Hundreds of Sunni Deaths. *New York Times* (November 5): 1.
43. This discussion of the interagency process draws from Peter Feaver's (2011) detailed analysis.
44. Michael Abramowitz and Robin Wright, 2007. Bush to Add 21,500 Troops in an Effort to Stabilize Iraq. *Washington Post* (January 11). http://www.washingtonpost.com/wp-dyn/content/article/2007/01/10/AR2007011002437.html.
45. The committee was chaired by former secretary of state James Baker and Lee Hamilton. See Iraq Study Group (2006).
46. He also folded in efforts and personnel from other reviews initiated elsewhere in government.
47. Indeed, Hadley is credited by many in the know, including the president, of putting an alternative US strategy together and pulling the bureaucracy along (Feaver 2011: 27; Woodward 2008: 320–321). For others, authorship is an issue for which the historic jury is still out (Gordon and Trainor 2012: 308).
48. Keane subsequently declined the offer to command US forces in Iraq (Ricks 2009: 104).
49. Deputy National Security Advisor J. D. Crouch led the assessment.
50. I am indebted to Peter Feaver, who served in the Bush administration as a White House adviser on Iraq, for elucidating this point in a personal email exchange.
51. Unlike Robert McNamara, to whom he was often compared, he "resigned" but knew he had been fired. On McNamara's firing, see chapter 2.
52. Rumsfeld submitted his "resignation" in early November, effective mid-December 2006.
53. New York Times, 2006. Rumsfeld's Memo of Options for Iraq, *New York Times*, (December 3). http://www.nytimes.com/2006/12/03/world/middleeast/03mtext.html; and Michael A. Fletcher and Peter Baker, 2006. Bush Ousts Embattled Rumsfeld: Democrats Near Control of Senate. *Washington Post* (November 9). http://www.washingtonpost.com/wp-dyn/content/article/2006/11/08/AR2006110801180.html. Indeed, in the coming weeks Bush would concede publicly that the United States was not "winning" in Iraq. Peter Baker, 2006. U.S. Not Winning War in Iraq, Bush Says for 1st Time. *Washington Post* (December 20). http://www.washingtonpost.com/wp-dyn/content/article/2006/12/19/AR2006121900880.html.
54. Michael A. Fletcher and Thomas E. Ricks. 2006. Experts Advise Bush Not to Reduce Troops. *Washington Post* (December 12). http://www.washingtonpost.com/wp-dyn/content/article/2006/12/11/AR2006121100508.html.
55. On the role of presidential experience in this regard, see Saunders (2017).
56. On the role of General Pace, see Feaver (2011: 89).
57. Hadley and other senior NSC staff members had contact with Petraeus in developing the surge strategy (Woodward 2008: 299–300).

58. Army Field Manual 3-34 (Marine Corps Warfighting Publication 3-33.5). 2006. *Counterinsurgency* https://www.hsdl.org/?abstract&did=468442
59. To be sure, the US military command in Iraq, under General Casey, had long recognized that it was combating an insurgency and must engage in "full spectrum counterinsurgency operations" (Wright et al. 2008: 177). Various commanders—in the early years of the US war effort, in Tal Afar in the north of Iraq and elsewhere—opted for a counterinsurgency approach. Yet the application of the approach had been "uneven" (Mansoor 2013: 21).
60. The new US strategy held the potential of countering a major Coalition disadvantage: regardless of who inflicted a given death, the local population can easily blame those who stand apart culturally and physically from them, inflict casualties easily—without apology—and serve, by their presence, as a painful reminder of the more tranquil time, before those troops invaded the country. In a study of local opinion in Afghanistan, for example, Lyall et al. (2013) establish that US forces were blamed for NATO-inflicted civilian deaths, whereas the Taliban did not similarly lose public support when inflicting casualties.
61. Importantly, associating the strategy with the surge does not mean that enlarging the US force in Iraq alone was sufficient to defeat the insurgency.
62. The guidelines in the revised counterinsurgency manual alone called for a larger force (Gordon and Trainor 2012: 331).
63. For opposing views, downplaying the value of the US troop surge, see Desch (2011/2012) and McCary (2009).
64. The memo proved diplomatically problematic when published by the *New York Times* before a planned trip by Bush to meet Iraqi prime minister Nuri al-Maliki (in Jordan). Sheryl Gay Stolberg and Edward Wong, 2006. Iraq's Premier Abruptly Skips a Bush Session. *New York Times* (November 30). http://www.nytimes.com/2006/11/30/world/middleeast/30prexy.html.
65. New York Times, 2006. Text of U.S. Security Adviser's Iraq Memo. *New York Times* (November 29). http://www.nytimes.com/2006/11/29/world/middleeast/29mtext.html.
66. Others question whether the surge was guided by meaningful strategy. In the words of one prominent critics, "As 'a strategy of tactics,' and abstract principles, it hardly constituted strategy in a meaningful sense, that is, 'choice, options, and the wisest use of resources in war to achieve policy objectives'" (Gentile 2011/2012: 2–3).
67. Peter Feaver, personal email exchange.
68. On the activities of these programs, see Tarnoff (2008). As introduced in Iraq in 2005, the PRTs fell well short of the ideal that was envisioned, given enormous problems in obtaining supplies, acquiring funds, recruiting competent professionals, getting locals to cooperate openly with US personnel, and coordinating across government and civilian entities. As had become the norm, bureaucratic infighting continued between the (resource-light) State Department and (resource-rich) Defense Department over what was an appropriate military contribution to a State Department–led enterprise. The priority that the military gave to providing the security that would allow civilians to travel around the country would remain a consistent source of contention.
69. CERP funds come largely from the Economic Support Fund (traditionally administered by the State Department) and the Development Fund for Iraq (monies obtained from Iraqi oil revenues and seized Iraqi assets).
70. In March 2008 there were eleven PRTs and thirteen ePRTs operating in Iraq. See Perito 2008a.
71. Rajiv Chandrasekaran, 2007. Iraq Rebuilding Short on Qualified Civilians. *Washington Post* (February 24): A1; and Kiki Munshi, 2007. Lessons Unlearned in Iraq. *Washington Post* (July 7): A15.
72. For the general's take on the situation at that time in Iraq, see Casey (2012: 108).
73. See Karen DeYoung, 2008. U.S., Iraq Scale Down Negotiations over Forces. *Washington Post* (July 13): A1; Karen DeYoung and Sudarsan Raghavan, 2008. U.S., Iraqi Negotiators Agree on 2011 Withdrawal. *Washington Post* (August 22): A1; Amit R. Paley, 2008. Maliki Demands

All U.S. Troops Pull Out by 2011. *Washington Post* (August 26): A6; and Ned Parker, 2008. Iraq Shakes Up Talks on U.S. Troop Pullout. *Los Angeles Times* (August 31). http://articles.latimes.com/2008/aug/31/world/fg-iraq31.
74. Ernesto Londoño, 2009. U.S. Troops Uneasy as Rules Shift in Iraq. *Washington Post* (January 12): A1.
75. The Sons of Iraq, which had joined forces with US troops against the insurgency, would soon be caught between their vengeful former compatriots in the al-Qaeda-linked insurgency and a distrusting Iraqi government that continued to treat many of these units as Baathist co-conspirators.
76. Al-Sistani announced (through an official spokesman) that he did not consider the slim majority vote in the legislature to have met his standard of widespread support. Although he did not call for a rejection of the agreement, he underscored inadequate protections in the document for Iraqi sovereignty and assets and suggested that the weakness of the Iraqi government would prevent it from standing up to the US in implementation. Sudarsan Raghavan and Saad Sarhan, 2008. Top Shiite Cleric in Iraq Raises Concerns about Security Pact. *Washington Post* (November 30): A19.
77. Glenn Kessler, 2016. On Iraq Withdrawal, Democrats Airbrush Out Details. *Washington Post* (October 9): A8.
78. He nevertheless chose to stick with the Iraqi leader rather than risk unsettling the existing Iraqi order, open defiance of US wishes, or actions that might increase the US commitment to Iraq (Gordon and Trainor 2012: 635).
79. At that point, around fifty thousand US advisory troops remained in the country (Cordesman and Khazai 2014: 8, 216); active US combat forces left Iraq in the summer of 2010 (Cordesman and Khazai 2014: 216).
80. By September 2010, US combat troops had exited Iraq, leaving behind roughly fifty thousand advisory troops; special operations forces; and others to advise, train, and otherwise assist Iraqi security forces (Cordesman and Khazai 2014: 216).
81. Indeed, US officials had greatly exaggerated Iraq's willingness to accept a large US *civilian* footprint—which included a sprawling embassy complex and a five-figure labor force—once US troops had *finally* left the country.
82. On the program collapse in the US government (and the State Department in particular), see Jeff Gerth and Joby Warrick, 2016. Promises Unfilled: How a State Department Plan to Stabilize Iraq Broke Apart. *Washington Post* (August 16): A1.
83. The prior violence had homogenized many areas of conflict; indigenous conflict had declined as militant groups "ran out of people to kill." Mixed areas, including Nineveh province to the north and Diyala province to the northeast of Baghdad, continued to witness recurrent violence.
84. Robinson (2008: 156–158); and Joshua Partlow, 2007. Maliki's Office Is Seen Behind Purge in Forces. *Washington Post* (April 30): 1.
85. Alissa J. Rubin, 2009. Maliki Pushes for Election Gains, Despite Fears. *New York Times* (January 26): 1; and Jim Michaels, 2009. Chain of Command Concerns Raised in Iraq. *USA Today* (February 23): 2A.
86. The same sectarian loyalists, whose appointments General Petraeus had managed to thwart, would replace competent commanders once US forces were withdrawn (Petraeus 2017: 165).
87. Ned Parker, 2010. Secret Prison Revealed in Baghdad. *Los Angeles Times* (April 19). http://articles.latimes.com/2010/apr/19/world/la-fg-iraq-prison19-2010apr19.
88. Leila Fadel, 2010. Sunni Awakening Officers Are Kicked Off Police Force in Iraq. *Washington Post* (September 27). http://www.washingtonpost.com/wp-dyn/content/article/2010/09/26/AR2010092603533.html
89. Max Fisher, 2010. Iraq's Security and Intelligence Gutted in Political Purges, New Cables Show. *The Atlantic* (December 3). https://www.theatlantic.com/international/archive/2010/12/iraqs-security-and-intelligence-gutted-in-political-purges-new-cables-show/67431/.

90. Dana Priest and Aaron Gregg, 2014. U.S. Confronts Difficulties in Arming Iraqi Air Forces with Missiles and F-16s. *Washington Post* (July 3). https://www.washingtonpost.com/investigations/us-confronts-difficulties-in-arming-iraqi-air-forces-with-missiles-and-f-16s/2014/07/03/3784ac22-0224-11e4-8572-4b1b969b6322_story.html.
91. In late 2011 the Iraqi government issued a warrant for the arrest on terrorism charges of the Sunni vice president, a fierce political opponent of the prime minister, who was then convicted, in absentia, of murder and sentenced to death. These events would not cease, of course, with the US military's departure from Iraq. In 2012 al-Maliki sanctioned the Asaib Ahl al-Haq militia, a radical, Iran-backed offshoot of the Sadrist militia that had targeted US troops, by allowing its leaders to return from exile in Iran and supposedly came to rely upon that militia for "armed support" of his political faction. David D. Kirkpatrick, 2014. Shiite Militias Pose Challenge for U.S. in Iraq. *New York Times* (September 16). https://www.nytimes.com/2014/09/17/world/middleeast/shiite-militias-pose-challenge-for-us-in-iraq.html. In 2013 the government provoked an outcry when Iraqi forces responded to peaceful protests—which had been growing for months after a raid on the home of the Iraqi finance minister, a Sunni, and the arrest of his bodyguards—with an armed assault that killed dozens of protesters in Anbar province.
92. "Maliki's tactic with Sunni leaders was to always co-opt some of them, either through legal threat or patronage, and then engage in 'negotiations' with those compromised individuals" (Sowell 2014: 60).
93. This included a favorable interpretation of the constitution that allowed him to lead the "largest bloc" after the 2010 parliamentary election by forming a majority coalition, though his electoral bloc did not receive the largest number of votes.
94. In 2011 Iraq ranked at 175, with Somalia leading the world at 182, in Transparency International's Corruption Perceptions Index. https://www.transparency.org/cpi2011/results.
95. World Bank, World Wide Governance Indicators. http://info.worldbank.org/governance/wgi/#home.
96. On this, see, for example, Ned Parker, 2009. Corruption Plays Key Role in Iraqi Justice. *Los Angeles Times* (June 29). http://articles.latimes.com/2009/jun/29/world/fg-iraq-security29.
97. Importantly, associating the strategy with the surge does not mean that enlarging the US force in Iraq alone was sufficient to defeat the insurgency.
98. Dana Hedgpeth, 2008. $13 Billion in Iraq Aid Wasted or Stolen, Ex-Investigator Says. *Washington Post* (September 23): A19.
99. Joshua Partlow, 2007. Maliki's Office Is Seen Behind Purge in Forces: Some Commanders Had Pursued Militias," *Washington Post* (April 30): A1.
100. James Glanz and Riyadh Mohammed, 2008. Premier of Iraq Is Quietly Firing Fraud Monitors. *New York Times* (November 18): 1.
101. See DeYoung, U.S., Iraq Scale Down Negotiations over Forces; DeYoung and Raghavan, U.S., Iraqi Negotiators Agree on 2011 Withdrawal; Paley, Maliki Demands All U.S. Troops Pull Out by 2011; and Parker, Agreement on U.S. Withdrawal from Iraq Said to Be in Peril.
102. Iraq differed from the United States socially, economically, and governmentally, which limited the portability of "a US-shaped process of logistics and upper-echelon planning capabilities, and a command culture that supported initiative and decision-making at the junior levels" (Cordesman and Khazai 2014: 232).
103. See, for example, Natalia Antelava, 2009. Illusion of Security in Iraq. *BBC News* (August 11). http://news.bbc.co.uk/2/hi/middle_east/8194799.stm; Andrew North, 2009. Corruption Undermines Iraqi Security. *BBC News* (August 28). http://news.bbc.co.uk/2/hi/middle_east/8226076.stm; and Marc Santora and Abeer Mohammed. 2009. After Blasts, Iraqi Officials Point Fingers. *New York Times* (August 22): 8.
104. Kevin Sullivan and Greg Jaffe, 2014. Maliki, U.S. Share Blame for Collapse of Iraqi Army. *Washington Post* (June 13). A1.

105. Missy Ryan and Erin Cunningham, 2014. Elite Iraqi Force on Way: U.S. Won't Rebuild Entire Army. *Washington Post* (November 28): A1.
106. Liz Sly, 2015. As Militias Dominate Iraq's War, Risks Grow. *Washington Post* (February 16): A1.
107. United Nations Human Rights Office of the High Commissioner. Staggering Civilian Death Toll in Iraq—UN Report. http://www.ohchr.org/EN/NewsEvents/Pages/DisplayNews.aspx?NewsID=16964&LangID=E.
108. Sly, As Militias Dominate Iraq's War.
109. Tamer El-Ghobashy and Mustafa Salim, 2017. Iraq's Top Shiite Cleric Backs Abadi with a Call to Reduce Militia Influence. *Washington Post* (December 16): A9.
110. Liz Sly and Aaso Ameen Schwan, 2017. After ISIS, Iraq's Real Test. *Washington Post* (September 14): A1.
111. Eric Schmitt, 2004. Iraq-Bound Troops Confront Rumsfeld over Lack of Armor. *New York Times* (December 8). https://www.nytimes.com/2004/12/08/international/middleeast/iraqbound-troops-confront-rumsfeld-over-lack-of.html.

Chapter 4

1. "Literally days after the Soviet invasion, Carter was on the telephone with General Mohammad Zia-ul-Haq offering him hundreds of millions of dollars in economic and military aid in exchange for cooperation in helping the rebels" (Galster 2001).
2. Lawrence Wright, 2011. The Double Game: The Unintended Consequences of American Funding in Pakistan. *New Yorker* (May 16). https://www.newyorker.com/magazine/2011/05/16/the-double-game
3. Joe Stephens and David B. Ottaway, 2002. From U.S., the ABC's of Jihad; Violent Soviet-Era Textbooks Complicate Afghan Education Efforts. *Washington Post* (March 23): A1.
4. John Kifner, 2001. Forget the Past: It's a War Unlike Any Other. *New York Times* (September 23). https://www.nytimes.com/2001/09/23/weekinreview/aftermath-forget-the-past-it-s-a-war-unlike-any-other.html.
5. The Pashtun constitute half of Afghanistan's population and most of the population of southern and eastern Afghanistan and reside in even larger numbers in the tribal regions on the Pakistan side of the border.
6. Dan Balz and Bob Woodward, 2002. America's Chaotic Road to War. *Washington Post* (January 27): A1.
7. As we know, even superficial resemblances are sufficient to trigger the full application of a historical analogy.
8. For an excellent discussion of World War II symbolism applied to the 9/11 attacks, see Dower (2010).
9. Balz and Woodward, America's Chaotic Road to War.
10. Michael R. Gordon, Eric Schmitt, and Thom Shanker, 2001. A Nation Challenged: The Combat. *New York Times* (September 19). https://www.nytimes.com/2001/09/19/world/nation-challenged-combat-scarcity-afghanistan-targets-prompts-us-change-strategy.html
11. Bob Woodward and Dan Balz, 2002. "We Will Rally the World," Bush and His Advisers Set Objectives, but Struggle with How to Achieve Them. *Washington Post* (January 28), A1.
12. Michael R. Gordon, 2001. After the Attacks: The Strategy. *New York Times* (September 17). https://www.nytimes.com/2001/09/17/world/after-the-attacks-the-strategy-a-new-war-and-its-scale.html
13. Gordon, Schmitt, and Shanker, A Nation Challenged.
14. Text: President Bush Addresses the Nation. *Washington Post* (September 20, 2001) http://www.washingtonpost.com/wp-srv/nation/specials/attacked/transcripts/bushaddress_092001.html
15. Bush chose to underscore the demands by including them in his speech, though he had previously charged Secretary of State Colin Powell with crafting the demands for a less-public

presentation to the Taliban through the government of Pakistan. Woodward and Balz, "We Will Rally the World," Bush and His Advisers Set Objectives; Dan Balz and Bob Woodward, 2002. A Presidency Defined in One Speech. *Washington Post* (February 1): A1.
16. John F. Burns, 2001. A Nation Challenged: The Taliban. *New York Times* (September 21). https://www.nytimes.com/2001/09/21/world/nation-challenged-taliban-afghans-coaxing-bin-laden-but-us-rejects-clerics-bid.html.
17. John F. Burns, 2001. A Nation Challenged: Last Chance. *New York Times* (September 18). https://www.nytimes.com/2001/09/18/world/a-nation-challenged-last-chance-taliban-refuse-quick-decision-over-bin-laden.html.
18. Luke Harding and Rory McCarthy, 2001. Sanctions Lifted as US Rewards Pakistan. *The Guardian* (September 23). https://www.theguardian.com/world/2001/sep/24/pakistan.afghanistan.
19. Balz and Woodward, America's Chaotic Road to War.
20. Bob Woodward and Dan Balz, 2002. At Camp David, Advise and Dissent. *Washington Post* (January 31): A1. In that regard, the administration was maintaining the approach of the prior administration and its own pre-9/11 thinking. On September 10, in a meeting of the National Security Council's Deputies Committee (which includes the second-in-command of the various departments and agencies involved in US national security), the participants had agreed to a three-phase strategy for dealing with the Taliban that would start by sending an envoy to meet with Taliban leaders to convince them to turn over bin Laden and shutter his terror infrastructure in the country (Ballard et al. 2012: 30).
21. Woodward and Balz, At Camp David, Advise and Dissent.
22. Woodward and Balz, At Camp David, Advise and Dissent.
23. Woodward and Balz, At Camp David, Advise and Dissent.
24. Woodward and Balz, "We Will Rally the World," Bush and His Advisers Set Objectives.
25. Gordon, After the Attacks.
26. Admittedly, Rumsfeld handwrote a qualifying sentence next to the typed text: "The U.S. needs to be involved in this effort to assure that our coalition partners are not disaffected." Notably, however, he did not strike out the other sentence. Donald Rumsfeld (to Douglas Feith), 2001. "U.S. Strategy in Afghanistan," National Security Council (October 16). https://nsarchive2.gwu.edu/NSAEBB/NSAEBB358a/index.htm
27. Donald Rumsfeld, 2001. Strategic Thoughts. Memorandum for the President (September 30). https://nsarchive2.gwu.edu/NSAEBB/NSAEBB358a/index.htm.
28. It included, as members, the second-from-the-top officials at the NSC, CIA, State Department, and Defense Department.
29. Woodward and Balz, "We Will Rally the World," Bush and His Advisers Set Objectives; and Balz and Woodward. A Presidency Defined in One Speech.
30. The meetings took place September 15–16 at the Camp David presidential retreat.
31. Woodward and Balz, 2002. "We Will Rally the World," Bush and His Advisers Set Objectives; and Dan Balz, Bob Woodward, and Jeff Himmelman, 2002. Afghan Campaign's Blueprint Emerges. *Washington Post* (January 29): A1.
32. Patrick E. Tyler and Elaine Sciolino, 2001, Bush Advisers Split on Scope of Retaliation, *New York Times* (September 20). https://www.nytimes.com/2001/09/20/world/a-nation-challenged-washington-bush-s-advisers-split-on-scope-of-retaliation.html.
33. Tyler and Sciolino, Bush Advisers Split on Scope of Retaliation.
34. Bob Woodward and Dan Balz, 2002. Combating Terrorism: "It Starts Today." *Washington Post* (February 1): A1. As one defense official surmised, "Rumsfeld for whatever reason has decided that Iraq can wait" but "he hasn't given up on it." Tyler and Sciolino, Bush Advisers Split on Scope of Retaliation.
35. Rumsfeld had Iraq on his list of alternative targets; indeed, his initial proclivity, as conveyed to the vice chair of the JCS on September 11, was to hit Iraq (with its more inviting target set) and al-Qaeda simultaneously (Graham 2009: 285–291).
36. Woodward and Balz, "We Will Rally the World," Bush and His Advisers Set Objectives.

37. Eric Schmitt and Michael R. Gordon, 2001. Top Air Chief Sent: Ground Units Deployed, Joining Bombers and Supporting Planes. *New York Times* (September 21): A1.
38. The principals explicitly recognized hurdles to acquiring domestic support for the administration's global war effort, such as when they acknowledged a need to achieve an early US victory in the antiterrorism war, to prepare the US public for a long and difficult war, and to act first—and succeed—in Afghanistan. Woodward and Balz, At Camp David, Advise and Dissent; Woodward and Balz, Combating Terrorism; and Woodward (2002: 48, 81).
39. John F. Burns, 2001. After the Attacks: In Pakistan. *New York Times* (September 15). https://www.nytimes.com/2001/09/15/us/after-the-attacks-in-pakistan-us-demands-air-and-land-access-to-pakistan.html.
40. In exchange for its support, the Uzbek government presented the administration with an unrealistic wish list that included immediate NATO membership (Woodward 2002: 172).
41. Donald Rumsfeld, 2001. A New Kind of War. *New York Times* (September 27). https://www.nytimes.com/2001/09/27/opinion/a-new-kind-of-war.html.
42. Woodward and Balz, "We Will Rally the World," Bush and His Advisers Set Objectives.
43. US Department of State, Cable, "Deputy Secretary Armitage's Meeting with Pakistan Intel Chief Mahmud: You're Either with US or You're Not," September 13, 2001. https://nsarchive2.gwu.edu/NSAEBB/NSAEBB358a/index.htm Pakistan's president, Pervez Musharraf, eventually claimed that Armitage had threatened, through the ISI chief, to bomb his country "back to the Stone Age" if it failed to cooperate in the US-led effort against the Taliban regime. Suzanne Goldenberg, 2006. Bush Threatened to Bomb Pakistan, Says Musharraf. *The Guardian* (September 22). https://www.theguardian.com/world/2006/sep/22/pakistan.usa
44. US Embassy (Islamabad), Cable, "Musharaff: We are with You in your Action Plan in Afghanistan," September 13, 2001. https://nsarchive2.gwu.edu/NSAEBB/NSAEBB358a/index.htm.
45. US Department of State, Cable, "Secretary's 13 September 2001 Conversation with Pakistani President Musharraf," September 19, 2001. https://nsarchive2.gwu.edu/NSAEBB/NSAEBB358a/index.htm.
46. Woodward and Balz, "We Will Rally the World," Bush and His Advisers Set Objectives.
47. Celia W. Dugger, 2001. After the Attacks: An Uncertain Ally. *New York Times* (September 14). https://www.nytimes.com/2001/09/14/us/after-attacks-uncertain-ally-us-presses-pakistan-help-pry-suspected-terrorist.html.
48. They ultimately emerged with a set of "recommendations" for the cabinet and National Security Council. Dugger, After the Attacks.
49. Kifner, Forget the Past.
50. On these issues in historical context, see Hoyt (2015).
51. ISI and other Pakistani officials "see Afghanistan simultaneously as a source of irredentist magnetism attracting Pakistan's Pashtun population and as potential strategic depth against India" (Zakheim 2011: 109).
52. Burns, After the Attacks.
53. CENTCOM, however, had prepared, expecting that ten thousand to twelve thousand US troops would eventually be required to back the Northern Alliance and defeat the Taliban (Wright et al. 2010: 58–60).
54. Central Intelligence Agency. On the Front Lines: CIA in Afghanistan. https://www.cia.gov/about-cia/cia-museum/experience-the-collection/text-version/stories/on-the-front-lines-cia-in-afghanistan.html
55. Eric Schmitt and Michael R. Gordon, 2001. Top Air Chief Sent: Ground Units Deployed, Joining Bombers and Supporting Planes. *New York Times* (September 21): A1.
56. Gordon, After the Attacks.
57. Rumsfeld apparently deferred to Franks (Graham 2009: 308), but the two were generally operating from the same playbook.

58. On the Afghan model of combined air-ground operations, see Andres et al. (2005/2006); on its limitations, see Biddle (2003).
59. David Rohde and David E. Sanger, 2007. How a "Good War" in Afghanistan Went Bad. *New York Times* (August 12). https://www.nytimes.com/2007/08/12/world/asia/12afghan.html.
60. In Zakheim's view, that he did not learn about Haass's work "despite constant interface with other officials, both at State and other agencies, who dealt with Afghanistan—as well as with two ambassadors to that country—is sorry testimony to the state of disarray that governed the administration's approach to Afghanistan once the military mission seemed to be under control" (Zakheim 2011: 174).
61. The PRT program had its origins in the Coalition Humanitarian Liaison Cells that were initiated in early 2002.
62. In sum, "the provincial reconstruction team concept was sound, but there simply were not enough people, money, and time to realize its full potential"; "they remained selectively useful but insufficient to meet the country's huge needs" (Neumann et al. 2013: 59).
63. On this problem more generally, see Biddle (2014: 80). He observes that "poorly monitored 'capacity building' often makes the problem worse by supplying patronage networks with the money and resources needed to reward their allies, punish their rivals, and extract resources from the public more effectively."
64. The ISAF was formed in accordance with the Bonn agreement, which established the framework for Afghan governance.
65. Coordination would presumably improve as US troops arrived better trained for a COIN operation and the PRTs were better integrated within operations and the command structure within areas of operation (Wright et al. 2010: 292, 300).
66. By mid-2005, twenty-two PRTs were operating in Afghanistan, thirteen of them under US (rather than ISAF) direction (Wright et al. 2010: 308).
67. Rohde and Sanger, How a "Good War" in Afghanistan Went Bad.
68. Although the United States and its allies nonetheless invested in still another force—the Afghan Defense Force (ADF), created to guard local villages under the direction of local leaders—it, too, developed patronage relationships with local leaders (Grenier 2015: 52). By 2006 the AMF and ADF were disbanded (Grenier 2015: 54).
69. Put more strongly, the job of building the Afghan army was essentially "'contracted out,'" with the British charged with training noncommissioned officers, the French taking on officer training, and other states filling in the gaps (Rothstein 2012: 61).
70. According to the GAO (1975: 26), based on interviews with knowledgeable German officials, "Germany has viewed its role as one of advising and consulting with other donors and the Afghan government rather than as the major implementer or funding source for the police sector." Feith (2008: 154–155) concludes that Germany "focused its efforts on the narrowly conceived, long-term task of educating senior officers in multiyear courses—ignoring almost all of Afghanistan's immediate police related needs."
71. With the reorganization under the NTM-A, the CSTC-A was placed in charge of developing and professionalizing the Ministry of Interior and Ministry of Defense.
72. Indeed, in the early years of OEF the US military worked with various militia, organized nominally as the Afghan Military Force (AMF) and then the Afghan Security Forces (ASF), until 2006, when they were disbanded (Rynning 2012: 90).
73. Pamela Constable, 2009. Dispute Over Timing of Afghan Vote Turns Messy. *Washington Post* (March 5): A10; and Rajiv Chandrasekaran, 2009. Obama's War: A New Approach to Karzai. *Washington Post* (May 6): A1.
74. Chandrasekaran, Obama's War.
75. The evidence from building professionalized military forces provides little reason for optimism in answering that question (see Biddle et al. 2018).
76. North Atlantic Treaty Organization, ISAF's Mission in Afghanistan. (2001–2014). (archived) http://www.nato.int/cps/en/natohq/topics_69366.htm

77. Indeed, Rumsfeld wanted to keep US troops out of the ISAF, fearing that US allies might otherwise shirk their responsibilities (Feith 2008: 156).
78. The British force first pursued a broad counterinsurgency strategy in Helmand province; its small size, limited mobility, and large area of responsibility pushed it nonetheless to rely on firepower, with the perhaps inevitable results: an alienated local population, insufficient security gains, and the eventual British retreat to more defensive positions (Nagl and Weitz 2015: 172–174).
79. In September 2006, for example, the Canadians (who as of July commanded the southern region) took the lead in Operation Medusa, a conventional confrontation in Kandahar province, pitting thousands of ISAF troops against a large concentration of Taliban fighters attempting to hold ground. The two-week operation left over a dozen ISAF and many hundreds of Taliban fighters dead. Richard Norton-Taylor, 2007. Full Interview: General David Richards. *The Guardian* (January 21). https://www.theguardian.com/world/2007/jan/22/afghanistan.afghanistantimeline1.
80. The extent of the differences was betrayed indirectly by the chief of NATO, Jaap de Hoop Scheffer, when, at a late 2006 NATO summit, he remarked, "We have made real progress on caveats." BBC News, 2006. NATO Hails Shift on Afghan Combat. *BBC News* (November 29). http://news.bbc.co.uk/2/hi/europe/6195102.stm.
81. Indeed, Dutch troops engaged in intensive battles to clear the Taliban from Uruzgan province in subsequent years (Rietjens 2012: 78).
82. Richards himself would chafe at the restrictions, later describing the NATO command structure as "disorganized and unhelpful." Con Coughlin, 2012. General David Richards: Afghan Campaign Was Woeful. *The Telegraph* (October 19). https://www.telegraph.co.uk/news/uknews/defence/9045079/General-David-Richards-Afghan-campaign-was-woeful.html
83. Rohde and Sanger, How a "Good War" in Afghanistan Went Bad.
84. Kilcullen (2009, 64); Dexter Filkins, 2009. U.S. Sets Fight in the Poppies to Stop the Taliban. *New York Times* (April 28): 1; and Craig Whitlock, 2009. Diverse Sources Fund Insurgency in Afghanistan. *Washington Post* (September 27): A1.
85. James Dao, 2009. Afghan War's Buried Bombs Put Risk in Every Step. *New York Times* (July 15): 1; Karen DeYoung, 2009. Taliban Surprising U.S. Forces with Improved Tactics. *Washington Post* (September 2): A1.
86. As one counterinsurgency expert put it, "The Taliban appears to be applying an *exhaustion strategy* of sapping the energy, resources, and support of the Afghan government and its international partners, making the country ungovernable and hoping that the international community will eventually withdraw in exhaustion and leave the government to collapse under the weight of its own lack of effectiveness and legitimacy" (Kilcullen 2009: 52).
87. See http://icasualties.org/.
88. In July 2008, for example, forty-one people were killed in a suicide car bomb attack on the Indian embassy in Kabul. Abdul Waheed Wafa and Alan Cowell, 2008. Suicide Car Blast Kills 41 in Afghan Capital. *New York Times* (July 8). https://www.nytimes.com/2008/07/08/world/asia/08afghanistan.html.
89. In the deadly south of Afghanistan, roadside bombs, rocket attacks, and the occasional firefight were the weapons of choice. Drew Brown, 2008. In the South, Tenacious Taliban Fights On. *Stars and Stripes* (October 27). https://www.stripes.com/news/in-the-south-tenacious-taliban-fights-on-1.84562.
90. Carlotta Gall and Sangar Rahimi, 2008. Taliban Escalate Fighting with Assault on U.S. Base. *New York Times* (August 19) https://www.nytimes.com/2008/08/20/world/asia/20afghan.html; and John Bingham, 2008. Afghanistan Death Rate for British Troops Tops Height of Iraq Fighting. *The Telegraph* (August 27). https://www.telegraph.co.uk/news/newstopics/onthefrontline/2631658/Afghanistan-death-rate-for-British-troops-tops-height-of-Iraq-fighting.html
91. BBC News, 2008. US "Killed 47 Afghan Civilians." *BBC News* (July 11). http://news.bbc.co.uk/2/hi/south_asia/7501538.stm

92. Peter Baker, 2009. Could Afghanistan Become Obama's Vietnam? *New York Times* (August 22). https://www.nytimes.com/2009/08/23/weekinreview/23baker.html.
93. Karen DeYoung, 2009. Obama Announces Strategy for Afghanistan, Pakistan. *Washington Post* (March 28). http://www.washingtonpost.com/wp-dyn/content/article/2009/03/27/AR2009032700836.html
94. Rajiv Chandrasekaran, 2009. Civilian, Military Officials at Odds over Resources Needed for Afghan Mission. *Washington Post* (October 8): A1.
95. For a defense of the difficult decision to replace McKiernan, see Gates (2014: 344–345).
96. Anthony Blinken, Vice President Biden's national security adviser, was reportedly the sole dissenter. Chandrasekaran, Civilian, Military Officials at Odds over Resources Needed for Afghan Mission.
97. Chandrasekaran, Civilian, Military Officials at Odds over Resources Needed for Afghan Mission.
98. The White House, A New Strategy for Afghanistan and Pakistan (March 27, 2009). https://www.whitehouse.gov/blog/2009/03/27/a-new-strategy-afghanistan-and-pakistan
99. DeYoung, Obama Announces Strategy for Afghanistan, Pakistan.
100. COMISAF Initial Assessment (Unclassified), *Washington Post* (September 21, 2009). http://www.washingtonpost.com/wp-dyn/content/article/2009/09/21/AR2009092100110.html
101. Rajiv Chandrasekaran, 2009. In Kandahar, a Taliban on the Rise. *Washington Post* (September 14): A1.
102. Whereas the strategy revolves around protecting and serving the population, the Marines had a different set of priorities: they chose to locate in an area of active combat that could accommodate the entire force (including its logistical support apparatus and aircraft) and insisted further on operational autonomy (under the direction of a three-star Marine general at US Central Command). Rajiv Chandrasekaran, 2012. "Little America" Book Excerpt: Obama's Troop Increase for Afghan War Was Misdirected. *Washington Post* (June 22). https://www.washingtonpost.com/world/war-zones/little-america-excerpt-obamas-troop-increase-for-afghan-war-was-misdirected/2012/06/22/gJQAYHrAvV_story.html. See also Gates (2014: 340).
103. On this, see Ann Scott Tyson, 2009. Dearth of Capable Afghan Forces Complicates U.S. Mission in South. *Washington Post* (July 25): A9.
104. See ICG (2008); US GAO (2005: 22, 2009a); Pamela Constable, 2009. U.S. Troops Face a Tangle of Goals in Afghanistan. *Washington Post* (March 8): A1; Richard A. Oppel Jr., 2009. Corruption Undercuts Hopes for Afghan Police. *New York Times* (April 9): 1; and C. J. Chivers, 2009. Erratic Afghan Forces Pose Challenge to U.S. Goals. *New York Times* (June 8): 1.
105. Available at www.brookings.edu/reports/2008/02_weak_states_index.aspx and www.foreignpolicy.com/images/fs2008/failed_states_ranking.jpg (accessed September 1, 2009).
106. Walter Pincus, 2009. Analysts Expect Long-Term, Costly U.S. Campaign in Afghanistan. *Washington Post* (August 9): A8.
107. See www.transparency.org.
108. Bob Woodward, 2010. Military Thwarted President Seeking Choice in Afghanistan. *Washington Post* (September 27): A6.
109. Woodward, Military Thwarted President Seeking Choice in Afghanistan.
110. The president was reacting on these occasions against the well-worn practice of presenting a preferred middle option sandwiched between two nonviable options or multiple options that differed insignificantly from one another.
111. Steve Luxenberg, 2010. Obama Battles with Advisers over Afghan Exit Plan Detailed in Woodward Book. *Washington Post* (September 22): A8.
112. Rajiv Chandrasekaran, 2012. "Little America": Infighting on Obama Team Squandered Chance for Peace in Afghanistan. *Washington Post* (June 24). https://www.washingtonpost.com/world/national-security/little-america-infighting-on-obama-team-squandered-chance-for-peace-in-afghanistan/2012/06/24/gJQAbQMB0V_story.html.

113. David Ignatius, 2009. Obama's Skeptic in Chief. *Washington Post* (November 26): A27.
114. Michael O'Hanlon and Bruce Riedel, 2009. Why We Can't Go Small in Afghanistan. Brookings Institution (September 24). https://www.brookings.edu/opinions/why-we-cant-go-small-in-afghanistan/
115. Riedel maintained further that the Taliban would likely re-establish itself in Afghanistan, precipitating the collapse of the Afghan government, which would deprive the United States of bases for operating drone aircraft. He also maintained that US allies would likely take the US evacuation for abandonment and would then try to jump ship first.
116. Peter Baker, 2009. How Obama Came to Plan for "Surge" in Afghanistan. *New York Times* (December 5) https://www.nytimes.com/2009/12/06/world/asia/06reconstruct.html; and Neil Sheehan, 2010. Inside the Making of Obama's Vietnam. *Washington Post* (October 3): B1.
117. Greg Jaffe and Anne E. Kornblut, 2009. Narrowing of Mission Reflects Biden's Goal. *Washington Post* (December 3): A19; and Sheehan, Inside the Making of Obama's Vietnam.
118. Rajiv Chandrasekaran, 2009. Changes Have Obama Rethinking War Strategy. *Washington Post* (September 21): A1.
119. Helene Cooper, 2009. Karzai Using Rift with U.S. to Gain Favor. *New York Times* (August 29): 1.
120. BBC News, 2010. UN Envoy Peter Galbraith Denies Afghan Poll Fraud. *BBC News* (April 1). http://news.bbc.co.uk/2/hi/south_asia/8600249.stm
121. Ambassador Eikenberry's Cables on U.S. Strategy in Afghanistan. http://documents.nytimes.com/eikenberry-s-memos-on-the-strategy-in-afghanistan
122. Karen DeYoung, 2009. Afghan Envoy Assails Western Allies as Halfhearted, Defeatist. *Washington Post* (March 12): A14.
123. Baker, How Obama Came to Plan for "Surge" in Afghanistan.
124. Based on the results of a Washington Post-ABC News Poll conducted July 15–18, 2009, on a randomly selected sample of five hundred adults, as reported in Washington Post, 2009. Assessing Obama's War. *Washington Post* (July 22): A7.
125. Sentiment had turned against the war, though only 36 percent of the public thought that the United States was losing, and most thought that the United States could ultimately achieve its economic, political, and military goals in the country. These data are from a Washington Post-ABC News Poll conducted August 13–17, 2009, on a randomly selected sample of 1,001 adults, as reported in Jennifer Agiesta and Jon Cohen, 2009. Public Opinion in U.S. Turns against the War. *Washington Post* (August 20): A9.
126. Support for Afghan War Drops, CNN Poll Finds. CNN Politics.com (August 6, 2009). http://edition.cnn.com/2009/POLITICS/08/06/poll.afghanistan; and Poll: Support for Afghan War at All-Time Low. CNN Politics.com (September 15, 2009). http://edition.cnn.com/2009/POLITICS/09/15/afghan.war.poll.
127. On the deteriorating relationship, see Gates (2014: 335–386).
128. Baker, How Obama Came to Plan for "Surge" in Afghanistan.
129. Baker, How Obama Came to Plan for "Surge" in Afghanistan.
130. Anne E. Kornblut, Scott Wilson, and Karen DeYoung, 2009. Obama Pressed for Faster Surge. *Washington Post* (December 6): A1.
131. Baker, How Obama Came to Plan for "Surge" in Afghanistan.
132. Kornblut, Wilson, and DeYoung, Obama Pressed for Faster Surge.
133. Chandrasekaran, Civilian, Military Officials at Odds over Resources Needed for Afghan Mission; and Scott Wilson and Greg Jaffe, 2009. Obama Seeks Study on Local Leaders for Troop Decision. *Washington Post* (October 29): A1.
134. Press Briefing by Bruce Riedel, Ambassador Richard Holbrooke, and Michelle [sic] Flournoy on the New Strategy for Afghanistan and Pakistan (March 27, 2009). https://obamawhitehouse.archives.gov/realitycheck/the-press-office/press-briefing-bruce-riedel-ambassador-richard-holbrooke-and-michelle-flournoy-new-
135. Ignatius, Obama's Skeptic in Chief.

136. Karen DeYoung, 2009. With Narrower Military Goals, Obama Ups the Ante. *Washington Post* (December 2): A11.
137. Jaffe and Kornblut, Narrowing of Mission Reflects Biden's Goal.
138. Wilson and Jaffe, Obama Seeks Study on Local Leaders for Troop Decision.
139. Kornblut, Wilson, and DeYoung, Obama Pressed for Faster Surge.
140. Although the costs of operating in Afghanistan amounted to around $1 million annually per US soldier, troop numbers did not drive the costs of the US Afghan operation.
141. Rajiv Chandrasekaran, 2009. Troops Face New Tests in Afghanistan. *Washington Post* (March 15): A1.
142. Greg Jaffe, 2009. U.S. Commanders Told to Shift Focus to More Populated Areas. *Washington Post* (September 22) http://www.washingtonpost.com/wp-dyn/content/article/2009/09/21/AR2009092103704.html
143. Luxenberg, Obama Battles with Advisers over Afghan Exit Plan.
144. Ignatius, Obama's Skeptic in Chief.
145. Baker, How Obama Came to Plan for "Surge" in Afghanistan.
146. Woodward, Military Thwarted President Seeking Choice in Afghanistan.
147. DeYoung, With Narrower Military Goals, Obama Ups the Ante.
148. Baker, How Obama Came to Plan for "Surge" in Afghanistan.
149. Baker, How Obama Came to Plan for "Surge" in Afghanistan.
150. Baker, How Obama Came to Plan for 'Surge' in Afghanistan.
151. Baker, How Obama Came to Plan for 'Surge" in Afghanistan.
152. Rajiv Chandrasekaran, 2009. Afghan War Cost to Be Big Factor in Troop Drawdown. *Washington Post* (May 31): A1.
153. Washington Post, editorial. 2010. The Afghan Roller Coaster. *Washington Post* (June 17): A20.
154. Deployment specifics varied by location, though troops often deployed outside villages and cities to create working and living space or avoid a glaring US presence (O'Hanlon and Sherjan 2010: 41).
155. See Biddle (2014: 79). See also Jason Motlagh, 2010. Petraeus Toughens Afghan Rules of Engagement. *Time* (August 6). http://content.time.com/time/world/article/0,8599,2008863,00.html.
156. These units saw action despite public outrage over civilian deaths they had inflicted in prior nighttime raids. Eric Schmitt, 2009. Elite U.S. Force Expanding Hunt in Afghanistan. *New York Times* (December 26) https://www.nytimes.com/2009/12/27/world/asia/27commandos.html
157. Chandrasekaran, "Little America": Infighting on Obama Team.
158. Overview of the Afghanistan and Pakistan Annual Review. *New York Times* (December 16, 2010) https://www.nytimes.com/interactive/projects/documents/the-obama-administrations-overview-on-afghanistan-and-pakistan
159. Helene Cooper and David E. Sanger, 2010. Obama Cites Afghan Gains as Report Says Exit Is on Track. *New York Times* (December 16). https://www.nytimes.com/2010/12/17/world/asia/17afghan.html
160. Craig Whitlock and Greg Miller, 2010. Paramilitary Force Is Key for CIA. *Washington Post* (September 23): A1.
161. BBC News, 2011. Pakistan Outrage after "NATO Attack Kills Soldiers." *BBC News* (November 26). http://www.bbc.com/news/world-asia-15901363.
162. Salman Masood and Eric Schmitt, 2011. Tensions Flare Between U.S. and Pakistan after Strike. *New York Times* (November 26). https://www.nytimes.com/2011/11/27/world/asia/pakistan-says-nato-helicopters-kill-dozens-of-soldiers.html
163. Greg Miller and Bob Woodward. 2013. Secret Memos Reveal Explicit Nature of U.S., Pakistan Agreement on Drones. *Washington Post* (October 24). https://www.washingtonpost.com/world/national-security/top-pakistani-leaders-secretly-backed-cia-drone-campaign-secret-documents-show/2013/10/23/15e6b0d8-3beb-11e3-b6a9-da62c264f40e_story.html.

164. Helen Cooper and Thom Shanker, 2012. U.S. Refines Afghan Success before Conference. *New York Times* (May 17). https://www.nytimes.com/2012/05/18/world/asia/us-redefines-afghan-success-before-conference.html.
165. Peter Baker and Rod Nordland, 2010. U.S. Plan Envisions Path to Ending Afghan Conflict. *New York Times* (November 14). http://www.nytimes.com/2010/11/15/world/asia/15prexy.html?partner=rss&emc=rss.
166. CNN Wire Staff, 2011. Obama Announces Afghanistan Troop Withdrawal Plan. *CNN Politics* (June 23). http://www.cnn.com/2011/POLITICS/06/22/afghanistan.troops.drawdown/.
167. CNN Wire Staff, Obama Announces Afghanistan Troop Withdrawal Plan.
168. The White House, Statement by the President on Afghanistan (May 27, 2014). https://www.whitehouse.gov/the-press-office/2014/05/27/statement-president-afghanistan
169. Karen DeYoung, 2014. Obama to Leave 9,800 U.S. Troops in Afghanistan. *Washington Post* (May 27). https://www.washingtonpost.com/world/national-security/obama-to-leave-9800-us-troops-in-afghanistan-senior-official-says/2014/05/27/57f37e72-e5b2-11e3-a86b-362fd5443d19_story.html?tid=a_inl.
170. Mark Landler, 2014. U.S. Troops to Leave Afghanistan by End of 2016. *New York Times* (May 27). https://www.nytimes.com/2014/05/28/world/asia/us-to-complete-afghan-pullout-by-end-of-2016-obama-to-say.html.
171. Under the president's plan, ninety-eight hundred troops would remain by the beginning of 2015; roughly half that number would remain by the end of the same year, concentrated in Kabul and the base at Bagram. Even with the departure schedules, it is important to note that costs and staffing in Afghanistan owed largely to the massive infrastructure—the bases, facilities, logistical support, and equipment—supporting the entire US mission, including the training of Afghan security forces and reconstruction. Even by the end of 2015, when the United States had around ten thousand troops in Afghanistan, the United States had three times that number of defense contractors working in that country alone (although only around ten thousand of them were US citizens) (http://www.acq.osd.mil/log/ps/.CENTCOM_reports.html/5A_October2015_Final.pdf).
172. Statement by the President on Afghanistan, May 27, 2014. https://obamawhitehouse.archives.gov/the-press-office/2014/05/27/statement-president-afghanistan.
173. The occasion was widely remembered outside Afghanistan for the deadly US air attack on a Doctors Without Borders hospital there that followed.
174. Resources and personnel continued to flow across the border from Pakistan. David S. Sedney, 2015. Testimony before the Committee on Foreign Affairs; Subcommittee on the Middle East and North Africa. United States House of Representatives, December 2, 114th Cong., 1st Sess., pp. 14–15.
175. Mark Landler, 2016. For Obama, an Unexpected Legacy of Two Full Terms at War. *New York Times* (May 14). https://www.nytimes.com/2016/05/15/us/politics/obama-as-wartime-president-has-wrestled-with-protecting-nation-and-troops.html
176. Pamela Constable, 2017. Terror War in Kabul: "How Long Do We Have to Die?" *Washington Post* (March 10): A10.
177. Matthew Rosenberg and Michael D. Shear. 2015. In Reversal, Obama Says U.S. Soldiers Will Stay in Afghanistan to 2017. *New York Times* (October 15). http://www.nytimes.com/2015/10/16/world/asia/obama-troop-withdrawal-afghanistan.html.
178. Sarah Almukhtar and Karen Yourish, 2016. More Than 14 Years after U.S. Invasion, the Taliban Control Large Parts of Afghanistan. *New York Times* (April 19). https://www.nytimes.com/interactive/2015/09/29/world/asia/afghanistan-taliban-maps.html.
179. Institute for the Study of War. 2016. Afghanistan Partial Threat Assessment: June 30, 2016. http://www.understandingwar.org/backgrounder/afghanistan-partial-threat-assessment-june-30-2016.
180. UN News. 2016. Afghan Civilian Casualties Hit Half-Year Record, with 5,166 Dead or Maimed—UN. *UN News* (July 25). http://www.un.org/apps/news/story.asp?NewsID=54543#.V5ZNnHpM7nk.

181. Missy Ryan and Thomas Gibbons-Neff, 2016. Obama Approves New Steps to Fight Taliban in Afghanistan. *Washington Post* (June 11): A14; and Tim Craig, 2016. Progress Is Reported in Fight against the Taliban. *Washington Post* (July 17): A10.
182. Craig, Progress Is Reported in Fight against the Taliban.
183. Thomas Gibbons-Neff, 2016. NATO Expected to Keep Some Afghan Bases Open. *Washington Post* (June 16): A17.
184. Missy Ryan and Karen DeYoung, 2016. Closure in Afghanistan Falls Further Out of Reach for Obama. *Washington Post* (July 7): A1.
185. The counts excluded troops in country for fewer than 120 days, meaning that the physical count remained as much as 50 percent higher than the reported count. Wesley Morgan, 2017. Pentagon's Concealment of Total Troops in War Zones under Fire. *Politico* (August 26). http://www.politico.com/story/2017/08/26/mattis-tump-troop-numbers-war-zone-242055.
186. Craig, Progress Is Reported in Fight against the Taliban.
187. Pamela Constable and Mohammed Sharif, 2016. Battles Near Capital of Afghanistan's Helmand Province. *Washington Post* (August 14): A15.
188. Sayed Salahuddin, 2016. Taliban Advances on Former Stronghold. *Washington Post* (September 9): A8.
189. Sayed Salahuddin and Pamela Constable, 2016. Attacks at Afghan "Pentagon," Charity Steep Kabul in Fear. *Washington Post* (September 7): A9.
190. Thomas Gibbons-Neff, 2016. Afghans' Reliance on U.S. Strikes Increasing. *Washington Post* (October 17): A1; and Pamela Constable, 2016. Taliban Enters Strategic Southern Afghan City, Killing 14. *Washington Post* (October 11): A10.
191. The son of the network's head became a Mansour deputy.
192. Tim Craig, 2016. Grisly Killing Hints at New Level of Brutality by the Taliban. *Washington Post* (June 12): A14.
193. Craig, Grisly Killing Hints at New Level of Brutality by the Taliban.
194. Ryan and DeYoung, Closure in Afghanistan Falls Further Out of Reach for Obama.
195. Yalda Hakim, 2013. Afghanistan's Hamid Karzai Says NATO Caused "Great Suffering." *BBC News* (October 7). http://www.bbc.com/news/world-24433433.
196. Peter Baker and Rod Nordland, 2010. U.S. Plan Envisions Path to Ending Afghan Conflict. *New York Times* (November 14) https://www.nytimes.com/2010/11/15/world/asia/15prexy.html
197. Rod Nordland, Elisabeth Bumiller, and Matthew Rosenberg, 2012. Karzai Calls on U.S. to Pull Back as Taliban Cancel Talks. *New York Times* (March 15). https://www.nytimes.com/2012/03/16/world/asia/taliban-call-off-talks-as-karzai-urges-faster-us-transition.html.
198. Obama's eventual (May 2014) pledge to keep ninety-eight hundred troops in Afghanistan through 2015 assumed a signed agreement. DeYoung, Obama to Leave 9,800 U.S. Troops in Afghanistan.
199. Mark Mazzetti and Matthew Rosenberg, 2013. U.S. Considers Faster Pullout in Afghanistan. *New York Times* (July 8). https://www.nytimes.com/2013/07/09/world/asia/frustrated-obama-considers-full-troop-withdrawal-from-afghanistan.html.
200. Mazzetti and Rosenberg, U.S. Considers Faster Pullout in Afghanistan.
201. Karen DeYoung and Tim Craig, 2013. U.S. to Offer Afghans Assurances to Remove Hurdle in Post-2014. Deal. *Washington Post* (November 20). https://www.washingtonpost.com/world/asia_pacific/kerry-offers-to-write-letter-to-afghan-people-on-past-us-mistakes-kabul-officials-say/2013/11/19/11d16802-5159-11e3-9ee6-2580086d8254_story.html.
202. Karen DeYoung and Tim Craig, 2013. U.S., Afghanistan Agree on Language of Security Accord, Kerry Says. *Washington Post* (November 20). https://www.washingtonpost.com/world/national-security/us-afghanistan-agree-on-language-of-security-accord-kerry-says/2013/11/20/85136c40-521a-11e3-a7f0-b790929232e1_story.html
203. Obama's Full Letter to Afghan President Karzai on Security Agreement. NBCMiami (November 21, 2013) https://www.nbcmiami.com/news/national-international/Barack-

Obamas-Full-Letter-to-Afghan-President-Hamid-Karzai-on-Bilateral-Security-Agreement-232812761.html
204. Rod Nordland, 2013. Elders Back Security Pact That Karzai Won't Sign. *New York Times* (November 24). https://www.nytimes.com/2013/11/25/world/asia/afghan-council-approves-us-security-pact.html
205. The quotation is from a White House summary of the encounter. See White House, Readout of National Security Advisor Susan E. Rice's Meeting with President Hamid Karzai of Afghanistan (November 25, 2013). https://obamawhitehouse.archives.gov/the-press-office/2013/11/25/readout-national-security-advisor-susan-e-rices-meeting-president-hamid-
206. Azam Ahmed and Matthew Rosenberg, 2014. Karzai Arranged Secret Contacts with the Taliban. *New York Times* (February 3). https://www.nytimes.com/2014/02/04/world/asia/karzai-has-held-secret-contacts-with-the-taliban.html.
207. This is not to say that Karzai wanted US forces to depart. He appears to have believed that the United States had no desire to leave and coveted bases in Afghanistan (Neumann 2015: 14).
208. Carlotta Gall, 2014. In Afghan Election, Signs of Systemic Fraud Cast Doubt on Many Votes. *New York Times* (August 23). https://www.nytimes.com/2014/08/24/world/asia/in-afghan-election-signs-of-systemic-fraud-cast-doubt-on-many-votes.html.
209. Agreement between the Two Campaign Teams Regarding the Structure of the National Unity Government (September 25, 2014). http://www.stripes.com/news/full-text-of-the-power-sharing-agreement-for-afghanistan-1.304947
210. Tim Craig, 2014. Ghani Named Winner of Afghan Election, Will Share Power with Rival in New Government. *Washington Post* (September 21). https://www.washingtonpost.com/world/ghani-abdullah-agree-to-share-power-in-afghanistan-as-election-stalemate-ends/2014/09/21/df58749a-416e-11e4-9a15-137aa0153527_story.html.
211. Mujib Mashal, 2016. Afghan Panel Sets Election Date, Drawing Government Criticism. *New York Times* (January 18). https://www.nytimes.com/2016/01/19/world/asia/afghan-panel-sets-election-date-drawing-government-criticism.html.
212. Reuters, 2016. John Kerry Makes Surprise Visit to Kabul to Ease Tensions over Afghan Unity Pact. *The Guardian* (April 9). https://www.theguardian.com/world/2016/apr/09/john-kerry-afghanistan-coalition-government-unity.
213. Catherine Putz, 2016. 19 Months Later, Afghan Government Lacks Core Ministerial Leadership. *The Diplomat* (May 6). http://thediplomat.com/2016/05/19-months-later-afghan-government-lacks-core-ministerial-leadership/.
214. Pamela Constable, 2016. Tension Between Power-Sharing Afghan Leaders Becomes a Public Crisis. *Washington Post* (August 13): A7.
215. Michael D. Shear and Matthew Rosenberg, 2015. For Obama, Ghani Offers Hope of a Less Fractious Relationship. *New York Times* (March 22). https://www.nytimes.com/2015/03/23/world/asia/for-obama-ghani-offers-hope-of-a-less-fractious-relationship.html.
216. Jessica Donati, 2016. Afghan President Ashraf Ghani Starts New Effort to Fight Corruption. *Wall Street Journal* (April 25). https://www.wsj.com/articles/afghan-president-ashraf-ghani-starts-new-body-to-fight-corruption-1461594413
217. Pamela Constable, 2006. Afghan Leader Could Reform Himself Out of Power. *Washington Post* (September 3): A10.
218. Pamela Constable, 2016. Political Infighting Grips Afghanistan. *Washington Post* (November 18): A11.
219. To be sure, the monies allowed the president to cement alliances and local power brokers to acquire support by distributing largess (Suhrke 2015: 38–39) and gave them opportunities to buy the services of the many Afghanis who might otherwise turn to the insurgency. With or without the large infusions of US aid, profits from the opium trade purportedly corrupted government officials, from ministers and members of parliament to local police officials (Bayley and Perito 2011).

220. Chandrasekaran, Obama's War. Indeed, in the first post-Taliban decade, donors channeled only a fifth of development aid through the Afghan government; in turn, resources in the control of the central government were slow to reach, or inhibited from reaching, Afghan provinces and districts (ICG 2011: i–ii). Many local projects undertaken by the PRTs—a schoolhouse, for instance, that was built to accommodate more students than the surrounding villages could actually provide but is now collapsing—"saddled Afghanistan's impoverished provinces with infrastructure that wasn't completed, can't be sustained or didn't mesh with local needs." Shashank Bengali, 2013. U.S. Reconstruction Effort in Afghan Provinces Is Unfinished Work. *Los Angeles Times* (April 6). http://articles.latimes.com/2013/apr/06/world/la-fg-afghanistan-reconstruction-20130407
221. G. I. Dough, 2016. Afghanistan Waste Exhibit A: Kajaki Dam, More than $300M Spent and Still Not Done. *ProPublica* (January 19). https://www.propublica.org/article/afghanistan-waste-kajaki-dam-more-than-300-million-spent-still-not-done. See also Lutz and Desai (2015: 6–7).
222. "With the sharp contraction in foreign presence, formerly robust Afghan GDP growth rates slowed from 14.4% in 2012 to 3.7% in 2013 and to 1.3% in 2014, according to the World Bank" (SIGAR 2016: 4).
223. The deliberating influence of corruption is such that the Millennium Challenge Corporation, which the US government created to reward good governance based on multiple indicators, requires that all funded countries maintain a "passing" corruption score.
224. United States Department of State. Country Reports on Human Rights Practices for 2017. http://www.state.gov/j/drl/rls/hrrpt/humanrightsreport/index.htm#wrapper.
225. Indeed, Karzai had difficulty accepting the counterinsurgency philosophy that underpinned the policing program, for it at once legitimized the insurgency and delegitimized the government by creating "the impression of a legitimate resistance opposed to a corrupt government sustained by foreign, infidel troops" (Neumann 2015: 6).
226. Mujib Mashal, 2015. Afghan Plan to Expand Militia Raises Abuse Concerns. *New York Times* (October 16).https://www.nytimes.com/2015/10/17/world/asia/afghan-local-police-taliban.html
227. Military Times, 2016. Afghan Casualties Surged in 2015 Because of Increased Taliban Attacks. *Military Times* (January 4). http://www.militarytimes.com/story/military/2016/01/04/afghan-casualties-surged-in-2015-because-of-increased-taliban-attacks/78284814/.
228. Ian S. Livingston and Michael O'Hanlon. Afghanistan Index: March 31, 2016. Brookings Institution. http://www.brookings.edu/~/media/Programs/foreign-policy/afghanistan-index/index20160330.pdf?la=en.
229. In 2010, in Marja (in Helmand province), for example. When local troops were paired in battle with US Marines, observers noted an absence of independent leadership, camaraderie, and basic military skills like map reading and aiming a weapon before firing. C. J. Chivers, 2009. Erratic Afghan Forces Pose Challenge to U.S. Goals. *New York Times* (June 7) https://www.nytimes.com/2009/06/08/world/asia/08afghan.html; C. J. Chivers, 2010. Marines Do Heavy Lifting as Afghan Army Lags in Battle. *New York Times* (February 20) https://www.nytimes.com/2010/02/21/world/asia/21afghan.html; and C. J. Chivers, 2010. Afghan Army Advances in Training, If Not in Field. *New York Times* (October 12) https://www.nytimes.com/2010/10/13/world/asia/13kabul.html
230. Thomas Gibbons-Neff, 2016. In Afghanistan, Reliance on Commandos Becomes a Concern. *Washington Post* (October 9): A15; and Thomas Gibbons Neff, 2016. Afghans' Reliance on U.S. Strikes Increasing. *Washington Post* (October 17): A1.
231. In the words of US army Brig. Gen. Wilson Shoffner, in Afghanistan, "If soldiers are not getting paid or they are not getting fed properly or they are not getting leave, then you tend to have a problem with attrition. So the fix here is to make sure we have the right leadership in place." Andrew Tilghman, 2016. For Afghanistan in 2016, U.S. Plans to Deploy "Expeditionary Advise and Assist" Teams. *Military Times* (January 3). http://www.militarytimes.com/story/

military/pentagon/2016/01/03/afghanistan-2016-us-plans-deploy-expeditionary-advise-and-assist-teams/78079648/
232. Ben Farmer, 2012. NATO to Cut Funding for Afghan Force by Two Thirds. *The Telegraph* (March 22). http://www.telegraph.co.uk/news/worldnews/asia/afghanistan/9160579/Nato-to-cut-funding-for-Afghan-force-by-two-thirds.html
233. Lolita C. Baldor, 2013. Officials: NATO Considering Plan to Maintain Force of 352,000 Afghan Troops through 2018. *Associated Press* (February 21). http://www.startribune.com/nato-considering-keeping-larger-afghan-force-costing-2b-a-year/192297571/; and DeYoung, Obama to Leave 9,800 U.S. Troops in Afghanistan.
234. Yeganeh Torbati and Robin Emmott, 2016. Despite Fatigue, NATO Commits to Fund Afghan Forces to 2020. *Reuters* (July 9). http://www.reuters.com/article/us-nato-summit-afghanistan-idUSKCN0ZP0AC
235. Tim Craig, 2016. U.S. Seeking $15 Billion More for Afghan Forces. *Washington Post* (June 19): A18.
236. Ayaz Gul, 2015. Scores of Afghan Soldiers Defect to Taliban, Others Killed. *VOA* (November 14). http://www.voanews.com/content/scores-of-afghan-soldiers-defect-to-taliban-others-killed/3057852.html
237. Yochi Dreazen, 2017. Candidate Trump Promised to Stay Out of Foreign Wars: President Trump Is Escalating Them. *Vox*, August 25. https://www.vox.com/world/2017/8/25/16185936/trump-america-first-afghanistan-war-troops-iraq-generals
238. See Abrams (2017). See also Henry Nau, 2017. Trump's Conservative Internationalism. *National Review* (August 24). http://www.nationalreview.com/article/450742/donald-trumps-conservative-internationalism-foreign-policy-americas-best-interests
239. See James H. Lebovic, 2017. ISSF Policy Series: Lebovic on Elliott Abrams, "Trump the Traditionalist: A Surprisingly Standard Foreign Policy," August 23. https://networks.h-net.org/node/28443/discussions/191736/issf-policy-series-lebovic-elliott-abrams-%E2%80%9Ctrump-traditionalist.
240. Associated Press. 2017. Trump at 100 Days: "It's a Different Kind of Presidency." *Associated Press* (April 23). http://www.kcrg.com/content/news/Trump-at-100-days-Its-a-different-kind-of-presidency-420196774.html
241. Pamela Constable, 2017. Grim Take on Efforts in Afghanistan. *Washington Post* (May 1): A9.
242. Thomas Gibbons-Neff, 2017. Afghanistan to Boost Troops in Its Elite Commando Units. *Washington Post* (August 13): A18.
243. These low ratings were unprecedented for an administration in its "honeymoon" period, with a booming economy no less.
244. James Mattis, the new secretary of defense, was a four-star army general who had retired in 2013 as CENTCOM commander. His appointment required a special act of Congress to override the prohibition, initially passed in 1947, against recent veterans serving in that position. Trump's national security adviser, H. R. McMaster, was a three-star army general who had made a name for himself as an innovative war commander in Iraq (and as the author of a widely read book that critiqued the performance of the JCS in the Vietnam War). John F. Kelly, Trump's chief of staff (and former secretary of homeland security) was a retired four-star marine corps general who had commanded troops in Iraq and served most recently as head of the US Southern Command.
245. Missy Ryan and Greg Jaffe, 2017. Growing Military Clout Could Shift Foreign Policy. *Washington Post* (May 29): A1.
246. Philip Rucker and Robert Costa, 2011. "It's a Hard Problem": Behind the Decision; Debate, Infighting and Stalemate, and Finally a Bow to the Generals. *Washington Post* (August 22). https://www.washingtonpost.com/politics/its-a-hard-problem-inside-trumps-decision-to-send-more-troops-to-afghanistan/2017/08/21/14dcb126-868b-11e7-a94f-3139abce39f5_story.html

247. As Richard Haass (2017) has noted, however, unpredictability "can make sense as a tactic, but not as a strategy." See Kevin Sullivan and Karen Tumulty, 2017. Trump Promised an "Unpredictable" Foreign Policy: To Allies It Looks Incoherent. *Washington Post* (April 11). https://www.washingtonpost.com/politics/trump-promised-an-unpredictable-foreign-policy-to-allies-it-looks-incoherent/2017/04/11/21acde5e-1a3d-11e7-9887-1a5314b56a08_story.html

248. Pamela Constable, 2017. Afghans Hopeful Despite Government Woes. *Washington Post* (April 11): A17; Ethnic Minority Leaders Push for Afghan Reforms. *Washington Post* (July 2): A20; A Hodgepodge of Opposition Plagues Afghan President. *Washington Post* (August 14): A11; and Sharif Hassan, 2018. Ousted Afghan Strongman Still Calls the Shots. *Washington Post* (May 14): A8.

249. Then, the Obama administration exerted pressure without the explicit embrace, as in Trump's speech, of Pakistan's regional adversary, India, which could confound US attempts at influence. Pamela Constable, 2017. New Afghan Policy from Trump Angers and Alarms Pakistan. *Washington Post* (August 30): A20.

250. Phil Stewart and Idress Ali, 2017. Exclusive: Trump Eyes Hardening Line Toward Pakistan after Afghan War Review. *Reuters* (June 20) https://www.reuters.com/article/us-usa-pakistan-exclusive/exclusive-trump-administration-eyes-hardening-line-toward-pakistan-idUSKBN19B0C8

251. Pamela Constable, 2017. Many Pakistanis Are Smarting from Tillerson's Visit. *Washington Post* (October 26). https://www.washingtonpost.com/world/asia_pacific/many-pakistanis-are-smarting-from-tillersons-visit-but-the-prime-minister-is-taking-the-long-view/2017/10/26/97393f46-b9ca-11e7-9b93-b97043e57a22_story.html

252. Shaiq Hussain and Annie Gowen, 2018. Pakistani Officials: Trump "Contradicted the Facts" with Tweet. *Washington Post* (January 3): A8.

253. Shaiq Hussain and Annie Gowen, 2018. Pakistani Officials Decry U.S. Suspension of Military Aid. *Washington Post* (January 6): A10.

254. On these efforts, see SIGAR (2017: 94–98); Pamela Constable, 2017. Bolstering Elite Afghan Unit Seen as Key to Peace. *Washington Post* (May 24): A6; and Gibbons-Neff, Afghanistan to Boost Troops in Its Elite Commando Units.

255. Greg Jaffe and Missy Ryan, 2018. Up to 1,000 More U.S. Troops Could Be Headed to Afghanistan This Spring. *Washington Post* (January 22): A11.

256. Max Bearak, 2018. No Rest for U.S. Air Blitz in Afghanistan. *Washington Post* (January 17): A1.

257. Greg Jaffe and Missy Ryan, 2018. Did U.S. Kill Negotiating Partner or Fervent Foe? *Washington Post* (March 25): A1.

258. Pamela Constable, 2018. Ranks of Afghan Security Forces Have Dwindled, U.S. Reports. *Washington Post* (May 2): A14.

259. Dan Lamothe, 2018. High Stakes for New Army Unit in Afghanistan. *Washington Post* (February 12): A3.

260. About that, at least, Henry Kissinger was right in lamenting a popular addiction to a Vietnam-era withdrawal that would confound efforts to slow or reverse the pace.

261. Thomas Gibbons-Neff and Helene Cooper, 2018. Newest U.S. Strategy in Afghanistan Mirrors Past Plans for Retreat. *New York Times* (July 28). https://www.nytimes.com/2018/07/28/world/asia/trump-afghanistan-strategy-retreat.html.

262. Pamela Constable, 2018. U.S.-Taliban Talks in Qatar Could Be a Breakthrough. *Washington Post* (August 1): A9.

263. As one analyst put it, "At each major juncture, decision makers seemed to reach for the most expedient fixes without fully considering the context or consequences of their actions . . . as conditions worsened and the scale and scope of the operation slowly expanded, there was little reflection on the underlying assumptions of the mission" (Paris 2013: 545).

264. DeYoung, Obama to Leave 9,800 U.S. Troops in Afghanistan.
265. DeYoung, Obama to Leave 9,800 U.S. Troops in Afghanistan.

Chapter 5

1. The effectiveness of these people depends, however, on whether they can offer more than a "devil's advocate" view. Such a view can prove counterproductive should it come across as a "standard dissent," reinforce confidence in mistaken views that have now survived a "critical" airing, or seem like a less-than-serious argument when couched as the devil's advocate view.
2. On reputations and their formation, see Hopf (1994); Fettweis (2007/2008); and Mercer (1996).
3. On these challenges of obtaining influence over local governments, see Downes and O'Rourke (2016) and Ladwig (2016).

REFERENCES

Abrams, Elliott. 2017. Trump the Traditionalist: A Surprisingly Standard Foreign Policy. *Foreign Affairs* (July/August). https://www.foreignaffairs.com/articles/united-states/2017-06-13/trump-traditionalist.

Acacia, John. 2009. *Clark Clifford: The Wise Man of Washington*. Lexington: University of Kentucky Press.

Adams, Gordon, and Shoon Murray. 2014. An Introduction to Mission Creep. In *The Militarization of US Foreign Policy? Mission Creep*, ed. Gordon Adams and Shoon Murray, 3–21. Washington, DC: Georgetown University Press.

Allison, Graham T. 1971. *The Essence of Decision: Explaining the Cuban Missile Crisis*. Boston: Little, Brown and Company.

Andres, Richard B., Craig Wills, and Thomas E. Griffith. 2005/2006. Winning with Allies: The Strategic Value of the Afghan Model. *International Security* 30(3): 124–160.

Armitage, Richard L. 2009. An Interview with Richard L. Armitage. *Prism: A Journal for the Center of Complex Operations* 1(1): 103–112.

Arreguín-Toft, Ivan. 2005. *How the Weak Win Wars: A Theory of Asymmetric Conflict*. Cambridge, UK: Cambridge University Press.

Auerswald, David P., and Stephen M. Saideman. 2014. *NATO in Afghanistan: Fighting Together, Fighting Alone*. Princeton, NJ: Princeton University Press.

Avant, Deborah D. 1993. The Institutional Sources of Military Doctrine: Hegemons in Peripheral Wars. *International Studies Quarterly* 37(4): 409–430.

Baker, William D., and John R. Oneal. 2001. Patriotism or Opinion Leadership? The Nature and Origins of the "Rally 'Round the Flag" Effect. *Journal of Conflict Resolution* 45(5): 661–687.

Bakich, Spencer D. 2014. *Success and Failure in Limited War: Information and Strategy in the Korean, Vietnam, Persian Gulf and Iraq Wars*. Chicago: University of Chicago Press.

Baldwin, David A. 1979. Power Analysis and World Politics: New Trends versus Old Tendencies. *World Politics* 31(2): 161–194.

Ballard, John R., David W. Lamm, and John K. Wood. 2012. *From Kabul to Baghdad and Back: The U.S. at War in Afghanistan and Iraq*. Annapolis, MD: Naval Institute Press.

Barley, Nick. 2015. The NATO Training Mission-Afghanistan: A Game-Changer; Lest We Forget. *Small Wars Journal* (December 5). http://smallwarsjournal.com/jrnl/art/the-nato-training-mission-afghanistan-a-game-changer-lest-we-forget.

Barno, David W., Lt. Gen (ret.). 2007. Fighting "The Other War": Counterinsurgency Strategy in Afghanistan, 2003–2005. *Military Review* (September–October): 32–44.

Barrett, David M. 1988/1989. The Mythology Surrounding Lyndon Johnson, His Advisors, and the 1965 Decision to Escalate the Vietnam War. *Political Science Quarterly* 103(4): 637–663.

Bator, Francis M. 2008. No Good Choices: LBJ and the Vietnam/Great Society Connection. *Diplomatic History* 32(3): 309–340.

Baum, Matthew A., and Tim Groeling. 2010. Reality Asserts Itself: Public Opinion on Iraq and the Elasticity of Reality. *International Organization* 64(3): 443–479.

Bayley, David, and Robert Perito. 2011. *Police Corruption: What Past Scandals Teach about Current Challenges*. Special Report 294. Washington, DC: United States Institute of Peace. https://www.usip.org/publications/2011/11/police-corruption.

Behr, Timo. 2012. Germany and Regional Command-North: ISAF's Weakest Link? In *Statebuilding in Afghanistan: Multinational Contributions to Reconstruction*, ed. Nik Hynek and Péter Marton, 42–64. London: Routledge.

Bendor, Jonathan, and Thomas H. Hammond. 1992. Rethinking Allison's Models. *American Political Science Review* 86(2): 301–322.

Bensahel, Nora. 2006. Mission Not Accomplished: What Went Wrong with Iraqi Reconstruction. *Journal of Strategic Studies* 29(3): 453–473.

Bensahel, Nora, Olga Oliker, Keith Crane, Richard R. Brennan Jr., Heather S. Gregg, Thomas Sullivan, and Andrew Rathmell. 2008. *After Saddam: Prewar Planning and the Occupation of Iraq*. Santa Monica, CA: RAND Arroyo Center.

Berinsky, Adam J. 2009. *In Time of War: Understanding American Public Opinion from World War II to Iraq*. Chicago: University of Chicago Press.

Berinsky, Adam J. 2007. Assuming the Costs of War: Events, Elites, and American Public Support for Military Conflict. *Journal of Politics* 69(4): 975–997.

Best, James J. 1988. Who Talked to the President When? A Study of Lyndon Johnson. *Political Science Quarterly* 103(3): 531–545.

Biddle, Stephen. 2014. Afghanistan's Legacy: Emerging Lessons of an Ongoing War. *Washington Quarterly* 37(2): 73–86.

Biddle, Stephen. 2008. The New U.S. Army/Marine Corps Counterinsurgency Field Manual as Political Science and Political Praxis. *Perspectives on Politics* 6(2): 347–350.

Biddle, Stephen. 2003. Afghanistan and the Future of Warfare. *Foreign Affairs* 82(2): 31–46.

Biddle, Stephen, Jeffrey A. Friedman, and Jacob N. Shapiro. 2012. Testing the Surge: Why Did Violence Decline in Iraq in 2007? *International Security* 37(1): 7–40.

Biddle, Stephen, Julia Macdonald, and Ryan Baker. 2018. Small Footprint, Small Payoff: The Military Effectiveness of Security Force Assistance. *Journal of Strategic Studies* 41(1–2): 89–142.

Biddle, Stephen, Michael E. O'Hanlon, and Kenneth M. Pollack. 2008. How to Leave a Stable Iraq. *Foreign Affairs* 87(5): 40–58.

Birtle, Andrew J. 2008. PROVN, Westmoreland, and the Historians: A Reappraisal. *The Journal of Military History* 72(4): 1213–1247.

Boyle, Michael J. 2014. *Violence after War: Explaining Instability in Post-Conflict States*. Baltimore, MD: Johns Hopkins University Press.

Brands, Hal, and Peter Feaver. 2017. Was the Rise of ISIS Inevitable? *Survival* 59(3): 7–54.

Brands, Henry William, Jr. 1985. Johnson and Eisenhower: The President, the Former President, and the War in Vietnam. *Presidential Studies Quarterly* 15(3): 589–601.

Bremer, Paul, III. 2006. *My Year in Iraq: The Struggle to Build a Future of Hope*. New York: Simon and Schuster.

Brennan, Richard R., Charles P. Ries, Larry Hanauer, Ben Connable, Terrence K. Kelly, Michael J. McNerney, Stephanie Young, Jason Campbell, and K. Scott McMahon. 2013. *Ending the U.S. War in Iraq*. Santa Monica, CA: The RAND Corporation.

Casey, George W., Jr. 2012. *Strategic Reflections: Operation Iraqi Freedom, July 2004–February 2007*. Washington, DC: National Defense University Press.

Caverley, Jonathan. 2014. *Democratic Militarism: Voting, Wealth, and War*. Cambridge, UK: Cambridge University Press.

Chandrasekaran, Rajiv. 2007. *Imperial Life in the Emerald City: Inside Iraq's Green Zone*. New York: Vintage Books.

Clarke, Richard A. 2004. *Against All Enemies*. New York: Free Press.
Clifford, Clark M. 1969. A Viet Nam Reappraisal: The Personal History of One Man's View and How It Evolved. *Foreign Affairs* 47(1): 601–622.
CNA (Center for Naval Analysis). 2014. *Independent Assessment of the Afghan National Security Forces*. Alexandria, VA: Center for Naval Analysis.
Cohen, Eliot, Conrad Crane, Jan Horvath, and John Nagl. 2006. Principles, Imperatives, and Paradoxes of Counterinsurgency. *Military Review* 86(2): 49–53.
Coll, Steve. 2004. *Ghost Wars: The Secret History of the CIA, Afghanistan, and bin Laden, from the Soviet Invasion to September 10, 2001*. New York: Penguin Books.
Cordesman, Anthony, and Sam Khazai. 2014. *Iraq in Crisis: A Report of the CSIS Burke Chair In Strategy*. Washington, DC: Center for Strategic and International Studies.
Cosmas, Graham A. 2007. *The United States Army in Vietnam: MACV; The Joint Command in the Years of Withdrawal, 1968–1973*. CMH Pub. 91-7. Washington, DC: Center of Military History, United States Army.
Cosmas, Graham A. 2006. *The United States Army in Vietnam: MACV; The Joint Command in the Years of Escalation, 1962–1967*. CMH Pub. 91-6-1. Washington, DC: Center of Military History, United States Army.
Cuddy, Edward. 2003. Vietnam: Mr. Johnson's War, Or Mr. Eisenhower's? *The Review of Politics* 65(4): 351–374.
Daddis, Gregory A. 2011. *No Sure Victory: Measuring U.S. Army Effectiveness and Progress in the Vietnam War*. New York: Oxford University Press.
Desch, Michael C. 2011/2012. Correspondence: Civilians, Soldiers, and the Iraq Surge Decision. *International Security* 36(3): 180–191.
Dobbins, James, Seth G. Jones, Benjamin Runkle, and Siddharth Mohandas. 2009. *Occupying Iraq: A History of the Coalition Provisional Authority*. Santa Monica, CA: The RAND Corporation.
Dobbins, James F. 2008. *After the Taliban: Nation-Building in Afghanistan*. Washington, DC: Potomac Books, Inc.
Downes, Alexander B. 2009. How Smart and Tough Are Democracies? Reassessing Theories of Democratic Victory in War. *International Security* 33(4): 9–51.
Downes, Alexander B., and Lindsey A. O'Rourke. 2016. You Can't Always Get What You Want: Why Foreign-Imposed Regime Change Seldom Improves Interstate Relations. *International Security* 41(2): 43–89.
Dubik, James M. 2009. *Building Security Forces and Ministerial Capacity: Iraq as a Primer*. Best Practices in Counterinsurgency, Report 1. Washington, DC: Institute for the Study of War. www.understandingwar.org/report/building-security-forces-and-ministerial-capacity.
Dyson, Stephen Benedict. 2013. What Really Happened in Planning for Postwar Iraq? *Political Science Quarterly* 128(3): 455–488.
Eisenstadt, Michael. 2007. Iraq: Tribal Engagement Lessons Learned. *Military Review* 87(5): 16–31.
Fearon, James D. 1995. Rationalist Explanations for War. *International Organization* 49(3): 379–414.
Feaver, Peter D. 2011/2012. Correspondence: Civilians, Soldiers, and the Iraq Surge Decision. *International Security* 36(3): 191–199.
Feaver, Peter D. 2011. The Right to Be Right: Civil-Military Relations and the Iraq Surge Decision. *International Security* 35(4): 87–125.
Feith, Douglas. 2008. *War and Decision: Inside the Pentagon at the Dawn of the War on Terrorism*. New York: HarperCollins.
Fettweis, Christopher J. 2007/2008. Credibility and the War on Terror. *Political Science Quarterly* 122(4): 607–633.
Galster, Steve. 2001. *Afghanistan: The Making of U.S. Policy, 1973–1990*. Vol. II, *Afghanistan: Lessons from the Last War*. http://nsarchive.gwu.edu/NSAEBB/NSAEBB57/essay.html.
Garofano, John. 2002. Tragedy or Choice in Vietnam? Learning to Think Outside the Archival Box: A Review Essay. *International Security* 26(4): 143–168.
Gates, Robert M. 2014. *Duty: Memoirs of a Secretary at War*. New York: Alfred A. Knopf.

Gelb, Leslie H., with Richard K. Betts. 1979. *The Irony of Vietnam: The System Worked*. Washington, DC: The Brookings Institution.

Gelpi, Christopher, Peter D. Feaver, and Jason Reifler. 2005. Success Matters: Casualty Sensitivity and the War in Iraq. *International Security* 30(3): 7–46.

Gentile, Gian. 2011/2012. A Strategy of Tactics: Population-Centric COIN and the Army. *Parameters* 41(4): 1–12.

George, Alexander L., and Erik K. Stern. 2002. Harnessing Conflict in Foreign Policy Making: From Devil's to Multiple Advocacy. *Presidential Studies Quarterly* 32(3): 484–505.

Gigerenzer, Gerd, and Wolfgang Gaissmaier. 2011. Heuristic Decision Making. *Annual Review of Psychology* 62(January): 451–482.

Gilsinan, Kathy. 2015. The Pottery Barn Rule: The Syria Edition. *The Atlantic* (September 30). http://www.theatlantic.com/international/archive/2015/09/the-pottery-barn-rule-syria-edition/408193/.

Glad, Betty, and Michael W. Link. 1996. President Nixon's Inner Circle of Advisers. *Presidential Studies Quarterly* 26(1): 13–40.

Goldstein, Gordon. 2008. *Lessons in Disaster: McGeorge Bundy and the Path to War in Vietnam*. New York: Times Books, Henry Holt and Company, LLC.

Goodhand, Jonathan. 2015. Contested Boundaries: NGOs and Civil-Military Relations in Afghanistan. In *The Afghan Conundrum: Intervention, Statebuilding, and Resistance*, ed. Jonathan Goodhand and Mark Sedra, 49–67. London: Routledge.

Goodwin, Doris Kearns. 1991. *Lyndon Johnson and the American Dream*. New York: St Martin's Press.

Gordon, Michael R., and Bernard E. Trainor. 2012. *The Endgame: The Inside Story of the Struggle for Iraq, from George W. Bush to Barack Obama*. New York: Pantheon Books.

Gordon, Michael R., and Bernard E. Trainor. 2006. *Cobra II: The Inside Story of the Invasion and Occupation of Iraq*. New York: Pantheon.

Graham, Bradley. 2009. *By His Own Rules: The Ambitions, Successes, and Ultimate Failures of Donald Rumsfeld*. New York: Public Affairs.

Greenstein, Fred I., and John P. Burke. 1989/1990. The Dynamics of Presidential Reality Testing: Evidence from Two Vietnam Decisions. *Political Science Quarterly* 104(4): 557–580.

Grenier, Stephen M. 2015. United States: Examining America's Longest War. In *Coalition Challenges in Afghanistan: The Politics of Alliance*, ed. Gale A. Mattox and Stephen M. Grenier, 47–64. Stanford, CA: Stanford University Press.

Griffith, Thomas E. 1995. Strategic Air Attacks on Electric Power: Balancing Political Consequences and Military Action. *Strategic Review* 23(4): 38–46.

Haass, Richard N. 2017. Where to Go from Here: Rebooting American Foreign Policy. *Foreign Affairs* 96(4). https://www.foreignaffairs.com/articles/united-states/2017-06-11/where-go-here

Haass, Richard N. 2009. *War of Necessity/War of Choice: A Memoir of Two Iraq Wars*. New York: Simon and Schuster.

Halberstam, David, 1969. *The Best and the Brightest*. New York: Random House.

Hamilton, Donald W. 1998. *The Art of Insurgency: American Military Policy and the Failure of Strategy in Southeast Asia*. Westport, CT: Praeger.

Hanyok, Robert. J. 1998. Skunks, Bogies, Silent Hounds, and the Flying Fish: The Gulf of Tonkin Mystery, 2–4 August 1964. *Cryptologic Quarterly*. Center for Cryptological History, National Security Agency (Declassified). http://nsarchive2.gwu.edu/NSAEBB/NSAEBB132/relea00012.pdf.

Harvey, Frank P. 2012. *Explaining the Iraq War: Counterfactual Theory, Logic and Evidence*. Cambridge, UK: Cambridge University Press.

Haun, Phil, and Colin Jackson. 2015/2016. Breaker of Armies: Air Power in the Easter Offensive and the Myth of Linebacker I and II in the Vietnam War. *International Security* 40(3): 139–178.

Herring, George C. 1991. America and Vietnam: The Unending War. *Foreign Affairs* 70(5): 104–119.

Herring, George C. 1986. *America's Longest War: The United States and Vietnam, 1950–1975*. Philadelphia: Temple University Press.

Hoffman, Hugh F. T. 2017. Lessons from Iraq. In *Effective, Legitimate, Secure: Insights for Defense Institution Building*. Alexandra Kerr and Michael Miklaucic, 329–358. Washington, DC: Center for Complex Operations, Institute for National Security Studies, National Defense University.

Hoopes, Townsend. 1969. *The Limits of Intervention*. New York: David McKay Company, Inc.

Hopf, Ted. 1994. *Peripheral Visions: Deterrence Theory and American Foreign Policy in the Third World, 1965–1990*. Ann Arbor: University of Michigan Press.

Hoyt, Timothy D. 2015. Pakistan: A Tale of Two Allies. In *Coalition Challenges in Afghanistan: The Politics of Alliance*, ed. Gale A. Mattox and Stephen M. Grenier, 257–272. Stanford, CA: Stanford University Press.

Hughes, Ken. 2010. Fatal Politics: Nixon's Political Timetable for Withdrawing from Vietnam. *Diplomatic History* 34(3): 497–506.

Hulslander, Robert, and Jake Spivey. 2012. Village Stability Operations and Afghan Local Police. *Prism* 3(3): 125–138.

Hunt, Richard A. 2015. *Melvin Laird and the Foundation of the Post-Vietnam Military, 1969–1973*. Washington, DC: Historical Office, Office of the Secretary of Defense.

ICG (International Crisis Group). 2015. The Future of the Afghan Local Police. Asia Report No. 268. https://www.crisisgroup.org/asia/south-asia/afghanistan/future-afghan-local-police.

ICG (International Crisis Group). 2011. Aid and Conflict in Afghanistan. Asia Report No. 210. https://www.crisisgroup.org/asia/south-asia/afghanistan/aid-and-conflict-afghanistan.

ICG (International Crisis Group). 2010a. Loose Ends: Iraq's Security Forces Between U.S. Drawdown and Withdrawal. Middle East Report No. 99. https://www.crisisgroup.org/middle-east-north-africa/gulf-and-arabian-peninsula/iraq/loose-ends-iraq-s-security-forces-between-us-drawdown-and-withdrawal.

ICG (International Crisis Group). 2010b. A Force in Fragments: Reconstituting the Afghan National Army. Asia Report No. 190. https://www.crisisgroup.org/asia/south-asia/afghanistan/force-fragments-reconstituting-afghan-national-army.

ICG (International Crisis Group). 2008 Policing in Afghanistan: Still Searching for a Strategy. Asia Briefing No. 85. https://www.crisisgroup.org/asia/south-asia/afghanistan/policing-afghanistan-still-searching-strategy.

Iraq Study Group. 2006. *The Iraq Study Group Report: The Way Forward—A New Approach*. https://www.bakerinstitute.org/research/the-iraq-study-group-report/.

Iraq Survey Group. 2004. *Comprehensive Report of the Special Advisor to the DCI on Iraq's WMD*. US Central Intelligence Agency. https://www.cia.gov/library/reports/general-reports-1/iraq_wmd_2004/.

Isikoff, Michael, and David Corn. 2006. *Hubris: The Inside Story of Spin, Scandal, and the Selling of the Iraq War*. New York: Crown Publishers.

Janis, Irving L. 1982. *Victims of Group Think: Psychological Studies of Policy Decisions and Fiascoes*. Boston: Wadsworth.

Jensen, Benjamin M. 2016. *Forging the Sword: Doctrinal Change in the U.S. Army*. Palo Alto, CA: Stanford University Press.

Jervis, Robert. 2014. Serving or Self-Serving? A Review Essay of Robert Gates's Memoir. *Political Science Quarterly* 129(2): 319–331.

Jervis, Robert. 2010/2011. Policy and Politics in the United Kingdom and the United States: A Review Essay. *Political Science Quarterly* 125(4): 685–700.

Jervis, Robert. 2010. *Why Intelligence Fails: Lessons from the Iranian Revolution and the Iraq War*. Ithaca, NY: Cornell University Press.

Jervis, Robert. 1976. *Perception and Misperception in International Politics*. Princeton, NJ: Princeton University Press.

Johns, Andrew L. 1999. A Voice from the Wilderness: Richard Nixon and the Vietnam War, 1964–1966. *Presidential Studies Quarterly* 29(2): 317–335.

Johnson, Dominic D. P., and Dominic Tierney. 2006. *Failing to Win: Perceptions of Victory and Defeat in International Politics*. Cambridge, MA: Harvard University Press.

Jones, James L. 2007. The Report of the Independent Commission on the Security Forces of Iraq. http://csis.org/files/media/csis/pubs/isf.pdf.

Jones, Seth. 2013. *After the Withdrawal: A Way Forward in Afghanistan and Pakistan*. Prepared Statement before the Committee on Foreign Affairs, Subcommittee on the Middle East and North Africa and Subcommittee on Asia and the Pacific. United States House of Representatives, March 19, 113th Cong., 1st Sess.

Kadura, Johannes. *The War after the War: The Struggle for Credibility during America's Exit from Vietnam*. Ithaca, NY: Cornell University Press.

Kagan, Frederick W. 2012. A Case for Staying the Course. In *Afghan Endgames: Strategy and Policy Choices for America's Longest War*, ed. Hy Rothstein and John Arquilla, 97–114. Washington, DC: Stanford University Press.

Kahl, Colin. 2007. In the Crossfire or the Crosshairs? Norms, Civilian Casualties, and U.S. Conduct in Iraq. *International Security* 32(1): 7–46.

Kahneman, Daniel, and Amos Tversky. 1979. Prospect Theory: An Analysis of Decision under Risk. *Econometrica* 47(2): 263–291.

Kaiser, David. 2000. *American Tragedy: Kennedy, Johnson, and the Origins of the Vietnam War*. Cambridge, MA: Harvard University Press.

Kalb, Marvin, 2013. *The Road to War: Presidential Commitments Honored and Betrayed*. Washington, DC: Brookings Institution Press.

Kalyvas, Stathis N., and Matthew Adam Kocher. 2007. How "Free" Is Free Riding in Civil Wars? Violence, Insurgency, and the Collective Action Problem. *World Politics* 59(2): 177–216.

Katz, Andrew Z. 1997. Public Opinion and Foreign Policy: The Nixon Administration and the Pursuit of Peace with Honor in Vietnam. *Presidential Studies Quarterly* 27(3): 496–513.

Katzman, Kenneth, and Clayton Thomas. 2017. Afghanistan: Post-Taliban Governance, Security, and U.S. Policy. CRS Report to Congress (7-5700). Washington, D.C.: Congressional Research Service.

Kilcullen, David. 2009. *The Accidental Guerrilla: Fighting Small Wars in the Midst of a Big One*. New York: Oxford University Press.

Kimball, Jeffrey. 2004. *The Vietnam War Files: Uncovering the Secret History of Nixon-Era Strategy*. Lawrence: University Press of Kansas.

Kimball, Jeffrey. 1998. *Nixon's Vietnam War*. Lawrence: University Press of Kansas.

Kissinger, Henry. 1979. *Henry Kissinger: The White House Years*. Boston: Little, Brown and Company.

Kissinger, Henry. 1969. The Vietnam Negotiations. *Foreign Affairs* 47(2): 211–234.

Krause, Peter John Paul. 2008. The Last Good Chance: A Reassessment of U.S. Operations at Tora Bora. *Security Studies* 17: 644–684.

Krepinevich, Andrew F. 1986. *The Army and Vietnam*. Baltimore, MD: Johns Hopkins University Press.

Kuperman, Alan J. 1999. The Stinger Missile and U.S. Intervention in Afghanistan. *Political Science Quarterly* 114(2): 219–263.

Ladwig, Walter C., III. 2016. Influencing Clients in Counterinsurgency: U.S. Involvement in El Salvador's Civil War, 1979–92. *International Security* 41(1): 99–146.

Lake, David A. 2010/2011. Two Cheers for Bargaining Theory: Assessing Rationalist Explanations for the Iraq War. *International Security* 35(3): 7–52.

Lebovic, James H. 2017. Unipolarity: The Shaky Foundation of a Fashionable Concept. In *The Oxford Encyclopedia of Empirical International Relations Theories*, Volume 4, ed. William Thompson, 476–494. New York: Oxford University Press.

Lebovic, James H. 2010. *The Limits of US Military Capability: Lessons from Vietnam and Iraq*. Baltimore, MD: Johns Hopkins University Press.

Lebovic, James H. 2007. *Deterring International Terrorism and Rogue States: U.S. National Security Policy after 9/11*. New York: Routledge.

Lebovic, James H. 1996. *Foregone Conclusions: U.S. Weapons Acquisition in the Post-Cold War Transition*. Boulder, CO: Westview Press (HarperCollins).

Lebovic, James H. 1994. Riding Waves or Making Waves? The Services and the US Defense Budget, 1981–1993. *American Political Science Review* 88(4): 839–852.

Levy, Jack S. 1997. Prospect Theory, Rational Choice, and International Relations. *International Studies Quarterly* 41(1): 87–112.

Lewis, Bronwyn. 2014. H-Diplo/ISSF Forum on "Audience Costs and the Vietnam War." https://issforum.org/forums/audience-costs-and-the-vietnam-war.

Lewy, Guenter. 1978. *America in Vietnam*. New York: Oxford University Press.

Lian, Bradley, and John R. Oneal. 1993. Presidents, the Use of Military Force, and Public Opinion. *Journal of Conflict Resolution* 37(2): 277–300.

Lindblom, Charles E. 1959. The Science of "Muddling Through." *Public Administration Review* 19(2): 79–88.

Logevall, Fredrik. 2004. Lyndon Johnson and Vietnam. *Presidential Studies Quarterly* 34(1): 100–112.

Logevall, Fredrik. 1999. *Choosing War: The Lost Chance for Peace and the Escalation of War in Vietnam*. Berkeley: University of California Press.

Long, Austin. 2016. *The Soul of Armies: Counterinsurgency Doctrine and Military Culture in the US and UK*. Ithaca, NY: Cornell University Press.

Long, Austin. 2010. Small Is Beautiful: The Counterterrorism Option in Afghanistan. *Orbis* 54(2): 199–214.

Lunch, William L., and Peter W. Sperlich. 1979. American Public Opinion and the War in Vietnam. *Western Political Quarterly* 32(1): 21–44.

Lutz, Catherine, and Sujaya Desai. 2015. *US Reconstruction Aid for Afghanistan: The Dollars and Sense*. Providence, RI: Watson Institute for International Studies, Brown University.

Lyall, Jason, Graeme Blair, and Kosuke Imai. 2013. Explaining Support for Combatants During Wartime: A Survey Experiment in Afghanistan. *American Political Science Review* 107(4): 679–705.

Mack, Andrew. 1975. Why Big Nations Lose Small Wars: The Politics of Asymmetric Conflict. *World Politics* 27(2): 175–200.

Maley, William. 2015. Statebuilding in Afghanistan: Challenges and Pathologies. In *The Afghan Conundrum: Intervention, Statebuilding, and Resistance*, ed. Jonathan Goodhand and Mark Sedra, 17–32. London: Routledge.

Malkasian, Carter. 2008. Did the United States Need More Forces in Iraq? Evidence from Al Anbar. *Defence Studies* 8(1): 78–104.

Mansfield, Edward D., and Jack Snyder. 2005. *Electing to Fight: Why Emerging Democracies Go to War*. Cambridge, MA: MIT Press.

Mansoor, Peter R. 2013. *Surge: My Journey with General David Petraeus and the Remaking of the Iraq War*. New Haven, CT: Yale University Press.

March, James G., and Herbert A. Simon. 1993. *Organizations*. Cambridge, MA: Blackwell.

Markey, Daniel S. 2013. *A Pakistani Strategic Shift?* Prepared Statement before the Committee on Foreign Affairs, Subcommittee on the Middle East and North Africa and Subcommittee on Asia and the Pacific. United States House of Representatives, March 19, 113th Cong., 1st Sess.

Marsh, Kevin P. 2014. Obama's Surge: A Bureaucratic Politics Analysis of the Decision to Order a Troop Surge in the Afghanistan War. *Foreign Policy Analysis* 10: 265–288.

Mason, R. Chuck. 2012. *Status of Forces Agreement (SOFA): What Is It, and How Has It Been Utilized?* CRS Report to Congress (7-5700). Washington, DC: Congressional Research Service.

Mattox, Gale A. 2015. Germany: The Legacy of the War in Afghanistan. In *Coalition Challenges in Afghanistan: The Politics of Alliance*, ed. Gale A. Mattox and Stephen M. Grenier, 91–107. Stanford, CA: Stanford University Press.

McAllister, James. 2010/2011. Who Lost Vietnam? Soldiers, Civilians, and U.S. Military Strategy. *International Security* 35(3): 95–123.

McCary, John A. 2009. The Anbar Awakening: An Alliance of Incentives. *Washington Quarterly* 32(1): 43–59.

McDermott, Rose. 2001. The Psychological Ideas of Amos Tversky and Their Relevance for Political Science. *Journal of Theoretical Politics* 13(1): 5–33.

McMaster, H. R. 1997. *Dereliction of Duty: Lyndon Johnson, Robert McNamara, the Joint Chiefs of Staff, and the Lies That Led to Vietnam.* New York: HarperCollins.

McNally, Lauren, and Paul Bucala. 2015. *The Taliban Resurgent: Threats to Afghanistan's Security.* Afghanistan Report 11. Washington, DC: Institute for the Study of War.

McNamara, Robert S. 1995. *In Retrospect: The Tragedy and Lessons of Vietnam.* New York: Random House.

Mercer, Jonathan. 1996. *Reputation and International Politics.* Ithaca, NY: Cornell University Press.

Merom, Gil. 2003. *How Democracies Lose Small Wars: State, Society, and the Failures of France in Algeria, Israel in Lebanon, and the United States in Vietnam.* New York: Cambridge University Press.

Miles, Renanah. 2013. After War: Inside the U.S. Civilian Struggle to Build Peace. *Political Science Quarterly* 128(3): 489–516.

Mitzen, Jennifer, and Randall L. Schweller. 2011. Knowing the Unknown Unknowns: Misplaced Certainty and the Onset of War. *Security Studies* 20(1): 2–35.

Moe, Terry M. 1984. The New Economics of Organization. *American Journal of Political Science* 28(4): 739–777.

Moyar, Mark. 2014. Village Stability Operations and the Afghan Local Police. JSOU Report 14-7. MacDill AFB, Florida: Joint Special Operatioins University.

Nagl, John A. 2005. *Learning to Eat Soup with a Knife: Counterinsurgency Lessons from Malaya and Vietnam.* Chicago: University of Chicago Press.

Nagl, John A., and Richard Weitz. 2015. Counterinsurgency in Afghanistan: The UK, Dutch, German, and French Cases. In *Coalition Challenges in Afghanistan: The Politics of Alliance*, ed. Gale A. Mattox and Stephen M. Grenier, 170–183. Stanford, CA: Stanford University Press.

Neumann, Brian F., Lisa Mundey, and Jon Mikolashek. 2013. *The U.S. Army in Afghanistan: Operation Enduring Freedom, March 2002–April 2005.* CMH Pub. 70-122-1. Washington, DC: US Army, Center for Military History.

Neumann, Ronald E. 2015. *Failed Relations between Hamid Karzai and the United States: What Can We Learn?* Special Report 373. Washington, DC: United States Institute of Peace.

O'Hanlon, Michael E. 2010. Staying Power: The U.S. Mission in Afghanistan Beyond 2011. *Foreign Affairs* 89(5): 63–79.

O'Hanlon, Michael E. 2002. A Flawed Masterpiece. *Foreign Affairs* 81(3): 47–63.

O'Hanlon, Michael E., and Hassina Sherjan. 2010. *Toughing It Out in Afghanistan.* Washington, DC: Brookings Institution Press.

Pape, Robert A. 1996. *Bombing to Win: Air Power and Coercion in War.* Ithaca, NY: Cornell University Press.

Paris, Roland. 2013. Afghanistan: What Went Wrong? *Perspectives on Politics* 11(2): 538–548.

Perito, Robert M. 2011. *The Iraq Federal Police: U.S. Police Building under Fire.* Special Report 291. Washington, DC: United States Institute of Peace. https://www.usip.org/publications/2011/10/iraq-federal-police.

Perito, Robert M. 2008a. *Embedded Provincial Reconstruction Teams.* USIPeace Briefing. Washington, DC: United States Institute of Peace. https://www.usip.org/publications/2008/02/embedded-provincial-reconstruction-teams.

Perito, Robert M. 2008b. *Iraq's Interior Ministry: Frustrating Reform.* USIPeace Briefing. Washington, DC: United States Institute of Peace. https://www.usip.org/publications/2008/05/iraqs-interior-ministry-frustrating-reform.

Perito, Robert M. 2005. *The U.S. Experience with Provincial Reconstruction Teams in Afghanistan: Lessons Identified.* Special Report 152. Washington, DC: United States Institute of Peace. https://www.usip.org/publications/2005/10/us-experience-provincial-reconstruction-teams-afghanistan-lessons-identified.

Petraeus, David. 2017. Reflections by General David Petraeus, USA (Ret.) on the Wars in Afghanistan and Iraq. *Prism* 7(1): 151–167.

Petraeus, David. 2013. Foreword to *Surge: My Journey with General David Petraeus and the Remaking of the Iraq War*, by Peter R. Mansour. New Haven, CT: Yale University Press.
Pillar, Paul. 2014. *Intelligence and U.S. Foreign Policy: Iraq, 9/11, and Misguided Reform*. New York: Columbia University Press.
Prados, John. 2009. *Vietnam: The History of an Unwinnable War, 1945–1975*. Lawrence: University Press of Kansas.
Preston, Andrew. 2006. *The War Council: McGeorge Bundy, the NSC, and Vietnam*. Cambridge, MA: Harvard University Press.
Randolph, Stephen P. 2007. *Powerful and Brutal Weapons: Nixon, Kissinger, and the Easter Offensive*. Cambridge, MA: Harvard University Press.
Rapport, Aaron. 2015. *Waging War, Planning Peace: U.S. Noncombat Operations and Major Wars*. Ithaca, NY: Cornell University Press.
Rathbun, Brian C. 2007. Uncertain about Uncertainty: Understanding the Multiple Meanings of a Crucial Concept in International Relations Theory. *International Studies Quarterly* 51(3): 533–557.
Rathmell, Andrew, Olga Oliker, Terrence K. Kelly, David Brannan, and Keith Crane. 2005. *Developing Iraq's Security Sector: The Coalition Provisional Authority's Experience*. Santa Monica, CA: RAND National Defense Research Institute.
Reiter, Dan, and Allan C. Stam. 2002. *Democracies and War*. Princeton, NJ: Princeton University Press.
Rietjens, Sebastian. 2012. Between Expectations and Reality: The Dutch Engagement in Uruzgan. In *Statebuilding in Afghanistan: Multinational Contributions to Reconstruction*, ed. Nik Hynek and Péter Marton, 65–87. London: Routledge.
Rice, Condoleezza. 2000. Promoting the National Interest. *Foreign Affairs* 79(1): 45–62.
Ricks, Thomas E. 2009. *The Gamble: General David Petraeus and the American Military Adventure in Iraq, 2006–2008*. New York: Penguin.
Ricks, Thomas E. 2006. *Fiasco: The American Military Adventure in Iraq*. New York: Penguin.
Robinson, Linda. 2008. *Tell Me How This Ends: General David Petraeus and the Search for a Way Out of Iraq*. New York: Public Affairs.
Rosen, Stephen Peter. 1991. *Winning the Next War: Innovation and the Modern Military*. Ithaca, NY: Cornell University Press.
Rosenau, William, and Austin Long. 2009. *The Phoenix Program and Contemporary Counterinsurgency*. Santa Monica, CA: Rand (National Defense Research Institute).
Rothstein, Hy. 2012. America's Longest War. In *Afghan Endgames: Strategy and Policy Choices for America's Longest War*, ed. Hy Rothstein and John Arquilla, 59–81. Washington, DC: Stanford University Press.
Rovner, Joshua. 2011. *Fixing the Facts: National Security and the Politics of Intelligence*. Ithaca, NY: Cornell University Press.
Rudd, Gordon W. 2011. *Reconstructing Iraq: Regime Change, Jay Garner, and the ORHA Story*. Lawrence: University Press of Kansas.
Rumsfeld, Donald. 2011. *Known and Unknown: A Memoir*. New York: Sentinel.
Russell, James A. 2011. *Innovation, Transformation, and War: Counterinsurgency, Operations in Anbar and Ninewa Provinces, Iraq, 2005–2007*. Palo Alto, CA: Stanford University Press.
Rynning, Sten. 2012. *NATO in Afghanistan: The Liberal Disconnect*. Stanford, CA: Stanford University Press.
Sagan, Scott D., and Jeremi Suri. 2003. The Madman Nuclear Alert: Secrecy, Signaling, and Safety in October 1969. *International Security* 27(4): 150–183.
Saunders, Elizabeth N. 2017. No Substitute for Experience: Presidents, Advisers, and Information in Group Decision Making. *International Organization* 71(1): 219–247.
Saunders, Elizabeth N. 2012. *Leaders at War: How Presidents Shape Military Interventions*. Ithaca, NY: Cornell University Press.
Saunders, Elizabeth N. 2009. Transformative Choices: Leaders and the Origins of Intervention Strategy. *International Security* 34(2): 119–161.

Schelling, Thomas C. 1981. Vietnam Reappraised. *International Security* 6(1): 3–26.

Sedney, David S. 2015. *The Afghanistan Conundrum: How Should the US Approach the Rise of Insurgent Groups?* Prepared Statement before the Committee on Foreign Affairs; Subcommittee on the Middle East and North Africa. United States House of Representatives, December 2, 114th Cong., 1st Sess.

Sedra, Mark. 2015. The Hollowing-Out of the Liberal Peace Project in Afghanistan: The Case of Security Section Reform. In *The Afghan Conundrum: Intervention, Statebuilding, and Resistance*, ed. Jonathan Goodhand and Mark Sedra, 133–149. London: Routledge.

Sellen, Robert W. 1973. Old Assumptions Versus New Realities: Lyndon Johnson and Foreign Policy. *International Journal* 28(2): 205–229.

Selverstone, Marc J. 2010. It's a Date: Kennedy and the Timetable for a Vietnam Troop Withdrawal. *Diplomatic History* 34(3): 485–495.

Serena, Chad C. 2011. *A Revolution in Military Adaptation: The US Army in the Iraq War*. Washington, DC: Georgetown University Press.

Sharan, Timor. 2015. The Dynamics of Informal Political Networks and Statehood in Post-2001 Afghanistan: A Case Study of the 2010–2011 Special Election Court Crisis. In *The Afghan Conundrum: Intervention, Statebuilding, and Resistance*, ed. Jonathan Goodhand and Mark Sedra, 98–114. London: Routledge.

Sharan, Timor. 2011. The Dynamics of Elite Networks and Patron-Client Relations in Afghanistan. *Europe-Asia Studies* 63(6): 1109–1127.

Shimko, Keith L. 2017. *The Foreign Policy Puzzle: Interests, Threats, and Tools*. New York: Oxford University Press.

Shimko, Keith L. 2010. *The Iraq Wars and America's Military Revolution*. Cambridge, UK: Cambridge University Press.

SIGAR (Special Inspector General for Afghanistan Reconstruction). 2017a. *Quarterly Report to the United States Congress*. January 30. Arlington, VA: SIGAR. https://www.sigar.mil/pdf/quarterlyreports/2017-01-30qr.pdf.

SIGAR (Special Inspector General for Afghanistan Reconstruction). 2017b. *Quarterly Report to the United States Congress*. July 30. Arlington, VA: SIGAR. https://www.sigar.mil/pdf/quarterlyreports/2017-07-30qr.pdf.

SIGAR (Special Inspector General for Afghanistan Reconstruction). 2016. *Quarterly Report to the United States Congress*. January 30. Arlington, VA: SIGAR.

SIGIR (Special Inspector General for Iraq Reconstruction). 2012. Iraq Police Development Program: Lack of Iraqi Support and Security Problems Raise Questions about the Continued Viability of the Program. SIGIR 12-020. July 30. http://www.sigir.mil/files/audits/12-020.pdf.

SIGIR (Special Inspector General for Iraq Reconstruction). 2009. *Hard Lessons: The Iraq Reconstruction Experience*. Washington, DC: US Government Printing Office.

Sorley, Lewis. 1999. *A Better War: The Unexamined Victories and Final Tragedy of America's Last Years in Vietnam*. Orlando, FL: Harcourt, Inc.

Sowell, Kirk. 2014. Iraq's Second Sunni Insurgency. *Current Trends in Islamist Ideology* 17(August): 39–69.

Spector, Ronald H. 1993. *After Tet: The Bloodiest Year in Vietnam*. New York: Vintage Books.

Steinbruner, John D. 1974. *The Cybernetic Theory of Decision: New Dimensions of Political Analysis*. Princeton, NJ: Princeton University Press.

Suhrke, Astri. 2015. Statebuilding in Afghanistan: A Contradictory Engagement. In *The Afghan Conundrum: Intervention, Statebuilding, and Resistance*, ed. Jonathan Goodhand and Mark Sedra, 33–48. London: Routledge.

Sullivan, Marisa. 2013. *Maliki's Authoritarian Regime*. Middle East Security Report 10. Washington, DC: Institute for the Study of War.

Suri, Jeremi. 2008. The Nukes of October: Richard Nixon's Secret Plan to Bring Peace to Vietnam. *Wired Magazine* (February 25). https://www.wired.com/2008/02/ff-nuclearwar/

Suskind, Ron, 2004. *The Price of Loyalty: George W. Bush, the White House, and the Education of Paul O'Neill*. New York: Simon & Schuster.

Talmadge, Caitlin. 2015. *The Dictator's Army: Battlefield Effectiveness in Authoritarian Regimes*. Ithaca, NY: Cornell University Press.

Talmon, Stefan. 2013. *The Occupation of Iraq (Volume II): The Official Documents of the Coalition Provisional Authority and the Iraqi Governing Council*. Portland, OR: Hart Publishing.

Tannenwald, Nina. 2007. *The Nuclear Taboo: The United States and the Non-Use of Nuclear Weapons Since 1945*. Cambridge, UK: Cambridge University Press.

Tarnoff, Curt. 2008. *Iraq: Reconstruction Assistance*. CRS Report for Congress. Washington, DC: Congressional Research Service.

Taylor, Maxwell D. 1972. *Swords and Plowshares*. NY: Norton.

Tenet, George J. 2007. *At the Center of the Storm: My Years at the CIA*. New York: HarperCollins.

Thayer, Thomas C. 1985. *War without Fronts: The American Experience in Vietnam*. Boulder, CO: Westview Press.

Thies, Wallace J. 1980. *When Governments Collide: Coercion and Diplomacy in the Vietnam Conflict, 1964–1968*. Berkeley: University of California Press.

Thompson, Robert. 1966. *Defeating Communist Insurgency: The Lessons of Malaya and Vietnam*. New York: Praeger.

Tierney, Dominic. 2015. *The Right Way to Lose a War: America in an Age of Unwinnable Conflicts*. New York: Little, Brown and Company.

Trachtenberg, Marc. 2014. H-Diplo/ISSF Forum on "Audience Costs and the Vietnam War." https://issforum.org/forums/audience-costs-and-the-vietnam-war.

United Nations Security Council. 2008. Report of the Security Council Mission to Afghanistan, 21 to 28 November 2008. http://www.securitycouncilreport.org/atf/cf/%7B65BFCF9B-6D27-4E9C-8CD3-CF6E4FF96FF9%7D/CAC%20S2008%20782.pdf.

US Congress, Senate Select Committee on Intelligence. 2007. *Report on Prewar Intelligence Assessments about Postwar Iraq*. http://intelligence.senate.gov/prewar.pdf.

US GAO (General Accountability Office). 2005. *Afghanistan Security: Efforts to Establish Army and Police Have Made Progress, But Future Plans Need to Be Better Defined*. GAO-05-575. Washington, DC: GAO.

US Senate, Committee on Foreign Relations. 2009. *Tora Bora Revisited: How We Failed to Get Bin Laden and Why It Matters Today*. Washington, DC: Government Printing Office.

US Senate, Select Committee on Intelligence. 2004. *Report on the U.S. Intelligence Community's Prewar Intelligence Assessments on Iraq*. http://nsarchive.gwu.edu/NSAEBB/NSAEBB254/doc12.pdf.

Valentino, B., P. Huth, and D. Balch-Lindsay. 2004. Draining the Sea: Mass Killing and Guerilla Warfare. *International Organization* 58(2): 375–407.

Valentino, Benjamin A., Paul K. Huth, and Sarah E. Croco. 2010. Bear Any Burden? How Democracies Minimize the Costs of War. *Journal of Politics* 72(2): 528–544.

Van Staaveren, Jacob. 1977. The Air War Against North Vietnam. In *The United States Air Force in Southeast Asia, 1961–1973*, ed. Carl Berger, 69–100. Washington, DC: Office of Air Force History.

Warner, Geoffey. 2005. Review Article: Lyndon Johnson's War? Part II: From Escalation to Negotiation. *International Affairs* 81(1): 187–215.

Warner, Geoffey. 2003. Review Article: Lyndon Johnson's War? Part I: Escalation. *International Affairs* 79(4): 829–853.

Wilder, Andrew. 2015. *Assessing the President's Strategy in Afghanistan*. Prepared Statement before the Committee on Foreign Affairs; Subcommittee on the Middle East and North Africa. United States House of Representatives, December 2, 114th Cong., 1st Sess.

Wohlforth, William C. 1999. The Stability of a Unipolar World. *International Security* 24(1): 5–41.

Woodward, Bob. 2010. *Obama's Wars*. New York: Simon and Schuster.

Woodward, Bob. 2008. *The War Within: A Secret White House History 2006–2008*. New York: Simon and Schuster.
Woodward, Bob. 2004. *Plan of Attack*. New York: Simon and Schuster.
Wright, Donald P., James R. Bird, Steven E. Clay, Peter W. Connors, Scott C. Farquhar, Lynne Chandler Garcia, and Dennis F. Van Wey. 2010. *A Different Kind of War: The United States in Operation ENDURING FREEDOM (OEF), October 2001–September 2005*. US Army Combined Arms Center. Fort Leavenworth, KS: Combat Studies Institute Press.
Wright, Donald P., Timothy R. Reese, and the Contemporary Operations Study Team. 2008. *On Point II: Transition to the New Campaign; The United States Army in Operation IRAQI FREEDOM May 2003–January 2005*. US Army Combined Arms Center. Fort Leavenworth, KS: Combat Studies Institute Press.
Yetiv, Steve A. 2013. *National Security Policy Through a Cockeyed Lens: How Cognitive Bias Impacts U.S. Foreign Policy*. Baltimore, MD: Johns Hopkins University Press.
Zakheim, Dov S. 2011. *A Vulcan's Tale: How the Bush Administration Mismanaged the Reconstruction of Afghanistan*. Washington, DC: Brookings Institution Press.
Zelizer, Julian E. 2010. *Arsenal of Democracy: The Politics of National Security—From World War II to the War on Terrorism*. New York, NY: Basic Books.
Zhai, Qiang. 2000. *China and the Vietnam War, 1950–1975*. Chapel Hill: University of North Carolina Press.
Zimmerman, Rebecca S. 2015. The Afghan Government at War. In *Coalition Challenges in Afghanistan: The Politics of Alliance*, ed. Gale A. Mattox and Stephen M. Grenier, 15–30. Stanford, CA: Stanford University Press.

INDEX

Abadi, Haider al-, 114–15
Abdullah, Abdullah, 165–66
Abizaid, John P., 89–90, 93–94, 137
Abrams, Creighton, 49–50, 54–55
Abu Ghraib prison, 90
Acheson, Dean, 45–46
Adelman, Ken, 70
ad hoc argumentation, 190
administration changes, 12, 17. *See also* elections and electoral politics
adversary actions, 15
Afghan government
   and constriction of US mission in Afghanistan War, 119, 145–58, 179
   corruption problems, 135, 140–41, 146–47, 148, 151, 166, 168–69, 170, 171–72, 175, 176
   and extension of US mission in Afghanistan, 133, 178, 179
   institutional failings in, 139, 140–41, 164, 167, 168, 169–70, 171–72
   and security challenges in Afghanistan, 139
   and stabilization/development mission in Afghanistan, 134–35, 136–37
   and Taliban threat, 143–44
   and Trump policy on Afghanistan War, 176–77
   and US disengagement from Afghanistan War, 106, 160, 163, 179–80
   and US engagement in Afghanistan War, 123–24, 128
Afghanistan War
   and disjunction stage of decision-making process, 119, 133–45, 178–79
   and dynamics of planning to fail, 2
   and extrication stage of decision-making process, 119, 158–72, 179–80
   failure to meet objectives, 1
   and fixation stage of decision-making process, 119, 178
   and impact of biased decision-making, 190
   lessons from decisional stages of war, 183–84, 185–88, 189
   lessons of case studies, 181–82, 183
   and limitation of resources committed, 7–8
   and military innovation, 11
   and postwar security in Iraq, 73
   and public support for wars, 12
   and rational theory of war, 14–16
   and sources of bias in decision-making process, 2–3
   US disengagement from, 104–13, 179–80
   US engagement of military forces, 5, 122–32, 178
   and US regime change policy, 70–71
Afghan Local Police (ALP), 168–70
Afghan Militia Force (AMF), 138
Afghan National Army (ANA), 137, 138, 171–72
Afghan National Police (ANP), 138–39, 168–69
Ahmed, Mahmoud, 127–28
air/bombing campaigns
   and background of Vietnam War, 17
   and decisional context of Vietnam War, 44, 45
   disengagement of US military in Vietnam, 48, 49–50, 51–52, 56–57, 58, 59
   and disjunction in US prosecution of war, 34–38
   and early successes in Afghanistan War, 131
   and exit strategies for Vietnam, 56
   lessons from decisional stages of war, 184–85
   and non-rational explanations for US intervention in Vietnam, 27, 28, 29–31, 32, 33
   and US disengagement from Afghanistan War, 161–62
   and US engagement in Afghanistan War, 122
   and US engagement in Vietnam, 20, 21, 22, 23
   and Vietnam War, 61–62
Akhundzada, Haibatullah, 162–63

233

al-Askari mosque, 93
Allison, Graham T., 10
al-Qaeda
    and background of Afghanistan War, 121
    and constriction of mission in Afghanistan War, 147, 149, 150, 152–53, 157
    and early successes in Afghanistan War, 130–32
    and extension of US mission in Afghanistan, 133
    and justifications for US engagement in Iraq, 65
    and stabilization/development mission in Afghanistan, 134, 137
    and Trump policy on Afghanistan War, 175–76
    and US disengagement from Afghanistan War, 158–59, 160, 162–63
    and US engagement in Afghanistan War, 122–24, 125–26, 127, 129
ambiguous information
    and constriction of mission in Afghanistan War, 155–56
    and disjunction decision dynamic, 7
    and justifications for US engagement in Iraq, 68
    and occupation mission in Iraq, 83
    and organizational/bureaucratic influences, 10
    and public support for wars, 12
    and rational explanations for US engagement in Vietnam, 25–26
    and rational theory of war, 14
    and surge strategy in Iraq, 99
    and Trump policy on Afghanistan War, 173
Anbar Awakening, 90–91, 98, 102, 110, 111, 117
anchored thinking, 6
anecdotal evidence, 7
anti-Communist sentiment, 21, 23–24, 35–36, 47
Armitage, Richard, 71, 127–28
Army of the Republic of Vietnam, 60
assassination, 50, 58–59
assessment, continuous, 190
asymmetric conflicts, 2, 3–4, 12
attrition strategy, 39, 42, 50, 187. *See also* casualties
Authorization for Use of Military Force against Terrorists, 123
available resources, 16
"axis of evil," 122, 128–29

B-52 bombers, 52
Baath Party
    and expansion of US engagement in Iraq, 116–17
    and final resolution of Iraq War, 115
    and Iraqi institutional failings, 109, 111
    lessons from decisional stages of war, 187
    and US occupation mission in Iraq, 84, 85–86
Badr Organization, 91–92, 114
Baghdad Brigade, 109–10
Ball, George, 22

Baluchistan Province, 153, 158, 162–63
Barbero, Michael D., 114
Barno, David, 133–34, 136, 137
Basra, Iraq, 113
Bay of Pigs, 18–19
beliefs, 9–10
Betts, Richard, 12–13
biased decision-making
    and lessons of case studies, 189–92
    and mission of wars, 4
    psychological influences, 9–10
    and rational theory of war, 13–14, 15
    sources of bias in decision-making process, 2–4
Biden, Joe, 149, 150, 152–54, 155
bilateral security agreement (BSA), 164–65, 166
bin Laden, Osama
    and background of Afghanistan War, 121
    and constriction of mission in Afghanistan War, 157–58
    and early successes in Afghanistan War, 131–32
    and US disengagement from Afghanistan War, 159, 162–63
    and US engagement in Afghanistan War, 123–25, 126–27
Black, Cofer, 129
blockades, 22
Bonn agreement, 139–40
Bradley, Omar, 45–46
Bremer, Paul, 76–77, 82–85, 87–88
Brink Hotel, 21–22
Brookings Institution, 148
Bundy, McGeorge, 21, 22, 29, 30, 46
bureaucratic influences
    and civil aftermath of Iraq War, 79
    and complexity of decision-making process, 9
    described, 10–11
    and impact of biased decision-making, 191
    lessons from decisional stages of war, 186, 189
    and non-rational decision-making, 16
    and non-rational explanations for US intervention in Vietnam, 30
    and postwar security in Iraq, 74
    and sources of bias in decision-making process, 3
    and US engagement in Iraq, 116
Bush, George H. W., 5–6, 70
Bush, George W.
    and allied military contributions in Afghanistan, 141, 142–43
    and background of Afghanistan War, 119, 120–21
    and background of the Iraq War, 64
    and civil aftermath of Iraq War, 77, 79–80
    and constriction of mission in Afghanistan, 145, 146, 147, 148
    and constriction of mission in Iraq, 93, 117

and disengagement from Iraq War, 105, 106, 117–18
and dynamics of planning to fail, 1
and early successes in Afghanistan War, 129, 131–32
and engagement in Afghanistan War, 122, 125–27, 128, 129, 178
and extension decision dynamic, 5–6
and extension of military operations in Afghanistan, 178
and extension of military operations in Iraq, 81
and institutional failings in Afghanistan, 141
and justifications for US engagement in Iraq, 65–68, 69, 70
legacy of Iraq War in Afghanistan, 177
lessons from decisional stages of war, 183, 184, 187–89
lessons of case studies, 181–82
and occupation mission in Iraq, 82–83, 85
and postinvasion security in Iraq, 76–77
and rational theory of war, 14
and regime change policy in Iraq, 70–71
and security challenges in Afghanistan, 138
and security mission in Iraq, 88
and stabilization/development mission in Afghanistan, 134, 135
and surge strategy in Iraq, 7–8, 94–96, 97, 98–99, 104
and Taliban threat in Afghanistan, 143, 145
and Trump policy on Afghanistan War, 173
and US engagement in Afghanistan War, 123–25

Cambodia
and decisional context of Vietnam War, 44
and disengagement of US military in Vietnam, 51, 53–54, 57–58, 62
and US air campaign in Vietnam, 38
and US ground campaign in Vietnam, 38–40, 41, 42, 43
Camp Salerno, 144–45
Carter, Jimmy, 119–20
Cartwright, James, 153–54
Case-Church Amendment, 60
Casey, George W., 93, 94, 95, 96, 99–100, 104–5
casualties
and constriction of mission in Afghanistan War, 151
and legacy of the Vietnam War, 17
and public support for wars, 12, 62
and Taliban threat in Afghanistan, 144–45
and US ground campaign in Vietnam, 39, 62
and US security mission in Iraq, 88–89
Caverley, John, 12
cease-fires, 56
Central America, 120

Central Intelligence Agency (CIA)
and background of Afghanistan War, 119–20, 121
and constriction of mission in Afghanistan War, 157–58
and decisional context of Vietnam War, 45
and early successes in Afghanistan War, 129–30, 131–32
and justifications for US engagement in Iraq, 65–66, 67–68
and postinvasion security in Iraq, 76
and rational explanations for US engagement in Vietnam, 25–26
and security challenges in Afghanistan, 138
and Taliban threat in Afghanistan, 143
and US air/bombing campaigns, 38
and US engagement in Afghanistan War, 124
and US occupation mission in Iraq, 86
Chalabi, Ahmad, 76, 85–86, 111
Chamberlin, Wendy, 127
Cheney, Richard, 66, 68, 69, 71, 124–25, 126–27, 131–32
China
and constriction of US war effort in Vietnam, 46–47
and disengagement of US military in Vietnam, 51, 55–56
and disjunction in US prosecution of Vietnam, 61–62
and the Korean War, 34, 35
and rational explanations for US engagement in Vietnam, 24–25
and US air campaign in Vietnam, 34–36, 37
and US engagement in Afghanistan War, 126
and US ground campaign in Vietnam, 38–39
Christmas bombing campaign. *See* Linebacker I and II bombing campaigns
civilian casualties
and change in US military leadership, 96–97
and constriction of mission in Afghanistan War, 156
and constriction of mission in Iraq, 93
and final resolution of Iraq War, 114
and US disengagement from Afghanistan War, 161
and US ground campaign in Vietnam, 42
Clifford, Clark, 44–45, 46
Clinton, Bill, 70–71, 121, 123, 127–28
Clinton, Hillary, 148–49, 150
Coalition Provisional Authority (CPA)
and occupation mission in Iraq, 82–83, 84, 86, 87–88
and security mission in Iraq, 76–77, 89–90
cognitive research and biases, 2, 6
Cohen, Eliot, 95
COIN strategy, 147–48, 152, 153

INDEX

Cold War, 17–18, 21, 79, 116
collateral damage, 96–97.
    See also civilian casualties
colonialism, 17–18
Combined Forces Command-Afghanistan, 136
Combined Forces Land Component Command (CFLCC), 89–90
Combined Joint Task Force-7 (CJTF-7), 89–90
Combined Security Transition Command-Afghanistan (CSTC-A), 138–39
Commander's Emergency Response Program (CERP), 103, 136–37
comprehensive assessment, 190
conscription, 12, 54
constriction decision dynamic
    and the Afghanistan War, 119, 145–58, 179
    described, 7–8
    and the Iraq War, 64, 93–104, 117, 145
    lessons from decisional stages of war, 188–89
    and the Vietnam War, 17, 43–60
contingency planning, 191
Cooper-Church Amendment, 57
corruption
    and constriction of mission in Afghanistan War, 146–47, 148, 151
    and institutional failings in Afghanistan, 140–41, 166, 168–69, 170, 171–72
    and stabilization/development mission in Afghanistan, 135
    and Trump policy on Afghanistan War, 175, 176
cost-effectiveness, 6, 43, 153
Council of Colonels, 99–100
counterfactuals, 15
counterinsurgency strategies
    and allied military contributions in Afghanistan, 142
    and background of the Iraq War, 64
    and constriction of mission in Afghanistan War, 152–53, 156
    and constriction of mission in Iraq, 93, 117
    disengagement of US military in Vietnam, 49, 54–55
    implementation of US surge strategy, 101–2, 103, 104
    and institutional failings in Afghanistan, 169–70
    and Iraqi institutional failings, 112–13
    and Iraq War surge, 11
    lessons from decisional stages of war, 187–88
    and stabilization/development mission in Afghanistan, 133–34
    and US ground campaign in Vietnam, 40–42
    and US security mission in Iraq, 91–92
    and US surge strategy in Iraq, 93–101
counterterrorism, 149–50, 159–60, 161–62
covert operations, 120
Crocker, Ryan, 103
cruise-missile strikes, 121

Crumpton, Henry, 131–32
Cuban Missile Crisis, 10, 18–19

Da Nang airbase, 23
Dayton Accords, 148–49
de-Americanization, 52, 54–55, 62
de-Baathification, 84, 85–86, 109, 115, 116–17
decision dynamics
    and the Afghanistan War, 146–48
    and backdrop to Vietnam War, 17
    constriction dynamic described, 7–8
    disjunction dynamic described, 5–7
    and dynamics of planning to fail, 2
    extrication dynamic described, 8–9
    fixation dynamic described, 5, 20–33
    lessons from decisional stages of war, 183–89
    and non-decisions, 192
    and non-rational explanations for US intervention in Vietnam, 26–27
    reverse-engineering decisional problems, 191–92
Declaration of Principles, 105
deference to authority, 11, 24–25, 26–27, 36, 49, 82–85, 95–96, 186–87
Democratic Party, 12, 48, 145, 159, 188
Democratic Republic of Vietnam (DRV), 27
democratization and democratic governance
    and Iraq War, 1
    and justifications for US engagement in Iraq, 69
    and sources of bias in decision-making process, 3
    and surge strategy in Iraq, 98–99
    and US occupation mission in Iraq, 82
    and US regime change policy in Iraq, 72
    and US security mission in Iraq, 75–77, 88, 92
departure milestones, 8
deployment levels, 43–45, 93–94, 188
Desert Storm Operation, 5–6, 70, 74, 77–78
detachment in decision-making, 11
Dien Bien Phu, 50
disengagement of military forces
    and the Afghanistan War, 158–72, 179–80
    and Iraq War, 104–13, 117–18
    and stages of wartime decision-making, 8–9
disjoined tasks, 16
disjunction decision dynamic
    and the Afghanistan War, 119, 133–45, 178–79
    described, 5–7
    and the Iraq War, 64, 81–93
    lessons from decisional stages of war, 186–88
    and the Vietnam War, 17, 34–43
Dobrynin, Anatoly, 55–56
domestic political influences.
    See also public opinion
    and explanations for the Vietnam War, 27, 45
    and non-rational decision-making, 16

and non-rational explanations for US
    intervention in Vietnam, 27, 30–31
  public support for wars, 11–13
domino theory, 21
Donilon, Thomas, 149
draft, 12, 54
drone warfare, 149, 157–58
dual-war strategy, 62
Duck Hook operation, 51–52, 53–54

Easter Offensive, 57–58
economic costs of war, 54, 111–12, 167–68
Eikenberry, Karl, 137, 150–51, 155, 170
Eisenhower, Dwight D., 17–18, 19–20, 24
elections and electoral politics
  and civil aftermath of Iraq War, 79
  and constriction of mission in Afghanistan War, 145, 150
  and disengagement from Afghanistan War, 158–59, 160
  and disengagement from Vietnam, 48, 49, 56
  and institutional failings in Afghanistan, 165
  and public support for wars, 11–13
  and US occupation mission in Iraq, 84
  and US surge strategy in Iraq, 95
Emanuel, Raum, 150
embedded provincial reconstruction teams (ePRTs), 103
engagement of military forces
  and the Afghanistan War, 5, 122–32, 178
  and the Iraq War, 5, 64–81, 116–17
  and stages of wartime decision-making, 5
  and the Vietnam War, 61
escalation of conflicts
  and constriction of US war effort, 47
  and decisional context of Vietnam War, 43–44
  disengagement of US military in Vietnam, 53–54
  and exit strategies, 53–60, 62
  and non-rational explanations for US intervention in Vietnam, 32–33
  and US ground campaign in Vietnam, 43
exit strategies
  and disengagement from Afghanistan War, 159–60, 179
  and disengagement of military forces, 8–9
  and escalation of conflicts, 53–60, 62
  lessons from decisional stages of war, 187–88, 189
  and surge strategy in Iraq, 100–1
  and Trump policy on Afghanistan War, 176
  US departure from Iraq, 107
  and Vietnam War, 19–20
extension of military operations
  and the Afghanistan War, 133–45, 178–79
  and disjunction in US prosecution of Vietnam war, 61–62

  and Iraq War, 81–93
  and stages of wartime decision-making, 5–7
  and the Vietnam War, 17, 34–38
extrajudicial detention, 50
extrication decision dynamic
  and the Afghanistan War, 119, 158–72, 179–80
  described, 8–9
  and the Iraq War, 64, 104–13
  lessons from decisional stages of war, 189

Facilities Protection Service, 92
fallback options, 191
Fallon, William, 104–5
Faulkner, William, vii
Fearon, James, 13
Feith, Douglas, 65–66, 68, 69, 76, 80–81, 82, 125
fixation decision dynamic
  and the Afghanistan War, 119, 122–32, 178
  and engagement of military forces, 5
  and the Iraq War, 5, 64–81, 116–17
  lessons from decisional stages of war, 183–86
  and the Vietnam War, 61
Flournoy, Michèle, 152
"fog of war," 10
Ford, Gerald, 181
France, 17–18
Franks, Tommy, 67, 68, 81, 129, 132–33
Future of Iraq Project, 67, 79–80

Garner, Jay, 77–78, 79–80, 84, 85–86
Gates, Robert
  and constriction of mission in Afghanistan War, 146, 149–50, 152, 153–55, 156, 158
  and Taliban threat in Afghanistan, 145
  and US disengagement from Afghanistan War, 159
Gelb, Leslie, 12–13
Geneva Accords, 17–18
Ghani, Ashraf, 165, 166, 175
Giap, Vo Nguyen, 50
global war on terrorism, 14, 119, 120–21, 178
goal-directed policy, 15
goals of war, 15
Goldstein, Gordon, 18–19
Gorbachev, Mikhail, 121
gradual escalation strategy, 31, 32, 36
Great Britain, 119–20
Great Society Program, 24
ground campaigns
  and backdrop to Vietnam War, 17
  and disjunction in US prosecution of Vietnam war, 62
  and non-rational explanations for US intervention in Vietnam, 28, 30, 31, 32
  and US engagement in Vietnam, 23, 61
group dynamics, 26–27
groupthink, 6

guerrilla campaigns, 39–40, 55, 127–28. *See also* counterinsurgency strategies
Gulf of Tonkin Incident and Resolution, 21–22, 25–26, 57
Gulf War, 68, 74

Haass, Richard, 71, 134, 185
Hadley, Stephen, 94, 95–96, 98
Haiphong Harbor, 34, 58
Hamlet Evaluation System, 49–50
Hanoi. *See* North Vietnam
Hanoi, North Korea, 37
Haq, Asaib Ahl al-, 114
Haqqani network, 156
Harkins, Paul, 29–30
Harriman, Averell, 45–46
Hazaras, 121, 131, 140
Health Ministry (Iraq), 92
Helmand province, 147–48, 157, 160, 162, 167–68
Helms, Richard, 45–46
heuristics, 2–3
hierarchic politics, 109
historical analogies, 6
Ho Chi Minh, 17–18, 24–25
Ho Chi Minh trail, 37
Holbrook, Richard, 148–49, 151
hold-and-build operations, 144
humanitarian crises and assistance, 65–66, 76–79, 80–81, 125, 132, 133–34
Humphrey, Hubert, 26–27, 48, 51
Hussein, Saddam
 and background of the Iraq War, 64
 and civil aftermath of Iraq War, 80–81
 and expansion of US engagement in Iraq, 116–17
 and justifications for US engagement in Iraq, 65–67, 68, 69, 116
 lessons from decisional stages of war, 184, 185
 lessons of case studies, 181
 and postwar security in Iraq, 73–75
 and US occupation mission in Iraq, 84, 85–86
 and US regime change policy in Iraq, 70, 72
 and US security mission in Iraq, 89, 90, 91–92

improvised explosive devices (IEDs), 89, 102
incremental decision-making, 27–28, 61
Independent Commission on the Security Forces of Iraq (Jones Commission), 112
Index of State Weakness in the Developing World, 148
infiltrators, 38
informational deficiencies, 13–14
initiative in battle, 39–40
innovation, 11
institutional failings, 109–13
insurgency, 38, 39, 160–61

Integrity Commission, 109
Interagency Policy Group, 146–47
Interim Authority (Iraq), 76–77, 83
Interior Ministry (Iraq), 91–92, 112, 115, 116–17
International Security Assistance Force (ISAF)
 and allied military contributions in Afghanistan, 141–43
 and extension of US mission in Afghanistan, 178
 and institutional failings in Afghanistan, 168, 171
 and security challenges in Afghanistan, 138
 and stabilization/development mission in Afghanistan, 135–36
 and Taliban threat in Afghanistan, 143, 145
 and Trump policy on Afghanistan War, 173
 and US disengagement from Afghanistan War, 162
Inter-Services Intelligence (ISI) directorate, 120–21, 123–24, 127–28, 158
Iran, 105–6, 128–29
Iraqi Civil War, 109
Iraqi Defense Ministry, 107–8
Iraqi Governing Council, 83, 86–87, 116–17
Iraqi Parliament, 105–6
Iraqi Transitional Government, 91–92
Iraq Liberation Act, 70–71
Iraq Stabilization Group, 85
Iraq Study Group, 93–94
Iraq War
 background of, 64
 and change in US military leadership, 96–97
 de-Americanization, 52, 54–55, 62
 de-Baathification, 84, 85–86, 109, 115, 116–17
 and disengagement of US military, 104–13, 117–18
 and disjunction stage of decision-making process, 64, 81–93
 and dynamics of planning to fail, 2
 exit negotiations, 105–7
 and extension of military operations, 81–93
 and extrication stage of decision-making process, 64, 104–13
 failure to meet objectives, 1
 final resolution of, 113–15
 and fixation stage of decision-making process, 5, 64–81, 116–17
 and impact of biased decision-making, 190
 impact on Afghanistan War, 177
 and Iraqi institutional failings, 109–13
 justification for intervention, 64–70
 lessons from decisional stages of war, 183–85, 186–89
 lessons of case studies, 181–82, 183
 and limitation of resources committed, 7–8, 93–104, 117
 and military innovation, 11

INDEX

and mission creep, 6
and public support for wars, 12
and rational theory of war, 14–16
and regime change focus, 70–81
and sources of bias in decision-making process, 2–3
surge and counterinsurgency strategy, 93–96, 97–104
US engagement in, 5, 64–81, 116–17
and US engagement in Afghanistan War, 122–23
and US occupation mission in Iraq, 82–88
US security mission in Iraq, 88–93
Islamic fundamentalism and militancy, 102, 120–21, 127–28, 130, 160–61, 174
Islamic State, 107, 114, 115, 163, 173

Japan, 76
Jervis, Robert, 190
Johnson, Harold K., 41–42
Johnson, Lyndon B.
and air war in Vietnam, 34–36, 37, 38, 49–50, 51–52
and decisional context of Vietnam, 43–44
disengagement of US military in Vietnam, 48–49, 62
and engagement of US military in Vietnam, 5–6, 17, 20–23, 61–62
and ground war in Vietnam, 38–39, 43
lessons from decisional stages of war, 183, 184, 187, 188–89
lessons of case studies, 182
and limitation of military engagement in Vietnam, 7–8, 43–47, 49–50, 51, 62
and mission fixation explanation for US intervention in Vietnam, 29–33
and non-rational explanations for US intervention in Vietnam, 26–28, 29–33
and origins of Vietnam War, 19–20
pressures for policy changes, 43
and public support for wars, 12–13
and rational explanations for US intervention in Vietnam, 23–26
Joint Chiefs of Staff (JCS)
and background of Afghanistan War, 120
and constriction of mission in Afghanistan War, 146, 148, 150, 153–54
and disengagement from Iraq War, 104–5, 106, 107
and early successes in Afghanistan War, 129
and non-rational explanations for US intervention in Vietnam, 31, 32
and stabilization/development mission in Afghanistan, 137
and US engagement in Afghanistan War, 126
and US engagement in Vietnam, 20, 21–22, 23
and US ground campaign in Vietnam, 39–40

and US occupation mission in Iraq, 84
and US surge strategy in Iraq, 93–94, 96, 99–100
Joint Special Operations Command, 146
Jones, James, 146, 149

Kabul, Afghanistan, 160–61, 162, 167–68, 173–74
Kaiser, David, 28
kamikaze attacks, 122
Kandahar, Afghanistan, 121, 131, 136, 141–42, 147–48, 156, 157, 159, 160–61
Karzai, Hamid
and constriction of mission in Afghanistan War, 150–51
and early successes in Afghanistan War, 131
and institutional failings in Afghanistan, 140, 141, 163–65, 170
Keane, Jack, 94
Kennedy, John F., 18–20, 24–25, 27
Kent State shootings, 57
Kerry, John, 164, 165–66
Khalilzad, Zalmay, 136, 137
Khe Sanh, 39–40
"kinetic operations," 96–97
Kissinger, Henry
and final resolution of Vietnam War, 60
and US disengagement from Vietnam, 51–54, 55–56, 58–60
and US ground campaign in Vietnam, 39
Konduz, Afghanistan, 160–61
Korean War, 5–6, 34, 35–36
Kurds, 68, 86–87, 109, 114
Kuwait, 5–6, 75, 185

Laird, William, 53–54, 56
Laos
and backdrop to Vietnam War, 18–19
and decisional context of Vietnam War, 44
disengagement of US military in Vietnam, 51, 57–58, 62
and rational explanations for US engagement in Vietnam, 24–25
and US air/bombing campaigns, 37
and US ground campaign, 38–39
Lê, Nguyên Khang, 30
Lebanon, 79
legitimacy, 76
liberation, 82–93
limitation in resources committed
and the Afghanistan War, 145–58, 179
and Iraq War, 7–8, 93–104, 117
and stages of wartime decision-making, 7–8
and the Vietnam War, 62
limitation of bombing campaigns, 37
Linebacker I and II bombing campaigns, 58, 59
lobbying, 70. *See also* political-economic influences

Lodge, Henry Cabot, 45–46
Loya Jirga, 139–40, 164–65, 166
Lute, Douglas, 146, 149

MacArthur, Douglas, 76
Mahdi army, 90–91, 92, 102–3
Maliki, Nuri al-
    and disengagement from Iraq War, 105, 106–7, 108–9
    and final resolution of Iraq War, 114–15
    and Iraqi institutional failings, 109–11, 113
    and surge strategy in Iraq, 98–99
"Marshall Plan" in Afghanistan, 134
Mattis, James, 173
McCarthy, Eugene, 48
McChrystal, Stanley
    and constriction of mission in Afghanistan War, 146, 147–48, 150, 152, 153–56
    and institutional failings in Afghanistan, 169–70
McCone, John, 25–26
McKiernan, David, 89, 145, 146
McNamara, Robert
    and backdrop to Vietnam War, 18–20
    and constriction of US war effort, 46–47
    and decisional context of Vietnam War, 43–45
    and explanations for the Vietnam War, 26–28
    lessons from decisional stages of war, 187
    and limitation of resources for war, 7
    and non-rational explanations for US intervention in Vietnam, 30–31, 32, 33
    and rational explanations for US engagement in Vietnam, 24, 25–26
    and US engagement in Vietnam, 21, 22
    and US ground campaign in Vietnam, 43
military advisors, 20, 27
Military Assistance Command in Vietnam (MACV), 29–30, 36
military coups, 18
mining operations, 34, 51–52
Ministry of Interior (Afghanistan)
    and institutional failings in Afghanistan, 169–70
mission creep, 6, 23, 190
mission fixation, 29–33
mixed news, 7
Mueller, John, 12
mujahideen, 119–21, 140
Mullen, Mike, 107, 148, 150, 158
Multi-National Force-Iraq (MNF-I), 89–90
Multi-National Security Transition Command-Iraq, 96
Musharraf, Pervez, 127–28
myopia of policy makers, 2, 3–4

National Guard units, 45, 57, 138
nationalism, 130
National Liberation Front, 18
National Police (Iraq), 92–93, 112

National Security Action Memorandum 288, 27–28
National Security Advisor, 65, 84, 124, 149
National Security Council (NSC)
    and civil aftermath of Iraq War, 78–79, 80–81
    and constriction of mission in Afghanistan War, 152
    and early successes in Afghanistan War, 129
    and justifications for US engagement in Iraq, 67
    and non-rational explanations for US intervention in Vietnam, 28
    and rational explanations for US engagement in Vietnam, 25–26
    and surge strategy in Iraq, 98, 99–100
    and US engagement in Vietnam, 22
    and US occupation mission in Iraq, 85
    and US regime change policy in Iraq, 71
    and US surge strategy in Iraq, 94–95, 96
National Security Council Deputies Committee, 125–26
nation-building, 79, 103, 129, 133–35, 174, 175
NATO Training Mission-Afghanistan (NTM-A), 138–39
Navy Seals, 157–58
Near East Bureau, 79–80
neoconservatives, 69, 70
Neumann, Ronald, 154
New York Times, 150–51
Ngo, Dinh Diem, 18, 19, 32, 58–59, 183
Nguyen Van Thieu, 51, 53, 58–60
Nicholson, John W., Jr., 173
Nitze, Paul, 45–46
Nixon, Richard M.
    and declining public support for wars, 8
    disengagement of US military in Vietnam, 48, 49, 51–60, 62–63
    and engagement of US military in Vietnam, 34–35
    and final resolution of Vietnam War, 60
    lessons from decisional stages of war, 189
    lessons of case studies, 181–82
    and public support for wars, 12
non-decisions, 192
nongovernmental organizations (NGOs), 134–35
non-rational decision-making, 6, 26–33
North Atlantic Treaty Organization (NATO)
    and allied military contributions in Afghanistan, 141–42, 143
    and background of Afghanistan War, 119–20
    and constriction of mission in Afghanistan, 145, 146, 157–58
    and institutional failings in Afghanistan, 163, 164–65, 166, 170, 172
    and security challenges in Afghanistan, 138–39
    and stabilization/development mission in Afghanistan, 135, 136
    and Taliban threat in Afghanistan, 145
    and US engagement in Afghanistan War, 126

INDEX

Northern Alliance, 129, 131, 135, 138, 140
North Korea, 128–29
North Vietnam
   and backdrop to Vietnam War, 18, 19–20
   and constriction of US war effort, 44–45, 46–47, 62
   and disjunction in US prosecution of war, 34–36, 37, 38–41, 42, 43, 61–62
   Easter Offensive, 57–58
   and final resolution of Vietnam War, 60
   lessons from decisional stages of war, 184, 187
   and non-rational explanations for US intervention, 26–27, 29–31, 32, 33
   and rational explanations for US engagement in Vietnam, 24–26
   and the Tet Offensive, 15, 39–40, 44–45, 48, 50
   and US air campaign in Vietnam, 38
   and US disengagement from Vietnam, 48, 49–50, 51–58, 59–60, 62
   and US engagement in Vietnam, 20, 21, 22, 61
   and US ground campaign in Vietnam, 38–41, 42, 43
North Waziristan, 153, 157, 158, 160–61
NSC Deputies Committee, 67
nuclear weapons, 51–52, 68

Obama, Barack
   and background of Afghanistan War, 119
   and background of the Iraq War, 64
   and constriction of mission in Afghanistan War, 145–46, 147–48, 149–56, 157, 158, 179–80
   and declining public support for wars, 8
   and disengagement from Afghanistan War, 158–60, 161–62
   and disengagement from Iraq War, 105, 106, 107–8, 109, 117–18
   and final resolution of Iraq War, 115
   implementation of US surge strategy, 104
   and institutional failings in Afghanistan, 163–66, 168–69
   lessons from decisional stages of war, 185, 189
   and public support for wars, 12
   and *surge* in Afghanistan War, 7–8
   and Trump policy on Afghanistan War, 173–76, 177
   and US engagement in Afghanistan War, 123
occupation missions, 82–93, 116
Odierno, Raymond, 94, 96
Office of Military Cooperation-Afghanistan (OMC-A), 138–39
Office of Reconstruction and Humanitarian Assistance (ORHA), 76–79, 80, 81, 89–90
Office of Security Cooperation-Afghanistan (OSC-A), 138–39
Office of Security Cooperation in Iraq (OSC-I), 108
Omar, Mohammed, 121, 123–24, 131, 158, 162–63

one-war approach, 49–50
Operation ANACONDA, 131
Operation Enduring Freedom (OEF), 122, 141, 142, 178
organizational dynamics, 2, 3, 10–11, 16. *See also* bureaucratic influences
overoptimism, 27

Pace, Peter, 94, 96, 99–100
pacification, 41–43, 49–50. *See also* counterinsurgency strategies
Pakistan
   and background of Afghanistan War, 119–21
   and constriction of mission in Afghanistan War, 146–47, 148–49, 152–53, 155–56, 157–58
   and early successes in Afghanistan War, 130, 131–32
   and institutional failings in Afghanistan, 164
   and stabilization/development mission in Afghanistan, 135
   and Taliban threat in Afghanistan, 143–44, 178
   and Trump policy on Afghanistan War, 175
   and US disengagement from Afghanistan War, 160–61
   and US engagement in Afghanistan War, 123–24, 126–28
Panetta, Leon, 107, 158
"Parade of Horribles," 80–81
Pashtuns, 121, 135, 143–44, 171–72
path-dependency, 4
peacekeeping, 142
Pearl Harbor, 122
Pentagon attacks, 65
Petraeus, David
   and constriction of mission in Afghanistan War, 148, 150, 152, 155–57
   and disengagement from Afghanistan War, 159
   and disengagement from Iraq War, 104–5
   implementation of US surge strategy, 103
   and institutional failings in Afghanistan, 110, 169–70
   and leadership changes in Iraq War, 96
   and organizational/bureaucratic influences in decision-making, 11
   and Taliban threat in Afghanistan, 145
   and US surge strategy in Iraq, 96
Phoenix program, 50
Pillar, Paul, 67, 68
Plain of Jars, 37
planning to fail, 1, 191
Pleiku air base, 23
policy conflicts, 14
policy goals of wars, 2, 7
political-economic influences, 103–4
political ideology, 12, 109–11
political polarization, 12
political strategies, 39, 187

population-centric approaches, 97, 104
Powell, Colin, 65, 70, 71, 82–83, 84, 126–27, 185
power-sharing agreements, 166
Predator spy planes, 143
presidential approval ratings, 174
principal-agent relationship, 11
probabilistic information, 6
"A Program for the Pacification and Long-Term Development of Vietnam" (PROVN), 41–42
provincial-level commands, 109–10
provincial reconstruction teams (PRTs), 103, 135–37, 141–42
proximate goals of war, 2, 5, 16
psychological biases and influences, 2, 4, 9–10
public opinion
    and backdrop to Vietnam War, 17
    and constriction of mission in Afghanistan War, 151
    and disengagement from Afghanistan, 158–59
    and disengagement from Vietnam, 48
    impact of casualties, 12, 62
    implementation of US surge strategy, 102
    and Kent State shootings, 57
    lessons from decisional stages of war, 188
    and non-rational explanations for US intervention in Vietnam, 32–33
    public support for wars, 8, 11–13
    and rational explanations for US engagement in Vietnam, 24–25, 26
    and September 11 terrorist attacks, 126
    and US security mission in Iraq, 90

rational decision-making, 5–7, 8–9, 11, 13–16
Reagan, Ronald, 119–21
realists, 13, 15
reconstruction programs, 79, 134–35
regime change
    and background of the Iraq War, 64
    and civil aftermath of Iraq War, 77–81
    consequences of, 73–81
    and justifications for US engagement in Iraq, 67, 68
    lessons from decisional stages of war, 184–85
    premature focus on, 70–73
    and US detachment, 85–86, 88
    and US engagement in Iraq, 64–65, 116
    and US regime change policy in Iraq, 73
    and US security mission in Iraq, 73–77, 90, 112–13
regional military balance, 14
Republican Guard, 75, 91–92
Republican Party, 12, 48, 104–5, 158–59
reverse-engineering decisional problems, 191–92
Revolutionary Guards Corp (Iran), 114–15
Rice, Condoleezza
    and counterinsurgency strategy in Iraq, 94–95
    and institutional failings in Afghanistan, 164–65

    and justifications for US engagement in Iraq, 65, 70
    and US engagement in Afghanistan War, 124–25
    and US occupation mission in Iraq, 84, 85, 87–88
    and US regime change policy in Iraq, 71
Riedel, Bruce, 146–47, 149–50, 152
risk-taking, 6
Rogers, William, 53–54
rogue states, 69, 128–29
Rolling Stone, 155
Rolling Thunder bombing campaign, 23, 30–31, 36, 38, 45
Rostow, Walt, 45–46
Rudd, Gordon W., 81
Rumsfeld, Donald
    and allied military contributions in Afghanistan, 143
    and civil aftermath of Iraq War, 78–79, 80–81
    and counterinsurgency strategy in Iraq, 93–94
    and disengagement from Iraq War, 117–18
    and early successes in Afghanistan War, 129, 132
    and extension of US mission in Afghanistan, 133, 178–79
    and extension of US mission in Iraq, 81
    and justifications for US engagement in Iraq, 67, 68, 69–70
    on military shortcomings in Iraq, 115
    and organizational/bureaucratic influences in decision-making, 11
    and postinvasion security in Iraq, 76–77
    and postwar security in Iraq, 73–75
    and security challenges in Afghanistan, 138
    and stabilization/development mission in Afghanistan, 134, 137
    and Taliban threat in Afghanistan, 143, 145
    and US engagement in Afghanistan War, 123, 124–25, 126–27
    and US occupation mission in Iraq, 82–83, 84–86, 87–88
    and US regime change policy in Iraq, 71
    and US security mission in Iraq, 88, 90
    and US surge strategy in Iraq, 95
Rusk, Dean, 21, 22, 24, 45–46
Russell, James, 11
Russia. *See also* Soviet Union
    and air war in Vietnam, 34
    and constriction of US war effort, 46–47
    and disengagement of US military in Vietnam, 51, 55–56
    and the Korean War, 35
    military advisors in Vietnam, 34–35
    and rational explanations for US engagement in Vietnam, 24–25
    and US engagement in Afghanistan War, 126
    and US ground campaign in Vietnam, 38–39

INDEX

Sadr, Moqtada al-, 90–91, 98, 102–3, 105–6, 113
Saigon. *See* South Vietnam
Sanchez, Ricardo, 89–90, 93
Saudi Arabia, 119–20
sectarian conflict, 99, 112–13
security missions
   and allied military contributions in Afghanistan, 142
   and expansion of US mission in Iraq, 88–93
   and Iraqi institutional failings, 112–13
   and justifications for US engagement in Iraq, 115–17
   lessons from decisional stages of war, 187
   and surge strategy in Iraq, 102
self-interest, 191
September 11 terrorist attacks
   and background of Afghanistan War, 121
   as justification for US engagement Iraq, 65
   and US disengagement from Afghanistan War, 158–59, 162–63
   and US engagement in Afghanistan War, 122, 126, 128–29
   and US regime change policy in Iraq, 70–71
Shahi Kowt Valley, 131–32
Sharif, Mazar-e, 131
Shelton, Henry, 126
Shiite militia
   and background of the Iraq War, 64
   and constriction of US mission in Iraq, 93
   and expansion of US engagement in Iraq, 116–17
   and final resolution of Iraq War, 114–15
   implementation of US surge strategy, 102–3
   and Iraqi institutional failings, 109, 110–11, 112, 113
   lessons of case studies, 181–82
   and surge strategy in Iraq, 98, 99, 100–1
   and US occupation mission in Iraq, 86–87
   and US security mission in Iraq, 88, 90–92, 93
Shinseki, Eric, 74–75
signaling functions, 37, 38–39
Sistani, Ali al-, 87, 105–6
social costs of war, 54. *See also* civilian casualties
Somalia, 79
Sons of Iraq (SOI), 102, 105–6, 111
Sorley, Lewis, 49
South Vietnam
   and backdrop to Vietnam War, 17–18, 19–20
   and constriction of US war effort, 43–46, 47, 62
   and disjunction in US prosecution of war, 34, 35, 37, 38–41, 42, 43
   and final resolution of Vietnam War, 60
   lessons from decisional stages of war, 187
   and non-rational explanations for US intervention, 27–28, 29–31, 32–33
   and rational explanations for US engagement in Vietnam, 24–26

   and the Tet Offensive, 15
   and US air campaign in Vietnam, 37–38
   and US disengagement from Vietnam, 48, 49–50, 51, 52, 53, 54–60, 62
   and US engagement in Vietnam, 20–22, 23
   and US ground campaign in Vietnam, 38–39, 40–41, 42, 43
Soviet Union
   and background of Afghanistan War, 119–20, 121
   disengagement of US military in Vietnam, 51, 52
   and disjunction in US prosecution of Vietnam war, 61–62
   and early successes in Afghanistan War, 130, 131
   military advisors in Vietnam, 34–35
   and rational explanations for US engagement in Vietnam, 24–25
   and US engagement in Afghanistan War, 124
special forces, 40–42, 131
Special National Intelligence Estimate, 34–35
stability operations, 89, 103
stages of wartime decision-making. *See* constriction decision dynamic; disjunction decision dynamic; extrication decision dynamic; fixation decision dynamic
state building, 1, 5–6
status of forces agreement (SOFA), 105–6, 173
Stinger missiles, 120
Strategic Air Command, 52
Strategic Partnership Agreement (SPA), 164
strategy vs. tactics, 30
sunk-costs fallacy, 4, 6
Sunni insurgency
   and background of the Iraq War, 64
   and constriction of US mission in Iraq, 93
   and expansion of US engagement in Iraq, 117
   implementation of US surge strategy, 102–3, 104
   and Iraqi institutional failings, 109–11, 112
   and surge strategy in Iraq, 97–98, 99
   and US military leadership changes, 96–97
   and US occupation mission in Iraq, 86–87
   and US security mission in Iraq, 88, 90–92, 93
supplied information, 7
surface-to-air missiles, 34
surge
   and constriction of US engagement in Iraq, 117
   and counterinsurgency strategy in Iraq, 93, 94, 95–96
   and disengagement from Iraq War, 104–5
   implementation of, 101–4
   and Iraqi institutional failings, 109, 110, 111–12
   limits of, in Iraq, 97–101
   and US military leadership changes, 96
Syria, 186

tactics vs. strategy, 30
Tajiks, 121, 131, 140, 171–72
Taliban
    and background of Afghanistan War, 119, 120–21
    and constriction of mission in Afghanistan War, 147–50, 151, 152–53, 154, 155–57, 158
    and early successes in Afghanistan War, 129, 130–31, 132
    and extension of US mission in Afghanistan, 133, 179
    and the "global war on terrorism," 178
    and institutional failings in Afghanistan, 164–65, 167, 168, 170, 171, 172
    lessons from decisional stages of war, 184, 187–88
    and organizational/bureaucratic influences in decision-making, 11
    and postwar security in Iraq, 73
    and rational theory of war, 14
    and stabilization/development mission in Afghanistan, 133–35, 136–37
    and Taliban threat in Afghanistan, 143–45
    and Trump policy on Afghanistan War, 173–74, 175–77
    and US disengagement from Afghanistan War, 160–61, 162–63, 179
    and US engagement in Afghanistan War, 122, 123–24, 125, 126–28, 129
    and US regime change policy, 70
Tarin Kot, 162
Taylor, Maxwell, 27–28, 45–46
technological advantages in warfare, 132
temporizing, 190–91
Tenet, George, 66, 67–68, 71, 129
terrorism, 14, 174
Tet Offensive, 15, 39–40, 44–45, 48, 50
38th parallel, 35–36
Tora Bora, 131, 132
torture, 50
Trachtenberg, Marc, 19
Transparency International, 148
trilateral diplomacy, 51
Truman, Harry S., 5–6, 23–24
Trump, Donald, 173–77
tunnel vision, 6

unanticipated consequences, 32
uncertainty, 13–14
"unification" policy of North Vietnam, 58
United Nations (UN), 71, 114, 134–35, 141, 144–45, 150
United States Force-Iraq (USF-I), 108
UN Security Council, 121, 135
    and US engagement in Iraq War, 65, 76
    and US regime change policy in Iraq, 71

US Agency for International Development (USAID), 42, 79, 120–21, 134
US Air Force, 36
US Army, 99–100
US Army/Marine Corps Counterinsurgency Manual, 96
US Central Command (CENTCOM)
    and civil aftermath of Iraq War, 79
    and constriction of mission in Afghanistan War, 148, 150
    and disengagement from Iraq War, 104–5, 106, 108
    and early successes in Afghanistan War, 129, 132
    and extension of US mission in Afghanistan, 133
    and justifications for US engagement in Iraq, 67
    and stabilization/development mission in Afghanistan, 137
    and surge strategy in Iraq, 99–100
    and Taliban threat in Afghanistan, 145
    and US security mission in Iraq, 89–90
    and US surge strategy in Iraq, 93–94
US Civilian Operations and Revolutionary Development Support (CORDS) program, 49–50
US Congress
    and constriction of mission in Afghanistan War, 148
    and decisional context of Vietnam War, 44, 45
    and disengagement from Iraq War, 104–5, 108–9
    and disengagement from Vietnam, 60
    and engagement in Afghanistan War, 123–24, 126
    and engagement in Iraq War, 65, 69
    and exit strategies for Vietnam, 57
    lessons of case studies, 181
    and postwar security in Iraq, 74–75
    and rational explanations for US engagement in Vietnam, 25
    and surge strategy in Iraq, 93–94, 99
US Department of Defense
    and civil aftermath of Iraq War, 77–79, 80
    and constriction of mission in Afghanistan War, 152
    and decisional context of Vietnam War, 45
    and disengagement from Iraq, 108–9, 117–18
    and early successes in Afghanistan War, 130
    and institutional failings in Afghanistan, 172
    and justifications for US engagement in Iraq, 67
    and postinvasion security in Iraq, 76
    and postwar security in Iraq, 73
    and stabilization/development mission in Afghanistan, 134, 137
    and surge strategy in Iraq, 99–100

and US air/bombing campaigns, 38
and US engagement in Afghanistan War, 122, 124
and US occupation mission in Iraq, 87–88
and US security mission in Iraq, 89, 91
US Department of Justice, 91
US Department of State
and civil aftermath of Iraq War, 79–80
and decisional context of Vietnam War, 45
and disengagement from Iraq, 108–9
and justifications for US engagement in Iraq, 67–68
and postinvasion security in Iraq, 76
and postwar security in Iraq, 75–76
and US air/bombing campaigns, 38
and US engagement in Afghanistan War, 124
and US ground campaign in Vietnam, 42
and US security mission in Iraq, 91
and US surge strategy in Iraq, 94, 99–100, 103
US House of Representatives, 65, 104–5, 108–9. *See also* US Congress
US Marines
and constriction of mission in Afghanistan War, 147–48
and surge strategy in Iraq, 99–100, 101
and the Vietnam War, 23, 27, 36, 39–42
US National Intelligence Estimate (NIE), 66, 67
US Navy, 36
USS *Abraham Lincoln*, 81
US Senate, 25–26, 65, 66, 104–5. *See also* US Congress
USS *Maddox*, 25–26
USS *Turner Joy*, 25
Uzbekistan, 126–27, 130
Uzbeks, 121, 131

V Corps, 89–90
Vietcong
and backdrop to Vietnam War, 18
and decisional context of Vietnam War, 45
and disengagement of US military in Vietnam, 48, 50, 58
and non-rational explanations for US intervention in Vietnam, 29–30, 31, 32, 33
and the Tet Offensive, 15
and US air/bombing campaigns, 23, 37–38
and US engagement in Vietnam, 21–22
and US ground campaign in Vietnam, 39–41, 42, 43
Vietminh, 17–18
Vietnam War
backdrop to, 17–20
and constriction stage of decision-making process, 17, 43–60
and disengagement of US military, 48–60, 62–63

and disjunction stage of decision-making process, 17, 34–43
and dynamics of planning to fail, 2
and engagement of military forces, 5
engagement of US military, 20–33, 61
extension of military engagement, 34–43, 61–62
and extension of military operations, 5–6
failure to meet objectives, vii, 1
final resolution of, 60
and fixation stage of decision-making process, 61
and impact of biased decision-making, 190
impact on Afghanistan War, 177
legacy of, 61
lessons from decisional stages of war, 183–85, 186–87, 188, 189
lessons of case studies, 181–83
limitation of military engagement, 43–47, 62
and limitation of resources committed, 7–8
origins of, 18–20
and public support for wars, 12–13
and rational theory of war, 14–16
settlement negotiations, 38
and sources of bias in decision-making process, 2–3
and US air campaign, 34–38, 61–62
and US engagement in Afghanistan War, 122–23
and US ground campaign, 38–43, 61, 62
and US military leadership changes, 96–97
"Vietnamization" policy, 52, 53–55, 57–58, 62
village stability operations (VSO), 169–70

warlords
and institutional failings in Afghanistan, 139–40
and background of Afghanistan War, 121
and constriction of mission in Afghanistan, 153
and institutional failings in Afghanistan, 169, 170
lessons of case studies, 181–82
and security challenges in Afghanistan, 138, 139
and stabilization/development mission in Afghanistan, 135
"wars of necessity" vs. "wars of choice," 185
Washington Post, 84–85, 147
weapons of mass destruction (WMD)
and background of the Iraq War, 64
and justifications for US engagement in Iraq, 65–68, 69, 70
lessons from decisional stages of war, 184
and postwar security in Iraq, 75
and US engagement in Afghanistan War, 128–29
and US regime change policy in Iraq, 72

Westmoreland, William
   and decisional context of Vietnam War, 43–45
   and disengagement from Vietnam, 49–50
   and disjunction in US prosecution of war, 36
   and non-rational explanations for US intervention in Vietnam, 29–30
   and US engagement in Vietnam, 23
   and US ground campaign in Vietnam, 39–43
Wheeler, Earle, 39–40, 45–46
"Wise Men," 45–46

wishful thinking, 6
withdrawal from wars, 19–20.
   See also exit strategies
Wolf Brigade, 92
Wolfowitz, Paul, 67, 69, 74–75, 76, 126
World Bank, 44
World Trade Center attacks, 65, 122
World War II, 17–18, 34, 122

Zakheim, Dov, 134
Zhou Enlai, 55–56